THE PRAGUE SPRING
AND THE WARSAW PACT INVASION OF CZECHOSLOVAKIA, 1968

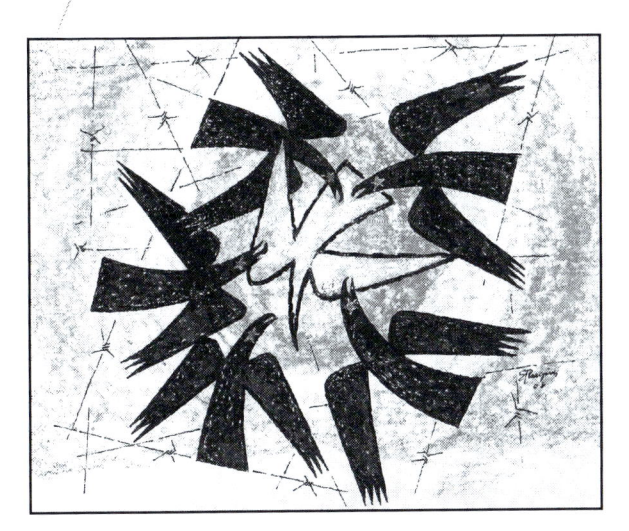

FORTY YEARS LATER

Compiled and Edited by

M. Mark Stolarik

Bolchazy-Carducci Publishers, Inc.
Mundelein, Illinois USA

This book is partially funded by the Chair in Slovak History and Culture at the University of Ottawa, and the Slovak-American International Cultural Foundation, Inc.

General Editor: Ladislaus J. Bolchazy
Cover Design & Typography: Adam Phillip Velez

The 'Prague Spring' and the Warsaw Pact Invasion of Czechoslovakia, 1968: Forty Years Later

Compiled and Edited by M. Mark Stolarik

© 2010 Bolchazy-Carducci Publishers, Inc.
All rights reserved.

Bolchazy-Carducci Publishers, Inc.
1570 Baskin Road
Mundelein, Illinois 60060
www.bolchazy.com

Printed in the United States of America
2010
by Publishers' Graphics

Paperback: ISBN 978-0-86516-751-3
Hardbound: ISBN 978-0-86516-757-5

Library of Congress Cataloging-in-Publication Data

The Prague Spring and the Warsaw Pact invasion of Czechoslovakia, 1968 : forty years later / compiled and edited by M. Mark Stolarik.
  p. cm.
  Essays and comments presented at an international conference held at University of Ottawa, Oct. 9-10, 2008.
  Includes bibliographical references and index.
  ISBN 978-0-86516-751-3 (pbk. : alk. paper)
  ISBN 978-0-86516-757-5 (hardbound)
 ISBN 978-0-86516-751-3, ISBN 978-0-86516-757-5 1. Czechoslovakia--History--Intervention, 1968--Congresses. 2. Czechoslovakia--History--Intervention, 1968--Influence--Congresses. 3. Warsaw Treaty (1955)--Congresses. 4. Geopolitics--Soviet Union--History--Congresses. 5. Europe, Eastern--Politics and government--1945-1989--Congresses. 6. Europe, Eastern--Politics and government--1989---Congresses. I. Stolarik, M. Mark, 1943-
  DB2232.P744 2010
  943.704'2--dc22

2010015521

CONTENTS

Preface v

Introduction, *M. Mark Stolarik* vii

The Czechoslovak Crisis of 1968 in the Context of Soviet
    Geopolitics, *Mikhail V. Latysh* 1

Reconsidering the Soviet Role in the Invasion of
    Czechoslovakia: A Commentary, *Matthew J. Ouimet* 19

The 'Prague Spring' and the Warsaw Pact Invasion as Seen
    from Prague, *Jan Rychlík*. 31

The 'Prague Spring' Revisited, *Michael Kraus*. 53

August 1968 as Seen from Bratislava, *Slavomír Michálek,*
    Stanislav Sikora 61

Commentary on "August 1968 as Seen from Bratislava,"
    Stanislav J. Kirschbaum 87

The 'Prague Spring,' Poland and the Warsaw Pact Invasion,
    Łukasz Kamiński 95

The 'Prague Spring,' Poland and the Warsaw Pact Invasion:
    A Comment, *Piotr Wróbel* 129

The Role and Activities of the SED, the East German State
and Its Military During the 'Prague Spring' of 1968,
Rüdiger Wenzke 137

Commentary on "The Role and Activities of the SED, the
East German State and Its Military During the 'Prague
Spring' of 1968," *Gary Bruce* 165

Bulgarian Participation in Suppressing the 'Prague Spring'
in August of 1968, *Ivana Skálová* 171

Bulgaria, the 'Prague Spring' and the Invasion of
Czechoslovakia: A Comentary, *Mark Kramer* 193

The 'Prague Spring,' Hungary and the Warsaw Pact
Invasion, *Csaba Békés* 203

Comments on "The 'Prague Spring,' Hungary and the
Warsaw Pact Invasion," *Peter Pastor* 225

Legitimacy, Nation-Building and Closure: Meanings and
Consequences of the Romanian August of 1968,
Dragoş Petrescu 237

Commentary on "Legitimacy, Nation-Building and
Closure: Meanings and Consequences of the
Romanian August of 1968," *Monica Ciobanu* 261

Notes on Contributors 269

Index 277

PREFACE

M. Mark Stolarik

The essays and comments that follow were presented at an international conference on "The 'Prague Spring' and the Warsaw Pact Invasion of Czechoslovakia, 1968," held on the 40th anniversary of these events at the University of Ottawa on October 9–10, 2008. Scholars from all the former Warsaw Pact countries presented papers based upon their research in archives of their countries that were long closed to such scrutiny. North American specialists served as commentators. These papers and comments represent the most up-to-date research on the tragic events of 1968 in Central Europe.

The conference was organized by the Chair in Slovak History and Culture at the University of Ottawa and was co-sponsored by the Embassies of the Slovak and Czech Republics. The Faculty of Arts of the University, as well as the President's office, contributed financially and materially to its success, as did the following: an anonymous donor, Sean Adams, the late Thomas J. Bata, the Slovak-American International Cultural Foundation, Inc., Branch 63 (Ottawa) of the Canadian Slovak League, Branch 28 (Windsor) of the Canadian Slovak League, the Czech and Slovak Association of Canada, the Comenius Institute of Montreal, the First Catholic Slovak Ladies Association, Global Uranium Corporation, John C. Haas, Dusan Miklas, Jaroslav Slaba, the Slovak Catholic Sokol, the Slovak Community Circle of Oshawa, the Slovak League of America Foundation, Mark and Anne Stolarik, Philip Taylor and family, and the United States Steel Corporation. Anne H. Stolarik helped with the local arrangements.

The conference organizer is grateful to all of the above, as well as to the 147 individuals who registered and participated in this undertaking. Their efforts demonstrated that both scholars and members of the wider community can come together to discuss matters of common interest.

INTRODUCTION[1]

M. Mark Stolarik

At 4:30 a.m. on August 21, 1968, Mark and Anne Stolarik were awakened by what sounded like the roar of jackhammers on the streets of the eastern Slovak city of Prešov in Czechoslovakia. Mark's first reaction was to curse the "stupid locals" for tearing up their streets at such an ungodly hour. "Why can't they wait until 8:00 a.m., as they do in civilized countries?" he complained to his groggy wife. To these newlyweds, and students from the University of Minnesota, this seemed like another example of the kind of communist arrogance and inefficiency that they had encountered since having entered the Czechoslovak Socialist Republic at the end of June that year. They had already grown used to not having hot water at all times, or even to having no water at all, in Anne's uncle's second-floor apartment at the "Sídlisko dukelských hrdinov" (Apartments of the Dukla Pass Heroes) on the west side of town.[2]

---

1 The author is grateful to Mark Kramer of Harvard University for having critiqued this Introduction.

2 In late 1944, elements of the First Czechoslovak Army Corps, led by Brigadier-General Ludvík Svoboda, together with the Red Army, broke through the Dukla Pass about 50 kilometers north of Prešov, and proceeded to drive the Germans out of Slovakia. For more on this operation see Miloslav Čaplovič and Mária Stanová, eds., *Karpatsko-duklianska operácia–plány, realita, výsledky, 1944–2004* (Bratislava, 2005).

Suddenly, there was a loud knocking on the apartment door. Now images of the dreaded secret police coming to get them raced through Mark's and Anne's minds. The secret police always came during the night, and Mark and Anne were foreigners in this communist country, subject to possible arrest at any time, they thought.[3] Andrej Krasnay, Anne's uncle and master of the house, gingerly approached the main door and asked "Who's there?" Mark and Anne could hear some muffled conversation after Andrej opened the apartment door, and a few moments later, he knocked on their glass bedroom door, opened it and announced "The Russians, Poles, East Germans, Hungarians and Bulgarians are invading us!"

Stunned by this news, Mark and Anne rose from their bed, looked out their balcony window, and saw a military helicopter circling overhead, while the din from the streets continued.[4] Now they understood that they were not hearing the sound of jackhammers, but of tanks! Not knowing what to do next, they hurriedly dressed and headed for the Dukla Hotel in the center of town, where Professor Timothy L. Smith, Mark's dissertation advisor from the University of Minnesota, was staying. When Mark knocked on Smith's third-floor door and announced that Czechoslovakia was being invaded by the Warsaw Pact, Smith reacted with surprise, because he could hear and see the tanks outside his window, but he had assumed that this was another Warsaw Pact exercise, similar to the one they had witnessed in June and July of that year.[5] Mark disabused him of this notion, and Smith suggested that they go downstairs to breakfast and consider their options.

Over breakfast Smith behaved like a typical American. He ate heartily (Mark and Anne merely poked at their scrambled eggs) and announced, "Well, we're Americans and this doesn't concern us. Let's go work in the archives." Smith then asked Anne to accompany him to the local city archives (he could not speak or read Slovak; she could), where he proceeded to badger the mayor

---

3   For a history of the "Štátna bezpečnosť [ŠtB]" (State Security) in Czechoslovakia, see Jan Pešek and Róbert Letz, *Štruktúry moci na Slovensku, 1948–1989* (Prešov, 2004), 119–254.

4   The author has a color slide of this helicopter.

5   These maneuvers, which took place from June 19 to June 30, 1968, but were then extended to July 11, were code-named "Šumava." As a form of "sabre-rattling," the Soviet Union did not withdraw its contingent until the end of July. The author has color slides of a portion of this army camped on a sideroad between the city of Žilina and the fortress of Strečno in north-west Slovakia in mid-July. See also "Documents 45-48 concerning the Šumava Exercises," in Jaromír Navrátil et al., *The Prague Spring 1968: A National Security Archive Reader* (Budapest, 1998), 191–205.

to let him and Anne into his records. The mayor kept repeating, in Slovak, that "due to the extraordinary circumstances, the archives are closed," which Anne kept translating, while Smith kept demanding that he open them. Finally, after many failed attempts to get the mayor to open his archives, Smith gave up and suggested that Anne join Mark, who was ostensibly working in the local state archives.

At the state archives, on the second floor of the former Lutheran Lyceum, just north of St. Nicholas Roman Catholic church on the town square, all the employees of the archives, along with Mark Stolarik, were looking out of the window, watching the Russian tanks roll by.[6] However, one researcher was hard at work—the elderly Mr. Grant, whom Mark had hired a few weeks earlier to translate Magyar-language documents for him. Mr. Grant, who was a descendant of a Scottish soldier who had fought in Central Europe during the Thirty Years' War, had been born and educated in the Dual Monarchy of Austria-Hungary. He was fluent in Slovak, German, Magyar and Latin. By the time of the invasion, he knew that Mark was looking for documents that pertained to Slovak emigration from Hungary before the Great War and was perfectly capable of finding and translating such documents without any supervision. Mark could not understand his nonchalance, and, after a few minutes of watching more tanks roaring by the open window, Mark asked Mr. Grant how he could keep working under such circumstances. Mr. Grant looked up at him and answered, "It's my fifth invasion," and then kept working. This answer caught Mark by surprise, and he had to quickly calculate when the previous four invasions had occurred. After having satisfied himself that Mr. Grant was telling the truth, Mark's heartbeat began to slow back to normal and he heaved a sigh of relief. Since Mr. Grant had survived four previous invasions, perhaps he, and Mark and Anne, would survive this one too.[7]

Survive they did. After three days of hurtling through the city, on the fourth day the tanks were quiet. They were now parked on side-streets at strategic locations—by the headquarters of the local army garrison, by the barracks of the paratroop regiment, by the train station, by the nearby radio

---

6   For a photo of this archives building and its interior, see Ferdinand Uličný et al., *Štátny archív v Prešove: Sprievodca po archívnych fondoch, I* (Bratislava, 1959), at the back of the book.

7   Author interview with Mr. Grant, August 21, 1968. The four previous invasions were in 1914 (the Russian General Brusilov offensive), the Hungarian Béla Kun invasion of Slovakia in 1919, the German invasion of Slovakia at the end of August 1944, and the Red Army invasion of November 1944. Mr. Grant had witnessed them all.

tower and so on.[8] Meanwhile, the citizens of Prešov reacted according to their age. On the first day of the invasion, middle-aged and older citizens lined up at the local stores and bought everything in sight. They had bad memories of the Russians' having looted their stores in 1945, as they were "liberating" them. Students, however, who had gone home for the summer holidays to their villages, started to pour into the city by 11:00 a.m. They quickly congregated into noisy groups and started to march towards the main crossroads of Dukla and Slovenská republika rád (Slovak Socialist Republic) streets, in front of the Bosák bank.[9] Here they chanted the old communist slogan "Všetci ľudia na chodníku nemilujú republiku" (People on the sidewalks don't love the Republic) and, when a break occurred in the procession of tanks, they quickly stepped into the street to stop them. Fortunately, the lead tank did stop and for three hours it was a standoff.[10] Finally, around 3:00 p.m., a Russian helicopter hovered overhead, and, suddenly, the lead tank lowered its cannon and started to swing it back and forth, while the students jumped out of the way. The same tank then started its engine with a roar and jerked ahead, just missing some students. The rest of the column followed it closely, not giving the students another chance to jump into the street to again stop the column.

Russian tank and soldier, Prešov, August 21, 1968.   *Photo Credit: M. Mark Stolarik*

---

8   The author has color slides of Russian soldiers and their vehicles at various locations in Prešov.

9   The American Slovak multi-millionaire, Michal Bosák of Scranton, Pennsylvania, had established this bank in the 1920's. The communists nationalized it after 1948. For more on Bosák, see Martin Bosák & Rudolf Bosák, *Michal Bosák: Americký bankár zo Šariša* (Prešov, 1998). A picture of this bank appears on page 131.

10 Author's color slides.

INTRODUCTION   xi

Russian vehicles stopped by students, August 21, 1968.   *Photo Credit:* M. Mark Stolarik

Russian scout car and tanks, Prešov, August, 1968.   *Photo Credit:* M. Mark Stolarik

Russian tanks, Prešov, August, 1968. *Photo Credit:* M. Mark Stolarik

Students blocking Russian vehicles, Prešov, August 21, 1968. *Photo Credit:* M. Mark Stolarik

The Whole World Supports Dubček, Brezovička, August, 1968.   ***Photo Credit:** M. Mark Stolarik*

As the students, and now the more self-assured citizens of Prešov, became more daring, anti-Russian posters began to appear on all the shop windows of the main square. Most told the Russians to go home, and some were even obscene. One featured a caricature of the hated Vasil Biľak, who hailed from Prešov and who was rightly suspected of having welcomed the Warsaw Pact invasion.[11] A huge white poster showed a Russian soldier, rising from a toilet bowl, where he had just relieved himself, with Biľak licking his rear! During the night the Russians tore down such posters. The next day new ones would appear. Later the Slovak archivists revealed to Mark that, after the first few nights, they (the archivists) tore down the posters before the Russians could get to them and the archivists hid them in the archives.[12] Also, on the first night

---

11 Biľak was one of five hard-liners in the leadership of the Communist Party of Czechoslovakia who had signed a letter that was delivered to Leonid Brezhnev, General Secretary of the Union of Soviet Socialist Republics, on August 3, 1968, asking for "support and assistance with all the means at your disposal" against so-called right-wing forces in Czechoslovakia. The citizens of Prešov did not know this, but suspected it, because, since May of 1968, Biľak had openly spoken out against the reforms of the 'Prague Spring.' For more on Biľak, see the chapters by Slavomír Michálek and Stanislav Sikora and by Jan Rychlík in this collection of essays.

12 Author interview with archivist Melánia Benkovská, August 24, 1968.

of the invasion, the Russian commander proclaimed martial law in the city, to begin at 10:00 p.m. At precisely that time, most of the citizens of Prešov appeared on the main square and denounced the Russians. When an armored scout car appeared, the furious citizens pelted it with rocks and bottles, and it quickly fled to the outskirts of town.[13] This happened every night that Mark and Anne remained in Prešov.

One week after the invasion, Timothy L. Smith decided that his students could no longer remain in Slovakia. He was particularly concerned about Oksana Dragan, his Ukrainian-origin graduate student, who was doing research on Ukrainians in Slovakia. A day earlier one of the Ukrainian professors from the Philosophical Faculty of Pavol Jozef Šáfárik University, which was located in Prešov, visited with Smith and strongly suggested that he and his students, particularly Oksana, leave as soon as possible. Apparently there were agents of the KGB in town, and they were arresting anyone suspicious.

So, on August 28, 1968, Smith and his students set out for Bratislava, at the other end of the country. As they traveled through northern Slovakia in separate Volkswagens, which they had purchased in Germany at the beginning of summer, the professor and his students had to pass many columns of Russian vehicles, which were traveling at slow speed. Often the columns were stopped by the side of the road, and Russian soldiers could be seen up in the apple and pear trees, picking the ripe fruit! Apparently, their supply trucks had not yet caught up with them. Mark also noticed that the locals had turned all the direction signs in the wrong direction, to confuse the Russians, forgetting that most Russian soldiers could not read the Latin alphabet. Fortunately, Mark had a good map of Czechoslovakia and was not fooled by the misdirected signs.

Anti-Russian graffiti appeared all across Slovakia, whether in villages or in cities. One large apartment tower just outside the city of Poprad, in the shadow of the High Tatras, had huge red letters painted on its side that read, from top to bottom, "DUBČEK."[14] A crane stood nearby, and it was clear how these letters came about. On the winding road beside the Váh river, between the cities of Ružomberok and Martin, one could read "Dubček je náš Jánošik" (Dubček is our Jánošik) painted on the slanted concrete walls

---

13   The author has a color slide of this armored car.

14   Alexander Dubček was the very popular First Secretary of the Communist Party of Czechoslovakia who led the effort to reform the communist system and create "socialism with a human face" in 1968.

holding up the hillsides.[15] In Martin, besides graffiti on guardrails that read "Rusi domov!" (Russians, go home!), one could read all about the invasion in the newly-resurrected *Národnie noviny*, official organ of the Matica slovenská.[16] In the lowland city of Trnava, fifty kilometers north of Bratislava, the streets were festooned with Czechoslovak flags and placards that read "Nie to čo nám nadikotvali okupanti, ale to čo cítime a myslime s Dubčekom a Svobodom" (We will not obey the occupiers, but rather what we feel and think with Dubček and Svoboda).[17] Finally, in the city of Bratislava, on Dostojevsky Street, someone had painted in large red letters the slogan "Nech žije Dubček a Svoboda" (Long Live Dubček and Svoboda) on the side of a grey building, while across the street, on a tool shed, was a banner that read "Moskva" (in Cyrillic letters) and an arrow pointed east.[18]

At the border crossing in nearby Petržalka, the border-guards were still armed Slovak soldiers. Even though a whole regiment of Russians was camped in the Petržalka city park, complete with tanks and artillery, only one lonely Russian private, with an AK-47 slung over his shoulder, sat on a bench and sullenly stared at the ground. When Mark asked the Slovak guards about the Russian, they replied, "We're ignoring him. You should too." After a perfunctory look at their passports and visas, the guards bade them farewell and the Minnesota caravan drove into Austria and freedom. Twenty-one years would pass before Czechs and Slovaks would once again enjoy the kind of freedom that they had tasted in 1968 in the so-called Prague Spring.[19]

---

15 Jánošík was an eighteenth-century social bandit, who allegedly stole from the rich and gave to the poor in northern Slovakia. He is considered a national hero by the Slovaks. For his story, see Patricia Krafcik, "Jánošík as a Symbol of Freedom in Communist Slovakia," *Slovakia*, 39, nos. 72-73 (2007), 63-80.

16 The author has several copies in his possession.

17 Ludvík Svoboda was the president of Czechoslovakia. Color slide in author's possession.

18 Color slides in author's possession.

19 The expression 'Prague Spring' was coined by western journalists to describe the 1968 reform movement in Czechoslovakia. It could just as well have been called the 'Bratislava Spring' because its leader, the Slovak Alexander Dubček, was First Secretary of the Slovak Communist Party from 1963 to 1968. It was he who slightly unscrewed the tap of censorship starting in 1963 and gave the impetus to the subsequent reforms. Since Dubček was located in Bratislava, western reporters did not notice him, because they were customarily based in Prague. Most Slovaks resent the term 'Prague Spring' and seldom use it (see the chapter by Michálek and Šikora). One of the very few western observers who correctly perceived the origins of the reform movement to have been in Slovakia was Stanley Riveles in his short article, "Slovakia: Catalyst of Crisis," *Problems of Communism*, 17 (May 1968), 1–9.

Many books and articles have been written about the 'Prague Spring' since it was crushed by the Warsaw Pact in 1968. Czech scholars sprang into action and hurriedly gathered and published as many documents as they could about the August events in a collection that came to be known as "The Black Book."[20] They followed this up with a collection of documents about the role and activities of the Central Committee of the Communist Party of Czechoslovakia in all of 1968.[21] At almost the same time, the western scholars Hugh Longhi and Paul Ello published what they considered to be the most important documents pertaining to Czechoslovakia in 1968.[22]

Western scholars subsequently wrote hundreds of articles and books about the 'Prague Spring' based on the published documents mentioned above, on the Czech and Slovak press, and on any other materials that they could access before the archives were closed to them during the period of "normalization" in Czechoslovakia, which lasted from the fall of 1969 to the fall of 1989.[23] Only after communism collapsed in Eastern Europe in the summer and fall of 1989, were the archives of these countries opened to scholarly scrutiny.

---

20 *Sedm pražskych dnů, 21.-27. Srpen 1968. Dokumentace* (Prague, 1968), translated and edited by Robert Littell, *The Czech Black Book* (London, 1979).

21 *Rok šedesátý osmý v usneseních a dokumentech ÚV KSČ* (Prague, 1969).

22 Hugh Longhi and Paul Ello, eds., *Dubček's Blue Print for Freedom: His Documentation on Czechoslovakia Leading to the Soviet Invasion, with a Profile by Hugh Longhi and Commentary by Paul Ello* (London, 1968).

23 Some of the best books on the subject written before 1989 are: H. Gordon Skilling, *Czechoslovakia's Interrupted Revolution* (Princeton, 1976); Galia Golan, *The Czechoslovak Reform Movement: Communism in Crisis, 1962–1968* (Cambridge, 1971) and *Reform Rule in Czechoslovakia: The Dubček Era, 1968–1969* (Cambridge, 1973); Robert Dean, *Nationalism and Political Change in Eastern Europe: The Slovak Question and the Czechoslovak Reform Movement* (Denver, 1973); Karen Dawisha, *The Kremlin and the Prague Spring* (Berkeley, 1984); Vladimir Kusin, *The Intellectual Origins of the Prague Spring: The Development of Reformist Ideas in Czechoslovakia, 1956–1967* (Cambridge, 1971) and *Political Groupings in the Czechoslovak Reform Movement* (New York, 1972); and Ivan Svitak, *The Czechoslovak Experiment, 1968–1969* (New York, 1971). Bibliographies include Michael Parrish, *The Czechoslovak Crisis: A Bibliography, 1968–1970* (Santa Barbara, 1971) and Michael Kraus, "The Thaw and the Frost: Prague and Moscow Nights, Ten Years After," *East Central Europe/L'Europe centre-est*, 6, no.1, (1979). An up-to-date bibliography may be found in Stefan Karner et. al., eds., *Prager Fruehling: Das internationale Krisenjahr, 1968*, vol.1, *Beitrage* (Vienna, 2008), 1249–77. For up-to-date analyses of the crisis, drawing on newly-available archival materials, see the essays in the Karner volume as well as Mark Kramer, "The Czechoslovak Crisis and the Brezhnev Doctrine," in Carole Fink, Philipp Gassert and Detlef Junker, eds., *1968: A World Transformed* (New York, 1998), 110–74.

Introduction

Almost twenty years after the fall of communism in Central and Eastern Europe and forty years after the Warsaw Pact invasion of Czechoslovakia, the editor of this volume organized a scholarly conference on this subject at the University of Ottawa. He reasoned that enough time had passed in order for scholars to have dug deeply into the previously-closed archives and to reveal what had hitherto been taboo. As a result, eight scholars from the former Warsaw Pact countries met at the University of Ottawa in October of 2008 and revealed their latest findings. An equal number of knowledgeable American and Canadian scholars commented on their papers.

Mikhail Latysh, an independent scholar in Moscow, presented many reasons for the actions of Leonid Brezhnev, and his Soviet Politburo, during 1968. He answered one of the most intriguing questions about the 'Prague Spring,' which has long bedeviled western historians: why did Leonid Brezhnev, on his visit to Prague in December 1967, not support Antonín Novotný, who was under attack by Alexander Dubček and his supporters on the Presidium of the Central Committee of the Czechoslovak Communist Party? According to Latysh, Novotný had insulted Brezhnev in the fall of 1964, shortly after the ouster of Nikita Khrushchev as General Secretary of the Communist Party of the Soviet Union. In a telephone call to Brezhnev, the new General Secretary, Novotný complained that the latter had not warned him of Khrushchev's impending ouster, and Novotný felt that he had deserved this courtesy, especially since Khrushchev had been on an official visit to Czechoslovakia in the summer of 1964. Brezhnev considered Novotný's telephone call to have been impertinent.[24]

In addition, Latysh pointed to the eagerness of Soviet generals to intervene militarily in order to halt the 'Prague Spring.' Russian generals unexpectedly attended the March 23, 1968, meeting of the members of the Warsaw Pact in Dresden, where the Czechoslovak delegation was severely dressed down by the Soviet Union, Poland, East Germany and Bulgaria. Furthermore, Russian generals unexpectedly arrived in Prague on May 9, 1968, to mark the celebration of the end of World War II, and they refused an escort as they visited various Czechoslovak army units. Indeed, a day earlier Marshal Yakubovsky, the commander-in-chief of Warsaw Pact forces, stationed in Poland, gave the order to invade Czechoslovakia, although he rescinded his command an hour

---

24 Gordon Skilling, in the most comprehensive treatment of the 'Prague Spring' published in the West, described Brezhnev's one-day visit to Prague on December 8, 1967, as being "shrouded in mystery." He offered no explanation for Brezhnev's lack of support for Novotný. Cf. Skilling, op.cit., 168–9 and note 22.

later. Finally, during the "Šumava" war games of June–July 1968 on Czechoslovak soil, the Russian commander told the Hungarian Minister of Defense that they were "dress rehearsals for the occupation."

Furthermore, according to Latysh, Soviet leaders were overly fearful about the proposed reforms of the 'Prague Spring' and totally miscalculated the level of support they had in Czechoslovakia. One of them rhetorically asked, "Do you know that the long-haired guys support Dubček?" Moreover, the Soviets expected at least fifty percent of the Central Committee of the Communist Party of Czechoslovakia to support the invasion, whereas most condemned it! Thus, after the invasion, according to Latysh, the Czechoslovak delegation in Moscow was in a position of strength, but did not realize it, and, in acceding to the "Moscow Protocol" of August 26, 1968, which justified the intervention, actually bailed out the Soviets!

Latysh concluded that the Warsaw Pact invasion taught the world two things: that communism could not reform itself and that invading one's neighbor solves nothing. That is why, according to him, the Soviet Union did not invade Poland when the Solidarity labor movement asserted itself in 1980–1981.[25]

Matthew Ouimet of the United States Department of State reminded us that Mikhail Latysh had access to Soviet Politburo working notes from 1968, which were provided by R.G. Pikhoia, the former Chief Archivist of the Russian Federation. Using these and other pertinent sources, Latysh was in a good position to try to answer six key questions about the Soviet-led invasion of Czechoslovakia in 1968: What was the nature of the 'Prague Spring'? When and why did the Soviets lose faith in Alexander Dubček? How early did the Soviets consider military intervention in Czechoslovakia? How well-informed was the decision to intervene? Could the intervention have been avoided? And, finally, why was the Warsaw Pact occupation so ineffective?

In answer to the first question, according to Ouimet, Latysh pointed to Dubček's loss of control over the reform movement and, hence, to "backsliding to the 1956 Hungarian version of developments." Ouimet questioned this interpretation by pointing out that both Dubček and defense minister Martin Dzúr were prepared to use force if they perceived their reforms were leading to "counter-revolution."

---

25 For a different view, see Mark Kramer, *Soviet Deliberations During the Polish Crisis, 1980–1981* (Washington, DC, 1999.). As the 'Prague Spring,' the Solidarity movement in Poland has received a great deal of attention by western historians. A good starting point is Timothy Garton Ash's *The Polish Revolution: Solidarity* (New York, 3rd ed., 2002).

As to the second question pertaining to the Soviets' loss of faith in Dubček, Ouimet pointed out that Latysh did not really answer it. Ouimet believes that the Soviets lost faith in Alexander Dubček after the Central Committee of the Czechoslovak Communist Party adopted the "Action Program" of April 1968, for the Soviets believed that this Program would lead Czechoslovakia back to capitalism and to withdrawal from the Warsaw Pact.

How early did the Soviets consider military intervention in Czechoslovakia? Ouimet noted that, according to Latysh, the decision had been made by June of 1968, when the Šumava war games got underway. However, Ouimet countered that these maneuvers were an exercise in intimidation and the Politburo had not yet reached a final decision.

How well-informed was the Soviet decision to intervene? According to Latysh, Dubček did not do enough to reassure the Soviets that he was not engaged in counter-revolution. Therefore, Ouimet agreed with Latysh that Moscow was left to its own resources to analyze the situation and chose to believe the most reactionary of its sources.

Could the intervention have been avoided? Latysh did not answer this question, but Ouimet indicated it could not have been because of the "sum-zero" logic of the Cold War.

Why was the Warsaw Pact occupation so ineffective? Latysh argued, and Ouimet concurred, that the Soviet leaders deluded themselves into believing that a majority of the Central Committee of the Czechoslovak Communist Party would support the invasion, as would a majority of the population. The exact opposite occurred; hence, the invading forces were greeted, not by flowers, but by bricks and hostile epithets. Ideology blinded the Soviets to reality.

Jan Rychlík of Charles University in Prague looked at the role of the Czechs in the 'Prague Spring' and surprisingly gave the Slovaks their due. He pointed out that the Slovak question was the "spark" that started the reform movement in communist Czechoslovakia because the Czechs regarded the republic as their nation-state and merely wanted to introduce economic and democratic reforms. The Slovaks, on the other hand, also wanted to federalize the state and the Communist Party, and that was why conservatives such as Vasil Biľak supported Dubček's efforts to overthrow the very conservative Antonín Novotný. By helping to promote Dubček to the position of First Secretary, Biľak cleared the way for himself to succeed Dubček as First Secretary of the Communist Party of Slovakia. Therefore, the Communist Party of Slovakia placed federalization before democratization. As a result, the National Assembly in Prague passed a Constitutional Law in June of 1968 which created a Czech National

Council as a counterpart to the already-existing Slovak National Council, something the Slovaks had been seeking since 1945. However, according to Rychlík, the conservative Alois Indra blocked the formation of a Czech Communist Party, with the result that the Act on the Federation of the Republic, which was signed into law on October 30, 1968, created an "asymmetrical federation," in which the Czechs would continue to dominate the government of the republic and the Czechoslovak Communist Party. Mikhail Latysh noted that Leonid Brezhnev had also opposed the creation of a Czech Communist Party because no Russian Communist Party existed in the Soviet Union. Rychlík concluded that federation, however imperfect, was the only reform that survived the invasion. Like most Czech and western historians, he was unaware that one other reform also survived—the resurrection of the Greek Catholic Church in Slovakia, which the communists had suppressed in 1950.[26]

Rychlík also agreed with Latysh's conclusion that while the military invasion was a success, the political result was a failure. Instead of finding widespread support for the invasion, the Warsaw Pact found only outrage, both by the leadership of the Communist Party of Czechoslovakia and on the part of Czech and Slovak citizens. Not only did the Extraordinary Congress of the Communist Party of Czechoslovakia, which met at Vysočany on August 21, 1968, denounce the invasion, but president Ludvík Svoboda refused to appoint the puppet government that was suggested to him by the Soviets. Indeed, the Soviets had kidnaped Alexander Dubček and other members of the Politburo, first into Poland and later into the Soviet Union, and were initially flummoxed by the widespread support for their prisoners all across Czechoslovakia. At this point, Rychlík pointed out, President Svoboda made a "fatal mistake." Instead of remaining in Prague and supporting the Vysočany Congress, he flew to Moscow and took with him the most conservative members of the Czechoslovak Party Presidium. In this way, he bailed out the Russians by having the Czechoslovak delegation sign the Moscow Protocol, which sanctioned the invasion.

---

26 While in Prešov in the month of July 1968, the author witnessed the re-taking of the Greek Catholic Cathedral by a committee of Greek Catholic laymen, one of whom was Andrej Krasnay, uncle of the author's wife. The author also met with the Greek Catholic Action Committee in Košice, which was led by the Rev. Ján Hirka, who would later be consecrated Greek Catholic eparch (bishop) of Prešov. For the history of the Greek Catholic church in Slovakia, see Ján Hric and Peter Šturák, *Prešovske biskupstvo* (Prešov, 1998).

Like Mikhail Latysh, Jan Rychlík concluded that the 'Prague Spring' demonstrated that reforming communism was impossible. He added that Dubček and his followers never renounced communism, nor did they contemplate leaving the Warsaw Pact. On this point, several historians disagree with Rychlík. They believe that Czechoslovakia was, indeed, heading for a social-democracy type of government, even though Dubček and his followers, fearing the wrath of Moscow, did their best to disguise their aims. Certainly Dubček's famous statement that he was trying to create "socialism with a human face" points in this direction.[27]

Unlike Rychlík, Michael Kraus from Middlebury College in Vermont stressed the role of Czech intellectuals in motivating and driving the 'Prague Spring.' He perceived the seeds for reform in the June 1967 Congress of the Union of Czechoslovak writers in Prague, which revealed a "restless intelligentsia" that produced the first draft of the Party's "Action Program" as early as February of 1968, just a month after Dubček's election as First Secretary. Interestingly enough, Kraus ignored the much earlier meeting of the Union of Slovak Writers in 1963, some of whose members, for the first time, criticized the communist system and encountered the wrath of Antonín Novotný.[28]

Kraus was also puzzled by certain actions or inactions by Dubček in 1968. He wondered why Dubček did not purge the conservatives from the Party apparatus, and he noted that the First Secretary accepted a certain amount of Soviet interference in Czechoslovak affairs. Slavomír Michálek and Stanislav Sikora would answer (and Rychlík would probably agree) that because Dubček believed in the democratic process (however limited at that time), he felt that he had to wait for the 14th Party Congress, scheduled for September of that year, in order to rid himself of the conservatives. As for accepting a certain amount of Soviet intervention, that was probably a tactic Dubček employed to try to mollify the Soviets, who were very suspicious of his actions. Indeed, the abolition of censorship by the Presidium of the Communist Party of

---

27 Skilling, *Czechoslovakia's Interrupted Revolution*, 843; Jiří Valenta and Jan Moravec, "Documentation: Could the Prague Spring Have Been Saved?" *Orbis: a Journal of World Affairs*, 35 (Fall 1991), 581–601. When interviewed by his biographer, Alexander Dubček suggested that "I was not so naive as not to see that it would only take time before the changes we made yielded to a full multiparty democracy. I knew that, and Brezhnev knew that, of course. So why won't the critics see it?" Jiří Hochman, *Hope Dies Last: The Autobiography of Alexander Dubček* (New York, 1993), 277.

28 Ibid., 89.

Czechoslovakia on March 4, 1968, as Kraus pointed out, "opened the floodgates to demands from below." After this, the public drove the reform process, and this, plus the Action Program, put Czechoslovakia on a collision course with other members of the Warsaw Pact. What remains unclear, according to Kraus, is how far the leadership of the Czechoslovak Communist Party was willing to go in the reform process. He suspects that they merely wanted to "liberalize" society while the general public wanted true democracy. According to Rychlík, the archives give us no answer. That may be because Dubček and his supporters were playing a dangerous "cat and mouse" game with the Warsaw Pact and did not want to reveal their true motives.

In looking at the 1968 reform era from a Slovak perspective, Slavomír Michálek and Stanislav Sikora, both from the Slovak Academy of Sciences in Bratislava, revealed the machinations that occurred in the Communist Party of Slovakia, which led to its insistence upon federation before democracy. In Slovakia the struggle was principally between two strong-willed individuals and their followers—Vasil Biľak and Gustáv Husák. Biľak initially posed as a Dubček supporter and reformer in order to have himself elected to the top Party post in Slovakia on January 23, 1968. However, after March 4th, as he observed the emerging public outcry for more freedom, Biľak began to have misgivings and by May 4–5, 1968, when he and other members of the Presidium met with the Soviet Politburo in Moscow, Biľak showed his true colors and echoed Soviet demands to halt the reform process. Gustáv Husák, who had been purged and imprisoned in the 1950's, and rehabilitated in the 1960's, felt that he deserved the position of First Secretary of the Slovak Communist Party. When he lost his first bid in January, he became an outspoken radical who even called for the dismantling of the Iron Curtain! As a result, Husák managed to have himself appointed Chairman of the Committee on the Preparation of the Act on Czechoslovak Federation on May 21, 1968. Taking advantage of his growing popularity, Husák also managed to persuade the Central Committee of the Communist Party of Slovakia to hold its future Congress on August 26, 1968, one month before the scheduled 14th Czechoslovak Party Congress in Prague. When the Slovak Party Congress met in August, the discredited Biľak, who had supported the invasion, was replaced by Husák as the First Secretary of the Slovak Communist Party. From this position of strength, Husák was able to replace Dubček as First Secretary of the Communist Party of Czechoslovakia on April 17, 1969. Thus, Michálek and Sikora concluded, both Biľak and Husák were opportunists who posed as reformers in order to gain popularity and move up in the Party ranks. Indeed, once Husák was firmly in charge, he had the Federation Act of 1968 (of which he was the principal author) amended in December of 1970 in order to allow even more concentration of his power in Prague.

Even though Michálek and Sikora were very critical of Gustáv Husák, they overlooked the fact that, weak as it was, the Federation Act of 1968 did finally grant the Slovaks equality with the Czechs, and, in the final analysis, it permitted the peaceful dissolution of the federation on January 1, 1993.[29]

Stanislav Kirschbaum of York University in Toronto rightly pointed to Slovak demands for federation going back to 1945. He reminded us that Prague politicians returned to the pre-war philosophy of "Czechoslovakism" after the communist takeover of power in 1948. He also reminded us that the reform process in Czechoslovakia started in Bratislava in 1963, when Slovaks began to demand the rehabilitation of their countrymen who had been purged for "bourgeois nationalism" in the 1950's.

According to Kirschbaum, two questions still need to be addressed by future historians of 1968. First, how involved were Czech and Slovak citizens in the liberalization process and were there significant differences between the Czechs and Slovaks in this regard? Second, did individual Slovaks appreciate the difference between liberalization of the regime and the federalization of the republic? Like other scholars of 1968, Kirschbaum believes that federalization was the only reform that survived the Warsaw Pact invasion. On the other hand, he does see the connection between the federalization of 1968 and Slovak independence in 1993.

What most historians, whether from the East or the West, do not stress enough is the fortuitous existence of a separate Slovak Communist Party since 1939. Before then there had been only an all-national Czechoslovak Communist Party. However, since Czechoslovakia ceased to exist on March 15, 1939, and a semi-independent Slovak Republic, backed by Germany, had come into being on March 14, 1939, in May of that year the Comintern instructed true believers in Slovakia to form an underground Slovak Communist Party.[30] After the defeat of Nazi Germany in May of 1945, the collapse of the

---

29 The "Preamble" to the Constitutional Act No. 143/1968 contains the very important sentences, "We, the Czech and Slovak nations, ...recognizing the inalienable right to self-determination **even to the point of separation** [my emphasis]....." Cf. Jaroslav Chovanec, *The Czechoslovak Socialist Federation* (Bratislava, 1976), 21.

30 Anna Josko, "The Slovak Resistance Movement," in Victor S. Mamatey and Radomír Luža, eds., *A History of the Czechoslovak Republic, 1918–1958* (Princeton, 1973), 366–7.

Slovak Republic and the resurrection of pre-war Czechoslovakia, most prewar Slovak political parties were banned. Therefore, it would be members of the Slovak Communist Party who would carry on the tradition of demanding Slovak equality with the Czechs. Even though Prague centralists purged the Slovak Communist Party and either executed or jailed its leaders in the 1950's, nevertheless Slovak communists, led by Alexander Dubček, would lead the counterattack in the 1960's. The resulting federation of 1968 was one of their greatest victories, and to them must subsequently go the credit for having made the dissolution of the federation legally possible.

Łukasz Kamiński from the University of Wrocław in Poland detailed the reaction of Władysław Gomułka, First Secretary of the United Polish Workers' Party, to the reforms of the 'Prague Spring.' According to Kamiński, Gomułka reacted very negatively to news from Czechoslovakia in early 1968 because in March he, himself, was under attack by students and intellectuals for having bowed to pressure from the Soviets to close down the anti-Russian play *Dziady* by the nineteenth-century poet Adam Mickiewicz. Moreover, Gomułka was obsessed with the increasing strength of West Germany, and he also had an intense personal dislike of Alexander Dubček, whose popularity was growing while Gomułka's was fading. For all these reasons, at the Dresden meeting of the Warsaw Pact on March 23, Gomułka warned of a brewing "counter-revolution" in Czechoslovakia. Furthermore, on May 6, 1968, reacting to certain anti-Polish communist articles in Czechoslovakia's freed press, Gomułka had his Central Committee send a protest note to the Czechoslovak Central Committee. At the July 5, 1968, meeting of the Politburo of the Polish Central Committee, Gomułka even suggested that Poland invade Czechoslovakia on its own, in order to halt the reform process! Since this was impossible without Soviet permission, Poland's communist leadership gladly contributed the largest non-Soviet contingent to the invasion force of August 21, 1968.

Kamiński's main contribution to the conference was to detail the reaction of Polish society to the invasion. Utilizing the newly-opened archives of the Polish secret police, Kamiński discovered many instances of skepticism voiced by local communist leaders and their followers about the official reasons given for the invasion: 143 confiscated printed pamphlets denouncing the invasion, over 200 examples of anti-invasion graffiti in 49 towns and cities, and several hundred confiscated anonymous letters denouncing the invasion. In addition, several dozen Polish intellectuals resigned from the Polish Workers' Party in protest. Altogether, the secret police arrested eighty individuals for such actions. The biggest disappointment in this regard was the hierarchy of the

Roman Catholic Church. Only the bishop of Częstochowa openly denounced the invasion in one of his homilies. The rest of the hierarchy obeyed Stefan Cardinal Wysińszki's instructions to remain silent, as did the Roman Catholic members of the Polish Diet, lest church-state relations in Poland deteriorate.

Kamiński did remind us, however, that the first instance of self-immolation as a protest against the invasion occurred in Poland. On September 8, 1968, on the occasion of a giant harvest festival in Warsaw, Ryszard Siwiec, in front of a crowd of 100,000, which included Władysław Gomułka, soaked himself in lighter fluid and set himself ablaze. Even though he left a suicide note explaining the reason for his self-immolation, the police confiscated the note and announced that he was a drunk who had spilled alcohol all over himself and had accidentally set himself on fire! As a result, Polish society and the outside world did not discover the truth about this incident until the downfall of communism in Poland in 1989. While the case of the Czech student Jan Palach immolating himself in Prague on January 16, 1969, for the same reasons, is well-known in the West, very few people know that Michal Leučík, a Slovak soldier, did likewise on Liberators Square in the eastern Slovak metropolis of Košice on April 11, 1969.[31] His act was quickly covered up by communist authorities.

In spite of the numerous examples of protest that Kamiński detailed in his paper, he did admit that, generally speaking, the number of protests, relative to the total population, was very small. He blamed this dearth of protests on the "March events" in Poland and on the fact that many potential protesters were already in jail. He also alluded to the long history of Polish-Czech animosity, which was based partly on territorial disputes and partly on the Polish attitude that the Czechs had "not suffered enough" during the Second World War.

Michal Leučík, Košice, April 11, 1969
Photo Credit: *Courtesy of M. Mark Stolarik*

---

31 For instance, while Skilling devotes a few lines to Palach, he does not mention Leučík. Cf. *Czechoslovakia's Interrupted Revolution,* 818. For the case of Leučík, see František Honzák, *Dejiny Slovenska. Dátumy, udalosti, osobnosti* (Bratislava, 2007), 616.

Piotr Wróbel of the University of Toronto agreed that in Poland the level of protest against the invasion was minuscule. He suggested that it was much stronger among Poles abroad, especially in Paris, and this phenomenon merits more study. Furthermore, Wróbel observed that the Politburos of the other Warsaw Pact countries were not initially united in their reaction to the reforms underway in Czechoslovakia, possibly because a "generation gap" existed in these Politburos, and this also deserves more study. He also pointed to the rise of anti-Semitism in Poland and in the Soviet Union as a result of the 1967 Arab-Israeli war, and the subsequent charge that some of the reformers in Czechoslovakia were exponents of "Zionism." This, too should be studied. Finally, Wróbel asked whether the heavy involvement of the Polish army in the invasion of Czechoslovakia in 1968 was a prelude to the martial law proclaimed in Poland in 1981? This, too, awaits further study.

Rüdiger Wenzke from the Military History Research Institute in Potsdam, Germany, demonstrated that Walter Ulbricht, First Secretary of the Socialist Unity Party of the German Democratic Republic (GDR), was just as fearful, if not more so, about the reforms of the 'Prague Spring' as was his Polish counterpart. In late January of 1968 the Central Committee of the GDR expressed alarm about the "bourgeois liberals" in Czechoslovakia, and on March 11 the same body complained about "revisionist, openly bourgeois forces" in that country. At the infamous March 23 Dresden meeting of the Warsaw Pact, Ulbricht openly denounced the "counter-revolution" taking place in Czechoslovakia. In May and June of 1968, East Germany launched a press and media war against Czechoslovakia and began to spy upon its neighbor. When the Warsaw Pact began to plan military moves against Czechoslovakia, Ulbricht and his colleagues demanded that the GDR be included, even though initially the Warsaw Pact wanted to leave it out. As a result, the GDR did participate in the June–July "Šumava" exercises upon Czechoslovak soil.

However, when it came to invading Czechoslovakia itself, Wenzke continued, the GDR suddenly found itself sidelined. This was a tremendous humiliation to Ulbricht, and to the GDR and, as a result, the GDR did everything in its power to cover up the insult. The leadership of the GDR was so successful in pretending that its armed forces had, indeed, participated in the August 21, 1968, invasion, that most observers believed it was so until the collapse of communism in the fall of 1989!

Why did the Warsaw Pact not allow one of its most faithful allies to participate in the invasion of Czechoslovakia? According to Wenzke, discoveries in East German and Soviet archives, some made as recently as in the summer of 2008, showed that the Soviet Politburo cancelled the participation of the GDR in the invasion at the last moment because of appeals by some of the most conservative leaders of the Czechoslovak Presidium, who were afraid of the extreme outrage such participation would provoke among the Czech population. Thus, for the next twenty-one years, thanks to the skillful propaganda machine of the GDR, most western and eastern observers believed that the GDR had actually participated in the 1968 invasion of Czechoslovakia.[32]

In addition to having detailed this GDR hoax upon both East and West, Wenzke uncovered many instances of protest against the invasion of Czechoslovakia in the GDR, many more than in Poland. For instance, a few thousand leaflets and much graffiti appeared all over the GDR; the Lutheran church openly protested against the invasion, as did many members of the Communist Party. In all, 278 "comrades" were expelled from the Party, and 1,189 individuals were arrested by the police for their opposition to the invasion. Even twenty soldiers and five officers, including a captain and a lieutenant-colonel, were cashiered from the army for having opposed the invasion. Wenzke concluded that these protests laid the basis for an opposition movement to develop in the GDR, which would eventually overthrow the communist regime in East Germany.

Gary Bruce from the University of Waterloo agreed with most of Wenzke's findings. He showed that Walter Ulbricht genuinely believed that Czechoslovakia was undergoing a counter-revolution which had to be stopped. Furthermore, Ulbricht was utterly humiliated by the last-minute Soviet decision not to allow East Germany to participate in the invasion, and he and his successors scrambled to cover up this humiliation for the next twenty years. Thus, Bruce concluded, the 1968 Warsaw Pact invasion of Czechoslovakia was a "Pyrrhic victory" for the hard-liners in the GDR. They suffered international condemnation; Walter Ulbricht was soon deposed; and the dissidents began to prepare for 1989. In 1968 the dissidents had been atomized. By 1989 they were united. Furthermore, according to Bruce, Wenzke made a real contribution in detailing the opposition to the invasion in the GDR. The result of this opposition was that in 1989, when people took to the streets to demand their freedom, the armed forces hesitated to act against their own people and made the overthrow of communism possible.

---

32 As noted above, Mark and Anne Stolarik were informed in the morning of August 21, 1968, that East Germany had participated in the invasion. In Jaromír Navrátil *et.al., The Prague Spring 1968*, op.cit., which was published in 1998, the map on the inside front cover shows two East German divisions having invaded Czechoslovakia in August of 1968.

If Władysław Gomulka and Walter Ulbricht were excessively concerned about the "counter-revolution" underway in Czechoslovakia, the First Secretary of the Communist Party of Bulgaria, Todor Zhivkov, was absolutely irrational about it. As Ivana Skálová of the Regional State Archives in Prague showed, as early as March 6, 1968, at a meeting of the Presidium of the Bulgarian Communist Party in Sofia, Zhivkov pronounced the situation in Czechoslovakia "counter-revolutionary" and he proposed using the military to suppress it. Even though Bulgaria was not initially invited to the March 23 meeting of the Warsaw Pact in Dresden because Bulgaria did not border on Czechoslovakia, Zhivkov insisted on being invited and sent a delegation to participate. Meanwhile, Bulgaria clamped down on its press and started spying on Czechoslovakia as early as March of 1968. In a Warsaw Pact meeting in Moscow on May 8, Zhivkov once again called for military intervention in Czechoslovakia, as he did in Warsaw on July 15 and at Čierna nad Tisou in early August. He finally got his wish at the Warsaw Pact meeting on August 18, which authorized the invasion of Czechoslovakia on the twenty-first.

As Skálová illustrated, participation by the Bulgarian army in the invasion of Czechoslovakia was no easy matter. The Soviet Union had to first transport, by sea and by air, two Bulgarian regiments to the Soviet Union, from which they proceeded by land, accompanied by the Red Army, into eastern Slovakia. In the cities of Košice and Rožnava the outraged citizens erected blockades on the main roads and pelted the invading soldiers with rocks and other projectiles. This surprised many of the Bulgarian soldiers, most of whom thought they were on military maneuvers.

Since Bulgaria was ruled by the Stalinist Zhivkov, Skálová found very little evidence of protests against the invasion. Only one history professor was fired and a few of his students were expelled from university. However, the prominent playwright Georgi Markov fled the country in disgust, settled in London, and wrote a cycle of plays against the invasion. His work was broadcast on the BBC. The Bulgarian Secret Service assassinated Markov for his insubordination in 1978.

Skálová concluded that some historians were misled about Bulgaria's role in suppressing the 'Prague Spring' because original sources were unavailable until Todor Zhivkov was overthrown in 1989 and also because Zhivkov lied about his role in his published memoirs. Contrary to what Zhivkov wrote, he was, in fact, one of the most vehement opponents of the reforms underway in Czechoslovakia in 1968. Skálová explained his vehemence as a reaction to Bulgaria's insignificance in the Warsaw Pact. Apparently Zhivkov shouted the loudest because he was afraid that, otherwise, he and Bulgaria would be ignored.

Mark Kramer of Harvard University agreed with Ivana Skálová's findings and added some of his own. He revealed that Karen Dawisha, Gordon Skilling, Jiří Valenta and Fritz Ermarth did not know Todor Zhivkov's stand on Czechoslovakia in 1968 until the Bulgarian archives were opened in 1989. Now scholars know that Zhivkov was suspicious of Dubček from the start and, as a result, did not publish his portrait in the press after he was elected First Secretary of the Communist Party of Czechoslovakia in early January of 1968. Furthermore, in a meeting with Leonid Brezhnev in Sofia on March 6–7, 1968, Zhivkov already urged using force to suppress the reforms. He repeated these suggestions for the next several months and, after the invasion of August 21, he even proposed installing a military dictatorship in Czechoslovakia! Thus, his memoirs were a pack of lies.

On the other hand, as Csaba Békés of the Cold War History Research Center in Budapest informed us, János Kádár and the leadership of the Hungarian Socialist Workers' Party welcomed the reforms of the 'Prague Spring.' They hoped that the reforms in Czechoslovakia would complement similar initiatives in Hungary and also lead to the establishment of diplomatic relations with West Germany. However, since Kádár had led the repressions in Hungary after the Soviet invasion of 1956, he did not desire the same fate for Czechoslovakia. Therefore, according to Békés, Kádár met no less than nine times with Alexander Dubček in 1968 to urge him to proceed with caution. In other words, he acted as a mediator between the Warsaw Pact and Czechoslovakia and tried to prevent a military intervention until mid-July of 1968, at which time Władysław Gomułka, Walter Ulbricht and Todor Zhivkov turned upon Kádár and threatened to analyze the situation in Hungary as well. Having reluctantly acceded to a military solution at the July 14–15 meeting of the members of the Warsaw Pact in Warsaw (without the participation of either Romania or Czechoslovakia), Kádár still pleaded for three more summit meetings in the next month and also met with Dubček one last time, all to no avail. After the Warsaw Pact invaded Czechoslovakia on August 21, with the unenthusiastic military support of Hungary, Békés continued, Kádár pleaded for moderation by the Warsaw Pact. According to Békés, the "Moscow Protocol," which established a government of both reformers and hard-liners in Czechoslovakia, was a compromise between Kádár's views on the subject and those of Ulbricht and

Zhivkov, who proposed a revolutionary government of workers and peasants. That there were no bloody repressions in Czechoslovakia after the invasion (as there had been in Hungary in 1956) again reflected the "moderating influence" of Kádár upon Leonid Brezhnev. Therefore, Gustáv Husák, who replaced Alexander Dubček as First Secretary of the Communist Party of Czechoslovakia in April of 1969, could "consolidate" peacefully.

Peter Pastor of Montclair State University in New Jersey strongly disagreed with Békés's analysis. Rather than having played a mediating role between Dubček and Brezhnev in 1968, Pastor contended that Kádár acted as a "messenger boy" for Brezhnev and played a duplicitous role in the whole affair. Also citing newly-discovered documents in the Hungarian archives, Pastor charged that Kádár turned against the reforms in Czechoslovakia after the Prague *Literární listy* on June 16, 1968, published an article which accused Kádár of having ordered the execution of premier Imre Nagy in 1956. Pastor further asserted that scholars cannot trust Kádár's reports to his own Politburo because they were designed for "home consumption," and we do not have minutes of his meeting with Brezhnev at Yalta on August 12–15. Furthermore, Pastor rejected Békés's claim that the "Moscow Protocol" was a "compromise" between the wishes of Kádár and other members of the Warsaw Pact. Instead, insisted Pastor, it was a "dictate."

Even though Romania was a member of the Warsaw Pact, it did not participate in the 1968 invasion of Czechoslovakia. Instead, Nicolae Ceauşescu, First Secretary of the Romanian Communist Party, condemned the invasion from the balcony of Party headquarters in Bucharest on the very day it took place. Dragoş Petrescu of the University of Bucharest explained this condemnation as a clever move by Ceauşescu to promote his own vision for the future of Romania. This consisted of his version of nation-building through national communism and independence from the Warsaw Pact. Indeed, his balcony speech legitimized Ceauşescu's rule, because even his opponents admired him for his audacity in making it. Nevertheless, even though Ceauşescu denounced the invasion of Czechoslovakia, he also regarded Dubček as too lenient; he rejected the Czechoslovak reform process and stressed a return to Romania's "glorious" past through mass-mobilization, and the systematization of national culture. As a result, Ceauşescu turned Romania into a Stalinist state based upon a personality cult of himself and his family.

Monica Ciobanu of the State University of New York at Plattsburgh agreed with Petrescu's analysis and elaborated upon it. She pointed out that 1968 had two meanings for Romania: the end of a very brief period of liberalization

(1958–1968) and the beginning of an "ideological reconstruction" that led to a cult of personality. She also reminded us that Ceaușescu's balcony speech gave him international legitimacy into the 1970's, when he appeared as another "Tito" who had broken with the Soviet Union. As a result, he was invited to visit both the USA and China in 1970 and 1971. However, Ceaușescu was deceiving the outside world while reorganizing the secret police and placing members of his own family into the upper echelons of the Romanian Communist Party. The net result, according to Ciobanu, was that "in attempting to challenge Soviet hegemony, Romanian communism essentially reproduced its worst characteristics."

The articles and commentaries that appear in this book show that scholars have learned a great deal about the 'Prague Spring' and the Warsaw Pact invasion of Czechoslovakia since the downfall of communism in 1989 and the subsequent opening of previously closed archives. However, they also demonstrate that many questions remain unanswered and much more research remains to be done. These are challenges for a new generation of scholars in the search for the truth about the 'Prague Spring' and the Warsaw Pact invasion of Czechoslovakia in 1968.

The basic history of the 'Prague Spring' is well known in academic circles. However, to help the average reader better understand the articles and commentaries in this book, the following is a time-line of the most important events of 1967–1969 in Czechoslovakia.

October 30–31, 1967—A plenary meeting of the Central Committee of the Communist Party of Czechoslovakia (CC CPCs), Alexander Dubček, the First Secretary of the Communist Party of Slovakia (CPS), openly criticized Antonín Novotný, the First Secretary of the CPCs and President of the Republic, for having too much power.

Antonín Novotný invited Leonid Brezhnev, General Secretary of the Communist Party of the Soviet Union (CPSU), to visit Prague on December 8, in the hope that Brezhnev would help Novotný to stay in power. Brezhnev visited Prague but declined to support Novotný.

January 3–5, 1968—At the meeting of the CC CPCs, Novotný was removed as First Secretary and was succeeded by Alexander Dubček.

March 4, 1968—The Presidium of the CC CPCs began the process of abolishing censorship, which greatly alarmed most other members of the Warsaw Pact.

March 14–15, 1968—The Slovak National Council demanded that the Czechoslovak republic be federalized.

March 22, 1968—After facing severe criticism from the press, Antonín Novotný resigned as President.

March 23, 1968—Members of the Warsaw Pact (except Romania) met in Dresden, East Germany, and the Czechoslovak delegation received a severe dressing-down for its reform program.

March 30, 1968—Ludvík Svoboda was elected President of the Republic by the National Assembly in Prague.

April 1–5, 1968—A plenary session of the CC CPCs adopted the "Action Program" for the reform of Czechoslovak society.

May 4–5, 1968—A delegation of Czechoslovak leaders in Moscow was again warned by Soviet leaders that "counter-revolution" was taking place in Czechoslovakia and that steps should be taken to rein it in.

May 8, 1968—Top Party officials of the Warsaw Pact (minus Czechoslovakia and Romania) met to discuss the worrisome situation in Czechoslovakia.

May 10–23, 1968—Military maneuvers involving Polish and Soviet troops took place on Polish soil.

June 19–July 11, 1968—Military maneuvers code-named "Šumava" of the Warsaw Pact took place in Czechoslovakia.

June 24–28, 1968—The National Assembly in Prague adopted a law to prepare for the federalization of the republic and established the Czech National Council.

June 17, 1968—Ludvík Vaculík's "Two Thousand Words" Manifesto calling for complete freedom was published in *Literární listy* and other Czech newspapers. On the same day the CC of the CPCs denounced the Manifesto.

July 14–15, 1968—Leaders of the Warsaw Pact (minus Czechoslovakia and Romania) met in Warsaw to discuss the situation in Czechoslovakia.

July 30–August 1, 1968—Soviet and Czechoslovak leaders met at Čierna nad Tisou to discuss the situation in Czechoslovakia.

INTRODUCTION   xxxiii

August 3, 1968—Leaders of the Warsaw Pact (except Romania) met in Bratislava to further discuss the situation in Czechoslovakia. On the same day a letter from five hard-line members of the Czechoslovak delegation asking the Soviets for "fraternal assistance" was given to Petro Shelest of Ukraine, who passed it on to Leonid Brezhnev.

August 15–17, 1968—The Politburo of the Soviet Union decided to order the invasion of Czechoslovakia.

August 18, 1968—Leaders of Poland, East Germany, Hungary and Bulgaria, gathered in Moscow, and approved the invasion.

August 20–21, 1968—Armed forces of the Soviet Union, Poland, Hungary and Bulgaria invaded Czechoslovakia. On the morning of August 21 Alexander Dubček, and three other members of the Presidium of the CC CPCs were kidnaped by Soviet troops and flown, first to Poland, and then to the Soviet Union. On the same day the National Assembly and government of Czechoslovakia condemned the invasion.

August 22, 1968—The 14th Extraordinary Congress of the CPCs met at Vysočany, condemned the invasion, and re-elected Alexander Dubček as First Secretary.

August 23–26, 1968—The kidnaped Czechoslovak leaders, along with others flown in by Ludvík Svoboda, met with Soviet leaders and were browbeaten into signing the "Moscow Protocol," which justified the invasion.

August 26–29, 1968—The 14th Extraordinary Congress of the CPS met in Bratislava and elected Gustáv Husák as First Secretary.

September 8, 1968—Ryszard Siwiec immolated himself in Warsaw to protest the invasion.

September 27, 1968—Leaders of Poland, East Germany, Hungary and Bulgaria met with Soviet leaders in Moscow to discuss the Czechoslovak situation.

October 18, 1968—The National Assembly in Prague approved a treaty with the Soviet Union, which provided for the "temporary" stationing of Soviet troops on Czechoslovak soil.

October 30, 1968—In Bratislava Ludvík Svoboda signed into law the federation of Czechoslovakia.

January 1, 1969—The Czechoslovak Socialist Federation came into being.

January 16, 1969—Czech student Jan Palach immolated himself in front of the National Museum in Prague to protest the restoration of censorship and other restrictions on civil liberties.

March 21 and 28, 1969—The Czechoslovak national hockey team defeated the Soviet national team at the world championships in Stockholm, and these victories sparked anti-Soviet demonstrations in major cities across Czechoslovakia.

April 11, 1969—Slovak soldier Michal Leučik immolated himself in Košice.

April 17, 1969—Alexander Dubček was removed as First Secretary of the CC of the CPCs and was replaced by Gustáv Husák.

August 19–21, 1969—On the first anniversary of the Warsaw Pact invasion, demonstrations took place all across the republic.

September 25–26, 1969—A plenary session of the CC CPCs in Prague disavowed the August 21, 1968 resolution condemning the Warsaw Pact invasion, and the purge of the Party began, along with the "normalization" of society.

1

The Czechoslovak Crisis of 1968 in the Context of Soviet Geopolitics

Mikhail V. Latysh

The present contribution is based on materials in the AGC (Archives of the ČSFR Government Commission for the Study of the 1967–70 Events), located in Prague. Kept in the Archives are the verbatim reports of all talks which were held by the East European partners, minutes of the sittings of the Presidium of the Central Committee of the Communist Party of Czechoslovakia, the personal archives of Alexander Dubček and other leaders, ciphered messages of the Czechoslovak Ministry of Foreign Affairs, documents of the Ministry of State Security, interviews and materials of witness accounts in the Prosecutor's office received from prominent leaders of the 'Prague Spring' and from the leading officials who were responsible for the "normalization," as well as Polish, Hungarian and primarily Soviet materials bearing on the subject in question. Minutes of all the Soviet Politburo sittings relating to 1968 were contributed by the former Chief of the Archival Committee in Moscow, R.G. Pikhoya. Those materials make it possible to clarify some views of the Soviet leaders, the style and methods of Party diplomacy and factors which determined decision-making on foreign policy issues.

A certain degree of liberalization of the Soviet regime under Nikita Khrushchev (1953–1964), as well as the uncertain and contradictory nature of instructions which were sent from Moscow after Leonid Brezhnev had come to power, raised the level of autonomy of Moscow's European satellites to a certain extent and, at critical turning points in history, led to attempts at breaking free from the alliance with Moscow. Although Czechoslovakia's leaders stressed in every possible way loyalty to its commitments in the socialist bloc, there, too, dissociation from the Stalinist legacy took the form of searching for independent paths towards socialism (communism).

The 1968 crisis situation in Czechoslovakia makes one ponder the role of leaders in societies that are based upon totalitarian principles. The account by Jiří Pelikán, director of Czechoslovak Television, reveals the secret motives behind Brezhnev's reluctance to openly support Antonín Novotný in the latter's attempt to remain in power in late 1967.[1] Novotný had had strained relations with Brezhnev ever since Khrushchev's ouster, when Novotný, in a telephone conversation with Brezhnev, refused to accept the official version of Khrushchev's retirement for reasons of poor health. Finally, Brezhnev conceded that Khrushchev's retirement was attributable largely to his mistakes. At that point Novotný lost his temper and asked Brezhnev why he had not warned him earlier, for just a few months prior to that Novotný had accompanied Khrushchev during the latter's tour of Czechoslovakia, making a show of their comradely relations. Thus, the two leaders' personal enmity, to a great extent, contributed to the rise to power of the reformist wing of the Communist Party of Czechoslovakia.

In a telephone conversation with János Kádár in December 1967 (its minutes are to be found in the Hungarian materials sent to the Commission), Brezhnev explained: "The main reason for our difficulties, as I see it, is Novotný's desire to act exclusively on his own, his inability to cooperate with his colleagues in a collective leadership."[2]

The reform movement in Czechoslovakia, led from the top, had a chance at success, given the good mutual contacts between the reformers and the masses. The orthodox communist leaders might have been ousted from all levels of power on the wave of this new public activity. At that juncture, however, the Dubček government lost control of the reform process and was faced with the prospect of the country's backsliding to the 1956 Hungarian version of developments—a process of rather dangerous daydreaming which threatened the country's relations with its allies in the communist bloc.

---

1   AGC (Archives of the ČSFR Government Commission for the Study of the 1967–70 Events, Prague), J. Pelikán, October 18, 1990.

2   AGC Z/M, Telephone conversation between Brezhnev and Kádár, December 13, 1967.

Czechoslovak leaders received a stern warning for the first time at the Dresden meeting of Warsaw Pact leaders on March 23, 1968. It was preceded by a Politburo meeting in Moscow, at which some minor members of the Soviet leadership openly expressed distrust of Alexander Dubček. As P. M. Masherov put it: "I don't believe Dubček. He says one thing and does another. They are trying to change all the gains of Czechoslovakia in a peaceful way."[3] The Czechoslovak delegation at the Dresden meeting, experiencing an internal split, was subjected to scathing criticism, mostly by the leaders of Poland and the GDR for allegedly sliding towards counter-revolution. During a break in the session, Dubček and Oldřich Černík, shedding tears, approached Brezhnev, asking why hadn't he warned them, not opened their eyes to what was going to happen?[4] They were amazed by the absence of Romanian communists and the presence of military representatives. According to Brezhnev, these generals would render assistance in case of an emergency in Czechoslovakia.[5]

Czechoslovak leaders were summoned to Moscow on May 4, ostensibly to ask for a Soviet loan. But again they were reprimanded for their desire to get rid of the orthodox communists, who were considered to be the most reliable partners of the Soviets. Dubček again violated his informal promises. He commented that, "I try to smile when Brezhnev yells at me. He accuses me of saying yes, yes, and on coming back home fulfilling nothing."[6] But, by accepting Soviet rules of the game, he acknowledged the defense of socialism to be the concern of the whole socialist bloc, and by allowing a discussion of Czechoslovakia's internal problems, he replaced its foreign relations with party diplomacy. In the end, the Czechoslovak delegation was so perplexed by Soviet allegations that it obediently asked what it ought to tell the journalists about these negotiations.[7]

---

[3] Presidential Archives of the Russian Federation in Moscow (hereafter PARF), minutes of the meeting of the Politburo, March 15, 1968.

[4] PARF, Politburo meeting, March 25, 1968.

[5] AGC, O. Černík, R3, January 19, 1990.

[6] William Shawcross, *Dubcek* (London, 1970), 175.

[7] AGC Z/P2, meeting of the Communist Party of the Soviet Union (CPSU), the Polish United Workers' Party (PUWP), the Socialist Unity Party of Germany (SUPG), the Hungarian Socialist Workers' Party (HSWP) and the Bulgarian Communist Party (BCP) with the Communist Party of Czechoslovakia (CPCs), May 4, 1968.

The situation in Czechoslovakia was the main focus at the meeting of the five ruling East European Communist Parties held in Moscow on May 8, 1968. Even minor economic innovations, which prior to this period did not meet with objections by partners in the bloc, were now the object of criticism. Walter Ulbricht of the GDR asserted that "[Ota] Šik's reforms will prove a heavy burden on the working class. Intellectuals alone will benefit from them." While on the subject of an alleged offensive by counter-revolutionary forces, Ulbricht charged that "Czechoslovakia is governed by a secret service center, not by Černík, and this center is subordinated to Bonn, not Prague." Ulbricht was supported by Poland's Władysław Gomułka: "It is necessary to find the healthy core in the leadership and to support it. The main thing for them to do is to launch a struggle inside the Party, and we will support them."[8]

In order to support the Czechoslovak hard-liners among the military, the Kremlin resorted to "generals-diplomacy." In early May several high-ranking Soviet military officers arrived in Czechoslovakia, without any invitation, for the end of World War II anniversary commemoration. They explained their unexpected arrival by their desire "to visit their wartime colleague, President Svoboda," and, having refused the services of an escort, started paying visits to various military units to study the situation.[9] At the same time, orthodox Czechoslovak communists held consultations with Czechoslovak and Polish security officers. All these separate facts can be arranged into a logical system, if we accept the version that the Warsaw Pact leaders were looking forward to appeals for help from orthodox Czechoslovak communists, and upon receiving those appeals, they intended to transfer the war games, which were at that time held in Poland, to Czechoslovakia. As a result, either Soviet troops might come to stay in Czechoslovakia, or new leaders might come into power in Prague, who would be ready, at the allies' instructions, to reduce the sphere of action by the non-party opposition. The sensational testimony by General G. Yashkin, who in 1968 was commander of a tank division, corroborates this view. Marshal Ivan Yakubovsky, who inspected that division on May 8, gave it the task of crossing the Czechoslovak border and advancing in two directions. To Yashkin's question as to what should be done with the Czechoslovak tanks which were facing the Soviet troops on the other side of border, Yakubovsky answered, "Drive their tanks into the river and at 11:00

---

8 Ibid.
9 AGC, Minutes of a conversation with Colonel General G. Yashkin (no date or signature).

on May 9 cross the border to fulfill your task."[10] However, ten minutes later he cancelled his order. On this basis one may conclude that there was the possibility of an intervention and a top-echelon coup in Czechoslovakia as early as May of 1968. There was also a great degree of independence in the actions of the Soviet top brass, which was prepared to provoke a major international conflict in order to realize its strategic goals.

Incessant war games and maneuvers on Czechoslovak territory were now to be used to exert pressure on the disobedient ally. As a rule, they were timed to coincide with Czechoslovak Communist Party plenary meetings or other forums, when a struggle for power was expected to take place between Party reformers and traditionalists. The Hungarian defense minister, who had taken part in the war games "Šumava," reported to János Kádár that those games should be regarded as "a dress rehearsal for occupation." He also pointed out that, during the games, Czechoslovak servicemen had been treated in a humiliating manner.[11] Czechoslovak defense minister Martin Dzúr tried in vain to ascertain the date for the conclusion of these games.

Constant interference by Soviet aides in the work of the top Party bodies of Czechoslovakia was another important way of exerting pressure. As soon as members of the Czechoslovak Central Committee Presidium received materials to be discussed at its next sitting, copies were sent by Vasil Bil'ak (with his comments) to the Soviet Embassy, so that on the eve of the sitting either Soviet Ambassador S.V. Chervonenko sent a message from the Kremlin to Dubček or Brezhnev spoke with him on the telephone.[12] After the military intervention the mechanism of pressure was increased, and telephone calls from Moscow were made during the course of the CC Presidium sittings in Prague in order to influence the discussion and decision-making.

Brezhnev's letters to Dubček were often of an epic nature: "I am now sitting alone, it's late at night," he wrote to Dubček. Then Brezhnev described how he pondered the destinies of the world, which he regarded as an irreconcilable confrontation between the two systems. "At present imperialism cannot launch a head-on attack on us...it is trying to launch an offensive on the ideological front. Imperialism is looking for weak links in the socialist

---

10   Ibid.

11   AGC Z/M 12, Report of Hungarian defense minister L. Cinege to J. Kádár, July 5, 1968.

12   AGC, Simon B., R13, February 26, 1990.

camp," he wrote in reference to Czechoslovakia.[13] Erroneous interpretations of developments in Czechoslovakia and their over-dramatization were largely determined by distorted information sent from the Soviet embassy in Prague, and its choice of informants. The most gloomy forecasts by these informants (many of whom were from the entourage of former president Novotný) predicted that "events were headed in the direction of the restoration of capitalism," etc.[14] These were received by the Kremlin with great understanding, for they were in accord with the ideas of the Soviet ruling elite concerning the class struggle, its confrontation with imperialism and the right of the Party to interfere in all spheres of life.

The Soviet leadership received from those informants detailed information about every prominent figure in Czechoslovakia, especially those holding potentially reformist views, which were described as hostile to the USSR. In contrast to reform-communist intellectuals, the informants used lingo which was familiar and understandable to the Soviet elite, whose education was rather limited and who were over-ideologized. In their reports the informants freely labeled their colleagues in the Party as "Social Democrats," "Zionists," and "Italian-type Marxists." Many of the ruling leaders were accused of intending to turn the country into a new Yugoslavia, with the result that a new Little Entente would be formed to incorporate Czechoslovakia, Yugoslavia and Romania.[15]

After relations between the Communist Party of the Soviet Union and the Communist Party of Czechoslovakia had reached their lowest point, the situation resembled the 1948 rupture between the Soviet Union and Yugoslavia. The two sides felt the need for bilateral talks, which took place in late July—early August at Čierna nad Tisou, on the Soviet-Czechoslovak border. The CPSU Politburo, which took great pains to present itself as a collective leadership, did not wish to entrust this grave matter to only one leader or even to the leading three (Party boss Leonid Brezhnev, Premier Aleksei Kosygin, President Nikolaj Podgorny). Brezhnev opened the talks with a four-hour marathon speech, in which quotations from the Czechoslovak press were intermingled with accusations of playing into the hands of Western imperialism. He also accused the leaders of the 'Prague Spring' of their desire to smuggle

---

13 AGC, L. Brezhnev's letter to A. Dubček, April 11, 1968 (no date or signature).

14 AGC, Conversation of S. Prasolov with F. Havlíček on April 12, 1968, roll 9756, f.6, i.60, 1.242-258.

15 AGC, Roll 9756, f.5, i.60, c.300, II.,17-19, and II., 41-5.

counter-revolution into their country. Contrary to the version of a crisis among the Soviet leadership (which is widespread in Western publications), based upon different assessments of what then took place in Prague and of the split among certain Soviet branches of authority,[16] CPSU Politburo members from those departments showed great unity at the talks, which was indicative of the previous agreement and clear-cut distribution of their functions.

For instance, the leading ideologist Mikhail Suslov described the ideological chaos that prevailed in the Czechoslovak mass media; N. A. Shelepin, Chairman of the Trade Unions, spoke about Czechoslovakia's Trade Unions, having renounced their function of educating the masses; Petro Shelest discussed the impact of the 'Prague Spring' on both the nationalist movement in his Ukraine and Trans-Carpathian separatism.[17] Ideological issues—a sphere where the Soviet leaders were hardly well versed—were pushed into the background and geopolitical considerations given priority. A. Kosygin warned the Czechoslovak leaders: "You should take into account that your western border is also our border."[18] At the same time, as the verbatim reports of the Soviet-Czechoslovak talks show, the CPSU leaders' mentality was still dominated by stereotypes created by Soviet propaganda. Brezhnev quite seriously pointed to the alleged "indignation, expressed by our workers, and all working people" about persecution of individuals in Czechoslovakia with friendly sentiments towards the USSR and thus justified the Soviet pressure: "We are obliged to restrain the working class, our Party, for they demand that those responsible for it should be called to account."[19]

Soviet representatives of all ranks on many occasions failed to differentiate between important phenomena and some minor irritants. True, they reacted very sensitively to criticisms by the Czechoslovak press, which was no longer subjected to censorship. On the other hand, the use of obsolete US military hardware in the shooting of a film about World War II in Czechoslovakia was discussed as a subject of great importance at the meeting of the five communist

---

16 See Dimitri Simes, "The Soviet Invasion of Czechoslovakia and the Limits of Kremlinology," *Studies in Comparative Communism*, 8 (Spring–Summer), 1975.

17 AGC, D II/21, Fond 07/15, sv. 26, Talks between the CPSU and CPCs delegations at Čierna nad Tisou, July 29–August 1, 1968.

18 Ibid.

19 AGC, Verbatim Report of the Meeting of the Communist and Workers' Parties of Poland, Hungary, the GDR, Bulgaria and the USSR, August 18, 1968.

countries in Moscow on May 8. Similarly, exaggerated importance was attached to the activities of small associations of intellectuals, such as the group around professor Václav Černý, about whom the KGB sent special reports to Ulbricht, Gomułka and Todor Zhivkov of Bulgaria.[20] At one point in a discussion with Kosygin on a wide range of views held by those who supported the Communist Party of Czechoslovakia, Soviet Ambassador S. Chervonenko, who wished to reinforce Kosygin's arguments, exclaimed: "And do you know that the long-haired guys support Dubček?"[21]

Curiously enough, the Kremlin could not even reach agreement with its loyal partners in the leadership of the Communist Party of Czechoslovakia, more than half of whom could safely be described as allies of the Soviets while the other half dreamed about the "renewal of socialism," not its dismantling. For instance, at a meeting of the Czechoslovak Party Presidium, which discussed replying to a letter sent from Moscow, Antonín Kapek, one of the CPCs leaders, remarked, "I do not wish to be a member of a body which has contributed to the exacerbation of relations with the Soviet Union," and Vasil Biľak said that he approved of the Soviet pressure.[22] Moreover, Dubček declared at the sitting of the Presidium on August 12, "If I come to the conclusion that we are on the verge of counter-revolution, I'll ask the Soviet troops to move in myself."[23] In fact, had the Soviet leadership not been so afraid that Czechoslovakia might drift away from it and had its generals not been so keen on stationing their troops on Czechoslovak territory, the Prague reformists were prepared to take steps on their own to curtail democracy in order to maintain stability. On the eve of the Soviet intervention, defense minister Martin Dzúr discussed with his generals how to disperse demonstrators in front of the CPCs headquarters with the use of armored personnel carriers.[24] Dubček, meanwhile, told Ambassador Chervonenko about the new Law on the National Front, under which all organizations and parties not incorporated in it would be banned, disbanded or closed down by government agencies.[25]

---

20   Archives of the Russian Foreign Ministry, Fond 059, 1.58. p.-c.126, c.582, l., 196-7.
21   AGC, C. Císař, R.43, March 29, 1990.
22   AGC, D II/15, Fond Dubček, meeting of the Presidium of the KSCs, July 12, 1968.
23   AGC, B. Šimon, R 13, February 26, 1990.
24   AGC, M. Smoldas, R37, April 19, 1990.
25   Archives of the Russian Foreign Ministry, f.059, 1.58, p.-c.123, c.570, l.16-31, April 13, 1968.

Ciphered messages of the Czechoslovak Foreign Minister confirm that, by sending its troops into a neighboring country, the USSR could act without worrying about the Western reaction and without fear of triggering a war. A certain White House official named Davis warned Karel Duda, the Czechoslovak Ambassador to the USA, that "the USA will play the role of an observer" in any case.[26] And Charles Bohlen, an official of the State Department, in a personal conversation with Soviet Ambassador Anatoly Dobrynin, said that a military intervention, naturally, would complicate Soviet-US relations, but he did not think that the US would take any specific action.[27]

Brezhnev went on vacation to Crimea right after the August 3 Bratislava meeting. His comrade-in-arms, A. P. Kirilenko, was charged with the duty of dispatching to Crimea bulletins and estimates of the situation in Czechoslovakia. The mission of collecting data and compiling necessary recommendations had been carried out by a working group led by A. Blatov and included representatives of various departments. The estimates of the working group could not afford to discount the spirit of compromise engendered by Bratislava, which was prompted by an unprejudiced analysis. As it was recalled by one of the members of the group: "There were no grounds to force the spirit, since there was no way of expecting some sort of sharp turn on the part of Dubček, even if one proceeded from the fact that he had made up his mind to heed the voice of the allies and reinstate control over the press and narrow the space for the opposition."[28] It appeared that Kirilenko, while keeping in regular contact with Brezhnev, could not report to him in a way different from the estimates submitted by the working group. It is most probable that bulletins delivered to Crimea from Moscow were of minor importance to Brezhnev. The main line of communication that enjoyed his complete confidence became the telephone, linking him several times daily with the Soviet Embassy in Prague. This means of communication provided Brezhnev a direct link with Dubček's adversaries among the orthodox communists, and their reports were probably more radical than any interpretations on paper dispatched to Moscow by Chervonenko. Despite the temperate information from Moscow, Brezhnev cut short his vacation in the Crimea and returned to Moscow determined to act. His telephone conversation with Dubček on August 13 was

---

26   AGC, 6608, Washington, July 13, 1968.
27   AGC, 6794, Washington, July 19, 1968.
28   Author interview with V. Alexandrov, January 4, 1991.

the last straw, as the Czechoslovak leader failed to understand the urgency of the matter and promised some cosmetic changes to soothe Soviet worries, losing the last chance to avert a military intervention.[29] A rushed session of the Soviet Politburo was held to adopt a final decision and there were no hesitation about the timing.

On August 18, 1968, Brezhnev once again convened a meeting of the five "fraternal" parties in Moscow to create a decent facade of "international action" on the planned invasion. Brezhnev preferred to present things as though it was not he but objective reasons that provoked the military action (i.e., the failure to fulfill the commitments undertaken by the CPCs at Čierna and at Bratislava), and it was other leaders (Ulbricht and Gomułka), who had convinced him to adopt a decision which most suited his mentality. Nevertheless, Brezhnev was flattered by the opportunity to act as the leader of the bloc and was prepared to bear the brunt of the responsibility. The fact was that Ulbricht and Gomułka, as a rule, went even further than Brezhnev in denouncing the "Prague heresy," and Zhivkov spelled out what Brezhnev had not found it suitable to say himself. For instance, Zhivkov was the only one who had mentioned the possibility of a military solution at the previous Warsaw meeting.[30]

By August the Kremlin had driven itself into a position where every step placed it in a deliberately unfavorable situation and called for an escalation of tension to its logical end—military action. The military operation was launched, not for the sake of capturing some territory, but for seizing the country's leaders to prevent them from issuing instructions to their own people or applying to the West for help. Finally, the desire for a top-level coup in the CPCs Presidium was adopted. The idea was that "healthy forces" at a meeting of the Presidium would provoke a final split, vote non-confidence in the right-wing forces, and take over the Party and government leadership.[31] Despite the fact that Brezhnev mentioned a letter of invitation, which was expected

---

29 AGC, Telephone conversation of L. Brezhnev with A. Dubček, August 13, 1968 (no signature).

30 AGC, Z/M 15, meeting of the HSWP Politburo, July 15, 1968, with J. Kádár's report on the Warsaw meeting.

31 AGC, Verbatim Report of the meeting of the Communist and Workers' Parties of Poland, the GDR, Hungary, Bulgaria and the USSR in Moscow on August 18, 1968.

to be signed by fifty percent of the CPCs leadership in the course of a single day, no new versions of invitations have been found. Only one letter signed by Antonín Kapek and another signed by Alois Indra, Drahomír Kolder, Antonín Kapek, Oldřich Švestka and Vasil Biľak, have been found.[32]

Brezhnev's group was absolutely sure of the invasion's success. After all, he counted on the support of half of the central committee of the CPCs and of a considerable part of local Czechoslovak party functionaries. It was expected that, after they had been informed of the new government by the new Presidium, local Party officials would greet the arriving Soviet units with flowers, restore Party control, do all the necessary "dirty work" by arresting all those who deserved it and thus relieve the Soviet forces of the need to interfere in Czechoslovak internal affairs.[33]

It was a great mistake on the part of Brezhnev to judge the group of Czechoslovak orthodox communists from the position of the Soviet Union and CPSU practices. At that time public opinion polls did not exist in the USSR. The Soviet leadership oriented itself at best with ministers, and republican and regional leaders, and it regarded this narrow circle as the whole country. Brezhnev, whose domestic policy was aimed at securing their trust, viewed the situation in Czechoslovakia in the same light: if you secure the support of the majority (or close to it) in the Party leadership, and if you are absolutely sure that they would be supported by the leaders of a number of regions, then the logical conclusion was that the whole country would support you. That was confirmed by the system of analysis of selected information, in which private conversations were presented as the public mood. Since Soviet representatives in Czechoslovakia moved within certain circles on the basis of mutual trust, one could hardly imagine a better method of self-deception.

Furthermore, guarantees were received from President Ludvík Svoboda and defense minister Martin Dzúr, who had been informed about the planned invasion and warned that the Czechoslovak army should stay in its barracks. Early in the morning of August 21, General I. Pavlovsky, commander of the invading forces, and his chief of staff I. Yershov arrived at Dzúr's office and

---

32   AGC, Series K., CPSU Secretariat, Package 255, Kapek's letter (no date) and the letter of Indra, Kolder, Kapek, Švestka and Biľak, also no date, but most probably early August.

33   Author interview with M. Kuznetsov, November 28, 1991.

placed a telephone call to Soviet defense minister Andrej Grechko, who did not mince words while giving orders to Pavlovsky: "Tell Dzúr that if they fire just one shot, I'll hang him on the nearest aspen!"[34]

The flawless implementation of the military operation was in sharp contrast to the subsequent political improvisation and absurd subterfuge of Soviet propaganda. The Soviets failed in installing a puppet government or in preventing the convocation of the CPCs Party Congress, which strongly condemned the invasion. Nor did they win over President Svoboda, whose authority was meant to be used to justify the change in leadership. Moreover, the passive resistance by the people was a permanent factor against them. The invasion was also condemned by many of the future "normalizers"—Ľubomír Štrougal and Gustáv Husák among them. According to eyewitness accounts, Husák exclaimed at the meeting of Slovak Communist Party Presidium on August 21: "Now you can see what a mess that idiot Brezhnev has made!"[35]

K. T. Mazurov, who represented the Soviet Politburo in Prague and was working at the embassy under the alias of General Trofimov, sent panicky messages to Moscow: "They are now shouting in the streets: 'Where is Dubček, Smrkovský and Černík?' The right-wingers are rallying their forces and the left-wingers are passive... We suggest that you talk with Dubček and Černík. In the evening it may be too late, and they may start real fighting in Prague."[36] Finally, the Soviet leaders had to hold negotiations with the same CPCs representatives whom they had arrested and interned in the USSR. The Archives of the Czechoslovak Government Commission include an exceedingly dramatic shorthand report of the first meeting between Dubček, Černík and the Soviet Politburo, when the Czechoslovak leaders, who were worried and perplexed, were urged to make a reassuring address to their people, as if nothing had happened.[37] The Soviet leaders found themselves in a quandary because of their own recklessness, but the situation was saved by the loyalty of the Czechoslovak communists, who were afraid of clashes and bloodshed and agreed to sign a secret "Moscow Protocol," which legalized the Soviet military presence in Czechoslovakia until the situation "returned to normalcy" (its criteria were not specified).

---

34 Author interview with I. Yershov, January 17, 1991.
35 AGC, Antonín Ťažký, V 43.
36 AGC Z/P 6. K.T. Mazurov to A. Kosygin, August 22, 1968.
37 National Security Archive, Washington, D.C., Verbatim Report on the Talks between L. Brezhnev, A. Kosygin, N. Podgorny, G. Voronov, with A. Dubček and O. Černík on August 23, 1968.

Władysław Gomułka, then on visit to Moscow with other leaders of the Warsaw Pact, defined their intensions with regards to Dubček: "He might sign some kind of document which is certainly unacceptable to the counter-revolution. That will compromise him."[38] It was agreed during those talks that, soon after Dubček had carried into effect the most unpopular decisions to "normalize" the situation, he would have to resign, especially in view of the fact that President Svoboda had disassociated himself from him.[39]

Rumors were often spread in Western publications that Brezhnev and Kosygin had repented for the part they had played in the intervention, that they had allegedly admitted the erroneous nature of the military solution to the Czechoslovak question and had relieved of their duties those who were guilty of generating tension at that time (for instance, Shelest). However, the minutes of conversations with the heads of the Warsaw Pact prove that this was not the case. A month later Brezhnev said that the time that had elapsed "confirms both the need for our joint action and its urgency. Now we have ample evidence confirming the counter-revolutionary and anti-Soviet activity in Czechoslovakia."[40] In reply to a reproach by the high-ranking Czechoslovak official Josef Špaček that "the USSR had stabbed the world communist movement in the back," Brezhnev replied: "You underestimate the situation. In the next few years the world socialist camp will not expand naturally, and we are now trying to save what there is."[41]

Feeling that they could rely on the support of the CPSU, guaranteed by the Soviet military presence in Czechoslovakia, orthodox communists there sought to complete what had started. In their conversations with Soviet representatives they advised the Soviet side "to press on confidently and demand, primarily, consistent implementation of the commitments on cadre issues."[42] Another informant predicted that "Dubček's leadership will not stand the pressure, it will expand the scope of compromises and will eventually lose

---

38 AGC Z/P 4, Meeting between Brezhnev, Kosygin and Podgorny with Ulbricht, Kádár, Gomułka and Zhivkov in Moscow, August 24, 1968.

39 Ibid.

40 AGC Z/P 4, Meeting of the Communist and Workers' Party Leaders of Poland, Hungary, Bulgaria, the GDR and the USSR in Moscow, September 30, 1968.

41 AGC, J. Špaček, R 9, February 5, 1990.

42 AGC, M. Zimyanin's message to Brezhnev (report of V. Shuravsky on his discussion with O. Švestka, October 29, 1968. Roll 9757, f.5, i.60, c.301, 1., 334-43.

the trust of the Party, the country and the world."[43] Meanwhile, the head of the CPCs International Department told Soviet Ambassador Chervonenko that "The healthy forces are disappointed by the information that the CPSU is satisfied with the process of normalization. The steadily growing daily political pressure and ever greater claims, laid by the CPSU and other allies to the right-wing CPCs leadership, are the basic preconditions for genuine normalization." He supplemented his advice with specific proposals on cadre appointments and on the composition of the CPCs's Central Committee Secretariat.[44] The Soviet side was ready and willing to deal in minute detail with those appointments.

The Soviets followed to the letter the advice of the CPCs traditionalist communists. The latter now had a congenial spirit, so their conversations with the CPSU leaders, which earlier were in the nature of club discussions, now looked much like reports of district secretaries to superior Party bodies. Thus, Dubček's evasiveness and reluctance to discuss in substance the questions posed was rather irritating whereas his more pragmatic colleagues—Černík and Štrougal—very soon were only too ready to oblige the CPSU leaders. "I understand Comrade Brezhnev, that today mere assurances are not sufficient to restore our mutual trust. You need practical steps to prove it...the key issue is to do away with spontenaity in the development of our processes and ensure the Party's guidance in public affairs."[45] Brezhnev usually started by saying: "We have never imposed anything on you," and, in the same breath, contradicted himself by raising the issue of cadre appointments, i.e., he recommended pro-Soviet elements to be appointed to leading posts, or advised the removal from such posts of those whom he no longer trusted. The Kremlin leaders were firm in their negative attitude to seemingly radical reformers such as Josef Smrkovský, Čestimír Císař, Jiři Pelikán, and Zdeněk Mlynář. For instance, they described Mlynář as a "dodger," "a man whose name is not clear enough." After the allied troops' invasion of Czechoslovakia, Mlynář hurried to the Soviet Embassy and proclaimed that, "thank God, the troops had at last been introduced to the country, otherwise there would have been a

---

43 The Center for the Preservation of Modern Documentation in Moscow (CPMD), Roll 9757, f.5, i.60, c.301, 1.3-18, September 30, 1968.

44 CPMD, Roll 9757, f.5, i.60, c.301, 1.3-18, September 30, 1968.

45 AGC, The General Department, 1st Sector, No. 1824. Minutes of discussions between the CPSU and the CPCs delegations on October 3, 1968.

catastrophe. Later on he attended the clandestine 14th CPCs Congress, paid a visit to President Svoboda, together with a group of colleagues, and held talks about the formation of a new government. Here you have a man without firm principles and ideological guidelines."[46]

Czechoslovakia was then expected to follow the Soviet example to the letter. The Brezhnev leadership even objected to the formation of a separate Central Committee of the Czech Communist Party, citing the Soviet experience. "The Russian people, Brezhnev argued, who account for 67 percent of the population in the Soviet Union, do not have either a separate Party or a separate CC. And the Russians do not feel offended."[47] The Soviet policy of dictating what to do was so oppressive that, in putting forward a resolution on the Party's current position and tasks to be endorsed by the plenary meeting of the Central Committee of the CPCs, to be held in November of 1968, the Dubček team, which could foresee a clash with their orthodox opponents at the meeting, thought it wise to fly to Warsaw in order to secure the approval of Brezhnev, who had arrived to attend a regular Congress of the Polish United Workers' Party. Well aware that they were going to part with the 'Prague Spring' supporters and were bound to lose the people's trust, Dubček and his colleagues, jointly with the Soviet comrades, followed to the letter the proposed resolution, going even further than its orthodox formulas provided so that they verged on the absurd.[48]

The leaders of the 'Prague Spring' were yet to live through the relapse of the marshals' diplomacy. After the ice-hockey incidents in March of 1969, when the Czechoslovak national team defeated the national team of the Soviet Union, and students demonstrated on the streets of Prague and Bratislava, Soviet defense minister Andrej Grechko unexpectedly arrived in Czechoslovakia. He was met by the country's top brass, who informed him that the president was waiting for him. To this, Grechko shouted, "What president? What government? You will be brought to account for what has happened." He then drove off to Milovice, where the largest Soviet garrison was stationed.

---

46 AGC, The General Department, 1st Sector, P 1952. Verbatim report of the meeting between the leaders of the Communist Parties of Poland, Hungary, the GDR, Bulgaria and the USSR in Moscow, September 27, 1968.

47 AGC, Verbatim report of talks between the CPSU and CPCs delegations in Moscow on October 3–4, 1968. General Department, 1st Sector, No.1824 (no signature).

48 AGC, Verbatim report of the discussions between L. Brezhnev, V. Grishin, K. Katushev and A. Dubček, O. Černík, G. Husák on November 15, 1968 (no signature).

Grechko's talks with Martin Dzúr reached such a low point that the Czechoslovak defense minister could no longer stand the pressure and declared that the Soviet side should be grateful to him for the order he issued the previous August that his troops should not leave their barracks. In response Grechko rolled up his sleeves and showed him the scars of wounds he had received during the liberation of Czechoslovakia in 1944–45.[49]

The Kremlin rulers were persistent in their search for "hundred-percent reliable" nominations to top Party posts. This reflected an old CPSU tradition of relying on one person or on only one sphere which was absolutely trustworthy. Vasil Biľak was now the main interpreter of Moscow's view of events in Czechoslovakia, and he also held the monopoly on communicating with Moscow. According to Štrougal, every time Brezhnev left Czechoslovakia, he was accompanied by Biľak for some 12–14 hours of the trip by rail from Prague to the Soviet border. In this way Bil'ak realized his unlimited right to convey his own views to the Soviet leader and later present them as those of the Soviet leadership, especially on cadre matters.[50]

So it is now clear that the Kremlin insisted on normalization the way it was implemented in Czechoslovakia—with radical purges, expulsions from the Party of over a million members and brutal ideological pressure. This was determined by the choice of dogmatic leaders (with the Kremlin's approval) who exerted direct and indirect pressure both on the more moderate "normalizers"— Husák and Štrougal—and on political affairs in the country as a whole.

This was not the first time that the USSR engaged in conflict with a member of the Warsaw Pact. But it was the first time that the introduction of troops was made to seem a collective venture and launched against a partner who repeatedly declared his loyalty to the Warsaw Pact. The invasion of Czechoslovakia destroyed the illusion that had been widely believed in the West after the Berlin and Cuban crises, that concern for political and strategic stability, as well as closer ties with the West, would result in the transformation of communism into a more civilized, pluralistic movement. By resorting to military force, the USSR manifested its readiness to protect its sphere of influence in a style traditional for the great powers. The CPSU continued to regard itself as the vanguard, not only of its own working class, but of the working people of the whole world. Furthermore, it was ready to sacrifice the reputation of

---

49   AGC, M. Smoldas, R37, April 19, 1990.

50   AGC, L. Štrougal, R1, November 21, 1990.

the USSR in order to return errant peoples to complete domination by the Communist Party. The precise execution of the invasion of Czechoslovakia was in great contrast to the subsequent helpless political improvisations of the Soviet Union—its inability to set up a puppet government. This senseless launching of a 500,000-strong army with zero effect subsequently forced the USSR to apply greater caution, for instance, with reference to the Polish events of 1980–81. The 'Prague Spring' of 1968 turned out to be the last attempt at a reformation of communism. Its failure produced doubts about the communist system's ability to evolve. It also stirred up a search for ways to break away from totalitarianism within the framework of other political systems and outside the established structures of power.

2

Reconsidering the Soviet Role in the Invasion of Czechoslovakia: A Commentary

Matthew J. Ouimet

A quick glance at the archival sources used in Mikhail Latysh's paper immediately suggests that his narrative offers new insights into the Soviet role in the Warsaw Pact's 1968 invasion of Czechoslovakia. Russia's former Chief Archivist, R. G. Pikhoia, shared with Dr. Latysh Soviet Politburo working notes from the 1968 intervention. Pikhoia published details from some of these meetings more than a decade ago in the Russian journal *Novaia i Noveishaia Istoriia*, but the transcripts themselves remain largely unavailable to researchers.

So what do we learn that is new here? On the whole, the landmarks of existing interpretation remain as they have been for much of the past decade since earlier studies first offered a look behind the scenes at the 1968 Warsaw Pact intervention. What Latysh brings to the table first and foremost are a number of fascinating details that offer insights into six key questions. What was the nature of the 'Prague Spring'? When and why did the Soviets lose faith in Alexander Dubček? How early did the Soviets consider military intervention in Czechoslovakia? How well informed was the decision to intervene? Could the intervention have been avoided? And finally, why was the Warsaw Pact occupation so ineffective?

Hungary All Over Again?

One of the remaining ironies of the 'Prague Spring' is that after forty years of scholarship, its precise political character remains unclear. Did Alexander Dubček believe in the reform of the communist system? If left unmolested by outside intervention, would the 'Prague Spring' have revitalized bloc politics, established legitimacy for communist leaders, and transformed itself into a more sustainable alternative to democratic capitalism? Latysh implies that it might have, "given the good mutual contacts between the reformists and the masses." The failure of the reform program, Latysh writes, occurred largely because Dubček lost control of events. Czechoslovakia faced the prospect of "backsliding to the 1956 Hungarian version of developments" through "dangerous daydreaming which threatened the country's relations with its allies in the communist bloc."

However, the suggestion that Czechoslovakia in 1968 was headed towards open rebellion, à la Hungary in 1956, remains an open question. If left to their own devices, would the Czechoslovak Communists have abandoned their monopoly on political power? Would they have withdrawn from both the Council for Mutual Economic Assistance (CMEA) and the Warsaw Pact alliance? The most reactionary voices on the Soviet Politburo believed that they would relatively early in Dubček's tenure. Speaking at a March 21, 1968, Politburo meeting, KGB Chairman Yuri Andropov told his colleagues that "the methods and forms by which the work is progressing in Czechoslovakia remind one very much of Hungary."[1] Andropov had helped to coordinate the Soviet intervention in Hungary as ambassador to Budapest in 1956. He believed the 'Prague Spring' would trigger a swing away from communism toward western-style social democracy. This had been the fate of Hungary in 1956, and in his opinion would be the future of Czechoslovakia in 1968. So Andropov proposed readying the military for use in Czechoslovakia, should it become necessary.[2]

---

1 Politburo working notes cited in R.G. Pikhoia, "Chekhoslovakiia, 1968 god. Vzgliad iz Moskvy po dokumentam TsK KPSS" [Czechoslovakia, 1968: The View from Moscow According to the Documents of the CPSU CC], *Novaia i Noveishaia Istoriia*, no. 6 (1994), 10. This is the first of two articles based almost entirely on the holdings of the Russian Presidential Archives and Center for the Study of Contemporary Documents in Moscow. As Chief Archivist, Pikhoia worked with key documents and working notes that have since been reclassified. His analysis is, therefore, one of the most valuable sources we have on the details of how the Soviets perceived the 'Prague Spring.'

2 Ibid., 12.

Most of Andropov's colleagues were slower to define the 'Prague Spring' as a counter-revolution in the absence of open rebellion or violence in the streets. Nevertheless, over the course of the next few months, Moscow gradually lowered the bar on what constituted a counter-revolution. Czechoslovakia was not Hungary, and the Soviets had to address this incongruity while considering the question of intervention. Latysh offers compelling evidence that the leaders in Prague might have been prepared to limit their own reform program to avoid a conflict with Moscow. Dubček himself apparently told the Czechoslovak Central Committee Presidium in mid-August that if he thought the country was on the verge of counter-revolution, he himself would ask the Soviets to intervene. Defense minister Martin Dzúr and his generals, on the eve of the occupation, discussed how to disperse demonstrators from the Party's headquarters with armored personnel carriers. Politically, the proposed Law on the National Front was to have banned, disbanded or closed opposition organizations. If accurate, these revelations from Latysh suggest that events in Czechoslovakia could have turned out quite differently from the Hungarian rebellion, had the 'Prague Spring' played itself out.

Moscow Loses Faith in Dubček

Moscow's readiness to redefine the concept of counter-revolution turned chiefly on a lack of faith in Alexander Dubček. Latysh suggests that the first real evidence we have of this mistrust comes from the March 1968 Dresden summit. Only days after Andropov proposed planning for military intervention, several bloc leaders used the summit to accuse Dubček of counter-revolution. Leonid Brezhnev reinforced the message with his observation that the generals present would render military "assistance" if circumstances so required.

What Latysh does not address is how Moscow moved from supporting Dubček to accusations of counter-revolution in the space of only a few months. A known quantity by 1968, Dubček had served as First Secretary of the Slovak Communist Party for nearly five years. He supported legal and economic reforms that ultimately led to a showdown in December 1967 with Czechoslovakia's Stalinist leader, Antonín Novotný. When Moscow refused to support Novotný, Dubček replaced him as First Secretary of the Czechoslovak Communist Party, though Novotný held on to the presidency for a few more months. Moscow, it seemed, was comfortable with putting the real power into Dubček's hands. Yet three months later, Dubček faced charges of counter-revolution and thinly veiled threats of military intervention. Was that shift of Soviet perceptions sudden, or gradual? Existing accounts fail to track the shift with sufficient clarity, resulting in an artificial sense of inevitability.

Latysh addresses the Soviet frustration with Dubček in the months that followed the Dresden summit, underscoring a certain inconsistency in Dubček's attitude towards the Soviet leadership in the bloc. This is an important observation. Once the 'Prague Spring' was well under way, the issue of Moscow's slipping influence in Czechoslovakia rose quickly to the top of the Kremlin agenda. It is difficult to overestimate how alarmed the Soviets were at the publication of the reformist "Action Program" in April of 1968. The program included calls for greater political pluralism, effectively challenging the communist monopoly on power, and included limits on the Party's control over the Czechoslovak Interior Ministry. Such a move promised to compromise Moscow's network of agents in Czechoslovakia.[3]

The Soviets saw in these measures an open bid to remove Czechoslovakia from the socialist camp and claimed at the April CPSU Central Committee plenum the right of ideological self-defense.[4] By early May, Brezhnev spoke of the Action Program as "opening the possibilities for the restoration of capitalism in Czechoslovakia." Foreign minister Andrei Gromyko warned of counter-revolution that could lead to the "complete collapse of the Warsaw Pact."[5] The consensus for military action was expanding as Moscow began to lose its traditional levers of influence in Eastern Europe.

Exercises or Military Intervention?

Latysh correctly identifies the "Šumava" Warsaw Pact exercises in May–June 1968 as a prelude to military intervention. However, his contention that Soviet military leaders might have launched an invasion under cover of the exercises is too speculative. Latysh cites as evidence minutes from a conversation between Marshal Yakubovsky and the commander of a Soviet tank division, General Yashkin, conceding that the marshal reversed apparent orders to occupy Czechoslovakia only ten minutes after issuing them. This is quite a contention to make on the basis of a single exchange. One struggles to

---

[3] Eugen Steiner, *The Slovak Dilemma* (Cambridge, 1973), 171.

[4] Pikhoia, "Chekhoslovakia, 1968 god," 13; and Karen Dawisha, *The Kremlin and the Prague Spring* (Berkeley, 1984), 59-60.

[5] Pikhoia, "Chekhoslovakia, 1968 god," 15.

recall any comparable instance of military independence in the entire course of Soviet history. Could the Yakubovsky-Yashkin exchange have amounted to two military men preparing for the worst in a politically uncertain situation? The Šumava maneuvers were, after all, an exercise in intimidation directed at the Czechoslovak leadership. "After this," Brezhnev joked prior to the war games, "everyone will understand that you cannot play games with us."[6] Their objective was, as Latysh points out, to strengthen the orthodox communists in the Czechoslovak leadership, whom Moscow referred to as "healthy forces." But they relied wholly on the power of intimidation, rather than on the immediate use of force.

The intimidation seemed to work even before Šumava began. In the days immediately leading up to the exercises, Dubček offered several significant concessions to the visiting Soviet Premier Alexei Kosygin. Czechoslovakia would remain in both the Warsaw Pact and the CMEA, he said. The Czechoslovak Communist Party would retain its monopoly on political power and oppose any move towards multiparty democracy. Kosygin offered in exchange the promise that the exercises offered "necessary assistance," rather than outside intervention. Reassured, Dubček gave permission for them to commence.[7] Soviet and allied forces entered the country without incident and received orders to remain after the exercises concluded in late June.

Even after Šumava, the question of how best to leverage the Warsaw Pact presence in Czechoslovakia divided the Soviet leadership. Some in the Kremlin echoed Soviet Ambassador Chervonenko's concern that leaving the troops in Czechoslovakia could turn the whole country against Moscow, frustrating any political solution.[8] Others agreed with foreign minister Gromyko's insistence that military intervention had become unavoidable. Brezhnev decided in early July to step back and reassess whether Moscow had a clear grasp of the situation. At Dubček's urging, he ordered the withdrawal from Czechoslovakia of the forces that had participated in the Šumava exercises.[9]

---

6   Ibid.

7   Ibid., 15–16.

8   Ibid., 20.

9   Jiri Valenta, *Soviet Intervention in Czechoslovakia, 1968: Anatomy of a Decision*, revised and expanded ed. (Baltimore, 1991), 170; Dawisha, *The Kremlin and the Prague Spring*, 189; Pikhoia, "Chekhoslovakia, 1968 god," 20.

Latysh quotes the Hungarian Defense Minister's reference to the exercises as a "dress rehearsal for occupation," and well they were. The reinsertion of Warsaw Pact forces into Czechoslovakia later that August did draw extensively on the lessons of Šumava. But it is unlikely that they were an early attempt to coerce a political solution in Czechoslovakia through military force. Moscow simply was not ready for decisive action in June of 1968.

The Role of Information and Ideology

Historians have long debated whether the Kremlin's response to the 'Prague Spring' was well informed, suggesting that more accurate reporting, or less ideological discussion, might have resulted in a more measured Soviet response. Here again, Latysh seems to blame Dubček for frittering away the prospect of a "modus vivendi" with Moscow. Latysh counts as "allies of the Soviets" more than half of the Party leadership in Prague and says the remainder sought the "renewal of socialism, not its dismantling." He points to the planned Law on the National Front as evidence that Dubček's government was prepared to assert the Party's monopoly on power to shut down all independent public organizations. Dubček is quoted as saying on August 12 that if he thought the country was on the verge of counter-revolution, he would invite the Soviets in himself. Moreover, Latysh argues, Prague was well aware that the United States and its allies would not respond meaningfully to a Soviet military intervention. Nevertheless, Dubček failed "to understand the urgency of the matter" as late as his mid-August discussions with Brezhnev.

This is an important point. How could Dubček say to the man who held in his hands the fate of Czechoslovakia, "Do whatever you think is necessary"? Brezhnev himself warned Dubček that he did not realize the gravity of his own suggestion.[10] The August exchanges with Brezhnev suggest that Dubček was either unwilling or unable to deliver on the promises of the Bratislava Declaration. It is difficult not to reach this conclusion even forty years later. If the reformers in Prague were planning to limit the scope of their initiatives, this was not at all apparent in these eleventh-hour conversations. Instead, Moscow was left to sort out the future prospects of the reform process, for both Czechoslovakia and the broader socialist alliance. In the zero-sum calculus of the Cold War, the Kremlin's response hinged on how it read the trajectory of the 'Prague Spring.'

---

10 Valenta, *Soviet Intervention in Czechoslovakia*, 188.

Left to its own devices, Latysh argues, the Kremlin deliberately painted itself into a corner until the only logical course of action was military. The select, even distorted, information that Ambassador Chervonenko forwarded to Moscow married well with the ideologically charged debates already raging in the Kremlin. It fostered the impression that the 'Prague Spring' was heading towards a restoration of western-style democracy in Czechoslovakia. Latysh does not mention the KGB, but its officers also warned of Western encroachment on Czechoslovakia in their reports to the Kremlin. Convinced that Bonn and other Western capitals were promoting counter-revolution, KGB personnel fabricated evidence to that effect.[11] The Kremlin apparently never saw reports from KGB officials in New York challenging these allegations, as intelligence authorities in Moscow had them destroyed.[12] But how much did all of this matter in Moscow's decision to send troops into Czechoslovakia?

Fundamentally, the question of a dominant power, occupying a weaker country boils down to the question of national sovereignty. Latysh demonstrates that the Soviet leadership thought little about Czechoslovak sovereignty. Premier Kosygin's remarks to Dubček at Čierna nad Tisou were especially revealing. Czechoslovakia and the USSR, he said, "together have only one border—the one that abuts the West and separates us from the capitalist countries." Dubček would hear words to this effect again from Brezhnev himself following the August intervention. On that occasion, Dubček was told that Czechoslovakia lay on territory that the Soviet Army bought "at the cost of enormous sacrifices" in World War II, and so Moscow would never leave it. "The borders of that area," Brezhnev declared, "are our borders as well."[13]

Soviet commentators would later remark that the so-called Brezhnev Doctrine of Limited Sovereignty was essentially a creation of western political observers, never formally adopted in the Kremlin. Yet, these unguarded remarks from Kosygin and Brezhnev in the summer of 1968 suggest that limited sovereignty was very much a part of the Kremlin's policy in Czechoslovakia. It seems unlikely that a less impassioned discussion about the future of the

---

11 Christopher Andrew and Vasili Mitrokhin, *The Sword and the Shield: The Mitrokhin Archive and the Secret History of the KGB* (New York, 1999), 252–5; Christopher Andrew and Oleg Gordievsky, *KGB: The Inside Story* (New York, 1990), 483.

12 Oleg Kalugin, "KGB poka ne meniaet printsipov…" [The KGB Has Not Yet Changed its Principles], *Komsomol'skaia Pravda*, 20 June 1990, 2.

13 Zdeněk Mlynář, *Nightfrost in Prague: The End of Humane Socialism*, tran. Paul Wilson (New York, 1980), 240.

'Prague Spring' would have changed this.[14] Czechoslovakia and its runaway reform program bore directly on the political fortunes of the Soviet Union itself in the Kremlin's mindset. Greater clarity into the situation on the ground would not likely have changed Moscow's strategic calculations.

What about its tactics? Would greater clarity have resulted in a more effective intervention? Quite possibly. A key misconception was Moscow's belief that large numbers of pro-Soviet Czechs and Slovaks were waiting anxiously for outside intervention against the reformers. Most of the Politburo sustained this belief despite Premier Kosygin's insistence that rumors of a "second center" in Prague were highly exaggerated. Kosygin held that Dubček and his allies were the only hope for controlling developments in Czechoslovakia, arguing in late May for a shift in Soviet attitudes towards the reformers.[15] Ukrainian Party leader Petro Shelest disagreed, citing assurances from First Secretary of the Slovak Communist Party Vasil Biľak of a viable "second center," and Kosygin's moment passed.[16]

What would have happened had Shelest not carried the day? Years later, in early 1979, the Kremlin postponed its intervention into Afghanistan on the grounds that communist authorities in Kabul had no real support. In December 1979, Moscow sent troops in anyway, worried that the United States had co-opted the communist authorities in Kabul.[17] It seems likely that similar reasoning would have prevailed in 1968, even if Kosygin's argument had received a full hearing. The zero-sum logic of the Cold War would likely have proven more compelling than rational political discourse between the reformers and Moscow.

---

14 One might offer the case of Poland in 1980–81 as evidence that the Soviets might well have shown greater restraint under different conditions. However, the circumstances that held the Soviet hand in Poland—fear of Western economic sanctions and action by the Polish authorities against the reform movement—were highly unlikely in 1968.

15 Pikhoia, "Chekhoslovakia, 1968 god," 17.

16 Ibid., 17–18.

17 Vladimir Bukovskii, *Moskovskii Protsess* [Moscow Process] (Moscow, 1996), 307–20. Bukovskii gained access to hundreds of archival records from the Center for the Study of Contemporary Documents and the Russian Presidential Archives, lengthy excerpts from which he published in this book along with his own commentary. See also G. M. Kornienko, *Kholodnaia Voina: Svidetel'stvo ee uchstnika* [The Cold War: Testimony of its Participant] (Mezhdunarodnye Otnosheniia, 1995), 191–5.

Why Was the Warsaw Pact Occupation so Ineffective?

The confusion that resulted from Moscow's belief in a viable "second center" within the Czechoslovak Party is now the stuff of legend in the annals of the August intervention. Latysh's insights into this aspect of the 'Prague Spring' are most interesting. Brezhnev, we learn, held that a majority of the Czechoslovak Party's Central Committee was behind the intervention. According to Latysh, he concluded further that broad Party support meant broad *popular* support behind the intervention from the majority of Czechs and Slovaks. Was the Soviet self-deception that comprehensive? Latysh offers little to demonstrate the depth of Moscow's conviction beyond the way events played out. Nevertheless, the events themselves do betray remarkable confidence among the Soviet leadership that the intervention would be bloodless. Consider Soviet defense minister Grechko's warning to his Czechoslovak counterpart, Martin Dzúr, at the start of the invasion: if even one shot was fired in resistance, he would hang Dzúr from the nearest aspen tree. This is not the attitude of someone who expects to face another Hungary. It may be that the Kremlin's ability to believe its own ideological rhetoric was far greater than many historians have allowed.

Latysh suggests that the initial responses of several key players were not as one might have expected. Gustáv Husák, Moscow's eventual choice to succeed Dubček in 1969, reportedly told the Slovak Party Presidium on August 21, "Now you can see what a mess that idiot Brezhnev has made." Latysh also cites a Soviet after-action report placing Zdeněk Mlynář, a leading Dubček ally, in the Soviet embassy at the start of the intervention, where he allegedly welcomed the occupation as necessary to stave off a catastrophe. This version of events does not square with Mlynář's own autobiographical *Nightfrost in Prague*, which describes in moment-by-moment detail how Soviet troops detained Mlynář and other members of the Czechoslovak Presidium at the start of the intervention. The conclusion of the Soviet report, "Here you have a man without firm principles and ideological guidelines," strikes one more as character assassination than as fact. Nevertheless, it would be interesting to look into the question more thoroughly.

Perhaps the best moment Latysh recounts from the normalization is the encounter between Grechko and Dzúr that occurred after the March 1969 hockey riots. The drama of Grechko's rolling up his sleeves to show Dzúr the scars from wounds he received during the Soviet liberation of Czechoslovakia is simply wonderful. Dzúr contended that the Soviets ought to be grateful to him for confining Czechoslovak forces to their barracks in August. Grechko responded with physical "evidence" that it was Dzúr and his countrymen who ought to feel grateful to Moscow for their liberation from the Nazis. More broadly, Grechko's gesture was fully consistent with Kosygin's argument at Čierna nad Tisou and Brezhnev's conversation with Dubček at the Moscow talks in August. In each instance, the Soviet leadership claimed the right to act as it deemed necessary in Czechoslovakia. It had earned that right through its defeat of the Nazis in World War II. And it would use that right to protect Soviet interests in the Cold War.

Conclusion

Latysh reasons that Moscow used force against the 'Prague Spring' "to protect its sphere of influence in a style traditional for the great powers." In part, this claim captures the kind of zero-sum, Cold War thinking that would brand as "counter-revolutionary" efforts to strengthen communism in Eastern Europe. But in what sense was it traditional for great powers to violate the sovereignty of their allies over troublesome political reforms? Certainly, this happened in East Germany in 1953, in Hungary in 1956, and in Czechoslovakia in 1968. But is it really possible to identify examples of this type of behavior outside the Soviet bloc? The Cold War did involve military intervention from both sides in proxy wars around the world. However, the Soviets were unique in the rough treatment of their allies.

Latysh argues that this treatment stemmed, at least in part, from the ideological conviction that the CPSU was the vanguard of the international working class. Moscow, he contends, was "ready to sacrifice the reputation of the USSR" to safeguard the communist monopoly on power beyond its own borders. While these particular assertions may take the point a bit too far, the broader point, that the Soviet leaders took their ideology seriously, is indisputable. The discussions, memoirs, and Politburo meetings referenced here and elsewhere illustrate the extent to which communist ideology featured in Soviet reasoning. The Kremlin's world view was steeped in Marxist-Leninist terminology that defined friends and enemies, threats and opportunities. This has been one of the more important—even surprising—revelations that have come out of the Soviet and East European archives.

A corollary to the Latysh argument is that Soviet ideological convictions interpreted the 'Prague Spring' reforms as a threat to political stability in the bloc. While the emergence of a vibrant civil society may well have strengthened the political legitimacy of Dubček's government, it necessarily chipped away at the communist monopoly on power across the whole socialist bloc. It also opened the door to closer relations with the Western powers, which the Soviets regarded as a political defeat in the zero-sum East-West standoff. In time, moreover, that political defeat could strengthen the Western military posture vis-à-vis the Warsaw Pact.

The inherent problem with this view, of course, was that any effort to reform communist rule in practice would look like counter-revolution. This was the "Achilles heel" of the entire system after 1968. Moscow worked hard to impose a single model of orthodox communist rule across the entire bloc, leaving its member states little flexibility. Its "normalization" subsequently hobbled the ability of the bloc states to cope with the twin crises of political legitimacy and economic stagnation. As Latysh points out, this process, begun in August 1968, set the stage for the collapse of communism two decades later.

3

The 'Prague Spring' and the Warsaw Pact Invasion As Seen From Prague

Jan Rychlík

In the 1960's the communist regime in Czechoslovakia gradually fell into a deep political crisis, and most Czechs hoped it would lead to serious social and political reforms. There were several reasons for the Czechs' dissatisfaction with their society. The first was that the process of de-Stalinization and political rehabilitation of the victims of the Stalinist era did not take place in Czechoslovakia in 1956 as it had in Poland and Hungary. Antonín Novotný, First Secretary of the Central Committee of the Communist Party of Czechoslovakia (CC CPCs) since 1953, was himself partly responsible for the repressions of the Stalin-Gottwald period (1948–1953). Novotný, who became president on November 19, 1957, was not interested in reforms or political rehabilitations. He feared that if the former high Party officials were rehabilitated, they would demand to return to their functions and political life. Thus, most of the victims of the political purges remained in prison after 1956 and in most cases were only pardoned, but not rehabilitated, in 1960, when Czechoslovakia adopted a new constitution.[1] Juridical and political rehabilitation finally took place in 1963, under pressure from Moscow.

The rehabilitation of former political prisoners, who were often former high communist officials, weakened the confidence of Czech society (including rank-and-file members of the Communist Party) in the Novotný

---

1   This was also the case with Gustáv Husák, who was sentenced to life imprisonment in 1954.

regime. Since the full truth about the political repressions of the fifties was not revealed in 1963, various intellectuals started gradually to question the legitimacy of the regime. In addition, a new generation with no memory of the pre-war capitalist system and the German occupation emerged in the middle of the sixties. This generation did not compare its way of life and standard of living with pre-war Czechoslovakia, as did their parents, but rather with the contemporary situation in neighboring democratic countries such as Austria and the Federal Republic of Germany.[2] It goes without saying that, in such a comparison, communist Czechoslovakia was the loser.

The second reason was economic. While in the 1950's, despite many difficulties, the Czechoslovak economy grew, in the 1960's it stagnated. The third Five Year Plan, adopted by the Communist Party Congress on July 5–7, 1960, and formally approved by the National Assembly on November 17, 1960,[3] was absolutely unrealistic. It announced an increase in production of 56 percent by 1965! The collapse of this Five Year Plan indirectly forced Novotný to start thinking about economic reform. Opening a discussion about the economy of Czechoslovakia, however, had political repercussions.

Antonín Novotný, as Party boss and president, was very powerful, but his position had weakened by the middle of the sixties. The fall of Nikita Khrushchev in 1964 deprived him of Soviet political support because the new leader, Leonid Brezhnev, was not interested in Novotný. Meanwhile, the rehabilitated victims of the purges of the fifties were gradually undermining Novotný's position in the Central Committee. In addition, young intellectuals, such as writers, poets and scientists, were also clamoring for more freedom of expression. The growing opposition to Novotný became visible mainly after the 13th Congress of the Communist Party held on May 31–June 4, 1966. By then it had become obvious that substantial political and economic reform would be necessary. The reformers did not want to destroy the communist system, but rather to make it more flexible and adaptable. In the Czechoslovakia of the mid-1960's there was no politically relevant segment in Czech society thinking about switching to a standard capitalist and democratic system.

---

2   From 1963 on, it became possible for Czechoslovak citizens to visit relatives living legally in the West. Travel was liberalized even more in 1965 when the Passport Act was passed (Law No. 63/1965). Also, tourists from the West started to visit Czechoslovakia in large numbers after 1963. See Jan Rychlík, *Cestování do ciziny v habsburské monarchii a v Československu. Pasová, vízová a vystěhovalecká politika 1848-1989* (Prague, 2007), 65.

3   Law No. 165/1960.

Therefore, the fall of Antonín Novotný and the beginning of a process of democratization and an attempt at reform, which would bring together socialism and democracy, was not directly connected with the demand for more freedom and democracy, but with the dissatisfaction of the Slovaks with the centralist regime. While on the Czech side the lack of freedom was seen as the biggest problem, mainly by intellectuals, in Slovakia the liquidation of Slovak autonomy, which meant all decisions were made in Prague, was rightly seen as the main problem. The Slovak executive organ—the Board of Commissioners—was abolished by the new constitution in 1960, and the Slovak National Council (SNC) [the Slovak Parliament] was deprived of all its powers. As a consequence, in Slovakia, the reorganization of Czechoslovakia as a federation was seen as a suitable solution to local dissatisfaction. Under this banner were united the communists, non-communist intellectuals, the ex-*ludáks* (the adherents of the wartime Slovak state) and also the neo-Stalinists, who saw in federation an opportunity for better participation in the political power of the Czechoslovak state. The Czech reformers, for tactical reasons, supported this cause because they viewed it as an opportunity to remove Novotný. It was no surprise that the Slovak question was the spark which started the reform movement in Czechoslovakia.[4]

It all began with the scandal that erupted during Novotný´s visit to Slovakia on August 25–27, 1967. When Novotný visited the *Matica slovenská*, the leading Slovak cultural institution in Martin, Juraj Paška, the executive director, asked Novotný to allow the *Matica slovenská* to establish contacts with Slovak institutions abroad and to collect books and newspapers published by those institutions. Novotný refused both requests and accused the *Matica slovenská* of Slovak "bourgeois nationalism." He abruptly left the *Matica* building and refused to accept presents prepared for him and his wife.[5] Novotný´s behavior increased the opposition against him.[6] Within a short time, a strong coalition formed within the Presidium of the Central Committee of the Czechoslovak

---

4   For more on this topic see Jan Rychlík, "From Autonomy to Federation," in Jiří Musil, ed., *The End of Czechoslovakia* (Budapest, 1995), 193–5.

5   AMS (Archív Matice slovenskej – Archives of Matica slovenská, Martin), J. Paška, Novotný´s visit to Martin in 1967.

6   SNA (Slovenský národný archív-- Slovak National Archives, Bratislava), f. (fond - fund) ÚV KSS, secretary Alexander Dubček, k. (krabica – box) 2396, a. j. (archívna jednotka - archive unit a.j.) 3. Informácia o konflikte so s. Novotným v Matici slovenskej [Information about the conflict with comrade Novotný at the Matica slovenská].

Communist Party,[7] consisting of Slovak and Czech reform communists and Slovak nationally orientated conservatives. Alexander Dubček, the First Secretary of the Communist Party of Slovakia (CPS),[8] started the move against Novotný. On October 30–31, at the plenary session of the Central Committee, Dubček announced that the crisis has its roots in the internal system of the Party itself. He criticized the "accumulated functions," that is, that Novotný was simultaneously the First Secretary of the Czechoslovak Communist Party and the President of the Republic, which gave him dictatorial powers.[9] Novotný accused Dubček of defending "narrow local interests," meaning Slovak nationalism. On November 1, 1967, Dubček rejected Novotný´s accusations.

At the beginning of November 1967, Novotný left Prague for Moscow to attend the celebrations of the fiftieth anniversary of the Great October Socialist Revolution. In Moscow he tried to obtain the support of Soviet leader Leonid Brezhnev. During his absence from Prague, as the opposition against Novotný increased among members of the Central Committee and the population at large, a secret agreement was reached among the majority of the Communist Party secretaries that Novotný should be removed. At the next meeting of the Presidium of the Central Committee on December 5, many members defended Dubček and criticized Novotný.[10] Then, the Presidium of the Central Committee of the Communist Party of Slovakia openly supported Dubček at its meeting on December 8, 1967.[11] Brezhnev, who arrived secretly in Prague on the same day, gave Novotný no support.

---

7   Since the 12th Congress in 1962, the leading body of the Communist Party of Czechoslovakia was called the *předsednictvo* (*predsedníctvo* in Slovak) which we translate as Presidium. It is equivalent to the Soviet Politburo.

8   The Communist Party of Slovakia (CPS) was a regional organization of the KPCs in Slovakia, not a separate political party. The decisions of the CC CPCs and its Presidium were binding on all Party members, including the CPS. The CPS had its own Central Committee and its own Presidium subordinated to the CC CPCs. There was no Communist Party of the Czech Lands. The relationship of the CPCS and the CPS was modelled on the situation in the USSR, where the republican organizations were regional organizations of the Communist Party of the USSR. There was no Communist Party of the Russian Federation.

9   NA ČR (Národní archiv České republiky – National archives of the Czech Republic, Prague), f. ÚV KSČ, 01, a. j. (archívní jednotka – archive unit) 117, Meeting of the Central Committee on October 30–31, 1967, pp. 29–35. See also: Jitka Vondorvá, Jaromír Navrátil, Jan Moravec, *Komunistická strana Československa. Pokus o reformu Prameny k dějinám československé krize v letech 1967–1970* (further cited as PDČSK). Díl (part) 9., svazek (volume) 1, (Prague, 1999), doc. 2, p. 29.

10 NA ČR, f. ÚV KSČ, 02/1, Presidium 5. 12. 1967.

11 SNA, f. ÚV KSS, predsedníctvo, schôdza 8. 12. 1967.

The Presidium of the CC of the CPCs met again on December 11, and its session lasted until December 14. By now, the Presidium had divided into two camps: supporters of Novotný—A. Novotný, Jozef Lenárt, Michal Chudík, Bohumil Laštovička, Otakar Šimůnek and candidates to the Presidum Antonín Kapek and Miroslav Pastyřík—and opponents of Novotný—Jiří Hendrych, Drahomír Kolder, Alexander Dubček, Oldřich Černík, Jaromír Dolanský and secretaries of the Central Committee Ľubomír Štrougal, Vladimír Koucký and Štefan Sádovský.[12] The dividing line did not follow the nationality of the Presidium members, because in Novotný´s bloc were two Slovaks, Michal Chudík and Jozef Lenárt, and the majority of Novotný´s opponents were Czechs. In the period of the so-called normalization, that is, after the Soviet-led invasion, anti-Novotný members Drahomír Kolder, Lubomír Štrougal and Novotný´s supporters Jozef Lenárt remained; on the other hand, former pro-Novotný and anti-Novotný members of the Presidium were among those fired and persecuted, e.g., B. Šimůnek, A. Dubček, O. Černík, Š. Sádovský.

No final decision was made in early December of 1967 because of the deadlock.[13] But the conflict escalated at the Central Committee session of December 19–21.[14] On December 21 the session was interrupted for the Christmas holidays. It continued on January 3, 1968, simultaneously with the meeting of the Presidium. On January 5 Novotný resigned as the first secretary but remained in the Presidium and also retained the post of president. On the same day Alexander Dubček was elected the First Secretary of the Communist Party of Czechoslovakia.[15]

The public knew nothing about the discussions of the Central Committee, in which many members called for democratization and some Slovak members also called for federalization. The first information became available only at the end of February. The official statement published in the party daily, the Prague *Rudé právo,* on January 6, 1968, merely informed the public about the resignation of Novotný and his replacement by Dubček. It also announced that the Presidium of the Slovak National Council would present to the Central Committee an analysis of the functions of the Slovak national organs. The

---

12   NA ČR, f. ÚV KSČ, 02/1, sv. 51, a.j. 53 – Presidium 11. 12. 1967.

13   NA ČR, f. ÚV KSČ, 02/1, sv. 52, a.j. 55 – Presidium 14. 12. 1967.

14   NA ČR, f. ÚV KSČ, 01, Central Committee December 19–21, 1967.

15   NA ČR, f, ÚV KSČ, 02/1, sv. 55, a. j. 66, point 0/3, see also: sv. 57, a. j. 62 – extraordinary meeting 4. 1. 1968.

secret decision (resolution) of the Central Committee, which was not published, ordered the government and the Presidium of the SNC to present to the Central Committee proposals for a new division of powers between the central government and the SNC.[16]

In January of 1968 the struggle between the progressive and conservative wings, as well as between centralists and federalists, was still only an internal struggle within the narrow limits of the Central Committee. The "progressives," however, soon decided to extend the discussion to the rank-and-file members of the Party and shortly after to the public. On January 21, 1968, Josef Smrkovský published in the daily *Práce* (Labor)[17] an article titled "O co dnes jde" (What is it all about?). He was the first Party official who partly revealed what was behind the replacement of Novotný. Two days later Jan Štern, the editor of *Práce*, published the first open attack on Novotný. Public criticism against Novotný and his regime was soon extended to criticism of the entire period after the communist coup of 1948, even though the coup itself remained taboo during the whole of 1968. Fabricated political processes and repressions against the opponents of the regime in the 1950's were openly criticized. In Slovakia the abolition of Slovak autonomy was criticized as well. Thus, the January plenary session had opened the way to gradual democratization and more freedom for society. On February 26, 1968, the first draft of the Action Program of the Communist Party was adopted, including the promise of more freedom of the press and, in the longer run, the federalization of Czechoslovakia. On March 4, when the Presidium of the Central Committee decided to abolish preliminary censorship,[18] it opened a completely new period. Soon the press, radio and television were out of the control of the Communist Party and became really free, a situation completely unknown in the communist system.

At the end of March 1968, the democratization process was accelerated by the so-called Šejna affair. General Jan Šejna, a high Communist Party official at the Ministry of National Defense, a close associate of Novotný and personal friend of his son, was discovered to have misused for many years army property

---

16   *Rok šedesátý osmý v usneseních a dokumentech ÚV KSČ*. (Prague, 1969), 20. NA ČR, f. ÚV KSČ, 01, a. j. 119, p. 101, also PDČSK, doc. 4, p. 43..

17   *Práce* was the daily of the Central Committee of the Revolutionary Trade Union Movement (ROH) and the Central Council of the Trade Unions (ÚRO), the official Trade Union Congress subordinated to the Communist Party.

18   *Rok šedesátý osmý...*, s. 33.

on a large scale. At the beginning of February an investigation into his activities was opened. The police, however, could not arrest him, because he was a deputy in the National Assembly. While the parliamentary committee discussed lifting his immunity, Šejna, with his mistress and his son, escaped on February 26 via Hungary and Yugoslavia to Italy.[19] Before his departure, he contacted the American CIA, which promised him assistance once he was out of Czechoslovakia. Indeed, the CIA transported Šejna from Italy to the USA. Despite the fact that Šejna was a suspected criminal, he was given political asylum in exchange for military secrets which he revealed to the Americans.[20] Šejna's escape spelled the political end of Novotný. On March 23 he resigned as President of the Republic. One week later, on March 30, the National Assembly elected General Ludvik Svoboda, a hero of the Soviet Union, as the new president.

While in the Czech part of the country the public discussion was connected mainly with the problem of democratization, in Slovakia the demand for federation soon took precedence. This was natural. The Czechs considered Czechoslovakia their nation-state from its beginning in 1918. The Slovaks did not see the situation that way. They believed that federation might give them some sort of their own (Slovak) statehood and simultaneously maintain the advantages connected with the existence of Czechoslovakia. There was one danger, however. If, under the banner of federation and Slovak national interests, the conservatives and neo-Stalinists united with true democrats and reform communists, separating the issue of federalization from that of democratization, the result would be only a federalized totalitarian communist system, which would be of little use to the Slovaks.[21] The danger became real when, at the session of the Central Committee of the Communist Party of Slovakia on January 22, 1968, Vasil Biľak, a neo-Stalinist, was elected the First Secretary of the CPS. In his first speech in this function he reduced the January plenary meeting of the CC of the CPCs to the personal problems of Novotný and the problem of Slovakia's place in Czechoslovakia.[22] The issue

---

19   ABS (Archív bezpečnostních složek – Archives of the Security Organs), f. AMV (Archiv Ministerstva vnitra ČSSR – Archives of the Ministry of Interior of ČSSR), collection of microfilmes, roll A 24-963 (police investigation of Šejna's escape).

20   In America Šejna presented himself as a freedom fighter, which had nothing to do with reality.

21   As we know, this is exactly what happened in the period of the so-called normalisation, after 1969.

22   SNA, f. ÚV KSS, Plenary session of the Central Committee of the KSS on January 22, 1968.

of democratization was dropped from the agenda, and Gustáv Husák, who was then considered to be one of the reform communists, was not co-opted into the Central Committee. The reform-minded communists, to whom at the beginning of 1968, for tactical reasons, Gustáv Husák belonged, and non-communist intellectuals soon became aware of the danger of further political developments in Slovakia. The discussion about the relationship between federalization and democratization was started by Július Strinka in the Slovak weekly *Kultúrny život* on April 5, 1968, when he stated that federation would mean nothing if in Slovakia decisions would still be made by the "political inspectors" and "Tatar figures." There were many people in Slovakia who were not satisfied with Biľak's leadership of the Party. The reform communists, who had strong positions in the Bratislava Party organization led by Jozef Zrak, tried repeatedly to get rid of the conservatives, including Biľak.[23] Their attempts had little effect. Generally speaking, the reformers in Slovakia were not strong enough to remove Biľak and other hard-liners.

The problem of federation was decided at the meeting of the Slovak National Council on March 14–15, 1968. The deputies removed the Chairman (Speaker) of the SNR Michal Chudík, a centralist and a trustee of Novotný, and adopted a resolution asking for a constitutional codification of federation.[24] The resolution was approved by the Central Committee of the Communist Party of Slovakia.

On April 5, 1968, the session of the Central Committee of the Communist Party of Czechoslovakia approved the "Action Program." It was the first complex program proposing the democratization of society and political life. The Communist Party was to remain the leading force in the country, but it was ready to accept some concessions and reforms towards a more open society.[25] Economic reforms giving more autonomy to factories were proposed; freedom to travel abroad and to emigrate was to be given; and freedom of the press and speech were to be restored. Czechoslovakia was to be federalized.[26]

---

23 Miloš Marko, during the "normalization," the director of Slovak radio and one of the hard-liners, confirmed in 1971, that "revisionists" (i.e., reformers) had strong positions in the Party organization in Bratislava. See Marko, M., *Čierne na bielom* (Bratislava, 1971), 82.

24 SNA, f. SNR, IV. volebné obdobie, 16. schôdza 14–15. 3. 1968.

25 *Rok šedesátý osmý...*, 103–46.

26 Ibid., 120-21.

On April 8, 1968, President Ludvík Svoboda appointed Gustáv Husák as one of the vice-chairmen of the new government of Oldřich Černík. The new cabinet announced the governmental program on April 24. Its main aim was to implement the Action Program approved on April 5. For that reason, a special Constitutional Committee for the preparation of the federation was established under Gustáv Husák. This committee, together with the Economic Committee under Ota Šik, was to prepare the draft of the Constitutional Law on the Federation. On June 24, 1968, the National Assembly passed Constitutional Law No. 77/1968, under which a Czech Parliament—the Czech National Council—was established as the equivalent of the Slovak National Council. The draft of the Constitutional Law was ready before the Soviet occupation and was approved by the Presidium of the Communist Party on August 13.[27] The draft was based on the proposals of the special committee of the Slovak National Council and the CC of the SCP. According to the draft, the unitary Czechoslovak Socialist Republic was to be divided into two semi-independent states—the Czech Socialist Republic and the Slovak Socialist Republic—each having its own parliament (the Czech and Slovak National Councils) and its own government. Common affairs were to be in the purview of the federal government and a bicameral Federal Assembly. The Czechoslovak case differed from other federations in one respect: the Upper House of the Federal Assembly (the House of Nations) consisted of 75 deputies elected in the Czech Republic and 75 deputies elected in the Slovak Republic. In most cases, the Czech and Slovak deputies voted separately and a consensus was required. The Constitution had no solution if a consensus was not reached. Such a situation could hardly happen during the communist dictatorship when the Parliament played only a minor (if any) role. But after the fall of communism in 1989, it led to the political deadlock in June of 1992 and subsequently to the dissolution of the federation at the end of the same year.

The success of the federation in 1968 also required the federalization of the Communist Party. This meant that the Communist Party of Slovakia was to be made relatively independent and a new Communist Party of the Czech Lands was to be established. The Central Committee of the CPCs at its session of May 29–June 1 decided to do so. The preparatory committee for the establishing of the Communist Party of the Czech lands was set up under the

---

27   NA ČR, f. ÚV KSČ, 02/1, sv. 81, aj. 126, No. P 4675.

ultraconservative neo-Stalinist Alois Indra.[28] Because the federalization of the Communist Party was absolutely incompatible with the principle of "democratic centralism" on which all Communist Parties were based, Alois Indra sabotaged the preparatory work. The existence of two Communist Parties was also included in the draft of the organizational order of the CPCs.[29]

The reformers (or the "progressive wing") in the Communist Party were aware that the radical changes in the Party could not be accomplished by the existing party apparatus and the Central Committee elected at the 13th Party Congress in 1966. Despite the fact that there were many reformers on the Central Committee, there were still many members connected to Novotný. The proposed radical changes required a totally new Central Committee and so would require holding an extraordinary Party Congress. The idea of such a Congress was first proposed for the agenda at the April session of the Central Committee but it was rejected. The reformers were also unable to significantly change the composition of the Presidium. Although some reform-minded members of the lower party structures were co-opted, some conservatives became members of the Presidium, where the conservatives held strong positions in the Secretariat (Vasil Biľak, Drahomír Kolder, Alois Indra). On the surface, the "progressives" and the "conservatives" were in a position of parity. But this meant that the democratization process would end in deadlock.

The April plenary session (April 1–5, 1968) opened with a public discussion of society. As a side effect, it led to the further mobilization of civil society and of some non-communist political parties, tolerated since 1948 but playing no role in the system (the Czechoslovak Socialist Party and the Czechoslovak People's Party in the Czech Lands and the Party of Freedom and the Party of Slovak Revival in Slovakia). New political organizations such as The Club of Active Non-Party Members (*Klub angažovaných nestraníků*—KAN) or the organization of former political prisoners (K-231)[30] existed only in the Czech lands. In Slovakia the Society for the Defence of Human Rights tried to register as a political subject. The Social Democratic Party, which had been

---

28 *Rok šedesátý osmý...*, 224.

29 Ibid., 282-4.

30 The name of the club referred to Law No. 231/1948 "On the Protection of the People's Democratic Republic." This extraordinary law served as the legal basis for the persecution of opponents of the regime. The law was technically valid for only two years, but in 1950 its provisions were incorporated into the new Penal Code No. 86/1950.

forcibly merged with the Communists in 1948, established a Preparatory Committee. In the press, an open discussion about the existence of opposition political parties was started by Václav Havel.[31] Churches started to play an active role in public life, mainly in Slovakia. All this meant that the process of democratization was gradually getting out of the control of the Communist Party. The May Day celebrations (May 1, 1968) changed from an official government parade to manifestations of the claims of all citizens. In the Party itself, the lower organizations became active and refused to blindly obey the Central Committee and its Presidium which—seen from the Marxist-Leninist perspective—meant the violation of the principle of "democratic centralism." All this led to open criticism of the situation in Czechoslovakia by the Soviet Union and most of its allies.

From the very beginning, the Soviet leadership was dissatisfied with developments in Czechoslovakia. Alexander Dubček was elected First Secretary of the CPCs without the prior consent of Moscow, which was unprecedented. At the beginning, however, the Soviet leadership considered Dubček to be "their man," because he had lived and studied in the Soviet Union. But already at the meeting of the Political Advisory Committee of the Warsaw Pact in Sofia on March 6–7, 1968 (Romania did not take part), the Czechoslovak Party leadership was criticized by Walter Ulbricht (the GDR Party leader) and Władysław Gomułka (the Polish Party leader). Even stronger criticism against Dubček´s leadership emerged at the meeting of the representatives of the Warsaw Pact countries in Dresden on March 23. Here Walter Ulbricht sharply criticized Alexander Dubček for "revisionism" in the Communist Party of Czechoslovakia.

As we know today, the possibility of eventual military intervention in Czechoslovakia was already discussed in the USSR at the end of February. Concrete preparations in the Soviet army started in April. Leonid Brezhnev was probably dissatisfied with the regional party conferences which took place in April. Preparations for a military invasion were started secretly by the Soviet General Staff. Brezhnev, however, preferred a political solution. On May 4–5 a Czechoslovak Party delegation was invited to Moscow. Dubček was again criticized by Brezhnev for being too soft vis-à-vis the "rightist elements." According to Brezhnev, there was an imminent danger of "counter-revolution" similar to that which took place in Hungary in 1956. The Soviet leadership

---

31   *Literární noviny*, April 4, 1968.

asked Dubček to remove the "anti-socialist elements" from the Presidium and the Central Committee and to restore "order," that is, to return—if necessary by force—to the Soviet model of socialism. Dubček, Smrkovský and Černík defended democratization in Czechoslovakia but promised to fight against the anti-communist elements.[32]

Immediately after the delegation's return from Moscow, a session of the Presidium and the Secretariat took place on May 7–8. Here, for the first time, Vasil Biľak openly criticized Dubček for doing nothing vis-à-vis "the danger from the right." In other words, he repeated the same accusations which Dubček had heard in Moscow. After Drahomír Kolder made the same charge against Dubček, it became obvious that there were Soviet agents—both Czechs and Slovaks—in the Presidium, who represented Moscow and informed Brezhnev of all Party decisions. But even Oldřich Černík and Josef Smrkovský, the reformers, recognized the "danger from the right." The main question was whether or not they should hold an extraordinary Party Congress. Dubček tried to find a compromise.[33]

At the plenary session of the Central Committee on May 29–June 1, the Central Committee suspended Party membership for Antonín Novotný and his close associates, which decreased the number of conservatives, but it also agreed to convene an extraordinary Party Congress on September 9, before the new district and regional conferences of the Communist Party were to be held.[34] Dubček and the reformers hoped that the Congress would confirm the new political line and would remove the conservatives from the Party leadership. At the same time, a conservative group was formed (D. Kolder, A. Indra, V. Biľak, O. Švestka, E. Rigo, A. Kapek, O. Volejník, M. Jakeš), which was, in fact, a "fifth column" for Moscow. As we know today, on May 8 a secret meeting of General Secretaries of the five Communist Parties of the Warsaw Pact (known later simply as "the Five") took place in Moscow and decided to try to organize "healthy forces" (e.g., conservatives, Leninists) in the Czechoslovak Presidium and the Central Committee. Brezhnev hoped that this group would be able

---

32 See Václav Kural a kol., *Československo roku 1968. I. díl. Obrodný proces* (Prague, 1993), 83-4.

33 PDČSK, 9/1, doc. 60, pp. 399-408, doc. 61, pp. 450-51.

34 There was also the question of whether or not the extraordinary congress of the Communist Party of Slovakia should take place before the 14th Congress of the CPCs or after that. After a long discussion in Slovakia, the Central Committee of CPS decided to hold its session on July 18, and to hold the Slovak Party Congress on August 26, 1968, that is, before the 14th Congress of the CPCs—see *Pravda* (Bratislava), July 19, 1968.

to seize power with the help of the centrists and reverse the democratization process in Czechoslovakia. Its members took their instructions from Moscow, usually via the Soviet Embassy in Prague. Brezhnev's hopes were not quite unrealistic; even some reformers felt that the situation was no longer under the control of the Communist Party. In spite of their reform program, they were still communists first and, afraid of new developments, denounced the attempts to form new political organizations. The final resolution published on June 1 talked about the "danger from the right." Attempts to organize new political parties and political opposition were criticized as were the press and other media, which were now totally out of the control of the Communist Party.[35]

The conservative and neo-Stalinist group was even stronger in the Central Committee of the Communist Party of Slovakia, which held its session on May 22–23. First Secretary Vasil Biľak repeated the accusation launched by Moscow and tried to establish an anti-Dubček platform.[36] In his memoirs Biľak proudly wrote that he openly informed the members of the Central Committee about the "danger from the right," about the concerns of the Soviet leadership and of the danger of "counter-revolution"[37] If we can believe these memoirs (which were written before 1989), the Central Committee did not accept the pro-Soviet resolution because of Dubček´s personal intervention.[38]

The resolution of the Central Committee of the CPCs from June 1 can be evaluated as a failed attempt to appease both reformers and conservatives. The reformers and the non-communists saw the resolution as an effort to slow down the democratization process. On June 27, 1968, the Czech writer Ludvík Vaculík published his "Two Thousand Words" manifesto. Here he reacted to the resolution and called upon citizens to accelerate the process of democratization, that is, to stand openly against the leadership of the Communist Party if the conservatives took power. The manifesto was directed toward the district Party conferences where the delegates for the 14th Party Congress were to be elected and was in this aspect quite clear: the conservatives should not be elected. Citizens were also called upon to be active in the defense of the freedom of the press and other rights.[39]

---

35   Rok šedesátý osmý..., 214–18.
36   SNA, f. ÚV KSS, stenografický záznam zo zasadnutia ÚV KSS 22.-23. 5. 1968.
37   Vasil Biľak, Paměti, II (Prague, 1991), 32–4.
38   Ibid., 36–7.
39   Literární noviny, June 27, 1968.

The Presidium of the Central Committee denounced the "Two Thousand Words" on the same day—June 27.[40] Negative attitudes were also expressed in the Slovak National Council, which assembled on that day.[41] But, they had no effect. The manifesto gained the support, not only of ordinary citizens and rank-and-file Party members, but also of some lower Party organizations. In addition, it became obvious that the regional Party committees in Prague, Brno and Bratislava had pro-reform majorities and, in case of open conflict, would probably not obey instructions from above.[42] For Moscow, the manifesto and the situation in some regional organizations was further proof that the Presidium of the Communist Party of Czechoslovakia was not in full control, either over society or over the Party. On July 3 the Soviet Party leadership sent a letter to the Czechoslovak leaders claiming that the Communist Party of Czechoslovakia was, in fact, no longer a Party "of the Leninist type." Brezhnev also asked other Communist Parties of the Warsaw Pact to send similar letters. Soon thereafter the Czechoslovak Party leadership was invited to Warsaw, where the leaders of the Communist Parties of the Soviet Union, the German Democratic Republic, Poland, Hungary and Bulgaria were to meet and discuss the Czechoslovak case on July 14–15.[43]

The Presidium of the Central Committee discussed the letters and the invitation to Warsaw on July 8 and 12. Dubček proposed bilateral consultations and also consultations with Romania and Yugoslavia first. But Drahomír Kolder organized a conservative platform that accepted the invitation to Warsaw and repeated the previous accusations. At the end of the discussion the Presidium refused to accept the invitation to Warsaw and asked for bilateral consultations instead.

The "Letter of the Five" sent to the Czechoslovak leadership sharply criticized Dubček and his policy. According to the letter, developments in Czechoslovakia were dangerous for other socialist states because Czechoslovakia could become "a gap" in the Warsaw Pact. The danger of German "revanschism" (an attempt at revenge for its defeat in World War II) and "American imperialism" as a threat to independence and socialism in Czechoslovakia

---

40 Rok šedesátý osmý..., 229.

41 SNA, f. SNR, IV. vol. obd., 17. schôdza, 27. 6. 1968.

42 Moravský zemský archív (Moravian Land Archives) (MZA) (Brno), f. KV KSČ (Regional Committee of KSČ), i. č. (inventární číslo - number) 6, k. 7, a.j. 597. See also M. Marko: op. cit., 82.

43 Rok šedesátý osmý..., 235.

were also mentioned. The letter requested the immediate dissolution of anti-socialist organizations in Czechoslovakia, restoration of government control over the press and an aggressive policy against "revisionist" and "rightist" powers. At the end, the representatives of the "Five" assured the Czechoslovak leadership that it could rely on "full solidarity and support from the side of brother socialist countries."[44]

The Presidium of the Central Committee of the CPCs obtained the letter through diplomatic channels on July 16 and immediately reacted. After an internal discussion, it refuted the accusations and stated that each socialist country was responsible for the development and defense of socialism on its own soil. It also gave assurances that Czechoslovakia remained a trusted member of the Warsaw Pact and Comecon (Council on Mutual Economic Assistance).[45] Discussions about the content of the letter continued on the next day. In the end the Presidium proposed a relatively mild answer, which tried to explain the Czechoslovak position and offered bilateral consultations.[46] The Central Committee of the CPCs, which was summoned on July 19, approved the draft.[47]

During June and July pressure by the Soviet leadership increased and military intervention became more likely. Already from May 10 through 17, large joint Polish-Soviet military maneuvers took place in Poland near the Czechoslovak border. At the same time, the Soviet general staff renewed its request for Soviet military bases in Czechoslovakia. This request had been made to Novotný in the spring of 1967. Novotný had refused, and the response of Dubček's leadership to the new request was also negative. Finally, on June 20, large joint maneuvers of the Warsaw Pact under the code name "Šumava"[48] started in Czechoslovakia. After they concluded, the Soviet army postponed its departure from Czechoslovakia until the beginning of August.[49] The aim all these actions was clear: to make both the leadership and the population of Czechoslovakia nervous. Meanwhile, Brezhnev still

---

44 *Rok šedesátý osmý...*, 240.

45 Ibid., 241–2.

46 Ibid., 249–50.

47 Ibid, 258–9.

48 The Czech name for the mountains at the border with Bavaria, in German known as the Böhmerwald.

49 The Soviet units which were in Czechoslovakia during "Šumava" returned on August 21.

believed that "healthy forces" would force Dubček to stop the democratization process, which the Soviet leadership saw as the road back to capitalism and the subsequent departure of Czechoslovakia from the Warsaw Pact. On July 22, the Soviet Union agreed to a bilateral meeting and to the Czechoslovak request that it be held on Czechoslovak soil.

The new meeting took place on the Czechoslovak side of the Czechoslovak-Soviet border, at the railway station Čierna nad Tisou, from July 29 until August 1.[50] The Soviet delegation consisted of the whole Politburo and the Czechoslovak side encompassed the whole Presidium. The Soviet delegation stayed overnight in Užhorod and every morning came by special train to Čierna nad Tisou. The fact that the Czechoslovak delegation was composed of all Presidium members meant the participation of the pro-Soviet fifth column.[51] The plenary session of both delegations did not have much significance, however. The decisive meeting took place between Dubček and Brezhnev in the Soviet train on the third day, July 31. According to Dubček's memoirs, Brezhnev asked him whether it would be possible to invite the other members of the "Five." Dubček agreed, with the proviso that the Warsaw letter of the "Five" would not be the basis of the negotiations and that there would be "new relations" between the CPCs and other Communist Parties of the "Five." Brezhnev agreed.[52] On the other hand, Brezhnev claimed that Dubček agreed with the necessity to stop the "counter-revolution" in Czechoslovakia, to restore control over the media and to remove from the Presidium members who were considered by the Soviets to be *personae non gratae* (the first persons mentioned were František Kriegel, the Chairman of the National Front, that is, the would-be coalition of the legally acting political parties, and Josef Pavel, the Minister of the Interior). Biľak, in his memoirs, made the same claim and disagreed with Dubček's speech on August 1, the day of the last plenary session.[53] Official statements issued after the meeting only confirmed that the representatives of the "Five" would meet again with the Czechoslovak leadership in Bratislava on August 3.[54]

---

50   Today the station is at the border between Slovakia and Ukraine.

51   V. Biľak, op. cit., 76–80.

52   Jiří Hochman, ed., *Naděje umírá poslední. Vlastní životopis Alexandra Dubčeka* (Prague, 1993), 179–80.

53   Biľak, op. cit., 83–84.

54   *Rok šedesátý osmý...*, 262–3.

The meeting in Bratislava and the subsequent declaration were considered to be a great victory for Dubček. There was no reference to the Warsaw letter, and the declaration contained the assurance that each Communist Party would decide how to solve problems according to its national specifics and local conditions. The reformers interpreted this sentence as approving the specific Czechoslovak road to socialism and the promise of non-interference in Czechoslovak domestic affairs. They probably saw a similarity with the Belgrade declaration of 1955, which ended formally the break between the Soviet bloc and Yugoslavia and in which the specific road for Yugoslavia was approved by Nikita Khrushchev. Nevertheless, the text of the Bratislava declaration contained a much more important clause that specified that the defense of socialism was the common duty of all socialist countries.[55] This sentence, which Dubček considered only as "Stalinist rhetoric,"[56] was in fact the nucleus of the subsequently well-known "Brezhnev Doctrine" and meant the justification of the possible invasion of Czechoslovakia. In Bratislava Vasil Biľak, in the name of the conservative group (Kolder, Indra, Švestka, Kapek, Biľak), secretly handed to Petro Šelest, the First Secretary of the Communist party of Ukraine (a member of the Soviet delegation), a letter asking for military intervention in the name of socialism.[57]

Soon after the Bratislava meeting, Brezhnev came to the conclusion that Dubček was unable or unwilling to eliminate "rightist elements" and to restore "order" according to classical communist standards. On August 16, members of the conservative group, led by Kolder and Indra, met at the Communist Party hotel in Orlík (a recreation center on the Vltava). Here a new memorandum was prepared for Brezhnev and the secret plan was worked out. The conservative group promised to seize power in the Presidium at its planned session on Tuesday, August 20, if the military intervention took place on the same evening. The new Presidium would then issue a resolution approving the invasion. After the invasion, a new "revolutionary government" was to be

---

55 Ibid, 264.

56 J. Hochman, op. cit., 180–1.

57 V. Kural, op. cit., 144. Kapek had given the Soviet delegation a similar letter in Čierna nad Tisou.

appointed in a scenario similar to that in Hungary in 1956.[58] The decision to intervene was approved first at the secret meeting of the Soviet Politburo and then at the new meeting of the "Five" in Moscow on August 18.[59] The Czechoslovak conspirators counted on their supporters in the state and security apparatus. Colonel Viliam Šalgovič, Deputy Minister of the Interior and Chief of State Security, was to play the main role. Šalgovič, who during the Second World War had deserted from the Slovak army on the eastern front to Ukrainian partisans, was most likely an agent of the Soviet Security Service and was taking directions from Moscow.[60] The conspirators also relied on Karel Hoffman, the Director of Central Communications, who was to seize control over radio and television.

The conspirators' plan failed. They were unable to change the program of the Presidium and to open the discussion "about the situation in the Party" after Čierná nad Tisou and Bratislava. The Party Presidium first discussed preparations for the Extraordinary Party Congress. A resolution warning of imminent danger of counter-revolution was prepared by members of the Secretariat Kapek and Indra only after 8:00 p.m. After a long discussion, most of the members rejected the proposed text. The discussion continued until 11 p.m., when a message arrived that Soviet paratroopers had occupied the Prague Ruzyně Airport and that elements of the Soviet, East German, Polish, Hungarian and Bulgarian armies had crossed the Czechoslovak border.[61] In these circumstances the conservatives lost the chance that their resolution would be accepted. On the contrary, a resolution and an appeal to the public denouncing the occupation was approved. There were seven votes for the latter resolution (Dubček, Černík, Kriegel, Špaček, Smrkovský, Barbírek and Piller) and four against (Kolder, Biľak, Rigo and Švestka). Kapek and Indra, as

---

58 The text was sent to Moscow in advance. A short announcement that the Warsaw Pact armies came at the invitation of the Czechoslovak Communist Party and the government was published in all Party newspapers of the invading countries on August 21 (see for example: *Rabotničesko delo*, 21. 8. 1968). Because both the Presidium of the CPCs and the government denounced the invasion, it was obvious that the Soviet Union was to blame for the invasion, For the full text, see *Sedm pražských dnů. Dokumentace. 21. – 27. 8. 1968*, 2nd. edition, (Prague, 1990) 29-32 (the so-called "Black Book," 1st ed., Prague, 1968).

59 V. Kural, op. cit., 153–5.

60 About Šalgovič, see Jan Pešek et. al., *Aktéri jednej epochy* (Prešov, 2003), 305–6.

61 The army of the GDR stayed near Dresden in reserve. The Czechoslovak leadership did not know this.

members of the Secretariat, who were not members of the Presidium, did not have the right to vote.[62] Two "mild conservatives"— Barbírek and Piller—on whom the conspirators counted, and who had been ready to vote for Kapek's resolution, changed their minds. The approved resolution was immediately published.[63] In the early morning of August 21, Soviet occupation forces seized Dubček and other reform members of the Presidium and interned them, first at the Soviet military base in Legnica (in Poland) and later in Ruthenia (the former Podkarpatská Rus).

The invasion, under the code-name "Dunaj" (the Danube), was a military success but a political failure.[64] The Soviets wrongly counted on traditional "Russophilism" among Czechs and Slovaks. Instead, the attitude of the civil population—both Czechs and Slovaks—toward the occupiers in general, and toward the Soviet army in particular, was openly hostile. "Russophilism" evaporated overnight and has never returned. On August 21 certain members of the Central Committee decided to immediately start the extraordinary Party Congress in Prague-Vysočany. The Congress denounced the invasion. There were no members of the conservative group in the new Presidium and Central Committee. The attempt of the invaders to install a puppet government also failed because President Svoboda refused to appoint it. The National Assembly and the government denounced the occupation.[65]

The Soviet leadership did not know what to do until President Svoboda offered the Soviet forces a solution: he denounced the invasion but simultaneously asked Soviet Ambassador Chervonenko to arrange for him to travel to Moscow. Svoboda's proposal for direct negotiations with Brezhnev was politically naive and a fatal mistake. He did not help anyone but the Soviets. In addition, he included in his delegation the conservatives Biľak, Indra and Piller, the first two of whom had no mandate and, in fact, openly cooperated with the invading forces. The reformers were represented only by Party Secretary Zdeněk Mlynář, who also represented the "Vysočany" Congress. The Czechoslovak delegation, led by Svoboda, left Prague on August 23 on a special aircraft. The plane landed in Bratislava, where it picked up Gustáv Husák, and

---

62   According to Zdeněk Mlynář, a reform member of the Secretariat, nobody at this meeting dared to openly defend the invasion. See Mlynář, *Mráz přichází z Kremlu* (Prague,1990), 170.

63   *Rudé právo*, 21. 8. 1968 (special edition). See also *Rok šedesátý osmý...*, 297.

64   See Antonín Benčík, *Operace Dunaj. Vojáci a pražské jaro. Studie a dokumenty* (Prague, 1994).

65   *Sedm pražských dnů...*, 51, 57–9.

then continued to Moscow. Dubček, Černík and other interned members of the Presidium were transported to Moscow on the same day and "added" to the Czechoslovak delegation.[66] The representatives of the "Five" assembled in Moscow, but the Czechoslovak "delegation" refused any discussions with the representatives of other Warsaw Pact countries.

The negotiations in Moscow belong to the most tragic moments of modern Czech and Slovak history. The term "negotiations" is a misnomer. The majority of the reform members of the Czechoslovak "delegation" were in fact Soviet internees, or prisoners, and had no freedom of action. Other members—Biľak and Kolder—were Soviet agents. In addition, Gustáv Husák, after a secret meeting with Brezhnev, offered him his services. It is hard to say whether or not it was Husák's idea to annul the extraordinary Party Congress under the pretext that the Slovak delegates were not sufficiently represented, but he did argue this in Moscow. On August 26 the Czechoslovak "delegation" was forced to sign a secret protocol according to which Dubček agreed to make the required personnel changes and to halt most of the reforms. The Extraordinary Congress was to be proclaimed "null and void." In addition, the presence of Soviet forces on Czechoslovak soil was to be legalized by a special Czechoslovak-Soviet Treaty. The Czechoslovak side also agreed that Czechoslovak citizens who openly participated in the preparation of the invasion would not be persecuted. All members of the Czechoslovak delegation, with the exception of František Kriegel, signed the document.[67] The Moscow Protocol was kept secret. The full text was published only after the fall of the communist regime.[68]

The "delegation" returned from Moscow on August 26. On the same day the Extraordinary Congress of the Communist Party of Slovakia opened in Bratislava. The Congress denounced the invasion and proclaimed its full support of the Vysočany Congress.[69] Husák immediately returned to Bratislava. On August 27 Husák appeared at the Congress and informed the delegates about the Moscow negotiations. On the next day, August 28, he appeared again and

---

66 Z. Mlynář, op. cit, 228–30.

67 The following members of the Czechoslovak "delegation" signed the Moscow Protocol: L. Svoboda, A. Dubček, O. Černík, J. Smrkovský, G. Husák, V. Biľak, F. Barbírek, J. Piller, A. Indra, B. Šimon, J. Špaček, O. Švestka, E. Rigo, J. Lenárt, M. Jakeš, Z. Mlynář, V. Koucký, General M. Dzúr and B. Kučera. As we can see, the delegation was a mixture of different people. Bohuslav Kučera was the Chairman of the Czechoslovak Socialist Party.

68 See the text in V. Kural, op. cit., 201–5.

69 SNA, f. ÚV KSS, k. 2072, fasc. 219–Mimoriadny zjazd KSS.

denounced the Vysočany Congress under the pretext that the Slovaks were underrepresented. After secret negotiations and under Husák's pressure, the Congress of the CPS on August 28 revoked its acceptance of the 14th Party Congress in Prague.[70] But the Congress of the SCP was not proclaimed illegal, and Husák was elected First Secretary of the Communist Party of Slovakia.

On August 27 and 28, 1968, the Central Committee of the CPCs elected in Vysočany listened to the report of Bohumil Šimon and Josef Smrkovský about the "negotiations" in Moscow. After lengthy discussions, the new members of the Central Committee resigned, and by this act they annulled the whole Congress. On August 31 the newly elected members were co-opted to the old Central Committee as were the members of the new Presidium. By this trick the Central Committee and the Presidum obtained a pro-reform majority.[71]

The fact that the delegation returned to Prague, and Dubček and most other reformers remained in their functions led to the illusion that the reforms would continue. Dubček himself believed that he had chosen the "lesser evil" when he accepted the Moscow Protocol. But the dismantling of the reforms started almost immediately. The non-Communist organizations such as KAN, K-231 or the Social Democratic Party, were not registered by the Ministry of the Interior and were dissolved. Censorship was restored. At the November 14–17 session of the Central Committee, the conservative members launched a frontal attack against the reform movement. Dubček was forced, step-by-step, into a deeply pro-Soviet position. Finally, on April 17, 1969, Dubček was replaced by Gustáv Husák as First Secretary of the Communist Party of Czechoslovakia. Husák then started the period of so-called normalization, that is, the return to a standard communist system.[72] Public demonstrations on the first anniversary of the invasion were used as a pretext for taking the "hard line" of normalization—massive purges of the Communist Party and total restoration of Party control.

The only aspect of reform that was realized was federalization of the Republic. This was approved by a special Constitutional Law on October 28, 1968, and came into effect on January 1, 1969. The Constitutional Law No. 143/1968 was based in principle on proposals approved before August 21. But,

---

70   Ibidem, p. 202. See also *Pravda* (Bratislava), 29. 8. 1968.

71   *Rok šedesátý osmý*..., 304–8. See also Vojtěch Mencl et. al., *Československo v roce 1968. Vol. II., Počátky normalizace,* (Prague, 1993), 7–8.

72   See Zdeněk Doskočil, *Duben 1969. Anatomie jednoho zvratu* (Prague, 2006).

because of the political developments after April 1969, the federation soon lost its significance. The communist system cannot exist in a real federation. After December 1970, the federation became fictional. All decisions were again made by the Communist Party Presidium in Prague, led by Gustáv Husák, who from 1975 was also the President. The fact that Husák himself was a Slovak (like Biľak, the main ideologist) was of little importance to the Slovaks.

There remain several questions and problems connected with the Czechoslovak reform movement. According to the Soviet explanation, the Communist Party of Czechoslovakia was no longer a Party of the Leninist type because the system of democratic centralism was violated and revisionist and right-wing elements penetrated the Presidium and Central Committee. In the opinion of the Polish leader Władysław Gomułka, after the 14th Congress the CPCs would in fact become a Social Democratic Party. But, according to the documentation in Czech and Slovak archives, despite all the changes, the CPCs remained a Leninist Party. The principle of democratic centralism, incompatible with real democracy, was maintained. Again, according to Moscow, "counter-revolution" in Czechoslovakia would lead to the departure of Czechoslovakia from the Warsaw Pact and to the occupation of the country by the German *Bundeswehr* and the US Army. But as we know (and as the Soviet leadership knew in August of 1968), the American administration had no intention of intervening in Czechoslovakia. Moreover, according to Czech and Slovak documentation, nobody in the Communist Party was thinking about leaving the Warsaw Pact.

There is another important question: if the Warsaw Pact had not invaded, would the communist system in Czechoslovakia have really developed into a new model of socialism, or would it have collapsed? The Czech and Slovak archives do not provide an answer and we cannot say for sure. However, the failure of "perestroika" in the USSR under Mikhail Gorbachev and developments in Eastern Europe in 1989–1991 proved that reforming the communist system was impossible.

4

The 'Prague Spring,' Revisited

Michael Kraus

Jan Rychlík's fine paper, thoroughly documented from the newly accessible archives, makes a number of valuable observations. My comments supplement them and suggest additional perspectives in four areas.

Concerning the origins of the 'Prague Spring,' Rychlík rightly identifies three factors at work: the state of the economy and the widespread sense that the existing economic system had exhausted its potential; the festering issue of political rehabilitation of the victims of repression; and the Slovak question. Noting the asymmetry in Czech and Slovak perceptions in the mid-1960's, his thesis is that while the Czechs saw "the lack of freedom…as the biggest problem," for Slovaks the burning issue was the dissatisfaction with the centralist regime in Prague and, in particular, what he calls "the liquidation of Slovak autonomy." He argues that "the Slovak question was the spark which started the reform movement in Czechoslovakia."

While I fully agree that these three (to a significant extent, overlapping) factors were at work and that Slovak grievances with Prague's centralism played a key role in the origins of the 'Prague Spring'—indeed, the Slovak question was inseparable from Alexander Dubček's rise to power—we should note one additional source of pressure for change from below, namely, the restive intelligentsia. Its demands for the removal of state controls on the written and spoken word reflected deeper societal strivings for an emancipation from the clutches of state ideology. Karel Kaplan concluded his recent survey of the roots of the Czechoslovak reforms by noting that, by the second half of 1967, Czechoslovakia was in the throes of a profound crisis. Echoing the sentiments of many fellow citizens, prominent writers criticized the regime at the June 1967 Congress of the Union of Czechoslovak Writers and demanded changes in accordance with the country's democratic traditions. As one of them, Ludvík Vaculík, stated, the communist regime had solved "not a single human problem" after twenty years of being in power.[1] This represented an unprecedented critique of the communist establishment by the Party's own writers.

It is often asserted that in 1968 change in Czechoslovakia was initiated and led by the Communist Party. But given the complex relationship between the state and society, this proposition needs amending. As the "Two Thousand Words" manifesto (written by the same Vaculík) in June of 1968 put it, "…the process could have started nowhere else. For after twenty years the communists were the only ones able to conduct some sort of political activity. It was only the opposition inside the Communist Party that had the privilege to voice antagonistic views."[2] As Václav Havel aptly illuminated this issue in 1978:

> The Prague Spring is usually understood as a clash between two groups on the level of real power: those who wanted to maintain the system as it was and those who wanted to reform it. It is frequently forgotten, however, that this encounter was merely the final act and the inevitable consequence of a long drama originally played out chiefly in the theatre of the spirit and the conscience of society... One thing, however, seems clear: the attempt at political reform was not the cause of' society's reawakening, but rather the final outcome of that reawakening.[3]

---

[1] Quoted in Karel Kaplan, *Kronika komunistického Československa: Kořeny reformy 1956–1968* (Brno, 2008), 516. Apart from those cited below, among classic studies of 1968 are: Galia Golan, *The Czechoslovak Reform Movement: Communism in Crisis, 1962–1968* (Cambridge, 1971) and *Reform Rule in Czechoslovakia: The Dubček Era, 1968–1969* (Cambridge, 1973); Vladimir Kusin, *The Intellectual Origins of the Prague Spring: The Development of Reformist Ideas in Czechoslovakia, 1956–1967* (Cambridge, 1971) and *Political Groupings in the Czechoslovak Reform Movement* (New York, 1972).

[2] Jaromír Navrátil, ed., *The Prague Spring 1968* (Prague, 1998), 179.

[3] "The Power of the Powerless," in Jan Vladislav, ed., *Václav Havel: Living in Truth* (London, 1990), 60.

Kaplan's study provided new evidence for Havel's interpretation, for he documented mounting demands for change on many levels of society by the mid-1960's. In Kaplan's words, on the eve of 1968 "the time for change had come: the society was pregnant with reforms."[4]

Second, Rychlík rightly emphasizes the division at the top of the Czechoslovak Communist Party, especially in the Presidium, into the progressive versus the conservative wings of the Party, or simply, reformers versus conservatives. This often made any resolute Czechoslovak response to Soviet demands difficult, if not impossible, to contemplate. He also points out that these factions did not always overlap with the centralist versus the federalist divisions on the Slovak question. Not only did Dubček lack a reform-minded majority in the Presidium or the Central Committee, but as Rychlík argues, a number of conservatives in the top leadership either were, or were acting as, Soviet agents. They were informing Moscow of confidential deliberations in Prague, arguing on behalf of Soviet interests, basically comprising what Rychlík calls a "Fifth column for Moscow." Indeed, one of the virtues of his contribution is its portrayal of the interplay of domestic factions with Soviet interests and pressures. After April, but probably even earlier, Moscow expected and encouraged the so-called healthy forces to wrest power from the reformers, either with or without Dubček's blessing.

It is not entirely clear why Dubček did not or could not—as the Party's First Secretary—make greater use of his unmatched powers of appointment to effect more sweeping personnel changes. Apparently for the first three months, at the Presidium level, Dubček was still preoccupied by the struggle with Novotný. Following Novotný's resignation at the end of March, Dubček's leadership, "a product of behind-the-scenes conflicts and compromises," was, according to Zdeněk Mlynář, one of its new members, "a self-defeating conglomeration of incongruent political forces."[5] By one estimate, during the eight months of the 'Prague Spring,' out of 250,000 Party "nomenklatura" positions, only about 100 top functionaries were replaced. Needless to say, the underlying continuity of the Party's apparatus immensely complicated Dubček's decision-making. To be sure, changes in the composition of the Central Committee were being contemplated in connection with the upcoming September 1968 Party Congress. As a result, basically the same Central

---

4   Kaplan, op. cit., 775.

5   Zdeněk Mlynář, *Nightfrost in Prague: The End of Humane Socialism* (New York, 1980), 110.

Committee that approved Novotný's replacement by Dubček and supported the Action Program also endorsed the Soviet-imposed post-invasion plans and the replacement of Dubček by Gustáv Husák in 1969.[6]

A third and related question, given these divisions at the top, is how can one account for the blazing speed with which the reform agenda, namely, the so-called Action Program, was adopted? Rychlík rightly notes that by February 1968, the first draft of the Action Program of the Communist Party was adopted by the Presidium. How is one to explain that it took less than a month from the moment it was commissioned to create a rather elaborate and comprehensive statement of intended political and economic changes? The answer, it seems, is that the reformist agenda had been crystallizing over a number of years. Specialized teams, primarily at various institutes of the Czechoslovak Academy of Sciences, had been preparing position papers on what would become the key aspects of reform: in the economy, loosening of the clutches of the Party on individual enterprises; in politics, reducing the hierarchical structure and control of the Party and giving more authority to people lower down; finally, the federalization of the political system would place the Czechs and the Slovaks on a more equal footing.

When the Party leadership approved the Action Program, it understated and disguised the real policy differences at the top and postponed the conflict over the underlying agenda. Simply put, for the conservatives the Action Program was the maximum, something they agreed to under pressure in the hope that they would be able to slow down, if not completely sabotage, in its implementation. For them it was the beginning of the end. The radical reformers, by contrast, saw the Action Program as the end of the beginning.

However, when on March 4, 1968, the Presidium abolished preliminary censorship, it opened the floodgates to demands from below. This decision gave rise to a free press, radio and television and became a major factor in the rapid resurrection of elements of civic society and in the re-pluralization of Czechoslovak society in the form of independent organizations such as KAN, the Club of Active Non-party members, or K-231, the organization of former political prisoners.

---

6   See Jan Pauer, "Sovětská intervence a restaurace byrokraticko-centralistického systému v Československu, 1968–1971," in Jindřich Pecka a Vilém Prečan, eds., *Proměny pražského jara, 1968–1969* (Brno, 1993), 174. Pauer mentions that his data does not include the June 1968 elections to regional committees in the Party, which resulted in about 700 new appointments.

This newly emergent configuration of political forces also put Dubček and the reformers into an unsustainable political situation. In order to bolster their strength in the struggle with the conservatives inside the Party, and by extension, their Soviet sponsors, the reformers increasingly relied on public support. Public support, in turn, grew commensurately with the openness of the media, the revelations from the archives, the criticism of the Soviet model, the emergence of the civic society, the pluralization of politics, and so on. These very developments, however, comprised changes that Moscow found unacceptable and demanded be undone. Further, Dubček never attempted to set firm boundaries to Soviet interventions in Czechoslovak internal affairs. As early as February of 1968, Dubček only too eagerly accepted Brezhnev's intervention into a text of his own speech on the anniversary of the February 1948 communist takeover of Czechoslovakia and thereby opened the doors to similar interventions to come. (In his post-1989 autobiography, Dubček downplayed this incident, stating that at Brezhnev's request, he removed only two innocuous paragraphs. As it turns out, however, Brezhnev requested that six paragraphs be deleted—and Dubček willingly obliged).[7]

As early as the March summit meeting in Dresden, Soviet leaders and their East German and Polish counterparts introduced the notion that a creeping counter-revolution was unfolding in Czechoslovakia. That is why none of the Warsaw Pact countries published the contents of the Action Program in April. And by July, the Soviets informed their Prague comrades that their Party could no longer be considered Leninist, a most serious charge in the lexicon of Marxism-Leninism. In short, the tactics that gave Dubček and the reformers rising support and growing legitimacy at home were precisely what put them on a collision course with the requirements for the control and the cohesion of the Soviet bloc. Arguably, Dubček's own idealism and fervent belief in "socialism with a human face," along with his rising popularity—which grew commensurately with his resistance to Soviet demands—blinded him and the reformers to the perils of outside intervention. Contemplating the possibility of Soviet intervention in his post-1989 autobiography, Dubček flatly asserted that, at "no point between January and August 20, in fact, did I believe that it

---

[7] Jiří Hochman, ed., *Naděje umírá poslední: Vlastní životopis Alexandra Dubčeka* (Prague, 1993), 147–8. These passages were omitted from the English edition of the same book.

would happen."[8] "The reform movement" concluded Kaplan, "got so much support from the public that the internal opposition to reforms had no prospect of defeating them."[9] Ultimately, the Soviet-led invasion took place after Moscow had lost whatever remaining faith it still had that the "healthy forces" inside Czechoslovakia could succeed in stemming the tide on their own.

Finally, Rychlík's references to "democratization" and to "the democratization process" raise the questions of how far the reforms of the political system actually went and how far they might have gone had it not been for the Warsaw Pact intervention. To be sure, words such as democracy and democratization appeared with great frequency in the vocabulary of the 1968 reformers, including in the Party's Action Program. But the latter was riddled with contradictions, proclaiming the need for the rule of law, freedom of travel and freedom of the press, while affirming the primacy of Marxism-Leninism and of the principle of "the leading role of the Party" at the same time. The Party was going to "win its supremacy through democratic political means," without permitting the existence of opposition parties.

In this connection, we should note that political scientists make a useful distinction between the notions of "liberalization" and "democratization." The former is conventionally understood to refer to a "mix of policy and social changes," such as relaxation of censorship over the media, somewhat greater space for trade union activities, "the releasing of most political prisoners, the return of the exiles…and most important, the toleration of opposition." By contrast, democratization "entails liberalization but is a wider and more specifically political concept. Democratization requires open contestation over the right to win control of the government, and this in turn requires free competitive elections, the results of which determine who governs…" Therefore, "there can be liberalization without democratization."[10] It would seem, then, that while in 1968 Czechoslovakia was in the throes of liberalization, democratization in the foregoing sense remained outside the scope of

---

8   Jiří Hochman, ed., *Hope Dies Last: The Autobiography of Alexander Dubček* (New York, 1993), 128.

9   Kaplan, op.cit., 776.

10 Juan J. Linz & Alfred Stepan, *Problems of Democratic Transition and Consolidation: Southern Europe, South America, and Post-Communist Europe* (Baltimore, 1996), 4. For another perspective arguing that the 1968 reforms "in intention and execution amounted to only the liberalization of a Leninist regime," see Kieran Williams, *The Prague Spring and its Aftermath: Czechoslovak Politics, 1968–1970* (Cambridge, 1997).

change contemplated by the Action Program. As Zdeněk Mlynář, one of the main architects of the Action Program, observed (speaking of the end of June 1968): "The regime was still a totalitarian political system that had yet to be democratized. The proposed changes in the political system were still only on paper, with one serious exception: freedom of expression really existed."[11]

Short of the Warsaw Pact invasion, could Czechoslovak communism have reformed itself? Rychlík concludes that the archives give no answer to this question but that the failure of "perestroika" in the Soviet Union two decades later suggests that "reforming the communist system was impossible." Disagreeing with Rychlík thirty years ago, Gordon Skilling in his monumental *Czechoslovakia's Interrupted Revolution*, concluded that "...the Prague experiment seemed doomed to failure for external reasons rather than inherent domestic ones."[12] According to Skilling, "barring outside intervention, the process of change would have been accelerated rather than slowed down or blocked, and would eventually have produced a thoroughly revised socialism, democratic in form, and national in content." But as Skilling's volume amply documents, other voices outside the Party, including Václav Havel, did not consider the Party's program a genuine guarantee of democracy and called for the creation of opposition parties. Philosopher Ivan Svitak put it most succinctly when in July of 1968 he wrote: "We want democracy, not democratization. Democratization is a minimal program on the way to democracy."[13] In going beyond the Party-orchestrated vision of limited pluralism, these voices had to be squelched in the aftermath of August 21, 1968—until 1989. It is revealing that in early 1990, Alexander Dubček in an interview with his biographer stated that "the Prague Spring would have led to a pluralist, multi-party society such as Havel was now creating." Thus, as the same source concludes: "By 1989 communism was dead even in the heart of the man who had given it a human face."[14]

---

11 Mlynář, op.cit., 139.

12 H.Gordon Skilling, *Czechoslovakia's Interrupted Revolution* (Princeton, 1976), 842–3. For a consideration of alternative strategies and outcomes of the Prague Spring, see the recent essay by Oldřich Tůma, "Nejhorší možná varianta: Srpen 1968," *Soudobé dějiny*, 2/2008, 318–40.

13 Ibid., 357.

14 William Shawcross, *Dubček* (Revised and updated, New York, 1990), 228–9.

5

August 1968 as Seen from Bratislava

Slavomír Michálek, Stanislav Sikora

In order to understand the Slovak role in the Czechoslovak reform process of 1968, we have to briefly outline the emancipation efforts of the Slovaks after 1945. During the Slovak National Uprising (SNP) of August 1944, the leaders of the rebellion organized themselves into a Slovak National Council (SNC), to replace the government of the Slovak Republic (1939-1945), which was allied with Nazi Germany. Even though the uprising was crushed by the German army in September–October 1944, and the SNC had to go into hiding, it resurrected itself towards the end of the war, as the Slovak Republic was disintegrating along with Nazi Germany.[1] On April 5, 1945, in the city of Košice, the Slovak National Council was officially recognized by returning president Edvard Beneš and by Klement Gottwald, the leader of the Czechoslovak Communist Party, who returned from the Soviet Union in the wake of the Red Army with a "Popular Front" government.[2]

The powers of the Slovak National Council and its executive branch, the Board of Commissioners, whose Chairman was the communist politician Gustav Husák, were initially very broad. A paradoxical situation existed where the central Czechoslovak government in Prague, in which the Slovaks

---

1   For a history of the Slovak National Uprising, see Jozef Jablonický, *Povstanie bez legiend* (Bratislava, 1990).

2   For the text of the "Košice Program," see "Košický vládny program," in *Dokumenty slovenskej národnej identity a štátnosti, II* (Bratislava, 1998), 407–8.

had their proportionate representation, did not actually govern Slovakia. Without the consent and agreement of the SNC, the government's decisions in the legislative area were not valid in Slovakia. Furthermore, in the area of governmental and executive power the SNC continued having full powers.[3] It was, therefore, necessary to adjust Czech-Slovak relations by means of political agreements and relevant legal regulations.

The first two so-called Prague Agreements (June 2, 1945; April 9–11, 1946) gave the Slovak national bodies quite broad powers even though they did not contain the idea of federation being promoted by the Slovak resistance politicians before the end of World War II and right after it. The radical breakthrough happened only after the first parliamentary elections on May 26, 1946, when almost all Czechoslovak political parties (including the Slovak communists) decided to paralyze the election victory of the Democratic Party in Slovakia. The Third Prague Agreement, adopted by the all-state National Front on June 27, 1946, was a dramatic intervention into the power of the Slovak National Council.

Pursuant to this agreement, the SNC had to submit its proposed legislation to the government in Prague before its submission to the General Assembly in order to assess whether or not this legislation contradicted the laws of the central government. It was left to the discretion of the central government as to what it considered to be a national issue and what should be left to the SNC. At the same time, the Slovak commissioners were subordinated and responsible to their equivalent ministers in Prague. Furthermore, the central government or its individual ministers were entitled to exercise their powers in Slovakia over and above the SNC or its commissioners. Thus, the Slovak national bodies became powerless institutions held in bondage by the central government.[4]

The powers of the Slovak national bodies were incorporated into the Constitution of May 9, 1948, in an almost identical way. Then the classical attributes of communist regimes came into play—centralization and concentration of power in the highest bureaucratic bodies of the Communist Party of Czechoslovakia (CPCs). In the Constitutional Act No. 47/1950 on adjustments in public administration, it was stipulated that, for the purpose of public

---

3   M. Barnovský, *Na ceste k monopolu moci. Mocenskopolitické zápasy na Slovensku v rokoch 1945– 1948* (Bratislava, 1993), 43.

4   Ibid., 112.

administration, flexibility and practicality, the government could "adjust the competence of ministries, commissioners and other bodies of public administration by means of regulations; establish new ministries, commissioners as well as other bodies of public administration; cancel ministries, commissioners as well as other bodies of public administration." This amendment to the Constitution was often used by the central government for endless reorganization of ministries and commissioners, the final effect of which could not be doubted: to concentrate political and economic control of society to the maximum extent into one center—in Prague.

This development finally culminated in the Constitution of the Czechoslovak Socialist Republic (ČSSR) of July 11, 1960. The powers of the Slovak national bodies now became illusory. Instead of drafting a budget for Slovakia, the SNC could only draft its own budget—as a social organization! The SNC ended up in a situation where it had to try to find some kind of work that would be socially essential and meaningful. Based on the words of its Chairman Jozef Lenárt in 1962–1963, it was a useless organization: "Nobody wanted anything from me in this position. Nobody ever invited me anywhere from the government. I did not receive any governmental materials, I simply received a state salary and if I had not learned about the issues at the Party Presidium, I would not have learned anything from the state about what was happening in this Republic."[5]

Further complications, which were of crucial importance for the position of the Slovak nation in Czechoslovakia, came from abroad. At the 12th Congress of the Communist Party of the Soviet Union (CPSU) a thesis was adopted "On the development and convergence of nations and nationalities," whose main (hidden) agenda was to deal with the separatist tendencies of non-Russian nations, national minorities and ethnic groups in the Soviet Union. This thesis was immediately adopted by the CPCs Presidium, chaired by Antonín Novotný. In his presentations, this "convergence" was often understood as "merging" and resembled the much-hated (in Slovakia) interwar "Czechoslovakism."

Alexander Dubček started to deal with this problem immediately after his accession to the position of the First Secretary of the Central Committee of the Communist Party in Slovakia (CC CPS) in April of 1963. However, he had to respect the Constitution of the ČSSR, as well as the fact that the

---

5   J. Lenárt at the meeting of Central Committee of the CPCs on January 3–5, 1968. Documents of the Institute for Contemporary History of AS ČR (State Archives of the Czech Republic). J. Lenárt was a member of the Presidium of the CPCs by virtue of being Chairman of the SNC.

word "federation" became taboo in the Czechoslovak political environment after the publication of the controversial 'samizdat' by the historian Miloš Gosiorovský, "K niektorým otázkam vzťahov Čechov a Slovákov v politike Komunistickej strany Československa" (On some Issues of the Relationship between the Czechs and the Slovaks in the Communist Party of Czechoslovakia) in March of that year.[6] Dubček, therefore, focused his attempts at increasing the powers of Slovak national bodies within the asymmetric state model, as incorporated in the Constitution of the ČSSR.

Dubček and his supporters demonstrated this struggle in 1967 in discussions over the contents of the upcoming Act on National Committees—regional and local bodies of state administration. At the meeting of the Central Committee of the Communist Party of Czechoslovakia (CC CPCs) in March of the same year, Dubček requested that the SNC, according to the new Act, should approve the budgets of National Committees in Slovakia. This request, as well as the demand that Bratislava again become the capital of Slovakia (a status it had lost in the 1960 Constitution), was rejected. This showed that, if relations between the Czechs and the Slovaks were to be improved, Novotný had to be removed as First Secretary of the CPCs.[7]

The process of democratization in the Czechoslovak Socialist Republic got underway after the CC of the CPCSs meeting on January 3–5, 1968. This was a follow-up to the earlier period of the so-called pre-Spring—the process of cautious liberalization of the regime, which started at the beginning of the 1960s as a consequence of the détente politics of the great powers and also internal developments in Czech and Slovak society. The ultimate factor for its start-up was the resignation of Antonín Novotný as First Secretary of the CPCs and his replacement by Alexander Dubček.

Dubček came from a family of workers. His father was not only one of the founding members of the Communist Party of Czechoslovakia, but also a romantic communist who was always willing to help to build a "better future." That is why in 1925 the Dubček family moved to the Soviet Union, to the Kirghiz Soviet Socialist Republic. The elder Dubček participated in an industrial cooperative of Czechoslovak workers and farmers called Interhelpo, established for the purpose of helping build the first workers' state in the world.

---

6   For more details see M. Londák, S. Sikora, H. Londáková, *Predjarie. Politický, ekonomický a kultúrny vývoj na Slovensku v rokoch 1960–1967* (Bratislava, 2002), 87–8.

7   Ibid., 93–4.

Alexander Dubček was only four when the family moved to the Soviet Union. However, in the 1930's he experienced the repressive atmosphere of Stalin's monstrous purges of the Party and society, which significantly influenced his later activities.[8] He also inherited his father's idealism, but even Stalinism did not shake his belief in communism. Rather, Dubcek's communism was more humanistic.

In 1938 the Dubček family returned to Czechoslovakia. Alexander was trained as a machinist and then worked in the ammunition factory in Dubnica nad Váhom. During the existence of the Slovak Republic (1939–1945), he participated in illegal anti-Nazi activities and even in the Slovak National Uprising. He entered politics in 1949 as a Secretary and later as the Chief Secretary of the Communist Party of Slovakia's Regional Committee in the Trenčín district. Subsequently he held all positions within the Communist Party of Czechoslovakia. He was the Chief Secretary of the CPS Regional Committee, the First Secretary of the Central Committee of the CPS, a Secretary of the CC CPCs and the First Secretary of the CC CPCs. In 1955–1958 he was able to study at the University of Political Affairs of the Central Committee of the Communist Party of the Soviet Union in Moscow.

As far as Dubček's character and his political beliefs are concerned, it is important to note that opinions about him differ widely. Regarding whether those who judge him have positive or negative views, it is important to note whether those who judge him are Czechs or Slovaks.

Those who disapproved of him, and continue to disapprove of him, claim that Dubček was an average politician who lacked imagination, was a naïve weakling, and was not suited for his position. He has been condemned by many because he was a communist. Those who admire him emphasize his positive attitude towards people and emphasize his humanity.[9]

In our opinion, Dubček's alleged naïveté is out of the question. Those who know how the Communist Party of Czechoslovakia operated at that time understand that a naïve person would never have been able to move up all its levels from the position of a regional secretary to the position of the First Secretary of the Central Committee of the Communist Party. One of Dubček's main beliefs was in the necessity of the radical reform of socialism.

---

8   A. Dubček, *Nádej zomiera posledná* (Bratislava, 1998), 79–80.

9   Historians who disapprove of him: Jitka Vondrová, Jan Pauer, Jiří Suk (Czechs). Historians who admire him: Antonín Benčík, Ivan Laluha, Ján Uher (Slovaks).

In that he believed in this without reservations, he might be called an idealist, but without idealism mankind would not have made any progress.

The intra-Party coup connected with removing Novotný from power accorded fully with the regime of totalitarian dictatorship and its cabinet politics: occurring behind closed doors as a struggle for power at the top of the Party bureaucracy. That was the reason some historians named this period the "January silence."[10] During the "January silence" the leadership of the Communist Party of Czechoslovakia did not witness any other significant changes, beyond the resignation of Novotný and his replacement by Dubček. Despite the fact that the confrontation between the reform and conservative members of the leadership of the CPCs took place at the session of its Central Committee on January 3–5, 1968, the door to real reform of socialism of the Soviet type was slightly cracked open.

Slovak communists in this period can be divided into three main groups: reformers, dogmatists and middle-of-the roaders. We will introduce some of them with short remarks, step-by-step. Even in the Slovak part of the Republic the "changing of the guard" occurred at the highest levels of the political structure: Vasil Biľak was elected as the First Secretary of the Central Committee of the Communist Party of Slovakia at its session on January 22–23, 1968. This did not involve a crisis in the leadership of the CPS, as Dubček's successor was his colleague and ally against the clique of President Antonín Novotný. Dubček's unanimous election was accompanied by long applause. During his inaugural speech, Biľak revealed himself to be a follower of the anti-Novotný wing in the leadership of the CPCs. He distanced himself from the "old methods" of the Party and supported the efforts to push through more progressive reforms.[11]

During this session of the CC of the CPS, where the conclusions of the session of the CC of the CPCs in January were adopted with enthusiasm, an attempt was made to rehabilitate Gustáv Husák, who had been purged and imprisoned in the 1950's for his alleged "bourgeois nationalism." Husák's supporters tried to co-opt him into this highest political body in Slovakia. Many of his followers in the CC of the CPCs demanded his return. But there was still personal antipathy from the mid-1960's between Husák, on the one hand, and Dubček and Biľak on the other, so this effort failed.

---

10   V. Kural, a kol., *Československo roku 1968*. I. (Prague, 1993), 30.
11   Slovak National Archives, Bratislava, f. CC of CPS, box no. 1877.

Developments on the Slovak political stage after the sessions of the CC of the CPCs and the CC of the CPS in January were akin to developments at the headquarters of the Communist Party of Czechoslovakia. Slovakia had its own "Novotný" at whom the reformers aimed their attacks because they considered him to be a protagonist of all that was conservative, dogmatic and antidemocratic in the CPS and also in Slovak society. He was Michal Chudík, the Chairman of the Slovak National Council, a member of the chairmanship of the CC of the CPCs and also of the CC of the CPS and the most loyal follower of Novotný in Slovakia.

In the middle of February 1968, in the ČSSR and also in Slovakia, one of the most significant processes of democratization started unfolding, with great repercussions in the media, above all, in the press. On March 4 the chairmanship of the CC of the CPCs decided to abolish censorship. Act No. 84/68, dated June 26, 1968, which constituted the official abolition of censorship, only confirmed the previous status quo.[12] The real abolition of censorship in the middle of February 1968 and the follow-up establishment of freedom of speech in the mass media were among the first noticeable results of the "after-January" developments. The rise of critical journalism was impossible to compare with anything over the previous twenty years. The media started exposing the torture of political prisoners during interrogation, fabricated political proceedings, forced labor camps, forced collectivization of agriculture and the so-called socialization of trade licenses, the persecution of priests and believers. However, the press pilloried not only the "small fry," but also top communists such as Josef Stalin and his 1950's henchmen in Czechoslovakia, Klement Gottwald, Antonín Zápotocký, Antonín Novotný, Viliam Široký, Václav Kopecký, Karel Bacílek and many others. Important figures in Slovak history, such as Milan R. Štefánik, who had been dismissed by the communists as a bourgeois politician, were rehabilitated by the press. In addition, questions regarding the anti-Fascist resistance in Slovakia during World War II., e.g., the Slovak National Uprising, the destinies of the soldiers and partisans who fought in the SNP, civil units of the uprising, etc., started being evaluated more critically. Periodicals seeking higher circulations published even the details of the brutal purges and manipulated political proceedings in the Soviet Union in the 1930's and after World War II.

---

12   S. Sikova, "Rok 1968 a politický vývoj na Slovensku," (manuscript) p. 37.

In the middle of this democratization process, the "Action Program of the Communist Party of Czechoslovakia" (AP CPCs) was adopted at the session of the Central Committee of the Communist Party on April 1–5, 1968. Its main goals were to radically reform socialism of the Soviet type in the ČSSR and to guide the democratization process in order to produce "socialism with a human face." This would be achieved by means of reform, i.e., an original synthesis of eastern socialism and western democracy. Moreover, the AP CPCs could be evaluated as the very first attempt at a complex reform of this socialism in the entire "socialist camp," which was the name of the zone of the Soviet satellites in Europe at that time. The project was aimed at the whole political, economic-social and cultural system.

Despite the fact that the AP CPCs contained revolutionary changes in comparison to its previous status, it did not succeed in guiding political developments because the program was published only at the beginning of April 1968. By then a revived civil society had reached such strength that it was impossible to fit it into this "Action Program." Society had progressed much further in its visions of the future.

The Communist Party of Slovakia followed the example of the Communist Party of Czechoslovakia and developed its own Action Program based on the decision of the CC of the Communist Party of Czechoslovakia's Chairmanship on February 2. Newly formed working groups participated in the preparation of the Action Program of the CPS. In all, about 400 people participated in this process.

After a short period of intensive work, these teams submitted the proposal of the Action Program of the Communist Party of Slovakia (AP CPS) to the CC of the CPS. However, it was put aside because disputes about its contents became part of a struggle between the reform and dogmatic wings in the leadership of the Communist Party of Slovakia. The AP CPS shared the same destiny as the AP CPCs. It did not influence social developments. Adopted only at the end of May 1968, it was more or less conservative. Only national emancipation took center stage in the whole stream of Slovak efforts to create a Czecho-Slovak federation.[13]

The basic division of reformers and conservatives already existed before January 1968, and it lasted until the end of March, when it began to erode for intra-political and, above all, foreign-political reasons. The reform-communist

---

13   Ibid., 50.

activities of the "progressive communist" groups, as the reformers were called, were very moderate. They mainly sought the elimination of the "distortion of socialism" and the "wrong methods of Party work." At this time they could be seen as potential reform communists.

Alexander Dubček, who was the First Secretary of the CC of the CPS until the beginning of January 1968 and then the First Secretary of the CC of the CPCs, was the leading personality during this time. He framed his vision about the reform policy of the CPCs at the 7th session of the Collective Farm Union (JRD) on February 1, 1968, when he stated:

> We are not changing the main course of internal or foreign policy. We have to give serious thought to how to speed up the socialist development of our country and what attitudes and methods to select in the new phase, which is defined by new social structures, a swift start of a revolution in science and technology and the closely connected urgent tasks of science, culture and the economy.[14]

These quite moderate requirements of "improvement" of socialism and its adaptation to new circumstances and Dubček's careful methods of enforcing these requirements classified him as a moderate reform communist, and he had a wide range of political followers in Slovakia. Later he moved from the program point of view to the platform of the Action Program of the Communist Party of Czechoslovakia, but he was never a radical.

Ironically, Vasil Biľak was initially the closest supporter of Dubček among the moderate reform communists in Slovakia. In the period 1962–1968, Biľak was the Ideological Secretary of the CC CPS and then its First Secretary. This is surprising because Biľak, with his political profile, represented more the visions of a typical dogmatic member of the Party machinery, which he displayed through his activities in the spring of 1968.

There were also many supporters of Alexander Dubček in the machinery of the CC of the CPCs. For instance, there was Ján Uher, who played an important role in the rehabilitation of the Slovak so-called bourgeois nationalists. Viliam Šalgovič was another example who, in the first phase of the reform process, could have appeared as a moderate reform communist, but was not. From 1962 to 1968, Chairman of the Central Supervisory and

---

14 J. Vondrová, J. Navrátil, J. Moravec, J. *Komunistická strana Československa. Prameny k dějinám československé krize v letech 1967–1970*, zv. 9/1 (Brno, 1999), 63.

Auditing Commission of the Communist Party of Slovakia, Šalgovič tried very hard to rehabilitate many members of the CPS. Because of this, towards the end of May 1968, Dubček promoted him to the rank of colonel and Deputy Minister of State Security, better known as the ŠtB (the Czechoslovak Secret Police). However, the Soviets then recruited Šalgovič into the KGB (the Soviet Secret Police), and he worked for them during the Warsaw Pact invasion of Czechoslovakia.[15]

Many other top communists in Slovakia also initially supported Dubček's reforms. Anton Ťažký was one of Dubček's closest friends and supporters in 1968. In 1967 Jozef Zrak, another close friend and supporter of Dubček, was an emissary—Chairman of the Committee of the Slovak National Party for the National Board. We could think of him as a "Minister of the Interior." Hvezdoň Kočtúch and Viktor Pavlenda, Slovak economists who were significant supporters of Dubček, were, from 1965 on, champions of economic reform, which was known as "The new concept of national economic management." At the same time, they also criticized that reform concept, because it was prepared for the Czech part of the Republic and did not respect specific Slovak economic conditions.[16] These individuals served Dubček as resource-persons when he was trying to gain more power for Slovak national bodies and to change the Slovak economic structure by the construction of new plants for the consumer goods industry, including the final phase of production. František Zupka, who was an important trade union official, also belonged to the group of moderate supporters of reforms. His disputes with the leadership of the Party were mainly about how a trade union should carry out its duties—to argue for the economic and social interests of the workforce—when the workforce also had to be the "transmission gear" of communist power. Zupka, who decried the problems of trade unions and trade unionists and the exercise of power from the top by the Party, consequently demanded power be divided among economic, Party, and trade unionist bodies. These opinions led him into sharp disputes with Novotný. Robert Herenčár, the Chairman of the Slovak Central Committee of the Czechoslovak Socialist Youth Movement (from the end of June, 1966) cannot be forgotten. He was the one who, even before 1968, had sowed the seeds of a new democratic structure in the youth movement in Slovakia.

---

15 J. Pešek, a kol., *Aktéri jednej éry na Slovensku 1948–1989* (Prešov, 2003), 307.

16 For more information, see M. Londák, *Rok 1968 a ekonomická realita Slovenska* (Bratislava, 2007).

Ondrej Klokoč, an employee of the Party press, belonged to the group of moderate reform communists. Klokoč, as the editor-in-chief of the daily *Pravda* in the early 1960's, made himself famous when he drew attention to the participation of Viliam Široký, who was the Prime Minister of the ČSSR at that time, in illegal political proceedings in the late 1940s and at the beginning of the 1950's.

Three famous Slovak writers—Ladislav Novomeský, Vladimír Mináč a Ladislav Ťažký—also were important moderate reform communists. In this period they very often appeared in the press or in public as outstanding personalities of Slovak cultural and political life. They kept their own, still unpopular opinions during the liberalization process. Ondrej Pavlík, a famous Slovak expert in the field of pedagogy, belongs with them in terms of generation and close relations.

More Slovak politicians were of two minds about whether they should join the new reform or the conservative group in the leadership of the CPCs. They supported Dubček "ad hoc," in specific cases, when they could intervene for his benefit in a tense political situation. The newly rehabilitated Gustáv Husák was an informal leading personality of these potential radical reform communists.

Slovakia also had dogmatic communists. As already mentioned, Michal Chudík was Novotný's closest supporter in Slovakia. In his youth he was brought up as "Viliam Široký's man" and played a very important role in the persecution of the "bourgeois nationalists" in the CPS. In the autumn of 1963, after the fall of his political "tutor," he turned to Novotný, who supported him as an opponent of Dubček for the position of the First Secretary of the CC of the CPS until the end of 1967. He continued to support Novotný even at the time of the political crisis in the leadership of the CPCs towards the end of 1967 and at the beginning of 1968. After the fall of Novotný, Chudík fell too.

Jozef Lenárt was another reliable supporter of Novotný. In September of 1963 he became the Prime Minister of the Czechoslovak Socialist Republic. In 1965 he played a very important role in the creation of the "new concept of national economic management," which permitted a regulated market environment with relatively independent business subjects. During tense political situations he always leaned towards dogmatism, as, for example, at the end of 1967 and beginning of 1968 when he belonged to "the last of the Mohicans" who still supported Novotný.[17] Michal Sabolčík, who was forced

---

17   Z. Mlynář, *Mráz přichází z Kremlu* (Prague, 1990), 125.

by Novotný to take the office of some informal Dubček representative in the leadership of the CC of the CPCs, also firmly stood for the interests of Prague centralism against the moderate national-emancipation and democratization efforts of Dubček. From the dogmatic and centralistic position of an economist, he criticized the activities of Viktor Pavlenda who, as a supporter of modern economic theories, demanded the restoration of the powers of the Slovak national bodies in the framework of the "new concept of national economic management."

It was Dubček who originally won over Ján Janík for work in the CC of the CPS. In 1964 he became a Secretary of the CC of the CPS and from 1966 he was a member of the leadership of the CC of the CPS. Later, Janik preferred political security and initially backed Novotný. However, he supported the successive liberalization of the regime in Slovakia and national emancipation. Towards the end of 1967, when the power of Novotný and his supporters started waning, Janík without any remorse leaped into the Dubček camp. At the December session of the CC of the CPS in 1967 he criticized Novotný, mainly for his economic policy in relation to Slovakia.

An example of servility towards Novotný was Rudolf Cvik, the Chief Secretary of the CC of the CPS. Novotný took advantage of this extreme and aggressive dogmatic to organize direct attacks against Dubček. Another conservative member of the Communist Party of Slovakia who worked in the Slovak press was Bohuslav Chňoupek, who was the managing editor of the weekly *Predvoj* in the years 1965–1967.

Differences between the political streams at the top of the CPS were not, of course, perfectly clear, and many members of one stream kept close tabs on members of other streams. In principle, supporters of Novotný stood against the supporters of Dubček, and both these streams were against "radicals" and "liberals." Such a diversification of political forces in the leadership of the CPS (a very similar diversification was apparent in the CPCs, as well), also developed in district and regional structures and was in the end vulnerable, not only to important intra-political pressures but, above all, to foreign political pressure.

When Novotný's regime was eliminated, and the route to the reform of socialism was opened in the ČSSR, the situation in the Soviet Union was very different from the days of Nikita Khrushchev, who had attempted a moderate reform of socialism in the Soviet Union. After Khrushchev's fall from power in October of 1964, the twenty-year era of the Stalinist Leonid

Brezhnev and his successors, and the final decay of the Soviet system, began. Socialism of the Soviet type identified with the conservative process of political, economic and ideological structures, which appeared in the days of Stalin in the USSR and were reproduced in the states of the Soviet satellite zone with minor changes.

By 1968 the world situation had also changed. Rumors were circulating that relations between the USA and the USSR had became more relaxed and that an agreement about restrictions of strategic weapons was about to be prepared. President Lyndon Johnson and his administration did not want to put their own goals in relation to the Soviet Union at risk. Because Johnson himself had prearranged his visit to Moscow and cared about it very much, the USA took a rather reserved stand on developments in Czechoslovakia. It sympathized with the reform process but issued mild proclamations after the invasion.[18] In addition, American diplomacy, according to the directions of Secretary of State Dean Rusk, was supposed to only "demonstrate informally and tactfully that the USA welcomes gladly the steps of Czechoslovakia towards liberalization."[19] Certain liberal and conservative groups in Western Europe were not happy about developments in the Czechoslovak Socialist Republic. The French minister of foreign affairs Michel Debré called the process of democratization in the ČSSR "an accident on the highway." He became very concerned about this deviation from the old arterial roads of the bipolar world.

The West European Left, which then considered the socialist system in Central Europe to be developed in terms of civilization, welcomed the changes in the Czechoslovak Socialist Republic. Thanks to this admiration, the idea of a "the third way" between capitalism and the Soviet model was created, but the Left's admiration of events in Czechoslovakia was tempered by the deepening doubts of members of the Warsaw Pact.

Via facti, developments inside the Soviet bloc determined its views and position. After the negotiations of "the Six" in Dresden on March 23, 1968, and harsh criticism of Czechoslovakia, Dubček still withstood Brezhnev's pressure. However, another "dressing down" of the prominent members of the Communist Party of Czechoslovakia occurred in Moscow on May 4–5, 1968. Soviet members severely criticized the reform process in the ČSSR. In their opinion,

---

18   For more on the reaction of the USA, see S. Michálek, *Rok 1968 a Československo. Postoj USA, Západu a OSN* (Bratislava, 2008).

19   O. Kořínek,, *Pozývací list 1968* (Bratislava , 2006), 19.

there was a "creeping counter-revolution" in Czechoslovakia which, thanks to its unfettered press, would lead to a decline in Czechoslovak power structures. Three out of four members of the Czechoslovak delegation—Dubček, Oldřich Černík and Josef Smrkovský—defended the reform policies in accordance with the tradition established in Dresden. They also pledged friendship with the Soviet Union. Still, they accepted the Soviet criticism.[20] And there was another typical feature of the negotiations in Moscow: although Dubček and his reform supporters thought that they had only exchanged views, Brezhnev was sure that he had given them orders which had to be fulfilled.

Unlike the negotiations in Dresden, where the Czechoslovak delegation gave, more or less, the impression of unity and defended the process of democratization, in Moscow it was different: the First Secretary of the CC of the CPS, Vasil Biľak, expressed his full sympathy with Soviet concerns. He emphasized that in Slovakia, where he was the highest political representative, the situation was not so critical as in the Czech part of the Republic.[21]

The results of the negotiations in Dresden and Moscow demonstrated that the international conditions for the continuation of the reform process in Czechoslovakia were going from bad to worse. In addition, the constriction of maneuvering space for the assertion of the relatively independent politics of the CPCs inside the Soviet bloc was clear. The consequence of this very negative reality revealed itself at the joint negotiations of the chairmanship and secretariat of the CPCs on May 7–8, 1968, immediately after their return from Moscow. At these joint negotiations, the differentiation of the original wing, which was against Novotný, revealed itself. One group separated from this wing to collaborate with the Soviet Union to "rescue" socialism in the ČSSR. Some historians, in their efforts to distinguish this new group from the original Novotný conservatives, named it a "neo-conservative" wing of the Communist Party of Czechoslovakia. The relations between this newly formed "neologism" and the original conservatives were quite complicated, despite their very close attitudes and characteristics. Peace between them came about only after the occupation of the ČSSR in August of 1968, in the first phase of the so-called normalization.

---

20 V. Bystrický, a kol., *Rok 1968 na Slovensku a v Československu* (Bratislava, 2008), 98–102.
21 O. Kořínek, *Pozývací list*, 30.

In the spring 1968 Vasil Biľak became the leader of the Slovak neo-conservatives. After a short career as a moderate reform communist, this typical dogmatist, conservative and patron of the Party machinery, moved into his natural political and ideological arena. His activities had not only an intra-political, but also a foreign-political, dimension.

With regard to Biľak's foreign-political activities, he began to get involved in this sphere a little bit earlier then in the intra-political sphere. According to the diary of the First Secretary of the CC of the Communist Party of Ukraine, Petro Shelest, which was revealed to the public in the mid-1990s, in April 1968 Biľak expressed interest in meeting with him. Shelest reciprocated because he was afraid of the possible unfavorable impact of the events in Czechoslovakia on his neighboring Ukrainian Soviet Socialistic Republic. He had heard that Ukrainian intellectuals and students were influenced by the activities of revisionist and antisocialist forces in Czechoslovakia. When Biľak and Shelest met in Uzghorod on May 24–25, 1968, Biľak painted a bleak picture of the situation in the ČSSR. He also mentioned the existence of a right-wing-opportunistic "second center" of the CPCs, where he placed Josef Smrkovský, Ota Šik and Čestmir Císař. Biľak also assured Shelest of the existence of "healthy forces" in the CPCs, including Drahomír Kolder, Jozef Lenárt, Alois Indra, Ján Janík and himself. In the end he asked Shelest to give these "healthy forces" in the CPCs a helping hand through the leadership of the Communist Party of the Soviet Union.

In the sphere of internal policy, Biľak acted as a protector of the machinery of the CPCs, which was constantly attacked by society at all levels, but mainly at the lowest, district level (where it was closest to the citizens). As a result of these attacks, Biľak felt threatened by what he called the "anarchy" of the mass media. His fear can best be illustrated by his closing speech at the session of the CC of the CPS on May 22–24, 1968. He answered the question as to whether or not the Party should once again control the media by using the army and the people's militia as follows: "That would be the last straw. Believe me, if it became that bad, we would do it."[22] At the meeting of the chairmanship of the CC of the CPCs on July 12, 1968, he alone, of all the conservative members of this body, declared in favor of the participation of the Czechoslovak delegation at the summit of the members of the Warsaw Pact in Warsaw on July 14–15, 1968, which was supposed to be another judicial proceeding against "heretical" Czechoslovakia.

---

22 Slovak National Archives, Bratislava, f. CC CPS, box no. 1880.

Biľak's supporters among the Slovak neo-conservatives could be divided into at least three groups. The first were some of the Biľak's "tribesmen" from the wing of the Slovak moderate reform communists who, in the spring of 1968, proved that they were more "anti-Novotný" than reformers of socialism. Šalgovič, Kodaj and Zupka belonged to this group. Viliam Šalgovič opposed any reforms and supported the occupation of Czechoslovakia by the armed forces of the Warsaw Pact. Samuel Kodaj, who represented one of the top military leaders of the Eastern Military Zone, was not able to accept the reform policies of the Communist Party of Czechoslovakia and, above all, the hectic way in which they were pursued. Towards the end of July 1968, when the manifesto of the radical reform forces, the "Two Thousand Words," was published, he asked that the people's militias be put on full alert, that a state of emergency by declared, and that the authors of the document be criminally prosecuted. In the end, the trade unionist rebel František Zupka also inclined toward the group of neo-conservatives in the spring of 1968; it was beyond him to adopt the ideas of reform communism.

The other neo-conservative wing of the Communist Party of Czechoslovakia consisted of those politicians who were not very involved before January of 1968. Although they welcomed the reform of socialism in Czechoslovakia, they could not accept the rapid decline of the old power structure and the difficult birth of the new one. That was why they supported the platform of the dogmatic-conservatives. Hruškovič, Šlapka and others belonged to this group. Michal Hruškovič became an informal deputy to Biľak in the Chairmanship of the CC of the CPCs during the occupation of the Czechoslovak Socialist Republic in August of 1968.[23] It would be possible to also put Ján Janík into this group, but with some reservations. Initially he supported Novotný in Slovakia, but then he contributed to his downfall. When Dubček was voted into Novotný's office, Janík later commented, he cried for joy.

The members of the last (third) group, in the wing of Slovak neo-conservatives were not politically active before 1968 and even after January they waited to see which way the wind was blowing. After the sharp criticism of democratization in Czechoslovakia by the Warsaw Pact in March and May, they took the "right stand." Emil Rigo, since January 5, 1968, a member of the Chairmanship of the CC of the CPCs, belonged to this group. He was the only Slovak Roma who had achieved such a high position in Slovak politics.

---

23   J. Pešek, *Aktéri jednej éry*, 162–4.

Others, who made themselves known only later, during the first phase of "normalization," after the occupation of Czechoslovakia by the Warsaw Pact, were Ignác Janák and Ľudovít Pezlár.

The "Novotný conservatives" had varied destinies after January of 1968. Some of them, whose reputations were damaged because of their former collaboration with Novotný, were removed from Party offices step-by-step and never held prominent positions in politics again.

Over time, others were successful in overcoming the suspicion which the members of the neo-conservative group felt for them, merging with them to create a quite homogenous conservative stream in the leadership of the Communist Party of Slovakia. Jozef Lenárt, Bohuslav Chňoupek, and others belonged to this group. After Lenárt was removed from office at the beginning of January 1968, he joined the pro-Soviet, neo-conservative bloc in the Communist Party of Czechoslovakia, becoming an important member. Chňoupek showed his tendency towards neo-conservatism when, in his speech at the meeting of the Central Committee of the Communist Party of Czechoslovakiaon April 1–5, 1968, he criticized the reform policies of Dubček. Like others, he very often visited the Soviet embassy in Prague and informed it about political developments in the ČSSR.[24] As deputy minister of culture, he favored the occupation forces during the Warsaw Pact invasion.

The members of the reform wing of the CPCs, who were opposed to the conservative and neo-conservative streams, were divided into radical and moderate groups. The typical feature of the moderate stream was that its members considered the Action Program of the Communist Party of Czechoslovakia as the most extreme limit to which they could take things in practice. Dubček could be seen as a classic moderate reform communist.

The initial leader of the radical reform Slovak communists was Gustáv Husák. By the beginning of April, however, Husák as Vice-Chairman of the federal government, could stop posing as a radical and start behaving as a moderate reform communist (a centrist). He even became an informal leader of this wing of the Communist Party of Slovakia. Husák confirmed this switch during his speech at a meeting in Bratislava's "Dimitrovka" factory in May of 1968, when he dismissed his former radical supporters among journalists as "barking like dogs fighting over scraps."[25] Some of Husák's supporters had

---

24 S. Sikora, *Rok 1968 a politický vývoj na Slovensku*, 62–5.

25 Ibid., 67.

tried to get him a "job" in the Central Committee of the Communist Party of Czechoslovakia as early as January 22–23, 1968. However, Husák did not give up and in March he demanded the reconstruction of the whole political system. At sessions with citizens and students he denounced the past in a populist manner by, for instance, pointing to the barbed wires at the borders or the impossibility of travel to the West. In popular opinion polls from the end of 1968 Husák ranked fifth in a chart of the most trustworthy politicians in the Czech Republic. In Slovakia he came in second, right after Dubček.[26] At that time only a few people guessed that Husák was, in the words of his former supporter Ján Uher, the "indisputable supporter of Stalin and Stalin's policy with his whole disposition, nature of his character, thinking and exercising the leading tasks of the Party and that of the whole… Stalinism."[27]

While Husák was "riding the high waves" of the democratization process, his next goal was to replace Biľak as First Secretary of the CC of the CPS. Some historians are correct in their opinions that Husák, and some of his supporters, were more "anti-Biľak" than pro- democracy.[28] In fact, Husák's most important goal was to achieve a federative constitutional system of the Czechoslovak Socialist Republic, and he set about doing so in his position as Vice-Chairman of the federal government.

The first serious dispute between Husák and Biľak concerned whether the extraordinary session of the CPS should take place before or after the extraordinary 14th Congress of the CPCs. Biľak and his supporters insisted that it had to take place only after the nationwide meeting because the Congress of the CPCs would not necessarily accept the standpoints of the Congress of the CPS. In fact, Biľak and his followers relied on the hope that, after the meeting of the Congress of the CPCs, conservatives would win and the following Slovak Congress would have to accept its political direction. Husák and his supporters, on the contrary, believed that at the staff meeting of the CPS, held before the meeting of the CPCs, they would cleanse the CC of the CPS of its dogmatists. As a result of this "purification," the Slovak Congress would have the power to oblige the Slovak delegates to advance the interests of Slovakia

---

26   Slovak National Archives, Bratislava, f. CC CPS, box no. 1879.

27   S. Sikora, op. cit., 67.

28   V. Kural, J. Moravec, F. Janáček, J. Navrátil, A. Benčík, *Československo v roku 1968. 1. díl: obrodní proces* (Praha, 1993), 76–7.

first and foremost, through the federalization of the state and Party, at the meeting of the CPCs. In the end, after pressure from regional conferences of the CPS and also the city conference of the CPS in Bratislava, which were held at the beginning of July 1968, at the meeting of the CC of the CPS, the date of the congress of the CPS was fixed for August 26, before the congress of the CPCs. This was a major victory for Husák.

On July 5, 1968, Brezhnev telephoned Dubček and informed him that a meeting of the Warsaw Pact countries, similar to the one held on March 23 in Dresden, would take place very soon in Warsaw. Shortly thereafter Dubček received a letter informing him that this meeting would take place on July 15. The chairmanship of the CC of the CPCs discussed its participation at the Warsaw meeting and rejected Czechoslovak participation, possibly because the letter from the Soviet Politburo was written in such a rude manner that it also angered the conservatives. Another reason could be that, after their negative experiences at the "Dresden council," no one from the chairmanship of the CC of the CPCs wanted to experience a similar dressing-down.

At the end of his speech in Warsaw, Brezhnev made some proposals directed at the Slovak and Czech communists. They would be informed about the "collective evaluation of the situation in Czechoslovakia" by means of a "letter to the Central Committee of the Communist Party of Czechoslovakia." He openly demanded a coup in the leadership of the Czechoslovak Communist Party by means of the support of the "healthy core" (that is, the conservative and pro-Soviet wing) in its leadership. In order to avoid any doubts, he stated: "We have to tell the 'healthy core' that we are ready to give them a helping hand." At the very end of his speech he enunciated the basis of his formulation, which historians later called "The Brezhnev Doctrine"—"The defense of socialism is in our joint interest."[29]

In response, the leadership of the CPCs fell back on a well-known tactic also used at the summit in Dresden. They agreed with the Soviet and allied invectives but declared they addressed an extreme phenomenon, which could be solved by political means. In the end the Czechoslovak delegates offered a polite and diplomatic, but really consistent rejection of the Warsaw letter: "We don't see any pragmatic reasons which would give you the right to claim that our present situation is counter-revolutionary, that there is a direct threat to

---

29 S. Michálek, *Rok 1968 a Československo. Postoj USA, Západu a OSN* (Bratislava, 2008).

the foundations of the socialist system, that in Czechoslovakia the change in inclination of our foreign policy is being prepared or that there is a real threat of separation of our country from the socialist community."[30]

In accord with one of the conclusions of Brezhnev's speech in Warsaw, the highest Soviet representative proposed to Dubček a bilateral meeting of the Politburo of the CC of the CPSU with the chairmanship of the CC of the CPCs. At first, the Soviet leadership proposed Moscow, but, in the words of Dubček, "in the given situation the journey to Moscow would be really humiliating."[31] Although the city of Košice, which was proposed by Dubček, did not suit the Soviets, both sides agreed that the meeting would take place at Čierna nad Tisou on July 29–August 1, 1968, in the "Railwaymen's Club" at the local railway station.

The meeting of both delegations started with speeches by their leading personalities on July 29, 1968. On one side were Brezhnev, Kosygin and Suslov, and on the other Dubček, Černík and Smrkovský. Both sides repeated their well-known views, and very soon the negotiations reached a deadlock. It would seem that Brezhnev was only biding his time when he stated: "Let everybody speak." The Soviet delegation, as always, acted in uniformity. However, the disunited leadership of the Communist Party of Czechoslovakia had to reveal its weaknesses. This was the old political tactic "divide et impera."

Vasiľ Biľak spoke right after Suslov, the top ideologist of Brezhnev's neo-Stalinism. He affirmed enthusiastically: "comrade Suslov, I admit you are exactly right," then Biľak pronounced Brezhnev right in everything he had said, concluding:

> You sent us a letter from Warsaw where you wrote that the counter-revolution was beginning in our country. In the chairmanship of our Party I stated that I approved of 80 percent of the contents in the letter. I voted for the views of the chairmanship and also that of the Central Committee,... in order for the chairmanship to be unified and in the hope that it would do something that would prevent a quarrel from breaking out and would help us to come to an agreement.[32]

---

30 J. Vondrová, J. Navrátil, *Documents...*, vol. 4/1, p. 310.
31 A. Dubček, *Nádej zomiera posledná,* 180.
32 J. Vondrová, J. Navrátil, *Documents...*, vol. 4/2., p. 110.

This Vasil Biľak was a typical product of the machinery of the Communist Party of Czechoslovakia. Trained as a tailor, he was a conservative and dogmatist with a shady and Party-oriented education. Fearing democratization would bring an educated "core group" to control all structures of society, he was trying to make the most of his natural shrewdness and his wily nature to hold down a "job." Biľak was one of those members of the communist movement who saw its ideology, Marxism-Leninism, as a religion without God.

The Bratislava meeting of Czechoslovak Communists with the "Five" on August 3, 1968, produced a joint declaration that was supposed to demonstrate the "inseparability" of the Soviet bloc. Coming, as usual, from the Soviets, it contained many typical phrases on the unity of the "socialist camp." However, in practice it could serve as a pretext for military intervention. Specifically, the famous "Declaration of Six Communist and Labor Parties of the Socialist Countries" adopted in Bratislava states that all six countries pledge to "Support, protect and consolidate...the comforts, which nations achieved by means of heroic efforts, and the devoted work of mankind in each country, which are the joint international responsibility of all socialist countries. This is the united opinion of all participants at this meeting..."[33] This is another formulation of the "Brezhnev Doctrine" of the limited sovereignty of the member states of the Warsaw Pact, which could, if necessary, justify military intervention in one of the member states.

Despite such an ideological justification of possible intervention, the Warsaw Pact countries headed by the Soviet Union would have felt that this excuse would cut no ice with worldwide public opinion. That is why they really welcomed what happened in some public toilet in Bratislava on August 3, 1968, at 8:00 p.m. Allegedly an agent of the Soviet Secret Police named Savčenko arranged for Vasil Biľak to meet with Petro Shelest, whereupon Biľak passed on to him a letter signed by Alois Indra, Drahomír Kolder, Antonín Kapek, Oldřich Švestka and Biľak. This "letter of invitation" stated, in part:

> In this difficult situation we appeal to you, dear comrades, leading representatives of the parties and governments. It is an appeal for your effective support and help by all means available, including military. Only with your help will it be possible to save Czechoslovakia from the imminent danger of counter-revolution and to preserve socialism.

---

33 Ibid., 152.

We are aware of the fact that this extreme step to protect socialism in Czechoslovakia is not easy for the Union of the Soviet Socialist Republics and for the Communist Party of the Soviet Union and also for all fraternal Parties and countries—participants at the meeting in Bratislava. We consider this declaration as an urgent supplication and appeal for your action and multilateral help, as we have used up almost all our energies and all other possibilities.[34]

In the period between the summit in Bratislava and August 21, 1968, the Czechoslovak moderate reform communists headed by Dubček found themselves in a delicate situation. The Warsaw Pact allies, led by the Soviet Union and its domestic minions, tried their utmost to stop the reform process in Czechoslovakia. Meanwhile, the radical reform communists, together with representatives of civil society, tried their hardest to speed it up. In such a situation Dubček, as the leader of the reform process in Czechoslovakia, saw the solution in "permanent apathy." Some historians characterize this as "vigilant tactics of a sly old fox, which accorded the most with the main requirement of his tactics—to gain time until the day of the meeting."[35] Others claim that it reflected "unskilful maneuvering" following Dubček's recklessness and total helplessness.[36] For Dubček, there was no way out, only to maneuver and to wait and see how things would develop.

The period of uncertainty and maneuvering after the meetings at Čierna nad Tisou and Bratislava was interrupted in a very dramatic way. On August 20, 1968, at 11 p.m., armed forces of the Warsaw Pact invaded the Czechoslovak Socialist Republic. Twenty-seven divisions consisting of more than 500,000 soldiers in 6,300 tanks, 2,000 pieces of artillery, 550 combat aircraft and 250 transport aircraft participated. On Slovak territory, 48,055 Soviet soldiers along with 10,372 Hungarian soldiers, as well as one Bulgarian regiment of about 1,000 soldiers, were committed to battle in the first phase of the military intervention. According to historians, it was the biggest military action in Europe since World War II.[37] This intervention by the armies of

---

34   O. Kořinek, *Pozývací list.*, 59.
35   S. Sikora, *Rok 1968 a politický vývoj na Slovensku*, 120.
36   For example, the Czech historian Jan Pauer.
37   J. Pauer, *Praha 1968. Vpád Varšavské smlouvy, pozadí, plánovaní, provedení* (Praha, 2004), 217, 322.

five "friendly countries'" put an end to the process of democratization. Now another period of the communist regime in Czechoslovakia began. Later it was called "normalization."

Shortly after the occupation of Czechoslovakia, some of the reform communists, including Alexander Dubček, assumed that something from the policy of "socialism with a human face" could be saved. That proved to be an illusion. Dubček himself had to resign on April 17, 1969. He was replaced by Gustáv Husák, who held office until December 1987, connecting his name with "normalization," or "goulash socialism."

The system of government in Czechoslovakia at the time of "normalization" was determined by the strategic interests of the Soviet Union, which wanted to stabilize its hegemony in this area by stationing Soviet troops in Czechoslovakia and firmly tying it to the Soviet Union. For more than two decades, Soviet control over the state was restored and the supremacy of orthodox communists over society was renewed. The doors to democracy did not open to Slovaks and Czechs until the end of 1989, as a result of internal and external factors.

Instead of a conclusion, a few remarks on issues connected with the Czech-Slovak federation are in order. After the reform communists took over the leadership of the CPCs in January of 1968, conditions were ripe for significant changes in the state organization of the ČSSR. Slovak and Czech social scientists agreed at a conference in Smolenice on March 6–8 that the only possible form would be a federation. This fact was confirmed in the Action Program of the CPCs adopted at the meeting of the CC of the CPCs on April 1–5, 1968. It noted that it was necessary "to make a significant change in the state organization of the Czechs and Slovaks. Therefore, the need arose with all solemnity to respect the advantage of a socialist federative organization as the reputable and approved form of coexistence of equal nations in a common socialist state." [38]

However, Slovak and Czech social scientists, as well as their political representatives, understood "federation" differently. In the Committee for the Preparation of the Act on Czechoslovak Federation, which functioned as of May 21, 1968, under the leadership of Gustáv Husák, arguments often broke out. The Slovaks wanted a *loose* federation, that is, the center of power

---

[38] J. Vondrová, J. Navrátil, J. Moravec, *Komunistická strana Československa. Prameny k dějinám československé krize v letech 1967–1970, zv. 9/1* (Brno, 1999), 333–4.

would be in two national states, the Czech Socialist Republic and the Slovak Socialist Republic. The federal government would only have charge over national defense, foreign policy, a common currency and the management of state material reserves. At the same time, the Slovaks sought some measures that would prevent the Czech nation's dominance over the Slovak nation. The Czechs preferred a *tight* federation, distinguished by a strong federal government at the expense of the national bodies. Prague would be the seat of the federal government, and the Czechs would prevail in its executive bodies. [39] Thus, the status quo would be maintained to a certain extent, securing for the Czechs continued domination of the state.

The Constitutional Act No. 143/1968 dated October 27, 1968, on the Czechoslovak Federation presented a compromise: Slovaks managed to obtain equality, but only in the federal government. They did not manage to secure strong powers for national bodies as they wished; the same applied to Czechs in relation to federal bodies.

However, federation as the attribute of political democracy par excellence requires democratic political conditions for its proper functioning. With the start of "normalization" in 1969, these conditions quickly disappeared. Moreover, even the "father of the federation," Gustáv Husák, misused the federalization process in order to seize power, just as he had done during the democratization process in 1968. After April 17, 1969, when Husák replaced Dubček as First Secretary of the Communist Party of Czechoslovakia, he sought to strengthen his political power but the Constitutional Law adopted at the end of October 1968 stood in his way. Because its balance of competence between the national and federal bodies was an obstacle to the centralization and concentration of political power in Prague, he had the Act amended on December 20–21, 1970.

The new Constitutional Act No. 125/1970 strengthened the federal bodies at the expense of the powers of the Czech Socialist Republic and the Slovak Socialist Republic in planning, foreign trade, the banking system, foreign currency management, internal security, etc. With the establishment of federal ministries of engineering, mechanical engineering, transportation and communications, the key industries of the economy were passed

---

39 In the 1960's, Slovaks made up 4.7 % of the CC of the CPCs apparatus and only 3.2 % of the central state bodies. Cf. J. Rychlík, *Češi a Slováci ve 20. století. Česko-slovenské vztahy 1945–1992* (Bratislava, 1998), 186.

into the competence of the federal government. The amendments to the former Constitutional Act on the Czechoslovak Federation, accompanied by the "normalization" of social life in the ČSSR, emasculated the federation. Consequently, if the opportunity arose sometime in the future, the Slovaks would once again seek a loose federation.

6

Commentary on "August 1968 as Seen from Bratislava"

Stanislav J. Kirschbaum

The paper by Slavomír Michálek and Stanislav Sikora on "August 1968 as Seen from Bratislava," focuses on the activities of the political groupings and personalities who were caught up in events that were seminal to the historical development of the Slovak nation and the creation of the Slovak Republic in 1993. What made the year 1968 so extraordinary is the fact that it witnessed two major, yet contradictory, developments in communist Czechoslovakia: a liberalization process and its brutal suppression through a military invasion from neighboring communist countries eight months later. These developments had a specific resonance in Slovakia with linkages not only to the creation and history of Czecho-Slovakia,[1] but to Slovak history as well.

The historical record unequivocally shows that Slovakia provided the impulse for the liberalization process that fully blossomed throughout Czechoslovakia during eight months in 1968. After six years of statehood and relative independence, Slovakia had been re-incorporated into Czechoslovakia in 1945 as a consequence of the Allies' decision to restore Czechoslovakia at the end of the Second World War. This resulted not only in a change of the political

---

1 I use the spelling with a hyphen when referring to the entire history of the state, a spelling that was introduced in the 1919–1920 Peace Treaties that created Czecho-Slovakia. The unhyphenated spelling is used when referring to specific periods when that spelling was officially used: 1920–1938 and 1945–1993. During the period 1990–1993, both spellings were used in the country; however, the unhyphenated spelling was used abroad.

elite in Slovakia, but, three years later, in the inclusion of Czechoslovakia in the Soviet sphere of influence and its subjection to a radical program of political, economic, and social change. Prague managed this revolutionary change and also incorporated, in its application to Slovakia, the ideology of the First Czechoslovak Republic that maintained the existence of a "Czechoslovak nation."[2] Slovakia's population was thus subjected to an ideological and political transformation process as well as the implementation of Czechoslovak interests, which the communist political elite defined as serving first and foremost Czech interests. Those Slovak communists who had fought during World War II for the restoration of Czechoslovakia and the imposition of a communist regime were targeted for elimination from political life in order to ensure full Slovak compliance to the new ideological and political order. They were found guilty of "Slovak bourgeois nationalism" in the early 1950's, and their place was taken by subservient Slovak politicians.

Slovak historical development could not, however, be suppressed with such radical measures. The war years when Slovakia had its own state had clearly shown that the Slovak nation was fully capable of governing itself and that it did not need to be managed by others. Even those Slovaks who, during the war, fought for the restoration of Czechoslovakia at the end of hostilities, did so with the aim of ensuring that the relations between Czechs and Slovaks would be on an equal footing, as expressed in the slogan *"rovný s rovním"* (as equals), which they proposed as the political and constitutional basis for the re-incorporation of Slovakia into the common state. However, Prague had other plans, as indicated above, and the country's communist leadership implemented its radical transformation program and pursued the objective of creating a "Czechoslovak nation." When major changes in the Soviet bloc in the 1960's made a challenge to the regime's policies possible, the Slovak communist political elite took the opportunity not only to redress the wrongs that were done to its members in the 1950's (the trials of the "Slovak bourgeois nationalists"), but above all to ensure the proper recognition of the one

---

2 Unlike the situation in the First Czechoslovak Republic (1920–1938) where the Slovaks were not recognized as a nation, the re-created Czechoslovak Republic of 1945 did recognize Slovak nationhood, but maintained that there also existed a Czechoslovak nation.

action that they had organized and led against the first Slovak Republic that was interpreted as Slovakia's return to Czechoslovakia, namely, the partisan uprising of 1944, which they called the Slovak National Uprising.[3]

The Soviet de-Stalinization campaigns of 1956 and 1960, as well as an economic crisis in the early 1960's, were opportunities adroitly used by the Slovak communist political elite to challenge the relations between the Czechs and Slovaks in their common state. They created a movement to redress historical wrongs that provided a major impetus to the nascent liberalization process made possible by the Soviet de-Stalinization campaigns. Beginning in 1963, they used a two-pronged approach that would be acceptable within the framework of communist politics: the full rehabilitation of those condemned in the 1950's and the recognition by the regime of the historical importance of the 1944 uprising. They achieved the latter in August 1964 during the twentieth anniversary celebrations of the Slovak National Uprising in the city of Banská Bystrica in the presence of Communist Party of Czechoslovakia (CPCs) leaders and also Nikita S. Khrushchev, First Secretary of the Communist Party of the Soviet Union; the rehabilitations took longer but by 1968, they had been achieved. Our two authors briefly present Slovak developments after 1945 from an institutional and political perspective.

The fact that the communist regime was being forced to redress past wrongs and accept new policies did not go unnoticed in the Czech Lands. Given the economic crisis in the country, the Czech communist elite became progressively involved in questioning the policies of the CPCs, in particular its economic policies.[4] Its reform wing pressured the regime to such an extent that by January 1968 a change in the top leadership took place, putting at the head of the CPCs Alexander Dubček, the First Secretary of the Communist Party of Slovakia (CPS), who had supported the Slovak movement for the historical rehabilitation of the Slovak National Uprising.

---

3   During the 1950's, the communist scholarship on the Slovak National Uprising was the object of deformations and misrepresentation. This was redressed by the preparation and eventual publication of memoirs and new studies. See, for example: Gustáv Husák, *Svedectvo o Slovenskom národnom povstaní* (Bratislava, 1964) and Jozef Jablonický, *Slovensko na prelome. Počiatky národnej a demokratickej revolucie* (Bratislava, 1965).

4   For an examination of these developments, see Galia Golan, *The Czechoslovak Reform Movement: Communism in Crisis 1962–1968* (Cambridge, 1971).

From January 1968 on, under his leadership, the liberalization process came into its own and influenced political life in Czechoslovakia during eight extraordinary months. As Prague was the capital city where many significant events took place pertaining not only to the country as a whole, but also to the future of communism and the Soviet bloc, this period of liberalization became known as the 'Prague Spring.'[5] However, many developments were also taking place in Slovakia at this time, some very specific to Slovak political life and Slovak historical development.

Michálek and Sikora present us with an analysis of the political situation in 1968 at the top echelons of the CPS, along with the background of the main leaders, namely, Vasil Biľak, Alexander Dubček, and Gustáv Husák. They discuss at length the role and importance of the Slovak communist elite, which soon became divided among reformers, dogmatists and middle-of-the roaders. As the situation evolved during the spring and summer and as it became clear that the neighboring communist states were uneasy with developments in Czechoslovakia, the alignments changed in the CPS. Michálek and Šikora do an excellent job of describing these new alignments and assessing their role in the final outcome of the liberalization process.

Although we get a good sense of the political situation in Bratislava during the spring and summer months of 1968, we are less informed on the Slovak perspective on the eight months of liberalization. Two questions need answers, which the literature has yet to provide: how different or similar to that of the population of the Czech Lands was the involvement of the population of Slovakia in the liberalization process? and how important to the Slovak people was the different approach to liberalization and federalization that expressed itself in the Slovak press, particularly in *Kultúrny život* and later in *Nové slovo*?[6] The latter question is especially important in view of the fact that the federalization of the state, passed into law on October 28, 1968, which created a Czech Socialist Republic and a Slovak Socialist Republic, is the one reform that survived the invasion of August and the imposition of "normalization" in 1969. Additional questions concerning federalization concern the debate that took place in the Slovak press on the type of federal system that best suited

---

5   For an excellent analysis of this period, see Galia Golan, *Reform Rule in Czechoslovakia: The Dubcek Era 1968–1969* (Cambridge, 1973).

6   For a brief analysis of this question, see Stanislav J. Kirschbaum, *A History of Slovakia: The Struggle for Survival*, 2nd edition (New York, 2005), 237–44.

Slovakia; the attitude of the various wings of the CPS to the federalization of the state; and the discussions between Czech and Slovak representatives on the federal system each side proposed. As CPS and CPCs archives of the period are now accessible to scholars, some answers should be found there.

It would also have been interesting to have had Michálek's and Sikora's overall assessment of the meaning of the 'Prague Spring' in Slovakia, and more specifically, for Slovak national development. Again, one can ask many questions: did the eight months of liberalization mark the beginning of the end of Czechoslovakia or was it merely a period that tested significantly the relations between the two nations? Even though this was still a time of one-Party rule with all that "democratic centralism" meant for Slovakia, did the events of 1968 result in a fundamental break between the Czech and Slovak communist elites? In the history of the common state after 1918, the Slovak political landscape always experienced a competition between two options: a Slovak and a Czechoslovak one. After 1948, the communist adherents of the Czechoslovak option governed Slovakia and imposed revolutionary change on the inhabitants of Slovakia; they ruled until 1963 when Dubček became First Secretary of the CPS. As Michálek and Sikora point out, he was a Soviet-trained communist and a faithful apparatchik, but he did support and even protect those in Slovakia who were pushing for a Slovak option, thereby incurring the wrath of the Czech leadership of the CPCs.[7] One can, therefore, ask whether the events of 1968 brought about a change in Slovak politics to such an extent that they inevitably led to the independence of Slovakia in 1993. Or was it nothing more than the end of what Ľubomír Lipták described for the early communist period as "politics in Slovakia," now replaced by "Slovak politics,"[8] yet at a time when a communist regime was still in place? Also, there is the question of the role of the policy of "normalization" that was imposed on the country after the Warsaw Pact invasion of August and its link to the preceding liberalization period.[9] Finally, one can also ask how "normalization" was applied to Slovakia, and what were its consequences for Slovak political development, now that the common state was functioning as a federation?

---

[7] For more on the role of Dubček in this period, see William Shawcross, *Dubcek* (London, 1970).

[8] Ľubomír Lipták, *Slovensko v 20. storočí* (Bratislava, 1968), 296.

[9] A good study of the liberalization and normalization periods is by H. Gordon Skilling, *Czechoslovakia's Interrupted Revolution* (Princeton, 1976).

To suggest that there is no direct link between the liberalization process of 1968 in Slovakia and Slovak independence in 1993 would fall into the realm of fantasy rather than good historical judgment. Specific as the events of 1968 were to communist politics and to the development of the Soviet bloc, that year also brought out two basic themes that mark the history of Czechoslovakia since its creation: the country's political, economic, and social development and Czech-Slovak relations. It is evident that the liberalization process was specific to the communist political, economic, and social program that was imposed on Czechoslovakia when the country found itself in the Soviet sphere of interest. It was an attempt to reform the political and economic system, to bring about "socialism with a human face," the expression that was used at that time. Its suppression by the Warsaw Pact invasion sounded the death knell of that experiment but even more so that of socialism as a viable alternative to liberal democracy and market economics. However, it would take another two decades before the system collapsed as part of a general rejection of the Soviet system throughout Eastern Europe. Nevertheless, while the debate on the reform of socialism was taking place during the eight months of liberalization, the question of Slovakia's economic position in and contribution to Czechoslovakia was raised, although not to the extent that it would be after 1989, when a socialist economic option was no longer viable and there was full freedom of expression. The focus at that time was primarily on the second theme for which a solution was proposed.

As far as Czech-Slovak relations are concerned, the federalization of Czechoslovakia, as a resolution of these relations, marked, in the first instance, the successful achievement of the goals of those who had fought in the 1944 partisan uprising (who are known in Slovak as *povstalci*). But federalization also had a broader meaning: it signalled the refusal of the Slovaks to be anything less than equal partners in a common state with the Czechs. Whether this equality could and would be respected was answered in the following two decades; the formal constitutional equality between the two socialist republics did not alter fundamentally the political relations between the two nations. When, in 1989, the communist regime was overturned and total freedom of expression returned to political life, the debates between Czechs and Slovaks and also among Slovaks indicated that each side had a very different conception of the common state and of its history (especially Slovakia's role in Czechoslovakia's economic development), and that these conceptions were, for all intents and purposes, unbridgeable.[10] The constitutional reform of 1968—federalization—had offered, theoretically at least, the best answer to the question that had already arisen in 1918, namely, how to organize and define Czecho-Slovakia as a state in which both nations could feel "at home." Its evident failure by 1989 (just like the failure of "Czechoslovakism" in 1939) pointed to the profound dissonance that existed between Czechs and Slovaks for which there was only one solution: state independence for both nations. It was put into effect the day after Czecho-Slovakia was dissolved on December 31, 1992.

Four decades after those eventful months in communist Czechoslovakia may be too short a time to give detached answers to many of these questions. However, future historical research based heavily on official documentation may not necessarily offer a truer picture of this period or of the role of personalities, but may clarify certain questions. The testimony of eye witnesses is also essential. The paper by Michálek and Sikora reflects the information that is available to us now from a variety of sources and a moment in time that many of us remember, perhaps even experienced, and allows us to have a better understanding of some aspects of an experiment that played such an important part in the historical development of the Slovak nation.

---

10   For an examination of these conceptions, see Kirschbaum, *A History*, 256–71.

7

The 'Prague Spring,' Poland and the Warsaw Pact Invasion

Łukasz Kamiński

1. Before the Invasion.

When Alexander Dubček became the new First Secretary of the Communist Party of Czechoslovakia (CPCs) on January 5, 1968, not many observers expected that this event would herald a new era. But, Władysław Gomułka was ill-at-ease with these changes. On February 7, 1968, Dubček met with Gomułka in Ostrava. To his astonishment, after having delivered a run-of-the-mill presentation of his intentions, Dubček listened to the Cassandra-like speech of "Wiesław" who frequently referred to his experiences from the post-October (1956) period. The leader of the Polish United Workers Party (PUWP) warned Dubček against denouncing Stalinism ("it will be possible to write elaborately on the period of the personality cult and all those events no sooner than in fifty years"), "activation of anti-socialist powers" and the appearance of postulates concerning "the second stage" of changes. Gomułka stressed the importance of vetting all Party members, which he was doing in Poland at that time, emphasizing that "the dogma-related issues were not dangerous, what was dangerous were the revisionist, the social-democratic and liberal-bourgeois issues." At the end of this meeting Gomułka pointed to the roots of his anxiety: "If the situation in your country was bad, hostile elements in our country would take heart. For instance, right now we've got problems with writers and students in connection with cancelling Mickiewicz's play Dziady (Forefathers' Eve)."[1]

Wiesław's concerns were justified. Despite the fact that the changes in Czechoslovakia (apart from personnel ones) were still not concrete, choosing a new Party leader aroused great hopes, not only among Czechs and Slovaks, but among their northern neighbors. Unfortunately, the opinions of Poles on the Czechoslovak transformation in the first weeks after the January plenum are very difficult to find in source materials. Both the security apparatus and the Party apparatus at that time were oriented towards reporting on social attitudes in connection with the issue of Dziady and the beginning of social protests. On the other hand, public opinion was more focused on the intensifying crisis in the state.

On February 29, 1968, the famous Polish writer Antoni Słonimski spoke about the hopes and concerns connected with the beginnings of the 'Prague Spring' during an extraordinary meeting of the Warsaw branch of the Association of Polish Writers (ZLP):

> Democratic and truly humanistic comments of our colleagues from Czechoslovakia are reaching us. They have managed to return meaning to words which have been falsified a hundredfold. We look with hope at events occurring in the country of our Czech neighbors. Those comments resemble our own words uttered ten years ago. But won't this breath of freedom, which has renewed the hopes of Czech writers bring one more disappointment, won't this end the same as our October freedoms?

Marek A. Wasilewski made a motion, which was not voted upon because the meeting was adjourned. In it he suggested that the writers issue the following dispatch: "Polish writers gathered at an extraordinary meeting of the

---

[1] „Protokół z rozmowy pierwszego sekretarza KC PZPR tow. Władysława Gomułki z pierwszym sekretarzem KC KPCz tow. Aleksandrem Dubczekiem (Ostrawa, 7 lutego 1968 r.)" [in:] *Zaciskanie pętli. Tajne dokumenty dotyczące Czechosłowacji 1968 r.*, foreword and preparation: A. Garlicki and A. Paczkowski (Warsaw, 1995), pp. 15–48. Original in: Archiwum Akt Nowych (Archive of Contemporary Documents), hereafter AAN, KC PZPR, XIA/33, pp. 250–334.

Warsaw branch of the ZLP send their brotherly greetings to Czech and Slovak writers, assuring them of their high regard and approval for their attitudes in the fight for cultural freedom.[2]

During the March events of 1968 in Poland, the impact of the 'Prague Spring' became clear. Leaflets issued before the rally of March 8 carried the following message: "We have the same rights as Czechoslovak students and the same means of defense." Pro-Czechoslovak banners also appeared during street demonstrations. As early as March 9, a famous slogan was chanted in Warsaw: "All Poland is waiting for its Dubček," which seems to indicate the earlier existence of this slogan. Three days later, in Częstochowa, students chanted "Long live Czechoslovakia" and "Long live Dubček." Some resolutions also referred to the transformation in the ČSSR. For instance, students in Poznań wrote: "We sympathize with and greet the heroic students in brotherly Czechoslovakia." References to the situation in Czechoslovakia also accompanied the last phase of the students' movement, the unsuccessful attempts at organizing an all-Poland protest on April 22, 1968. Two days earlier, leaflets calling for a rally in front of the Warsaw University of Technology were distributed. Some of them contained the following: "All Poland is waiting for its Dubček and that is why we support the 'Znak.'"[3]

The 'Prague Spring' for participants in the Polish March demonstrations of 1968 was a sign of hope that democratic transformation of the communist system was possible. Equally important was the hope that some of them might

---

2   „Stenogram z Nadzwyczajnego Walnego Zebrania Oddziału Warszawskiego Związku Literatów Polskich, Warszawa 29 lutego 1968" [in:] „Marzec '68. Między tragedią a podłością," Gregorz Sołtysiak and Józef Stępień, ed. (Warsaw, 1998), p. 100 (original in: AAN, KC PZPR, 237/XVIII-319, p. 45, also p. 166—the contents of Wasilewski's amendment).

3   Archiwum Instytutu Pamięci Narodowej (Archive of the Institute of National Remembrance), hereafter AIPN, MSW II, 968, Report, 20 April 1968, pp. 389–90; AIPN, 0296/99, vol. 1, Copy of the leaflet distributed on March 5, 1968, at Warsaw University, p. 9; *Informacja dotyczy sytuacji na terenie m.st. Warszawy w związku z wydarzeniami na Uniwersytecie Warszawskim* [in:] *Marzec 1968. Odgłosy na temat ekscesów na Uniwersytecie Warszawskim, ibidem*, s. 30; *Informacja dotyczy wydarzeń związanych z sytuacją w środowiskach studenckich, ibidem*, p. 30; *Odgłosy na temat ekscesów na Uniwersytecie Warszawskim, ibidem*, p. 30; *Informacja dotyczy wydarzeń związanych z sytuacją w środowiskach studenckich, ibidem*, p. 167; *Odgłosy na temat ekscesów na Uniwersytecie Warszawskim, ibidem*, p. 30; *Informacja dotyczy wydarzeń związanych z sytuacją w środowiskach studenckich, ibidem*, p. 219; J. Eisler, „Wpływ praskiej wiosny na polski Marzec '68" [in:] *Wokół praskiej wiosny. Polska i Czechosłowacja w 1968 r.*, ed. Ł. Kamiński, (Warsaw, 2004), pp. 27–30; *Wydarzenia marcowe...*, op. cit., p. 69.

count on the solidarity of Czech and Slovak colleagues. The Czechoslovak press, freeing itself from the manacles of censorship, more and more boldly wrote on the situation in Poland, openly condemning the anti-Semitic and anti-students' campaign. The most famous report on the March events, written by Jiří Lederer, was published in May by the weekly *Literární Listy*. In the period of "normalization" in Czechoslovakia he was sentenced to two years in prison for "maligning the state belonging to the world socialist order and its leaders." The Czechoslovak press also published numerous letters of solidarity with Polish students, scientists and researchers. Resolutions of similar content adopted during student rallies and demonstrations were sent to Poland. Unfortunately, most were intercepted by officers of the W division (correspondence control) of the Polish Security Service (SB). Protests were also delivered to the Polish embassy in Prague.[4] Invitations by Prague scientific institutions to come to Czechoslovakia as guest lecturers, which had been sent to Polish professors who had been fired (Bronisław Baczko, Zygmunt Bauman, Maria Hirszowicz-Bielińska, Leszek Kołakowski and Stefan Morawski), had far reaching consequences.[5] In May of 1968 rumors circulated regarding the possibility that students expelled from Polish universities might continue their studies in the ČSSR.[6]

On March 23, 1968, representatives of six states of the Warsaw Pact met in Dresden. This meeting, which was hurriedly convened (just two weeks after a similar meeting in Sofia), was devoted to an analysis of the situation in

---

4   Ł. Kamiński, "Marcowa solidarność", *Biuletyn Instytutu Pamięci Narodowej* (2003, no. 8–9), pp. 116–18.

5   Even before that, on March 28, employees of the Institute of Philosophy of the Czechoslovak Academy of Science issued a strong protest against the dismissals, at the same time demanding a halt to the anti-Semitic campaign and "infringement of basic human rights" (AAN, KC PZPR, 237/XVI-594, p. 83).

6   AAN, KC PZPR, 237/XVI-594, List organizacji wydziałowej Czechosłowackiego Związku Młodzieży Wydziału Fizyki Technicznej i Jądrowej do polskich kolegów, 13 March 1968, p. 87; AAN, KC PZPR, 237/XVI-615, Notatka służbowa [Memorandum], 21 March 1968, pp. 40–2; *ibidem*, Notatka [Note], 28 March 1968, pp. 63–6; AIPN, MSW II, 1266, Korespondencja napływająca z CSRS, zajęta przez Biuro „W", March 1968, pp. 2–5, 12–14; AIPN, IPN 0296/99, vol. 1, List studentów Wydziału Filozofii Uniwersytetu Karola w Pradze, 12 March 1968, p. 46; AIPN, MSW II, 968, Informacja dot. sytuacji na terenie m. st. Warszawy, 13 May 1968, p. 490; P. Blažek, „*Wszystko pójdzie w innym kierunku*". *Wpływ polskiego Marca '68 na praską wiosnę* [in:] *Wokół praskiej...*, op. cit., pp. 32–44.

Czechoslovakia. Because of the viciousness of its attacks on the transformations in the ČSSR, it is now known by historians as the "Dresden Tribunal." As we can see from the minutes of the session, one of the main prosecutors was the First Secretary of the Central Committee (CC) of the Polish United Workers Party (PUWP), Władysław Gomułka. Under the heading "theses for my speech," Gomułka wrote: "We agree with the assessment of comrade Brezhnev—the counter-revolution has begun—the process is developing." An analysis of this session allows us to conclude that "Wiesław" not only supported the Soviet leader, but he may even be considered a co-author of the "Brezhnev doctrine," stating:

> We have no intention of interfering in internal matters, but of course there are situations in which so-called internal matters affect the matters of the whole socialist camp. [...] Everything which happens in Czechoslovakia in a sense also affects our contracts, our arrangements and requires consultation, requires that we undertake certain measures, to say it openly, to block the way for counter-revolution.

Next Gomułka referred to the Polish and Hungarian experiences of 1956 where "everything also started with the writers." Finally, he presented a number of "proofs" that the situation in Czechoslovakia was headed in the wrong direction.[7]

Why did Gomułka have such great aversion towards to the events in the ČSSR, when just twelve years earlier he had been in the same situation as Dubček? By 1968 the leader of the PUWP had become a hard-line communist, and from this perspective the 'Prague Spring' seemed to be a deadly threat to the cohesion of the system, already strained by a number of violations of the Moscow Orthodox rules in previous years (Yugoslavia, China, Albania, Romania). In the context of March 1968, Gomułka could have feared the

---

7   J. Pauer, *Praha 1968. Vpád Varšavské smlouvy. Pozadi—Plánováni—Provedeni* (Prague, 2004), pp. 37–41; *Notatki Władysława Gomułki ze spotkania w Dreźnie 23 marca 1968 r.* [in:] *Zaciskanie...*, op. cit., pp. 49–60; *Stenografický záznam porady šesti komunistických stran v Drážďanech 23. března 1968* [in:] *Prameny k dějinám československé krize 1967–1970*, vol. 4/1: *Mezinárodní souvislosti československé reformy 1967–1970. Prosinec 1967 – červenec 1968*, prepared by J. Vondrová and J. Navrátil (Prague – Brno 1995), pp. 73–114 [English version in *The Prague Spring 1968. A National Security Archive Documents Reader*, prepared by J. Navrátil, A. Benčik, V. Kural, M. Michálkova, J. Vondrová (Prague, 1998), pp. 64–72].

consequences of liberal reforms—the strengthening of opposition trends in Poland. The March events in the Polish People's Republic (PPR) had revealed a significant weakening of his position so Gomułka, by "jumping the gun" on the others and showing a particular zeal, could have been trying to strengthen his position in the eyes of the Kremlin. Meanwhile, Gomułka exhibited an incredibly strong anti-German phobia and saw in the possible desertion of Czechoslovakia from the group of "People's democracies" that Poland could face a threat analogous to the one it faced in September 1939—the threat to its borders from the west and the south. The last factor was his personal dislike of Dubček. Gomułka talked with disdain, and sometimes even contempt, about the Czechoslovak leader during his meetings with Brezhnev. He continuously spelled the Czechoslovak First Secretary's surname with a "p" instead of "b"—making it sound nearly like the Polish equivalent of the word "asshole." Perhaps Dubček reminded him of unfulfilled hopes which Polish society had had in the autumn of 1956 and about Gomułka's incredible popularity which by 1968 was just a memory[8].

On May 6, 1968, an unprecedented event in the history of the relations among the states belonging to the Soviet bloc occurred—the CC of the PUWP and the government of the PPR issued to the CC of the Communist Party of Czechoslovakia (CPCs) and the government of the Czechoslovak Socialist Republic (ČSSR) a "Protest note against anti-Polish and anti-socialist attitudes in the Czechoslovak press, radio and television." It stated that "For many weeks the Czechoslovak press, radio and television have systematically produced biased, malicious and openly hostile information and comments on Poland." It then quoted a few examples of publications and comments which constituted "a brutal attack on Poland, our Party, and People's Power." Moreover, earlier diplomatic protests were ignored. The authors of the Protest Note also assumed that those "slip-ups" of the Czechoslovak mass media were convergent with "the campaign conducted by imperialist propaganda centers hostile towards the Polish People's Republic, such as Radio Free Europe and the circles of international Zionism which use for their slanderous,

---

8   Compare: J. Eisler, „Władysław Gomułka wobec Praskiej Wiosny," *Wiadomości Historyczne* (1998, no. 5), pp. 257–73; P. Machcewicz, „Do diabła z suwerennością". *Władysław Gomułka wobec Praskiej Wiosny* [in:] *Wokół praskiej...*, op. cit., p. 59–72; A. Paczkowski, „Władysław Gomułka versus Praska Wiosna," *Politicus* (1994, no. 1–2), pp. 39–45.

anti-socialist and anti-Polish aims the materials published in Czechoslovakia." Additionally, these actions did not meet with the "needed, resolute intervention on the part of your Party and your Government." That is why the note requested "the highest Party and state authorities of the Czechoslovak Socialist Republic to take a clear, public stance on those matters and to undertake energetic and effective measures which would immediately stop anti-Polish demonstrations, negative campaigns in the press, radio and television." The note concluded: "We want to express our faith that the gravity with which we present our stand on those painful matters to the respective authorities of the ČSSR will be fully appreciated."[9]

This document was not published, nor was the Czechoslovak answer to it. However, it became a pretext to organize a cycle of meetings of the basic organizations of the PUWP during which, for the first time, the attitudes of the authorities of the PPR towards the 'Prague Spring' were presented. During the meetings the "Note… was read together with the information on the situation in Czechoslovakia prepared on May 7, 1968." A sort of interpretation of the course of events in the ČSSR, it stated that Czechoslovakia was in "a state of political crisis," and the heads of the CPCs as a result of "the activities of revisionists and counter-revolutionaries […] have lost to a large extent the power to influence the process of correcting errors of the past." The authors assumed that the leadership of the CPCs was divided into three groups. The first was composed of revisionists aiming at the "liquidation of the People's Power, transformation of Czechoslovakia into a liberal bourgeois state which would lead to […] desertion from the socialist camp and Warsaw Pact and consequently connect with the West, and especially with the Federal Republic of Germany (FRG)." The next group—the center—"would like to take control over the situation but they have not enough courage to strongly defy revisionist tendencies" and that is why "they lag behind the events, are making more and more concessions in favor of anti-communist elements." The third group "representing the right standpoint" was aimed at "defending and strengthening the allies […] with brotherly socialist countries."

---

9   AAN, KC PZPR, XI/379, Nota Komitetu Centralnego PZPR i Rządu PRL do KC KPCz i Rządu CSRS z dnia 6 maja 1968 r., pp. 11–14; *Protokół nr 53 posiedzenia Biura Politycznego w dniu 6 maja 1968 r.* [in:] *Centrum władzy. Protokoły posiedzeń kierownictwa PZPR. Wybór z lat 1949-1970*, prepared by A. Dudek, A. Kochański, K. Persak (Warsaw, 2000), p. 403.

In the next part of the document a number of proofs were presented that the situation in Czechoslovakia "in recent days" had deteriorated, that "anti-communist forces" intensified their activities aiming at "the restoration of capitalist relations." In the meantime, "events in Czechoslovakia are not only an internal matter of a brotherly state." Rather, events in the ČSSR were of "vital importance" for the safety of the PPR, GDR and other states belonging to the Soviet bloc. That is why "we cannot under any circumstances agree with the counter-revolution that prevails in Czechoslovakia. The Soviet Union, as well as other states of the Warsaw Pact, cannot accept that." It was reported that "in direct connection with this situation" military maneuvers would be organized in the border areas "with the participation of Red Army units." At the same time, hopes were expressed that "healthy forces" would prevail in the leadership of the CPCs. Polish Party organizations were advised to "be on intense guard against all signs of hostile anti-socialist activities in our country, towards any attempts to spread havoc and disinformation among public opinion, towards the enemy's sabotage operations." Activists were entrusted with the task of explaining to society "the sense of events" in the ČSSR[10].

At the same time, the communist security apparatus started operations connected with the situation in Czechoslovakia. They were of two types—gathering information on the reactions of Polish society and gathering documents and information on the situation in Czechoslovakia. The latter were mostly gained during meetings with officers of the Czechoslovak security apparatus, border guards, and so on .[11]

Gomułka maintained his uncompromising stance during subsequent meetings of the "Warsaw Five" in Moscow and Warsaw. He promoted his theory that events in Czecho-slovakia were proof of the existence of "a new type of counter-revolution." Gomułka was more and more irritated by the lack of resolute action on the part of Brezhnev. During the meeting of the Politburo of the CC of the PUWP on July 5, 1968, an annoyed Gomułka shouted "To hell with sovereignty!"

---

10   AAN, KC PZPR, XI/379, Informacja dla organizacji partyjnych PZPR w sprawie sytuacji w Czechosłowacji, 7 May 1968., pp. 7–10.

11   AIPN, 0365/47, vol. 2, Tezowy plan przeciwdziałań niektórym tendencjom na tle wydarzeń w CSRS, 3 May 1968, no pagination; AIPN, 01283/565, part 1, Tezy dot.: kierunków działań pionu IV SB w związku z sytuacją w CSRS, 4 May 1968., microfiche; G. Majchrzak, „Operacja 'Podhale'" [in:] Wokół praskiej..., op. cit., p. 107.

He also considered the possibility of sending the Polish Army into Czechoslovakia without waiting for the Soviet Union. Of course this was impossible, but it showed Gomułka's determination to solve the Czechoslovak crisis by force[12].

At the end of July 1968 the next wave of Party meetings was held, during which the second letter of the CC of the PUWP on the situation in Czechoslovakia was read. The aim of the letter was to prepare Party members for the approaching intervention, which indicated that Gomułka's entourage did not believe in the success of the Czechoslovak-Soviet negotiations. The letter stated that, despite the declarations of the leaders of CPCs, the "pressure of reactionary forces is increasing" in Czechoslovakia, which are supported by the West and whose aim is to "change the composition of forces in Europe in favor of imperialism." Czecho-slovak refusal to participate in the meeting in Warsaw was treated as "the attempt to oppose other parties and socialist states under the banner of defending sovereignty" by the leaders of the CPCs, who at the same time did not want to fight with the "reactionary forces" and were aiming at transforming the Party into a Social Democratic Party and the ČSSR into a "democratic and bourgeois republic." Then, it was reported that "confidential contacts" maintained with West German politicians were to result in the opening of Czecho-slovakia to "western infiltration," especially by the intelligence services and "centers of sabotage." The next accusation referred to the lack of a CPCs response to the "Two Thousand Words" manifesto and revisionist forces in the mass media. The attention of the PUWP members was turned to the fact that the ČSSR "takes a very important place in the whole security system of socialist states." That was the root of this ominous declaration:

> We cannot let anyone challenge this alliance of our brotherly nations, we cannot let the balance of power change in favor of imperialism. The interests of socialism in Europe would be threatened. That is why we should give any necessary support needed to suppress the reaction and the foiling of imperialist plans of pulling Czechoslovakia out of the community of socialist states in Europe and to the Czechoslovak Communist Party and its activists, who remain faithful to the ideas of Marxism and Leninism, who are aware of their responsibility towards their own working class as well as world-wide socialist forces. It is our internationalist obligation.

---

12 *Wokół praskiej...*, op. cit., p. 192.

The letter ended with an appeal to remain vigilant against possible symptoms of hostile activities in the state and to explain "the vital sense of events in the ČSSR to society." At the last moment, was added: "Following the decision of the leadership of the Warsaw Pact, Soviet units on our territory are ready to march to the West," in connection with which society was urged to "warmly greet the Allied army."[13]

The anti-Czechoslovak propaganda campaign also intensified. There is no doubt that before August 21, dislike of the 'Prague Spring' was instilled into some part of Polish society through traditional anti-Czech stereotypes. The main anti-Czechoslovak propaganda focused on its alleged close relations with the Federal Republic of Germany and the threat to Poland from the south (recalling 1939), the alleged ingratitude of the Czechs for their liberation from German occupation, "too few victims and losses" suffered during the Second World War, and finally the alleged participation of "Zionists" in implementing the 'Prague Spring' reforms.[14]

Gomułka's radical stance resulted in the fact that the Polish People's Republic was the only one, apart from the Soviet Union, which contributed any significant military input into the invasion on Czechoslovakia. The Polish Army occupied about 20,500 square kilometers of territory. About 25,000 Polish soldiers took part in the intervention. They were equipped with 647 tanks, 566 armored personnel carriers, 371 cannons and 36 helicopters. Their main task was to blockade the Czechoslovak People's Army garrisons, to provide patrol services, and to engage in intense propaganda operations. Numerous leaflets, posters and brochures were distributed and, utilizing vehicles equipped with loudspeakers, radio broadcasts were aired.[15] Special units (assault and

---

13 AAN, KC PZPR, 237/VII-5790, vol. 1, Informacja [Information], no date, p. 198; AP Wrocław, KP PZPR Bolesławiec, 80/XIV/18, List do wszystkich organizacji partyjnych PZPR, 28 July 1968, no pagination. A similar letter at the same time was sent to the Party members from the Central Committee of the SED – compare AAN, KC PZPR, XIA/33, Notatka [Note], August 1968, pp. 696–7.

14 AIPN Wrocław, 053/570, Meldunki specjalne do CSK i Departamentu III MSW, 9 and 17 May 1968, pp. 2–3, 41.

15 From the territory of the PPR from August 24 until the end of September, twenty-four-hour radio broadcasts were aired in Czech on all wave lengths. From October 1, the broadcasting was limited to short and medium waves, and the time was also significantly shorter (three hours on each wave). The television station in Katowice aired a special program for the Czech minority in Teschen Silesia. In September alone 1,157,000 copies of propaganda materials directed at Czechs and Slovaks were published by the CC of the PUWP (leaflets, brochures, notices). AAN, KC PZPR, 237/XIX-348, Informacja o formach oddziaływania propagandowego na Czechosłowację, no date, pp. 93–6.

radio-electronic reconnaissance) participated in the operation of liquidating independent radio stations. Ten Polish soldiers died as a result of various incidents (road accidents, careless weapons handling, one suicide). There were also Czech and Slovak victims. On September 7, 1968, a drunk private Stefan Dorna opened fire on passers-by in Jičin. He killed two of them—Jaroslav Veselý and Zdeňka Klimešova—and wounded seven more, including two soldiers of the Polish Army. After being disarmed, the perpetrator was taken to Kłodzko where he was tried and sentenced to death. The sentence was later commuted to life imprisonment. The withdrawal of the Polish Army started at the end of October 1968. A solemn welcome of the army was organized in the territories of border districts, and military parades were organized in the city of Wałbrzych on October 27 and in Wrocław on November 4.[16]

2. Initial Reactions of Polish Society to the Invasion.

In the first days after the intervention, dislike of the activities of the Warsaw Pact Armies predominated in Poland. It was clearly visible in the wording used by Poles to describe "the brotherly assistance." Besides applying the adjectives: "erroneous," "illegal," "groundless," they called it a "not-legally binding act," a "brutal infringement of the norms of international law," an "invasion," an act of "violence," an "open aggression," an "attack," an "outrageous thing," a "regular armed invasion," a "dishonorable act," an "act of lawlessness," a "dirty trick, a "crime," an "occupation," a "provocation," "criminal home trespassing," an "act of aggression," an "assault," "lawlessness," a "violent act of lawlessness," a "great scandal," a "great fraud," an "outright aggression," a "violation of sovereignty," a "violent intervention," a "manifestation of villainy," and so on. We can only guess what was hidden behind the reports of the SB which mentioned that, when discussing the situation in Czechoslovakia, some persons used "various obscene and swear words" and "showered slander at the socialist régime and the USSR."

Reports by the official media that the intervention came at the request of the Czechoslovak authorities were commonly questioned. The technical director of one of the Warsaw unions stated that: "None of the workers believe that the Soviet army and Allied forces were asked by anyone to come to Czechoslovakia. [...] It is as true as the request of Seyss-Inqart to Hitler to come to Austria and the request of Hácha to Hitler to occupy Czechoslovakia." People

---

16   *Gazeta Robotnicza*, No. 260, 5 XI 1968.

demanded that they be informed of the names of the persons who were made such a "request." As in the case of other crisis moments, the trustworthiness of the dispatches of official publications was doubted: "What is written in the Polish press is not worth reading as it is a complete lie." The Security Service reported instead a significant increase of interest in the broadcasts of Radio Free Europe and other Western stations broadcasting in Polish. News heard from them was repeated by the people. After a few days, new doubts appeared—if the majority of the people and the ČSSR authorities were in favor of the intervention, "why does the process of appointment of the new government and Party leadership last so long?" In the province of Bydgoszcz many "provocative questions" were reported concerning the difference between "aggression" and "marching in" as well as "occupation" and "the stationing of troops."

The participation of the Polish Army in the occupation of Czechoslovakia was perceived by the public as a national disgrace, shame and violation of the traditions of liberty: "The participation of our troops in the occupation of the ČSSR is a dishonor for Poland, and I am personally ashamed that our troops unlawfully marched into the country as aggressors." "As Poles we must be ashamed that our troops became aggressors in Czechoslovakia." "The Polish army was used for dirty and mean purposes." "For the first time the Polish army will be used to suppress freedom and it is very bad." "I do not like the fact that Polish troops must play the role of a gendarmerie for the first time in our history. Our nation has been dishonored." "I feel like a bastard, I suffer from a moral hangover, it is a regular violent assault, the violation of any rules and agreements." "Listening to the radio communiqué on the statement of the government of the PPR, I was ashamed that I am a Pole and I felt like crying." On many occasions the opinion was expressed that Poland should replace its traditional banner: "For your and our freedom" with a new one: "For your and our enslavement." There were also concerns that participation in the intervention discredited Poland in the international arena: "Poland was condemned by international opinion because Polish troops marched into Czecho-slovakia. The Czech nation will become our enemy forever." One of the scientific workers at the University of Nicolas Copernicus expressed some hope that "Czechs, Slovaks and Moravians fully realize that Poles have nothing in common with that. Those are the acts of the leadership of the Party and how they extend their servility so far."

The participation of the PPR in the intervention aroused associations with Poland's takeover of Zaolzie (the Trans-Olza River territory in Silesia) in 1938, which for many years was exploited by communist propaganda. There were ironic remarks that "Rydz-Śmigły did not expect such an admirable performer of his ideas in the person of Wiesław." At the same time, it was stressed that "we occupied Zaolzie then on our own account, despite the fact that we did it together with the Germans; but now we occupy Zaolzie not for ourselves, but on someone else's orders and on someone else's account, acting as policemen." People sadly concluded that "we allow the Soviet Union to use us in the same way as Hitler did."

For many Poles the situation in Czechoslovakia was a benchmark for the position of their own country. On August 27 the Security Service in Katowice quoted a foreman from the Siemianowice mine: "Twenty years of brotherhood with the Soviet Union has not resulted in any improvement. Poland is the poorest of the socialist states and we watch it so calmly. Czechoslovakia is wiser and tried to stop this long-lasting occupation, which also affects us, once and for all. This is in our interest, it must also happen in our country." The questions were asked: "When are we going to be liberated from this tsar-like enslavement?" And postulates were raised: "the same could happen in our country."

Sometimes, fears were expressed that the intervention might become the root of a new worldwide conflict as "the USA will never accept the fact that the troops of the Warsaw Pact remain on the territory of Czechoslovakia." Many people expected the next target of Soviet aggression to be Romania or possibly the other dissidents from the Soviet bloc—Albania and Yugoslavia. One of the engineers employed in the Gliwice steelworks expressed it in the following manner: "Russians destroy everyone who thinks in a different way than they do. That is why sooner or later they will attack Romania and Yugoslavia, for their so-far anti-Soviet policies. They are only afraid of the Chinese and this keeps them from using force against them." In singular cases people saw a ray of hope in the possible armed conflict: "God help us with the outbreak of war. They would finally bring some order and they would hang and slaughter those with red *bumagas*."

Many persons perceived the Czechoslovak suppression as a failure of the communist system, rather than its success. It was assumed that "what happens right now in Czechoslovakia is the beginning of the end of communism." It was stressed that the Soviet Union had discredited itself in the eyes of world public opinion and showed its true nature: "The liberty banners voiced over the years by the USSR on freedom, non-aggression and self-determination are just platitudes, and it is regular Russian imperialism which aims at subordinating all of Europe." There were even very accurate forecasts of the effects of the invasion on the world communist movement: "In connection with the aggression in the ČSSR, the definite fall of the Communist International will take place and a new one will be established without the USSR, composed of Communist Parties and leftists from the West."

There are also relatively numerous examples of opinions which supported the intervention. It seems that the main motives behind such attitudes were fears, exaggerated by official propaganda, that Czechoslovakia might be under German influence:

> Of course the Soviets may be accused of infringing upon the sovereignty of Czechoslovakia as the intervention is connected with the internal affairs of the ČSSR and they did not manage to prove that it was at the request of Czechoslovak authorities. However, being a Pole and an inhabitant of Poland, I think that the intervention was necessary because otherwise the unlimited penetration of the ČSSR by the FRG would take place and that would endanger our borders. One may even be an enemy of communism and Soviet methods but he should accept those steps because of the "raison d'état."

There was also the issue, exploited by the authorities, of "too few victims and losses" suffered by the Czechs during the Second World War:

> The situation in the ČSSR is not good and that is because Czechs were not persecuted during the Second World War by the Germans in the same way as Poles were. That is why the Czechs perceive Germans as friends and they welcome them as brothers and do not want to talk to Poles. This situation will change when Czechs will be properly lined up by the USSR and other countries and the cronyism with Germans will end in the future. And this will happen when all countries deal with Jews. Let them beat Czechs a little, it will do no harm, they will start thinking sensibly.

The opinion that "order should have been brought into the ČSSR earlier, as it is an insincere nation" appeared relatively often. Such wording (the adjective *insincere* is the most often repeated one in opinions hostile to Czechs) shows the existence of still very strong prejudice and stereotypical perception of Poland's southern neighbor. In some opinions one may notice an astonishing mixture of real concerns (e.g., related to the outbreak of a new war) and communist propaganda: "The march of the allied armies into the ČSSR alone can tame the inclinations of Czech Jews to co-operate with the FRG and other capitalist countries. Irresponsible actions of Czech reactionaries and Zionists may lead the world to a new war."[17]

It seems that in the first days after the beginning of the armed intervention in Czechoslovakia, outrage and condemnation of the aggression dominated. With the passing of time, through the activities of the PPR propaganda, the circle of persons accepting the operation was gradually broadened. Unfortunately, because of lack of sociological sources (opinion polls) it is impossible to precisely reconstruct what was the percentage of particular attitudes in Polish society.

On August 21, 1968, at about 6 o'clock in the morning, meetings were organized for the secretaries of the Basic Party Organizations and the Enterprise Committees of the PUWP in the 'poviat' and district Party committees. The participants were informed about the need to organize open Party meetings on the very same day during which the letter of the CC of the PUWP, justifying the decision to use armed forces, and informing that the intervention was organized at the request of Czechoslovak comrades, was to be read. The letter recommended that Party organizations "explain to society the importance of events in Czechoslovakia for the security of our state and for peace in Europe, expose misinformation and lies of reactionary propaganda and oppose any attempts of spreading anxiety and panic."

The meetings, and especially the subsequent discussions concerning the materials presented, reflected the information chaos which prevailed in Poland at that time. Questions concerned: whether the FRG army marched into Czechoslovakia, whether Alexander Dubček ordered shooting at Warsaw Pact soldiers, whether people resisted the intervention, whether Dubček

---

17 The reactions mentioned above were based on reports of the "Podhale" operation sent from different provinces to the Central Management Post of the Ministry of Internal Affairs (MSW) in Warsaw (AIPN Warsaw, MSW II, 3831, 3834-3850), "Podhale" operation chronicle (AIPN Warsaw, 0296/109, vol. 2), information of the Cabinet of the Minister of Internal Affairs on the "Podhale" operation (AIPN Warsaw, MSW II, 2040), information of the 2nd Department of the MSW on the "Podhale" operation—domestic circles (AIPN Warsaw, MSW II, 3490), memorandums of the 3rd Department of the MSW on the comments and opinions connected with the situation in the ČSSR (AIPN, MSW II, 3833, 4772), reports of the "Poviat" Security Service structures of Katowice Province (AIPN Katowice, 0103/192 vol. 6 part 2-3), of Kraków Province (AIPN Kraków, no. 060/36 vol. XV) and of Wrocław Province (AIPN Wrocław, 053/805), informative notes on the situation in Kraków and Kraków Province (AIPN Kraków, 060/36 vol. XIV). See also Ł. Kamiński, „Zhańbione imię Polski na długie lata," *Biuletyn Instytutu Pamięci Narodowej* (2003, nos. 8-9), pp. 61–4.

was arrested, whether Marshal Grechko and Brezhnev resigned, whether Poland was to get Zaolzie back, etc.[18] People who feared that there might be a large-scale conflict asked about the reaction of the West, whether mobilization was planned, etc. People also asked whether personnel changes in the authorities of the ČSSR would follow; what was the stance of Romania and Yugoslavia on the intervention; whether the real power at the moment was exercised by the intervening forces or the Czechoslovak administration; how the ČSSR army behaved. During these meetings, Party officials called for a struggle against "hostile propaganda" and for counteracting the buying out of goods, military rumors, etc.

During the meetings on August 21, dissatisfaction with the USSR and its satellite activities was much broader than during previous waves of the POP meetings. The following questions were asked among others: "Maybe a plebiscite should be organized in Czechoslovakia on the choice of the new government wanted by the Czechoslovak nation." "As the agreement on non-intervention into the internal affairs of Czechoslovakia has been signed, why and how should one understand the entrance of the armies into Czechoslovakia?" "Why in Čierna nad Tisou did the Soviet comrades demand that some particular comrades be ousted and why did they interfere in the internal affairs of Czechoslovakia?" "Before the war we took some territory from Czechoslovakia, so why they are we entering that country again today?" "Czechoslovakia has its own army, so why do they need external help?" "Czechs have their own army, so what are the Soviet Warsaw Pact armies for?" "Why aren't we told the truth?" "Is the entrance of the Warsaw Pact armies in accordance with international law?" People also inquired about the difference between the intervention of the USSR in Czechoslovakia and the USA in Vietnam. They also asked why members of the CPCs, who represented the majority of the nation, asked for help and could not solve the problem on their own. Questions were also raised as to whether the intervention of the armies had been in accordance with the Warsaw Pact Statutes. People demanded better information on the events as well as the names of

---

18 The information chaos included the alleged blowing up of the embassies of the PPR and the USSR in Czechoslovakia, the issuing of weapons to civilians in the ČSSR, the conscripting of reservists, the killing of numerous soldiers of the Polish Army, the evacuations of hospitals in order to make room for the wounded, the internment of Czechoslovak politicians on the territory of the PPR, etc.

specific persons who had demanded help. These comments, which may be interpreted as a protest or at least distancing oneself from participation in the intervention, appeared at every third Party meeting in Lower Silesia! There were also silent meetings at which Party members just took cognizance of the presented information without taking the floor.[19]

Some Party members outside the meetings expressed much more radical opinions, which were scrupulously noted by SB informers. One of the workers at the Zabrze mine, a Party member, agreed with the incriminating letters:

> Russians right now dictate conditions to the world in the same way as Hitler did in 1939. Once such conditions were dictated by the swastika, today by a red star [...] Poles should remove the banner "for our and your freedom" from their platform as it is no longer in accordance with reality – and in sum the Polish press is hypocritical. Fortunately, we no longer use *Trybuna Robotnicza*[20] in the toilet, because if asses had eyes and could read what they write in it, they would instantly get sick.[21]

In the first days of the invasion, rumors forecasting the possibility of its transformation into an armed conflict intensified, and buy-outs of food products (salt, flour, sugar) were observed in many regions. The withdrawals from and payments into saving accounts of the PKO [Polish Savings Bank] also increased significantly[22].

---

19 Do wszystkich organizacji partyjnych, AAN, KC PZPR, 237/VII-5790 t. 1, pp. 269-72; ibidem, pp. 244–5, Informacja o pierwszych spotkaniach zorganizowanych w Komitetach Dzielnicowych w związku z listem KC PZPR i oświadczeniem rządu PRL, 21 Aug. 1968; ibidem, pp. 246–9, Informacja nr 82/S/68, 21 Aug. 1968; ibidem, pp. 254–5, Odpis dalekopisu [Copy of a teleprinter message], 21 Aug. 1968; ibidem, p. 256, Odpis dalekopisu [Copy of a teleprinter message], 21 Aug. 1968; ibidem, pp. 258–9, Zebrania POP na temat listu KC, bd; ibidem, pp. 274–7, Nastroje w związku z sytuacją w Czechosłowacji, no date; Ibidem, pp. 281–3, Przebieg zebrań POP na temat listu KC, bd; J. Ogonowski, op. cit., pp. 59–60; Ł. Kamiński, op. cit., pp. 143–5.

20 Organ of the Provincial Committee of the PUWP (KW PZPR) in Katowice.

21 Meldunek sytuacyjny [Situational report], AIPN Katowice, 0103/192 t. 6 part 2, no pagination.

22 Wzmożony wykup artykułów w niektórych województwach, AAN, KC PZPR, 237/VII-5790 vol. 1, p. 250; Notatka zbiorcza z informacji uzyskanych przez pracowników Wydziału d/w z Przest. Gosp. KW MO i jednostek terenowych w dniu 23 VIII 1968 r., AIPN Katowice, 0103/192 vol. 6 part 2, no pagination; Meldunek, AIPN Katowice, 0103/192 vol. 6 part 3, no pagination; Notatka dot. wypowiedzi i komentarzy w związku z sytuacją w Czechosłowacji, AIPN Warszawa, MSW II, 3833, no pagination; Notatki informacyjne, AIPN Kraków, 060/36 vol. XV, passim.

3. Leaflets and Wall Inscriptions.

From August 21, 1968, to the end of September 1968, there were 143 instances of distributing leaflets connected with the intervention in Czechoslovakia in at least 64 Polish towns and cities.[23] At the same time, over 200 pieces of graffiti appeared in 49 towns and cities.

The majority of the leaflets were printed in a few dozen or so copies, but some were duplicated in larger quantities and distributed in a few towns or cities. They were handwritten, printed on children's printers, re-written on typewriters, and in a few cases copied on stencil machines. Their content was mostly limited to one- or two-sentence long banners such as: "Halt the aggression on Czechoslovakia." "Gomułka, keep your hands off Czechoslovakia." "For our freedom and yours." "Long live our Czech brothers, out with Gomułka." "No more Soviet tyranny. We express solidarity with Czechoslovakia. The press lies." "The USSR keep your hands off the ČSSR." "We condemn the aggression of the Warsaw Pact armies on Czechoslovakia. Long live peace, freedom of speech and democracy." "We, Poles, no longer want wars, foreign armies keep out of Czechoslovakia, long live the government of Dubček." "Countrymen, fight for the freedom of the ČSSR." "Poles, let's condemn the aggression against the ČSSR. The press lies. Freedom for the ČSSR." "Withdraw the LWP (People's Army of Poland) from the ČSSR." "Keep your hands off the Czechs." "Long live Czechoslovakia." "Gomułka—the aggressor." "Long live Dubček." "We want a Polish Dubček." "Polish brothers take up arms, let's get rid of the communist regime, let's get rid of colonialism. We won't be one of the Soviet republics, long live a free Czechoslovakia." "The Polish nation has nothing in common with the dishonorable aggression of the USSR and its servants in Czechoslovakia. Gomułka's clique is the imposed occupational authority which does not represent the Polish nation. We will not let them disgrace the glorious banner of our nation, 'for our and your freedom.'" "Disgrace to the Bolsheviks, the bandits and their Warsaw servants for the assault on heroic Czechoslovakia." "Long live Czechoslovakia, no more Soviet SS members." "Let's get rid Soviet murderers in Czechoslovakia." "Imperialist communists hands off Czechoslovakia. Soviets, the ČSSR is not your homeland." "We completely dissociate ourselves from the activities of Polish authorities in Czechoslovakia—long live freedom." "Gomułka, we will never forgive you."

---

23 These calculations do not include numerous instances of the distribution of leaflets manufactured in Czechoslovakia and distributed on the territory of the PPR.

A few leaflets, however, had a more elaborate content, as the one which appeared on August 31, 1968, in Kraków :

> Poles, a horrible thing has happened. The good name of Polish soldiers famous for heroic fighting for honorable ideals, "For your and our freedom" has been disgraced as aggressors. Who is to blame for that, who issued the dishonorable order to send Polish troops against our brotherly socialist Czechoslovak state, whose only fault was that they did not want to order the nation about as it is done by our government, wanted to give to this nation great freedom? If we don't condemn this repugnant act of aggression which is only comparable with Hitler's deeds, the world will blame the whole Polish nation. We cannot let this happen. Germans from the GDR have understood it and they cut off this repugnant act of their government. Why shouldn't Poles do the same? We shouldn't let them make us sign dishonorable statements that we allegedly support the aggression, we shouldn't let them make us believe that the aggression has been necessary. Those are primitive lies. The last who managed to fool his nation and convince people of the rightness of criminal aggression was Hitler. If the good name of Poland is dear to us, let's tell the world that Poles have always detested all acts of violence and as always they support those who fight for freedom and not those who try to strangle it.[24]

The content of wall graffiti corresponds to the moods described above: "Get the armies out of Czechoslovakia" (Kraków, 22 Aug.). "No more Soviet aggression in Czechoslovakia. Soviets go home" (Milanówek, 22 Aug.). "Brezhnev—criminal and aggressor, we demand that the army be withdrawn from Czechoslovakia" (Ozimek, 22 Aug.). "Long live free Czechoslovakia" (Augustowo, 23 Aug.). "Communist Nazis keep your hands off Czechoslovakia, go home" (Janików, 23 Aug.). "Kremlin means blood and tears, long live the Czechs" (Karnin, 23 Aug.). "The aggression on the ČSSR disgraces Poland" (Poznań, 23 Aug.). "Long live the Czechs, get rid of Russia" (Włocławek, 24 Aug.). "This disgraceful Anzsluss won't be accepted" (Zakopane, 24 Aug.). "We demand that the Polish army be withdrawn from Czechoslovakia" (Anin, 25 Aug.). "Long live Dubček" (Borki Wielkie, 25 Aug.). "Disgraceful ČSSR occupiers" (Warszawa, 25 Aug.). "Soviets—murderers" (Sopot, 26 Aug.).

---

24 AIPN Kraków, 060/36 vol. 10.

"Let's get rid of Soviet imperialism" (Gdynia, 28 Aug.). "Death to the ČSSR occupiers" (Kraków, 28 Aug.). "Hitler 1938—Gomułka 1968" (Bochnia, 29 Aug.). In a few towns, drawings depicting the sign of equality between the Soviet star and the swastika appeared on walls.

4. Intelectuals' Protests.

Having heard that the armies of the Warsaw Pact marched into Czechoslovakia, several dozen persons, mostly employees of universities and the Polish Academy of Science (PAN) returned their Party membership cards in protest. The resignation from the Party of the employees of the PAN Institute of History Tadeusz Łepkowski, Bronisław Geremek and Krystyna Kersten had echoes far and wide.[25]

Just after the intervention, literary circles considered issuing a letter of protest (the initiative of Witold Dąbrowski). However, the idea was not put into practice because of fear of reprisal affecting the group of writers already weakened by the March events. As Wiktor Woroszylski said, collecting signatures for a document of that sort equaled "preparing a list of those to be arrested."[26]

The majority of Polish intellectualists could only note their pain and outrage in private. For instance, Stefan Kisielewski wrote in his diary:

> The Word became flesh: we have entered Czechoslovakia. We, that is to say Big Brother, GDR, Hungary, Bulgaria, PPR—the Warsaw Pact Five. We have entered literally—the army marched in. Today, at dawn one could hear heavy bombers flying overhead, also the tanks passed by—this is the shortest way to Prague. In the morning one could not buy newspapers, everything disappeared as if washed out. About lunchtime Sandauer junior showed me *Słowo*: with the Press Agency's communiqué on the cover page that "at the request of the Czechoslovak government (?!) the known countries extend military help against a reactionary and counter-revolutionary conspiracy which is supported by foreign countries." And just yesterday, exactly the same press lied to us that everything was all right in Czechoslovakia,

---

25 Notatka dot. wypowiedzi i komentarzy w związku z sytuacją w Czechosłowacji, AIPN Warszawa, MSW II, 3833, no pagination.

26 Informacja nr 6 dot. akcji „Podhale", AIPN Warszawa, 01283/565, microfiches.

and that discussions on the possibility of intervention were counter-revolutionary machinations. What a perfidy—what a masquerade! And now we march in and in what a repugnant role. And as always we play dirty with the Czechs—as in the case of Zaolzie, people reacted classically: they ran into shops and bought out everything. People are depressed, but one can also hear voices that the Czechs got what they deserved. Why have they attacked socialism and wheeled and dealed with the Germans? This nation has already been stupefied, especially here, where people feel neither safe nor at home. *Point de reverie*—goodbye eight-month-long Prague Spring idyll of freedom of speech! Muscovites did their job again—Paul was right: no international communism, no ideology, simply Soviet imperialism and nothing more! [...] "The Statement of the PPR government" on the invasion says that the "Polish government and...(allied governments), following the principles of indissoluble friendship and co-operation and in accordance with the existing alliance obligations, have decided to take into consideration the abovementioned request on extending necessary help to the brotherly Czechoslovak nation." And how to be a patriot. I feel like vomiting! "How hard to love and not to love."[27]

Only three persons dared to protest openly against the intervention. Sławomir Mrożek, who was in Paris, issued a statement published later in *Le Monde*:

> I am a Polish writer, not an emigrant, a member of the Association of Polish Writers. The news of the participation of the PPR government in the armed aggression against Czecho-slovakia shocked me. I protest against that aggression. I extend my solidarity to the Czechs and Slovaks, and especially to Czech and Slovak writers who are imprisoned and persecuted.

On September 1, 1968, a solidarity letter "To Czech and Slovak musicians organized in the Association of Composers in Prague and Bratislava" was issued by Zygmunt Mycielski.[28]

---

27 S. Kisielewski, *Dzienniki* (Warsaw, 1996), pp. 76-8.
28 E. Chwałko, „Praska Wiosna polskich intelektualistów," *Biuletyn Instytutu Pamięci Narodowej* (2003, nos. 8–9), pp. 87–98.

However, the most famous was a similar letter sent by one of the most illustrious of Polish writers, Jerzy Andrzejewski, to Edvard Goldstücker, the president of the Association of Czechoslovak Writers. As Stefan Kisielewski stated in his diaries: "It was beautifully written, in an incredibly courageous way—such a voice was needed, it rehabilitates Poland, explains that society has sealed lips, and liars and bastards talk instead of it."[29] Andrzejewski wrote:

> Dear Mr. President:
> Being full of respect and overcome with emotion, as well as bothered by anxiety connected with the situation in which Czech and Slovak writers find themselves as a result of tragic and regrettable events, I would like to ask you to express to your colleagues my great solidarity with them, real brotherhood with a Polish writer, who expresses only his own feelings and thoughts, but who also believes that he will find support among the vast majority of Polish writers, for whom truth, love, faithfulness, hope, patriotism and progress are still alive, and have not yet changed into stone.
>
> I would like you and your colleagues to know that in the days of your creative searches, so important for the future of the whole world, you have had friends among Polish writers and intellectuals revived by hope, and when you have gone through days especially important for you and your nations—we have been with you despite the fact that we have been deprived of freedom of speech in our own homeland.
>
> I am sure that you know that the most painful defeat is the feeling of hopelessness in the face of violence and coercion, and this defeat becomes even a harder burden when the best traditions of one's nation are insulted, freedom of speech is annihilated, and the truth trampled on. I realize that my voice of political and moral protest will not and cannot counterbalance the disgrace of Poland in the opinion of the whole world. But this protest emerged from outrage, pain and shame, and it is the only thing which I can do in the circumstances for you, your friends and colleagues. So please accept it with hope... But let's not talk about hope. Let's guard hope. Let's strengthen hope. Let's work for hope.[30]

---

29 S. Kisielewski, op. cit., p. 107.

30 *Nowe wstrząsy, część 1 Rok 1968 (Zeszyty Edukacji Narodowej – Materiały z dziejów Polski 1945–1980. Od października 1956 do grudnia 1970, part III)* (Warsaw, 1987), pp. 79–80.

The protests of intellectualists were quite limited. But we should keep in mind that those circles were pacified after the March events of 1968. The scale of reprisal applied then (especially towards scientists and writers) was so large that in August of 1968 fears of escalation prevailed.

5. Other Forms of Protest.

In the course of the "Podhale" operation, the SB intensified its control of correspondence, both between Poland and Czechoslovakia, as well as domestically. Nine percent of domestic correspondence included comments on the intervention, mostly of a hostile character, describing the "brotherly help" as aggression, unlawfulness or comparing it to the events of 1938 ("Exactly 30 years ago Hitler did the same"). In private letters many people expressed solidarity with Czechs and Slovaks: "I'm ashamed of the behavior of our government. Czechs haven't liked Poles, but now they will blow their top at the sight of Poles. I'm really sorry for them." Some complained about the passivity of Polish society: "The Polish government has made this dishonorable decision, because the Polish nation is passive and for unknown reasons inactive. The price of blindness has turned out to be high."

Among the correspondence confiscated by the SB officers are letters containing positive contents from the point of view of the PUWP: "We realize that it is no one else's interest but ours in Poland to keep the ČSSR in the socialist camp. No one wants 1939 to be repeated, and every Pole understands it, especially when the negotiations have been conducted with the FRG on the issue of giving back the Sudeten Mountains."

The SB also seized many leaflets sent to private persons and institutions. Dozens of letters of solidarity and telegrams were sent to the ČSSR embassy, and not all of them were anonymous. Part of this correspondence was directed to the addresses of embassies of Western countries with the request to pass them on to the Czechoslovak embassy. Similar letters were also sent to private persons and institutions in Czechoslovakia. In addition, hundreds of anonymous protest letters, against the participation of the PPR in the invasion, were sent to the top authorities (the government, the CC and the PUWP) as well as to editors' offices and radio stations: "To whom it may concern—to whom it may concern—I protest against the occupation of brotherly Czechoslovakia. And I demand the Army be withdrawn. Shame on the occupiers and their servants. Long live socialism."

Protests were also sent to foreign and international institutions (radio stations, the United Nations).[31] A few anonymous letters appeared, which were circulated in larger quantities and whose authors counted on bringing about a chain-letter in defense of the ČSSR:

> The circle of solidarity with the Czech and Slovak nations. Do not break the circle by imprudent or hasty actions. The Czech and Slovak nations wait for your help. Pass on this appeal. Awaken the conscience of the Polish nation against the dirty oppression and violence in the name of alleged brotherhood as exercised by Moscow. The Czech and Slovak nations have sent an appeal to the world. We want a referendum under the control and auspices of the UN. We want neutrality, we will choose the regime on our own. Please copy this appeal on a typewriter 5 times and send it to persons whom you consider able to understand it. Do not send it to people who belong to the PUWP, because out of cowardice that will break the circle. The people who belong to the Democratic Party are moneygrubbers and guzzlers without a heart and a soul. Do not send the appeal from the town in which you live. Don't send the appeal to your nearest and dearest, especially living in the same town. If possible, do not use a typewriter located in the town where you live. Avoid sending all envelopes at the same time, or address them in a different manner. Avoid the same type of envelopes, be careful, but remember the appeal, because one day your nation may need similar moral support. Do not break the circle.

A few anonymous satiric poems were also very popular. They made a mockery of pro-interventionist propaganda.[32] For many persons, especially those later engaged in opposition activities, the song by Jacek Tarkowski *Hradec Kralove* was very important:

---

31 Notatki służbowe dot. opracowania korespondencji w wymianie z Czechosłowacją i krajami zachodnimi za okres 21 VIII – 9 IX 1968, AIPN Warsaw, MSW II, 4455, passim; Zestawienie zatrzymanej korespondencji ze względu na treść w okresie od dnia 21 do 24 VIII 1968 r., AIPN Kraków, 060/36, vol. XI, p. 3; Biuletyny specjalne nr 1-4 z materiałów „W", ibidem, pp. 4–25.

32 The most famous one is 'List załogi zakładów im. Przyjaźni Polsko-Czechosłowackiej w Suwałkach do braci Czechów, wyśmiewający oficjalną propagandę' (*Nowe...*, op. cit., pp. 80–1).

[Heavy, sweltering and hot
are the nights of August]
    Ciężkie, duszne i upalne
    Są noce sierpniowe.
[Asleep are people, asleep is the town,
asleep is Hradec Kralove]
    Śpią już ludzie, śpi już miasto
    Śpi Hradec Kralove.

[A man is standing at the doorstep
And he cannot believe his eyes]
    Stał mężczyzna w progu domu
    I oczom nie wierzy:
[In Hradec Kralove, in Hradec Kralove
soldiers' steps, thunder]
    W Hradcu Kralovem, w Hradcu Kralovem
    Dudni krok żołnierzy.

[A woman, terrified,
through curtains is looking]
    A kobieta przerażona
    Patrzy zza firanki –
[In Hradec Kralove, in Hradec Kralove
Polish tanks thunder]
    W Hradcu Kralovem, w Hradcu Kralovem
    Dudnią polskie tanki.

[The Hradec days are no longer calm
The Hradec nights are poisoned]
    W Hradcu dni są niespokojne
    I noce zatrute –
[Soldiers' boots crush
the stone pavement of the town]
    Bruki miasta miażdży żołnierz
    Swym sołdackim butem.

[There was freedom and liberty,
There was democracy]
    Była wolność i swoboda,
    Była demokracja,
[In Hradec Kralove, in Hradec Kralove,
Polish occupation]
    W Hradcu Kralovem, w Hradcu Kralovem
    Polska okupacja.

[Not on your orders
the boots of soldiers thunder]
    Nie z Twojego to rozkazu
    Grzmią buty wojskowe
[But what have you done, what have you done
for Hradec Kralove?]
    Lecz co zrobiłeś, co ty zrobiłeś,
    Dla Hradec Kralove.

In the first days after the intervention, leaflets called for solidarity demonstrations at the embassy of the ČSSR in Warsaw or for protest demonstrations in front of the Soviet legation. Appeals for taking to the streets also appeared in Kętrzyn and Tarnów. However, no demonstration was organized.[33] Some inhabitants of Warsaw laid flowers in front of the Czechoslovak Cultural Center, but the SB instantly removed them.[34]

In 1991 the magazine *Karta* described the story of Michał Drejer (pseudonym) who, having heard about the intervention, crossed the "green border" and went to Czechoslovakia to participate in the fight against the occupiers.[35] Research in the archives of the Polish Institute of National Remembrance indicates that there could have been a few more such incidents.

---

33 Four citizens of Denmark unfolded a protest banner against the invasion in the second half of September and were arrested.

34 Meldunek informacyjny, AIPN Kraków, 060/36 vol. XV, p. 30; Informacja nr 5 dot. operacji „Podhale", AIPN Warsaw, MSW II, 2040, no pagination; Informacja nr 6 dot. operacji „Podhale", ibidem.

35 M. Drejer, „Mijanie granicy", *Karta* (1991, no. 3), pp. 122–34.

The most tragic form of protest was chosen by Ryszard Siwiec, a sixty-year-old accountant from Przemyśl who decided to shake the conscience of his countrymen by sacrificing his own life. Siwiec planned his protest very carefully: he acquired a pass for the Polish harvest festival in Warsaw, wrote his last will and testament, bought paint thinner, and prepared a white and red flag with the inscription "for your and our freedom." Finally, he recorded his political manifesto on tape, criticizing Soviet imperialism and the enslavement of smaller nations. His dramatic appeal ended with the words: "People who have a drop of humanity, a drop of human feeling in them, come to your senses! Hear my scream, the scream of a common man who loves his and the freedom of others more than anything else, more than his own life, come to your senses! It is not too late!"

On September 8, 1968, Siwiec rose early in the morning, blessed his five sleeping children, gave his watch to his eldest son and went to the railway station. On the train he wrote a letter to his wife in which he explained that: "I die to prevent the truth, humanity and freedom from being destroyed [...] I feel such inner calmness as never before." This letter was seized by the Security Service and reached the addressee twenty-five years later. In Warsaw Siwiec went to the Stadium of the 10th Anniversary of the PPR (Stadion Dziesięciolecia) where the Polish harvest festival was held in the presence of 100,000 people. Also present were the top government authorities headed by Gomułka and Prime Minister Józef Cyrankiewicz. When the folk dancers were performing, Siwiec scattered his leaflets and poured the paint thinner onto himself and set himself on fire. While burning, he continually shouted "I protest!" He pushed away persons who tried to extinguish the flames but was hustled into a car, probably belonging to the Security Services, after all his clothes had already burned away.

Ryszard Siwiec died on September 12, 1968. Despite the fact that thousands of people witnessed his immolation, he failed to achieve his goal. The Security Service informed the persons who stood nearby that it was a case of the spontaneous ignition of alcohol on a drunken man. Other rumors were spread in Przemyśl that Siwiec was a lunatic. Although there were rumors in Warsaw that someone burned himself to death during the harvest festival, no one connected that event with the intervention in Czechoslovakia. As Stefan Kisielewski wrote in his diary (on September 14): "They constantly say that someone poured petrol onto himself and set himself on fire during the harvest festival in the presence of Wiesio [Władysław Gomułka] and Józio [Józef

Cyrankiewicz]. But no one knows why." Only in the spring of 1969, after the self-immolation of Jan Palach in Prague, did Radio Free Europe broadcast the real information on Siwiec. His self-immolation finally became known in the 1990's, through the documentary "Hear my scream" by Maciej Dygas.[36] Ryszard Siwiec was posthumously awarded the Czech medal of Tomáš G. Masaryk, the Slovak medal of the White Double Cross and the Commander's Cross of Polonia Restituta.

6. The Stance of the Catholic Church and Lay Circles.

On August 21, 1968, Stefan Cardinal Wyszyński, the Primate of Poland, noted in his diary: "In the morning we received a very painful message that Soviet and Polish troops marched into Czechoslovakia to secure the socialist bloc [...] It is electrifying news. Its consequences—hard to predict."[37] Most bishops privately condemned the intervention as aggression, assault or even occupation, first-class imperialism and colonialism and a disgrace (Stanisław Jakiel), "villainy" (Aleksander Mościcki) or an "enormously dirty trick" (Wilhelm Pluta). Bishop ordinary of Częstochowa Stefan Bareła said: "The grave of freedom is being dug right now."

When considering the consequences of the intervention, it was assumed that war would result. A few (for instance, bishops Jakiel and Jerzy Modzelewski), predicted that "brotherly help" might be extended to Romania. Bishops of Katowice Herbert Bednorz and Juliusz Bieniek perceived the aggression of the armies of the Warsaw Pact as "a fiasco of the USSR politics" and "the beginning of the fall of communism," because "there is nothing more but Soviet imperialism, and communism has ended in smoke."[38] A similar opinion was

---

36   Akta sprawy R. Siwca, AIPN Warszawa, 01545/5, passim; S. Kisielewski, op. cit., p. 98; 8 września 1968 r.: żywa pochodnia na Stadionie X-lecia, no place of publication 1981.

37   Quotation after: P. Raina, *Kardynał Wyszyński, Czasy Prymasowskie 1967-1968*, vol. 8 (Warsaw, 1998), p. 197.

38   According to the report of Archbishop Kominek, noted by the SB, a similar opinion was expressed by Primate Wyszyński, who did not speak publicly on the issue ("Kominek passed on the opinion—allegedly of Wyszyński—that the USSR had pulled a fast one, but only 'as imperialist Russia, not as communist Russia—because everyone thinks that they have lost the battle for international communism.'" – AIPN Warsaw, 01283/566, microfiches). But, according to another MSW source, just before the intervention Wyszyński expressed the opinion that "the government of the PPR is currently in a very difficult situation and it would not be honorable to attack the Polish authorities" (ibidem). This statement corresponds with the contents of the discussions of Primate Wyszyński with the MPs from "Znak" (see below).

expressed by the Archbishop of Wrocław Bolesław Kominek, who on August 21, 1968, stated in a circle of trusted curia members that "in the long run it is the decay of communism [...] The working class and intelligentsia are against them. They still rely on tanks. It is Soviet greed." The suffragan of Kraków, Bishop Julian Groblicki, assumed that the invasion illustrated the defeat of Soviet strategy, of international revolution, and that the consequences would not be the fall of the system, but a return to "the old concept of solving political and ideological problems, typical of the Stalinist era."

The bishops stressed that participation in the intervention cost "Poland the loss of several years of authority and respect in the public opinion of the West." The apostolic administrator of the Diocese of Gorzów, Bishop Wilhelm Pluta, assumed that the entrance of the armies "is to the detriment of, not only Polish communists, but also Poles in general. In the West, they can still differentiate between communists and the Polish nation."

The majority of opinions of the hierarchs quoted above were expressed within a limited circle of trusted friends. The suffragan of Częstohowa, Franciszek Musiel, belonged to a small number of bishops who openly condemned the intervention in their homilies. Within two weeks of the armies' marching into Czechoslovakia, during canonic inspections of parishes and on other occasions, he preached that: "Large states impose on small states their will when the latter strive for freedom of speech and conscience. They face the threat of invasion by foreign armies;" and "We should fear for the fate of smaller nations, when a godless man will start to organize life in accordance with his will, when the Charter of Human Rights will be violated. The concept of freedom among godless persons—is freedom only for those who are with us—they will crush the bones of others and shoot at them with machine guns." "We do not want to impose enslavement on anyone, but we want a man and his nation, even the smallest one, to be free." "Each state, in accordance with the UN Charter, has the right to self-determination—we cannot let strong states march into small ones and violate their freedom."

Many bishops were very careful in expressing their opinions. They did not comment on the course of events and ordered their clergy not to do so. For instance, the suffragan of Warsaw, Bishop Wacław Majewski, ordered his priests "to keep quiet and refrain from commenting on events."

Some bishops openly supported the stance of the authorities. The bishop ordinary of Włocławek, Antoni Pawłowski, who according to the data of the IV Department of the Ministry of Internal Affairs (MSW), perceived the Czechoslovak authorities to be influenced by "international Zionism," stated that "We cannot allow Czechoslovakia to break free from our system [...] There was no other choice due to the threat posed by the FRG and that is why the actions of the authorities should meet with the support of clergy." Bishop of Płock, Marian Sikorski, spoke in a similar way: "What could we do in such a situation? We talk about Poland. Germans are just waiting to take our western lands and repeat 1939. You can hardly imagine what would happen if Germans took over Czechoslovakia. After that they would want our lands. In that case there was no other choice." Those comments indicate that even the hierarchs of the Catholic church were susceptible to communist propaganda which justified the intervention of the armies of the Warsaw Pact by the alleged threat posed by West Germany.[39]

The standpoint of priests was also diverse. As the "poviat" Security Service from Zabrze reported, priests "are mostly carriers of information broadcast by Radio Free Europe. It is extremely rare to find opinions such as the one stated by priest Kałuski who said: 'it is good that Soviet troops marched into Czechoslovakia because the Czech nation is insincere, and cannot be trusted.'"

Such an opinion was surprising to other clergymen: "On the one hand the clergyman criticizes the conduct of the USSR and is outraged by it, and on the other hand he is content that the Soviet Union got into a pretty mess which will result in the further loss of prestige and will make communism repugnant, not only to of the West, but also to socialist countries."[40]

On August 22, in the Warsaw Club of Catholic Intelligentsia, a group of activists met to discuss the situation. Among participants were: members of the Polish Parliament Tadeusz Mazowiecki, Andrzej Micewski, Wojciech Wieczorek and Zdzisław Szpakowski, who expressed their shock at the invasion and considered possible variants of future developments. Mazowiecki assumed that it was the result of a crisis in the CC of the Communist Party of the Soviet Union. Micewski speculated that there would be an increase

---

39   Collection of all comments of the bishops in: AIPN Warsaw, 01283/566, microfiches; Informacje dot. komentarzy w środowiskach kościelnych i katolickich na temat wydarzeń w Czechosłowacji, IPN Warsaw, MSW II, 3977, pp. 4–5, 10–12, 18–19; Informacja bieżąca Departamentu IV MSW z 22 VIII 1968 r., ibidem, pp. 8–9; Informacja dot. uroczystości kościelnych i wystąpień biskupów w dniu 25 VIII 1968 r., ibidem, pp. 23–4;

40   Meldunek sytuacyjny, AIPN Katowice, 0103/192, vol. 6, part 2, no pagination. A wider range of attitudes of the clergy (including non-Catholics) may be found in the reports of the Department IV of the MSW (AIPN Warsaw, MSW II, 3977; AIPN Warsaw, 01283/565, microfiches).

in extremist tendencies in Poland and an intensification of the struggle with communism, and in the Soviet bloc a "return to Stalinist methods." According to a secret collaborator, code-named "Anna," Mazowiecki "tried to discover the circumstances justifying the actions of the socialist countries towards Czechoslovakia, and he expressed the opinion that 'although it is very sad, what else could the Soviet Union have done?'"[41]

The MPs of the Znak Club at the meeting of September 6 discussed three possible reactions to the intervention of the Warsaw Pact troops in Czechoslovakia: issuing a statement with a protest note; taking the floor during debates in the Seym; or resigning their seats and abandoning Parliament. During the next meeting, held three days later, it was assumed that the MPs were ready to leave the Seym. On September 10, Primate Wyszyński met with the members of the Znak Club. Although he shared the outrage of the MPs, he proposed that they "act reasonably" and discuss the issue in more detail on October 10. Such a distant date was intentional. Andrzej Friszke remarked that "setting such a date [...] thwarted the demonstration effect and also calmed down emotions in Znak." At the end of September, the circle around *Tygodnik Powszechny* made an attempt to mobilize the MPs by sending Krzysztof Kozłowski and Marek Skwarnicki to Warsaw.[42]

The meeting of October 10 ended any doubts as to the further parliamentary representation of lay Catholics. Tadeusz Mazowiecki stated that "the last October element was rejected by the August fact" and, as a consequence, there is no reason for the existence of Znak at the Seym forum. In turn, Stanisław Stomma said that "It's time to accept the preponderance of testimony" and "protest against the intervention." Cardinal Wyszyński managed, however, to discourage the MPs from resigning their seats and even from the much more lenient variant suggested by Janusz Zabłocki, "accepting being squeezed out of the Seym." The Primate assumed that the liquidation of the Znak Club of MPs would weaken the Church in Poland. While convincing MPs that his concept was correct, Wyszyński stated that the decision of Gomułka to participate in the intervention was forced by the threat of direct occupation of Poland, which "limited" his responsibility.[43]

---

41   Information based on the account of comrade "Anna," AIPN Warsaw, 01283/565, microfiches.

42   A. Friszke, *Koło posłów „Znak" w Sejmie PRL 1957-1968* (Warsaw, 2002), pp. 95–96.

43   A note of the Primate from that meeting was published by Peter Raina, *Kardynał...*, pp. 203–6.

7. Repressions.

By the end of 1968, in the course of the Podhale operation, over eighty persons were detained, and a few dozen were arrested. Some of them were tried and convicted. For instance, Teresa Stodolniak was accused of "preparation and distribution of leaflets, posters and inscriptions containing false information on the events in Czechoslovakia which could arouse public unrest from August 21 to October 16, 1968 in Warsaw." Despite the fact that Teresa Stodolniak had two small children, the poviat court for the capital city of Warsaw sentenced her to one year in prison. The charges were: "exceptional intensification of ill will" and "social danger of the committed deed." The Court also stressed that "the activities of the accused, that is sending letters, handing out leaflets and posters [...] created a pretext for hostile elements, both internal and foreign, to express statements incompatible with the opinion of Polish society—it provided weapons for the spreading of opinions incompatible with the approach and assessment of citizens' attitudes towards the stance of the Polish Government and the Warsaw Pact." In other words, the accused was guilty of daring to interrupt the propaganda image of society which allegedly supported the intervention in Czechoslovakia on a mass scale.[44] In addition, a few hundred persons were summoned to "preventive and warning sessions," and several dozen were charged by the Penal and Administrative Committees.

At the end of October and the beginning of November 1968, the SB, in the course of operation "Akcja," broke up a group of persons who had produced and distributed leaflets starting in March. This group published and distributed relatively large editions (several hundred copies) of a few types of leaflets after August 21. At least thirty persons were detained and fourteen were arrested. Six more were subjected to surveillance; several dozen searches were carried out. Some of the arrested were released but the rest were sentenced to jail. Eight persons were released pending trial.[45] The following were found

---

44 Akt oskarżenia i wyrok w sprawie T. Stodolniak, the account of T. Stodolniak collected by Barbara Polak—in the document collection of the author.

45 They were Adam Sandauer, Michał Przybyło, Jadwiga Dziegiel, Ryszard Peryt, Michał Bogucki, Sławomir Kretkowski, Wiesław Dębowski, Marek Marzeński.

guilty: Romuald Lubianiec, Tadeusz Markiewicz, Wiktor Nagórski, Sylwia Poleska (one year in prison),[46] and Sławomir Kretkowski, Bogusława Blajfer, and Eugeniusz Smolar (one and a half years in prison).[47]

To a surprisingly large extent, Polish society in August of 1968 expressed solidarity with Czechs and Slovaks whose country was flooded by the armies of the Warsaw Pact. Of course, the scale of active resistance and help was smaller than in the autumn of 1956 when money was gathered on Polish streets for Hungary and hospitals were full of persons donating blood for the wounded. However, the political situation and social context were different. While in November of 1956 there was a peak in the liberalization and democratization process, in August of 1968 Polish society had been pacified after the March events. Hundreds of people were in jail and the emigration of thousands continued. Furthermore, reactions of solidarity with Hungary were a natural consequence of a centuries-old, nearly proverbial, friendship, but solidarity with Czechoslovakia required overcoming long-lasting prejudices, fueled by Party propaganda.

---

46 In fact, the sentences were more severe, but as a result of an amnesty they were cut in half.

47 Relacja z czynności operacyjno-śledczych wykonanych w sprawie kryptonim „Akacja", AIPN Warsaw, 0746/4, pp. 7–8; Meldunek specjalny, ibidem, pp. 9–10; Dot. sprawy kryptonim „Akacja", ibidem, pp. 39–41; Relacja z czynności operacyjno-śledczych wykonanych w sprawie kryptonim „Akacja", ibidem, pp. 79–94; Uzupełnienie do relacji z dotychczasowych czynności operacyjno-śledczych wykonanych w sprawie kryptonim „Akacja" (do dnia 25 XI 1968), ibidem, pp. 101–5; Relacja z czynności operacyjno-śledczych wykonanych w sprawie kryptonim „Akacja", ibidem, pp. 119–33; A. Friszke, *Opozycja polityczna w PRL 1945-1980* (London, 1994), p. 251.

8

The 'Prague Spring,' Poland, and the Warsaw Pact Invasion: A Comment

Piotr Wróbel

The 1968 'Prague Spring' and invasion of Czechoslovakia belong to the most important events of European history after World War II and have been described in numerous scholarly works. Yet, our knowledge about these events will remain incomplete as long as the most valuable Soviet archival collections are inaccessible in Russia. In this situation, the documents produced by the communist apparatuses of the former Soviet satellites and declassified after 1989 are of special importance. Several invaluable collections of these primary sources are located in the Polish archives and are being analyzed by Polish scholars. Particularly, historians linked to the Polish Institute of National Remembrance (IPN) are involved in this research. In September 2003, they organized a major international conference devoted to Poland and Czechoslovakia in 1968. Łukasz Kamiński, a Deputy Director of the Office of Public Education in the IPN, was one of the main organizers of this event and edited and published its materials.[1] His presentation at our conference is, at least to some extent, an outcome of this conference.

In his paper Kamiński reviews the international events leading to the Warsaw Pact intervention and the related activities of Władysław Gomułka, the First Secretary of the Central Committee of the Polish United Workers' Party (PZPR), who was hostile towards the 'Prague Spring.' Kamiński briefly describes how the communist authorities tried to prepare the atmosphere in

---

1 *Wokół praskiej wiosny. Polska i Czechosłowacja w 1968 roku,* ed. Łukasz Kamiński (Warsaw, 2004).

Poland before the intervention. A major part of his paper is devoted to Polish reactions to the intervention: comments made by Polish citizens during the first days of the military operations recorded by the Security Service (SB); leaflets and graffiti on the walls of Polish towns and cities; protests of Polish intellectuals; other forms of protest; reaction of the Catholic Church; and police repressions against Polish citizens involved in the protests. His presentation, based on meticulous research and written in an engaging way, concludes with the statement that "Polish society in August 1968 to a surprisingly large extent expressed solidarity with the Czechs and Slovaks whose country was flooded by the armies of the Warsaw Pact."

Several elements of Kamiński's presentation can be starting points for an interesting discussion. One may begin with the proportions of the described phenomena. The powerful and omnipresent Security Service (SB) did its best to record every critical comment and all the graffiti on the walls. It seems that the SB presented its discoveries in an exaggerated form, which exceeded the real danger of those comments, graffiti, and leaflets. Recording all of them and taking them at their face value can lead to the conclusion that there was, indeed, a massive protest and opposition in Polish society against the intervention. However, some of Kamiński's comments may provoke skepticism in this respect and may support arguments against his final conclusion.

It appears that, before July 1968, most Poles did not watch the 'Prague Spring' and the growing threat of the intervention closely because they followed, and frequently were completely overwhelmed by, the Polish internal crisis, later known as the March Events of 1968. The March Events, which Kamiński mentions, weakened the nuclei of Polish civic society and opposition. True, especially among the intellectuals, the invasion of Czechoslovakia caused a shock. Several dozen Polish writers and scholars returned their party cards, but only three intellectuals decided to openly protest, including Sławomir Mrożek, who lived at that time in Paris. Even in the Soviet Union, the writers protested more openly.[2] The reactions of Polish society were diverse. "It appears, however," claims Jerzy Eisler, the author of an important book on 1968 in Poland, "that indifference dominated at that time, indifference only partially justified by a lack of knowledge about the real character and course of events beyond our southern border."[3]

---

2   "In Defense of Czechoslovakia," *Problems of Communism*, XVII (Sept.–Oct. 1968), 59–65.
3   Jerzy Eisler, *Polski rok 1968* (Warsaw, 2006), 748.

Mieczysław Rakowski, the editor-in-chief of the prestigious weekly *Polityka*, a man very well connected and informed, carefully watched the events in Poland and Czechoslovakia. On August 30, 1968, he made the following entry in his diary:

> I learn something about the attitude of Polish society. It is not really as Radio Free Europe is bellowing. A significant number (*spora liczba*) of people believe that the Federal Republic of Germany wanted indeed to pluck Czechoslovakia out of the [communist] camp and that in this way our southern flank would be exposed. Others believe that a nation which dared to act against the Russians is simply stupid. Others are just ordinary nationalists: "Finally, we can show someone our power…" I believe that, in fact, it is the intelligentsia which is mostly against the invasion. Characteristically, after March, we used to get hundreds of letters, in which people condemned what was going on. Presently, only eight letters have arrived.[4]

Writer Stefan Kisielewski, another observer of the Polish political scene but a man of completely different views than Rakowski, formulated a very similar conclusion in his *Diaries*.[5] Many years later, Leszek Kołakowski recalled: "The atmosphere was depressing, but we could not do anything; we did not participate in any actions; they barely took place anyway."[6]

Also, the Catholic Church acted very cautiously. It was tired after its battles with the communist apparatus in the mid-1960's, was not ready for a new confrontation with the state, and intended to continue the existing, arduously achieved *modus vivendi*. To most Polish bishops (except for Wrocław Archbishop Bolesław Kominek and the suffragan of Częstochowa, Franciszek Musiel), the 'Prague Spring' was just an internal conflict in communist parties. Stefan Cardinal Wyszyński, Primate of Poland, was consistently silent about Czechoslovakia and, after the intervention, opposed any open protests both by the Church and the lay organizations close to it.[7]

---

4   Mieczysław F. Rakowski, *Dzienniki polityczne, 1967-1968* (Warsaw, 1999), 349.

5   Stefan Kisielewski, *Dzienniki* (Warsaw, 1996), 76.

6   *Czas ciekawy, czas niespokojny. Z Leszkiem Kołakowskim rozmawia Zbigniew Mentzel* (Cracow, 2007), 261.

7   Rudolf Vévoda, "Kościół katolicki w Polsce wobec praskiej wiosny oraz interwencji wojskowej w Czechosłowacji," *Wokół praskiej wiosny*, 82–96.

Altogether, writes Kamiński, only about ten to twenty people were imprisoned for the anti-intervention protests until the end of September 1968, and a similar number later landed behind bars. Is this a "surprisingly large extent"? On the other hand, Kamiński could have said more about protests of the Polish political emigration. Particularly the Polish émigré periodical *Kultura*, published in Paris, allocated considerable space to the 'Prague Spring' and to the intervention. In October 1968, a special issue of *Kultura* appeared, devoted entirely to the events in Czechoslovakia. *Kultura*'s statements were very strong: there were many mistakes in the history of Poland, "but, until now, the Poles have not had on their conscience a similarly shameful role like this one played presently by the Gomułka government."[8] Or "The Polish soldiers have been forced to accept a new shameful role of gendarmes who are supposed to quash a freedom movement in a brotherly country, operating under a slogan 'For our and your slavery.'"[9]

Another reason, only briefly mentioned by Kamiński, as to why many Poles did not protest against the invasion was their attitude towards the Czechs. Polish-Czechoslovak relations were bad throughout the entire interwar period because of the conflict over the Cieszyn (or Těšín) region and the Czechoslovak position during the Polish-Soviet and Polish-Ukrainian wars of 1918–1921. During World War II, the Czechoslovak government-in-exile moved from federation plans with Poland to collaboration with the Soviet Union. Slovakia, an ally of Germany during the war, occupied a small part of southern Poland. In 1945, Poland and Czechoslovakia were on the verge of a military conflict over some frontier regions. The final Polish-Czechoslovak border agreement was signed only in 1958. After 1945, Polish communists were afraid that Prague was "lagging behind" the rest of East Central Europe in its march towards a "people's democracy."[10] Many Poles looked down on the Czechs—allegedly a nation of "Shveiks," shared numerous anti-Czech stereotypes, and believed that Czechoslovakia had behaved cowardly in 1938–1939 when, by Polish standards, they should have resisted militarily. Finally, according to many Poles, Czechoslovakia did not suffer enough during World War II and received several things "on a silver platter," while the Poles had to fight for everything.

---

8 "Za nasz i wasz ... stalinizm," *Kultura*, no. 8/250-9/251 (Aug.–Sept. 1968), 72.

9 "Apel *Kultury*," *Kultura*, no. 10/252 (Oct. 1968), 3.

10 Andrzej Paczkowski, "The Polish Contribution to the Victory of the 'Prague Coup' in February 1948," *Cold War International History Project Bulletin*, 11 (Winter 1998), 141.

Władysław Gomułka was among the Poles who shared these sentiments. Openly hostile towards the 'Prague Spring,' he pressed the Soviet Politburo to intervene militarily in Czechoslovakia, at least from late March 1968.[11] Contrary to the evaluations of Kamiński and Paweł Machcewicz,[12] the author of the newest article on Gomułka's attitude towards the Czechoslovak reforms, the Polish First Secretary was not the only enemy and not the most zealous opponent of the Czechoslovak "crawling counter-revolution." All the communist leaders of the countries neighboring Czechoslovakia were afraid of a possible ideological "spill-over," watched the 'Prague Spring' very carefully, and pressed the Soviet Politburo to intervene. Petro Shelest, the First Secretary of the Ukrainian Communist Party and a member of the Soviet Politburo, had been interested in the Czechoslovak reforms well before the March 1968 conference of the communist leaders in Dresden. He was as strong a proponent of intervention as Gomułka and, most certainly, more influential in Moscow.[13] Even in relatively remote Moldavia and Albania, their communist leaderships were afraid of the Czechoslovak influence.[14] In Romania, which refused to participate in the invasion of Czechoslovakia and was itself on the edge of Soviet intervention, Nicolae Ceaușescu used the international crisis to stress the unity of all Romanian citizens, strengthen his position, and build a Front of National Unity.[15]

The most radical and the most persistent enemy of the Czechoslovak reforms was Walter Ulbricht, the First Secretary of the Central Committee of the Socialist Unity Party of Germany (SED) between 1950 and 1971. His government had been afraid of domestic ideological infection since 1956, when the unrest spread from Poland to Hungary. The East German services, scanning their neighbors for signs of trouble, spotted the first problems in Czechoslovakia

---

11 Paweł Machcewicz, "'Do diabła z suwerennością.' Władysław Gomułka wobec praskiej wiosny," *Wokół praskiej wiosny*, 59–72.

12 Ibid., 63.

13 Mark Kramer, "Ukraine and the Soviet-Czechoslovak Crisis of 1968 (part 2): New Evidence from the Ukraine Archives," *Cold War International History Project Bulletin*, 14/15 (Winter 2003-Spring 2004), 273–4.

14 H. Gordon Skilling, *Czechoslovakia's Interrupted Revolution* (Princeton, 1976), 708–10; Mark Kramer, "Soviet Moldova and the 1968 Czechoslovak Crisis: A Report on the Political 'Spill-Over,'" *Cold War International History Project Bulletin*, 11 (Winter 1998), 263.

15 J. F. Brown, "Rumania Today. I: Towards 'Integration,'" *Problems of Communism*, XVIII (Jan.–Feb. 1969), 15.

in 1963, when a literary conference "rehabilitated" a "decadent" and bourgeois writer Franz Kafka. Things became even worse for the SED when, in 1966, the Grand Coalition Government of Willy Brandt initiated a new *Ostpolitik* and tried to build a bridge over the West-East abyss. In January of 1967, Romania established diplomatic relations with the Federal Republic of Germany and, in August 1967, Prague exchanged trade missions with Bonn. In March 1968, Kurt Hager, an important SED ideologist and Politburo member, viciously attacked the changes in Czechoslovakia and ascribed them to West German influence. No comparable outburst occurred in Poland, or especially Hungary, where an attitude towards the Czech and Slovak reforms was more positive that in other countries of the region. Soon, the East German government began jamming German-language broadcasts from Prague, banned the Czechoslovak German-language *Volkszeitung,* restricted the travel of East Germans to Czechoslovakia, unleashed a propaganda campaign against the counter-revolution there, and pressed the Soviets for intervention.[16]

The scarecrow built out of anti-German feelings and propaganda images of the Federal Republic of Germany as an aggressive revanchist power ready to attack its Eastern neighbors worked very well in Poland. Many people did believe that the West Germans were behind the 'Prague Spring.' Gomułka's concept of foreign policy was based on his anti-German bias. He strongly believed that democratic changes in Czechoslovakia would strengthen the German and weaken the Polish position. It is also very likely that his zealously communist, pro-intervention attitude was supposed to help him in the internal struggle in the Polish United Workers' Party during the March Events. Gomułka wanted to appear as a strong ally of the Soviet leadership and, just like Ulbricht, Moscow's main partner in the management of Central European affairs.

The Soviet Politburo, however, was divided over the intervention, as were leaderships of other communist parties. The Czechoslovak conflict can be analyzed, therefore, in terms of transnational history: a struggle in communist Politburos between hardliners and more flexible and liberal politicians. Also, an analysis of a generational conflict could add to our understanding of the crisis. It is no coincidence that young people revolted in 1968 in several

---

16 Skilling, *Czechoslovakia's*, 675-81; Melvin Croan, "Czechoslovakia, Ulbricht, and the German Problem," *Problems of Communism*, XVIII (Jan.–Feb. 1969), 1–4; F. Stephen Larrabee, "Soviet Crisis Management in Eastern Europe," *The Warsaw Pact: Alliance in Transition?*, ed. David Holloway and Jane M. O. Sharp (Ithaca, NY, 1984), 121; Francois Fejto, "Moscow and Its Allies," *Problems of Communism*, XVII (Nov.–Dec. 1986)), 36.

countries in the West. Among the communist leaders, the older generation of Walter Ulbricht and Władysław Gomułka was defending itself against a new generation. Finally, it is interesting to note that the enemies of the 'Prague Spring' tried to reanimate the Zionist scarecrow. Some Polish newspapers, inspired by the infamous national communist Mieczysław Moczar, suggested Zionist involvement in Czechoslovakia. On August 17, *Krasnaya Zvezda*, the organ of the Soviet Army, described Zionism as an imperialist tool and praised the rebuff given to it in Poland.[17]

In October 1968, the émigré Leopold Labedz commented in *Survey* on the "moral defeat" of the intervention: "The paradox of the situation is that the ideological weakening of the Soviet leadership, both internal and external, pushes the Soviet leadership to actions which may be in effect more dangerous than the more cautious policy of Stalin (who did not invade Yugoslavia)."[18] Was there a similar paradox in Poland? Was the death of ideology in March and August of 1968 linked to the Polish crisis of 1970 and the communist government's reaction to it? On September 7, 1968, Rakowski noticed the visible participation of the Polish army in the political debate and the propaganda campaign against the Czechoslovak reforms. "I wouldn't be very surprised," he wrote, "if, in the nearest future, the army would play a growing role in the political life of our country."[19] Previously, on August 27, Rakowski concluded his entry in the following way: "It is interesting, among other things, that the Warsaw Pact established for the defense against NATO, was used for the first time as a tool of interference into the internal affairs of one of the allied states."[20] Did the Polish army start its march towards the Martial Law of 1981 in 1968?

---

17 Skilling, *Czechoslovakia's*, 674; Rakowski, *Dzienniki*, 345.

18 Leopold Labadz, "Czechoslovakia and After," *Survey*, 69 (Oct. 1968), 20.

19 Rakowski, *Dzienniki*, 352.

20 Ibid., 347.

9

The Role and Activities of the SED, the East German State and Its Military During the 'Prague Spring' of 1968

Rüdiger Wenzke

In order to appreciate the role of Walter Ulbricht in leading the criticism of the 'Prague Spring' in 1968, we need to understand the history of the German Democratic Republic and the role that Ulbricht played in its creation. As will be shown below, it was no accident that the most strident criticism of the Czech and Slovak reforms came from East Germany and its leader.

The unconditional surrender of the German Wehrmacht in early May of 1945 marked the end of World War II in Europe. Largely destroyed, Germany was occupied by the Allied forces. The victors ensconced themselves indefinitely in the four occupation zones into which Germany was divided.[1] The entire territory of what later became the German Democratic Republic (GDR) came under Soviet occupation—some 107,000 square kilometers inhabited by over 17.5 million people. Greater Berlin and its 4.4 million inhabitants were also divided into four sectors and placed under joint Allied administration.

Supreme governmental power in the Soviet Occupation Zone (SBZ) was exercised by the Soviet Military Administration in Germany (SMAD), which received its orders from Moscow. Vested with all powers, the SMAD was tasked with monitoring Germany's compliance with the terms imposed by the

---

1 Wolfgang Benz, ed., *Deutschland unter alliierter Besatzung 1945–1949/55. Ein Handbuch* (Berlin, 1999).

surrender in its zone as well as with administering the SBZ.[2] German communists played a key role in asserting Soviet interests in the Soviet Occupation Zone. In the last days of the war exiled German communists were flown from Moscow into central Germany. Their primary task was to effectively support the Red Army in the establishment and implementation of occupation rule. The head of the "Berlin Group" was Walter Ulbricht,[3] a functionary of the Communist Party of Germany who had been born in 1893 in Leipzig. From the very beginning, Ulbricht urged the transformation of society and the imposition of communist power in East Germany.

The Cold War, a process of mutual escalation in a bipolar international system that came into being after the Second World War, subsequently determined the basic political parameters in the East and West. The global conflict had reached Germany by mid-1946 at the latest. The Western powers, on the one hand, and the Soviet Union, on the other, were no longer willing to accept an enlargement of the zones of influence and power of their adversaries or a reduction in the size of their own.

Against this background, the Soviet Military Administration in Germany controlled and accompanied the transformation of the political system from an "occupation dictatorship" to a Soviet-style German dictatorship in the Soviet Occupation Zone. In the Eastern part of Germany, the reconstruction was exploited in the sense that communist power positions were established and stabilized. The latter was also in line with the ideas of the German communists and some social democrats who had formed the Socialist Unity Party of Germany (Sozialistische Einheitspartei Deutschlands—SED) in 1946 and unconditionally supported Soviet policy. Submissively dependent on Moscow, the SED increasingly distinguished itself in all fields of social life as a Stalinist-communist Party with an absolute claim to leadership.[4]

---

2   Jan Foitzik, *Sowjetische Militäradminstration in Deutschland (SMAD) 1945–1949. Struktur und Funktion* (Berlin, 1999); Norman M. Naimark, *Russians in Germany: The History of the Soviet Zone of Occupation 1945–1949* (Cambridge, MA, 1995).

3   Mario Frank, *Walter Ulbricht. Eine deutsche Biografie* (München, 2001).

4   On this, inter alia, Andreas Malycha, *Die SED. Geschichte ihrer Stalinisierung 1946–1953* (Paderborn, 2000).

On 7 October 1949, the German Democratic Republic (GDR) was established.[5] This completed the division of Germany under constitutional law. In addition to the communist Wilhelm Pieck, the elected GDR President, it was mainly Walter Ulbricht who, as Deputy Prime Minister and after 1950 as Secretary General of the SED Central Committee (from 1953 First Secretary), held the power. By that time, the SED leadership had largely gained control over its own Party, the administrative structures, mass organizations, and parts of the economic systems. Nevertheless, the Soviet Union continued to determine essential elements of GDR policy, focusing on questions of security and military policy. In addition, hundreds of thousands of Soviet soldiers remained stationed in East Germany.

By the early 1950's, the SED leadership had succeeded in consolidating its power and establishing a political system that enabled the adoption of the Soviet model of socialism. In the West, it became apparent that the Federal Republic would be integrated into a West European political and military alliance. The SED considered the Federal Republic a militarist state and the Western alliance system a threat to peace and the peoples of Europe. Against this background, the GDR was intended to form the political, economic and military counter-weight to West Germany in Europe, the first "bulwark" of the Eastern bloc on the border with "imperialism." In this context, the Soviet leadership in the spring of 1952 gave its permission for the GDR to create an army and to militarize society.

In July 1952, the 2nd Party Conference of the SED approved the "systematic building of socialism" in the GDR. However, the coercive measures this entailed, for example collective farming and repression of the private economic sector in industry, plunged the Ulbricht regime into a deep economic and supply crisis, the effects of which were increasingly felt by the population by the summer of 1953. On June 17, 1953, hundreds of thousands of people took to the streets in East Berlin and other GDR cities to demonstrate against SED policy.[6] It was only through the employment of Soviet troops that the mass protests could be stopped. The shock over the outbreak of the people's rage and resistance in June 1953 remained a trauma for East German communists for as long as the GDR existed.

---

5   On this, inter alia, Ulrich Mählert, *Kleine Geschichte der DDR* (München, 1998).

6   Torsten Diedrich, *Waffen gegen das Volk. Der 17. Juni 1953 in der DDR* (München, 2003).

In subsequent years Walter Ulbricht used the "carrot and the stick" approach to stabilize his regime. Although foreign policy events, such as the GDR's joining the Warsaw Pact in 1955, had already resulted in a certain strengthening of the SED state, the establishment of a regular army in 1956 was considered another expression of the increased sovereignty of the GDR. The National People's Army (Nationale Volksarmee—NVA) was meant to represent a new type of force in German military history, whose task was to defend peace and the "socialist achievements of the people" in the GDR against any attack. Its admission to the Unified Armed Forces of the Warsaw Alliance meant that it would be strictly modeled on the Red Army and be integrated into the joint military organization. Consequently, the purpose of the build-up of the NVA was to enhance the collective military power of the Warsaw Pact.[7]

Ultimately, however, Ulbricht ensured the continuation of his rule with the closing of the borders in 1961. It provided him with the opportunity to build GDR socialism according to his ideas. The mass flight to the West was stopped, after at least 2.6 million people had seized the opportunity to leave the GDR for a large variety of reasons in the period between 1949 and 1960.[8] After 1961, the majority of GDR citizens were forced to adjust to the socialist regime. For the subsequent twenty-eight years, the Berlin Wall became the symbol of the Cold War, the division of Germany, and the inhumanity of the SED regime.

Afterwards, the SED tried to win over the caged people in the GDR, especially the young, by launching social, educational and economic initiatives and reforms, as well as by temporarily easing ideological constraints in art and culture. At the same time, the military and security apparatus in the form of the National People's Army, the Border Troops, the police and the Ministry of State Security were systematically improved, and repression of political dissenters was increased. In its new constitution of 1968, the GDR presented itself with self-confidence and as a "socialist state of the German nation," strictly apart from the other German state.[9]

---

[7] Rüdiger Wenzke and Irmgard Zündorf, "Ein Eiserner Vorhang ist niedergegangen". Militärgeschichte im Kalten Krieg 1945–1968/70, in *Grundkurs deutsche Militärgeschichte*, vol. 3, ed. Karl Volker Neugebauer (München, 2008), 134–49.

[8] *Ulbricht, Chruschtschow und die Mauer. Eine Dokumentation*, ed. Matthias Uhl und Armin Wagner (München, 2003).

[9] On this, inter alia, Klaus Schroeder, *Der SED-Staat. Partei, Staat und gesellschaft 1949–1990* (München, 1998); Günther Heydemann, *Die Innenpolitik der DDR* (München, 2003).

The SED on a Collision Course with Dubček's Policies in 1968

"We will not, of course, interfere in the domestic affairs of the ČSSR and the Czechoslovak fraternal Party,"[10] affirmed a high-ranking representative of the East German communist leadership as late as the end of January 1968. In the months that followed, it became more than obvious that this was a lie. The Socialist Unity Party of Germany, under the leadership of Walter Ulbricht, was not only among the first Eastern bloc parties to criticize the events in the ČSSR, but also proved to be one of the fiercest opponents of the Czechoslovak reform process and thus a driving force for the military suppression of the 'Prague Spring' with its deliberate agitation, dissociation and, eventually, open confrontation.

It might, of course, be wondered why the SED took such a critical attitude towards Dubček and his policies, especially since Ulbricht regarded himself as a "closet reformer." It was he who sought his own solutions in the 1960s against the backdrop of economic crises emerging within the socialist camp. After the building of the Berlin Wall in 1961, which allowed "his" GDR to grow as a quasi-independent biotope, the SED chief soon focused on a so-called New Economic System of Planning and Leadership, which promised a more effective development of the economy. He also initiated modernizations in research and technology development which resulted in several economic successes in the early days. The GDR became, after all, the second strongest industrial power in the Eastern bloc. Despite some vague efforts at economic reform, under no circumstances did Ulbricht tolerate any deviations from the dogmas of absolute Party rule and the Marxist-Leninist ideology. Walter Ulbricht believed himself, at the age of seventy-five, to be on the right course with his neo-Stalinist policy. He was one of the most senior leaders of the communist movement and, in addition, considered himself one of the most successful among them. Full of self-confidence, he also regarded himself as a mentor of his counterparts in the so-called fraternal states on matters of ideology, domestic and, not least, foreign policy, although he also pursued very pragmatic objectives connected to the specific position of the GDR in Central Europe.

---

10   According to Lutz Prieß, Vaclav Kural, and Manfred Wilke, *Die SED und der "Prager Frühling" 1968. Politik gegen einen "Sozialismus mit menschlichem Antlitz"* (Berlin, 1996), 45, the person who delivered the paper at the 4th session of the SED Central Committee was the Secretary for International Relations of the SED Central Committee, Hermann Axen.

East Germany, as is well known, depended on the USSR in all important matters—politically, economically and militarily. Ulbricht knew that the GDR, which at the time had been recognized by just twelve states, would only be able to survive with the support of the USSR. East Germany, between two hostile systems, also felt its existence threatened by "imperialism," namely, by the Federal Republic of Germany. Any change in the political and military *status quo* in Central Europe, in whatever shape or form, gave rise to the spectre of the GDR's imminent incorporation into the Federal Republic. Hence, the Ulbricht Regime relied on the solidarity and support of the Eastern bloc and also had to be sure of its class comrades and alliance partners in neighboring Czechoslovakia.

For this reason, the GDR observed internal developments in the ČSSR in 1967–68 with particular interest. While relations between the two countries in previous years had not been free of tensions, they were still relatively normal.[11] The SED officials, therefore, saw no reason in January 1968 to deal explicitly with Czechoslovak issues in their weekly Politburo or Secretariat meetings. As early as at the 4th meeting of the SED Central Committee (CC) in late January 1968, however, the Party leadership began to express doubts about the new policy introduced under Alexander Dubček. In an internal speech, CC Secretary Hermann Axen referred to alleged initial tendencies toward a "bourgeois liberalization" in Czechoslovakia. He again justified the general interest of the SED in the Czechoslovak development by listing two factors, the joint responsibility at the western border of the alliance system to protect against any suspected Western intervention and the fear that the West might use certain events in the ČSSR to confront the GDR with the failings and deficiencies of its own politics.[12] The SED leadership, just like the Polish leadership, expressed its increasing concerns at an early stage to their "big brother," the USSR.[13]

By mid-March at the latest, after Party control of the mass media in the ČSSR had been relinquished, alarm bells started to ring in East Berlin. The SED Politburo and the Secretariat of the Central Committee became the most important decision-making bodies. State institutions, such as ministries, as well

---

11 Wolfgang Schwarz, *Brüderlich entzweit. Die Beziehungen zwischen der DDR und der ČSSR 1961–1968* (Munich, 2004).

12 Prieß, Kural, Wilke, *Die SED und der "Prager Frühling,"* 15 seq. and 43 seq.

13 Mark Kramer, *Die Sowjetunion, der Warschauer Pakt und blockinterne Krisen während der Breżnev-Ära*, in *Der Warschauer Pakt. Von der Gründung bis zum Zusammenbruch (1955–1991)*, ed. Torsten Diedrich, Winfried Heinemann and Christian F. Ostermann (Berlin, 2009), 273–336.

as other organizations, were mere executors of the Politburo's will. Neither the Parliament nor the Council of Ministers was involved in the decision-making process of the GDR in 1968.

Departments of the Central Committee and special working groups took over central functions and tasks and began, among other things, to analyze the documents of the Communist Party of Czechoslovakia (CPCs) and the daily situation in the neighboring country. One outcome of such an analysis was an internal SED paper, dated March 11, stating that there were revisionist, openly bourgeois forces in the ČSSR whose views were directed against the leading role of the Party and socialism in general.[14] Selected leadership cadres of the state, the Ministry of State Security and the National People's Army were informed about the Party's point of view regarding the situation in the ČSSR, which also tended toward supporting non-specified "healthy forces" in the neighboring country. The assessment that "open counter-revolutionary characteristics" were emerging in Czechoslovakia became the Party line. The SED, however, had as yet avoided speaking out in public against the ČSSR. It was not until the 5th session of the SED Central Committee on March 21 that Ulbricht openly set the course for a strict rejection of Czechoslovakia's reform politics. This happened, incidentally, without any discussions among the SED's own ranks and without talking to officials from the ČSSR or other countries. Moscow, too, was still silent.

The crucial event became the meeting of the leaders of the Warsaw Pact states (excluding Romania) in Dresden on March 23, 1968. Ulbricht again demanded with great urgency that the alleged "counter-revolution" in the ČSSR be resolutely opposed. His comments revealed, not only the East German communists' fear of a destabilization of the GDR, but also their determination to stop the political course of Dubček and his fellow reformers. "The conclusion reached in Dresden that a counter-revolution had broken out in the ČSSR eventually provided the reason for an intervention."[15] A contemporary

---

14   Federal Commissioner for the Files of the State Security Service of the former German Democratic Republic (BStU), Z 1564, 1–14, Information zur gegenwärtige Lage in der ČSSR vom 12.3.1968. See also Prieß, Kural, Wilke, *Die SED und der "Prager Frühling,"* 52.

15   Konstantin Hermann, "'Shortly you will stand in front of the tribunal.' The 'Tribunal der Fünf' in Dresden," in *Sachsen und der Prager Frühling*, ed. Konstantin Hermann (Beucha, 2008), 53–68; here, p. 67. An official protocol of the Dresden consultations probably does not exist. Previous research is, therefore, based primarily on a secretly-made stenographic transcript in the German language by order of the SED.

cartoon by Peter Leger in the Western media gave a very vivid image of the SED's attitude towards the Prague reforms. It showed East German "schoolmaster" Ulbricht in the classroom, standing at a lectern, and giving "student" Dubček a failing grade for his essay on "true socialism."[16]

To Walter Ulbricht, it was clear that, sooner or later, the increasing changes in the ČSSR, particularly in the politico-ideological realm, could spread to the GDR, especially since there was active tourism between the two countries. If democratization tendencies spilled out unchecked, questions regarding the historical and national legitimacy of the East German state, its relationship with the Federal Republic, the inhuman border regime, freedom of travel, etc. would become unavoidable. These were questions which the SED regime would not have been able to answer to the satisfaction of the people. Therefore, Ulbricht threatened Prague that he would not permit "rotten eggs to be imported into the GDR."[17]

In addition, the SED leadership repeatedly made clear to the fraternal parties the particular danger of any democratization emanating from the ČSSR, which it branded the outcome of the new *ostpolitik* (policy towards the East) of the West German federal government. Besides security considerations, it was very important to the GDR that no state of the Warsaw Pact enter into diplomatic relations with the Federal Republic of Germany prior to the latter giving up its claim to sole representation and recognizing the GDR. Ulbricht considered the Western concept of "change through rapprochement" to be just a method aimed at splitting the Eastern bloc. This policy would, in his view, have damaged chiefly the GDR—by further isolating East Germany and precluding the international recognition that was still lacking.

The SED was not only a trusted ally, follower and reliable junior partner of the Soviet Union in the dispute with the ČSSR; it was also a foremost pragmatic opponent, together with the Polish Party leadership, of Dubček's policies. After a phase of theoretical analyses and internal Party criticism, the East German communists from April 1968 on thought the time was ripe for action.

---

16   Ulbricht: Student Dubček, failure to achieve class objective! Pen drawing by Peter Leger, Germany 1968, in *Haus der Geschichte*, Bonn (www.dhm.de).

17   Quotation according to Lars-Broder Keil and Sven Felix Kellerhoff, *Deutsche Legenden. Vom „Dolchstoß" und anderen Mythen der Geschichte* (Berlin, 2002), 191.

Between Political Threat and Preparation for Intervention—The GDR at the Forefront of the Soviet Anti-reform Coalition

A smear campaign was launched on a large scale in the GDR media. The Party leadership instigated a press war against the ČSSR and its representatives, resulting in a sharper tone in May and June. A number of incorrect reports were published to create the impression that the Federal Republic of Germany and its armed forces supported the "counter-revolution" and thus endangered peace in Central Europe. Headlines such as "Bonn's massive interference in the domestic affairs of the ČSSR," or "Secret weapons cache near Karlovy Vary," were just a few that *Neues Deutschland*, the SED's main media organ, presented to its readers as official coverage.[18] Lies, half-truths and speculation were used to fuel fear among the country's own population about conflict and a third world war. There were those who were better-informed, though. The political information that the GDR leadership received through internal channels made it clear that the Federal Government in Bonn was instead pursuing a policy of "cautious waiting" rather than "provocatively" or openly standing up for the reformers in Czechoslovakia.[19] And military intelligence came to the conclusion, in a top secret estimate of the operational and tactical situation in the "NATO theaters of war Europe" for the month of July 1968, that "during the reporting period no activities were detected which suggest any basic increase in the level of combat readiness of NATO Forces in Europe and the occupation troops in West Berlin in general."[20]

---

18   *Neues Deutschland*. Zentralorgan der SED, Berlin (East), July 17, 20, 21, 1968.

19   Hans-Peter Schwarz, „Die Regierung Kiesinger und die Krise in der CSSR 1968," in *Vierteljahreshefte für Zeitgeschichte*, 47 (2, 1999) 159–86.

20   Bundesarchiv-Militärarchiv Freiburg (BA-MA), DVW 1/25799, p. 186, Aufklärungs-Sammelbericht Nr. 7/68 der Verwaltung Aufklärung des Ministeriums für Nationale Verteidigung vom 31.7.1968. Nor did the NVA intelligence forces detect any measures aimed at establishing higher or full combat readiness for the period until August 20, 1968.

Although several SED officials continued to state that they did not want to interfere,[21] they did just that. One practical measure in this respect was to establish contact with so-called positive or healthy forces, in other words, with opponents of Dubček within the CPCs, the state and the military. Also, the Ministry of State Security was instructed to undertake operational activities inside the ČSSR. It was to focus and spy on Western representatives, offices of correspondents or television teams within Czechoslovakia.[22]

The activities of the GDR's broadcasting media must also be regarded as obvious interference and as a further attempt to involve the GDR's own interests in the fight against the reformers. From July 22, 1968, Radio Berlin International aired a one-hour program in both the Czech and Slovak languages. Later "Radio Vltava" (Radio Moldau) broadcast programs from Dresden as a would-be Czechoslovak broadcasting station. This secret East German station was intended to support communists loyal to Moscow within the ČSSR and to counter the Czechoslovak pro-reform media.[23] Thus, the GDR took on an important role in the ideological offensive against the ČSSR.

The SED leadership was also included in the summit diplomacy of the Soviet anti-reform coalition from the very beginning. Although the relations between the Communist Party of the Soviet Union (CPSU) and the CPCs were the central axis of the dispute between the neo-Stalinist and reform communists, the Party leaderships in Bulgaria, Poland, Hungary and, of course, the GDR continued their joint efforts to intimidate, threaten and fight the course of reform in Czechoslovakia. At the meeting of the so-called "Warsaw Five"— Bulgaria, the GDR, Poland, Hungary and the USSR—in the Polish capital

---

21   Stiftung Archiv der Parteien und Massenorganisationen der DDR im Bundesarchiv (SAPMO-BArch), DY 30, J IV 2/3/1406, p. 13, Protokoll der Sekretariatssitzung des ZK der SED vom 15.5.1968 (Annex 1).

22   Monika Tantzscher, „Staatssicherheit mit ‚menschlichem Antlitz'. Die Folgen des Prager Frühlings für den tschechoslowakischen Staatssicherheitsdienst und seine Wechselbeziehungen zum MfS," in *Deutschland Archiv*, 31 (1998), 533–46.

23   Claus-Dieter Röck, „Invasion durch den Äther. Die Rundfunkpropaganda der DDR gegen die politische Reformbewegung in der ČSSR von 1968 ("Prager Frühling"). Struktur, Funktion und Resonanz des Geheimsenders Radio Vltava" (Phil. Diss, Leipzig, 2004).

in mid-July, Walter Ulbricht again emphatically evoked the dangers that the alleged counter-revolution posed to the socialist bloc and suggested "certain actions" to demonstrate the determination of the allied anti-reform forces.[24]

The basic decisions, however, were still made in Moscow. As is generally known, the CPSU Politburo decided only a few days after the Warsaw meeting to pursue a two-pronged policy which clearly supported both the military option and, yet again, the negotiating approach.[25] This Soviet course had immediate repercussions for the GDR. From that moment on, there is evidence that the Party and state organs of the GDR made a multitude of security-relevant and military preparations in the appropriate ministries, factories and organizations. These were particularly obvious within the GDR military, although kept secret from the public.

The National People's Army, officially founded in 1956, was the strongest armed force in East Germany. It followed the SED's line and was implicitly monopolized by its politics. Another of its specific features was its almost complete dependence on the Red Army, whose orders, military requirements and recommendations it had to follow. In the 1960's the GDR National People's Army had gradually been developed into a modern and well-trained

---

24 On this, inter alia, Manfred Wilke, „Die DDR in der Interventionskoalition gegen den ‚Sozialismus mit menschlichem Antlitz'," in *Prager Frühling. Das internationale Krisenjahr 1968. Beiträge*, ed. Stefan Karner et al. (Cologne-Weimar-Vienna, 2008), 421–46, as well as the associated documents volume *Prager Frühling. Das internationale Krisenjahr 1968. Dokumente*, ed. Stefan Karner et al., (Cologne, Weimar, Vienna, 2008) (=Veröffentlichungen des Ludwig Boltzmann-Instituts für Kriegsfolgen-Forschung Graz-Vienna-Klagenfurt, Sonderband 9/1 und 9/2); Antonin Benčik,"Walter Ulbricht, die SED und der Prager Frühling 1968," in *Zeitschrift für Geschichtswissenschaft*, 46 (1998), 700–09; Manfred Wilke, „Interventionspolitik: Die SED und der Prager Frühling 1968 und die polnische Demokratiebewegung 1980/81," in *Diktaturen in Europa im 20. Jahrhundert—der Fall der DDR*, ed. Heiner Timmermann (Berlin, 1996), 623–43; Prieß, Kural, Wilke, *Die SED und der „Prager Frühling,"* Jan Pauer, *Prag 1968. Der Einmarsch des Warschauer Paktes* (Bremen, 1995); Rüdiger Wenzke, *Die NVA und der Prager Frühling 1968. Die Rolle Ulbrichts und der DDR-Streitkräfte bei der Niederschlagung der tschechoslowakischen Reformbewegung* (Berlin, 1995); Rüdiger Wenzke, „Die mitteleuropäische Krise: Prag 1968," : *Vom Kalten Krieg zur deutschen Einheit. Analysen und Zeitzeugenberichte zur deutschen Militärgeschichte von 1945 bis 1995*. ed. Bruno Thoß (Munich, 1995), 157–78; Mark Kramer, "The Prague Spring and the Soviet Invasion of Czechoslovakia. New Interpretations (part 1)," in *Cold War International History Project Bulletin*, no. 2 (Fall, 1992), 1, 4–13; Mark Kramer, "The Prague Spring and the Soviet Invasion of Czechoslovakia. New Interpretations (part 2)," in Ibid., no. 3 (Fall, 1993), 2–13, 54 seq.[www.wilsoncenter.org.]

25 Michail Prozumenščikov, „Die Entscheidung im Politbüro der KPdSU," in *Prager Frühling. Das internationale Krisenjahr 1968*, 20541.

coalition force in the Eastern alliance.[26] Reliability, discipline, high combat readiness and a marked level of organization soon figured among its most outstanding features. Its predilection for "smart" ceremonial occasions, as well as its tough duty regime, soon earned it the nickname of "Red Prussians." In peacetime some 120,000 troops served in the NVA, with the officer corps being particularly loyal to the Party.

In 1968 the GDR National People's Army was included at an early stage in the preparations for the USSR's military action against the ČSSR. In response to the express wishes of the political and military leadership of the GDR, the defense minister, Army General Heinz Hoffmann, complained with unusual sharpness to the Supreme Commander of the Unified Armed Forces, Marshal Ivan I. Yakubovsky, "To my regret, I have to note that to this day the Ministry of National Defense of the German Democratic Republic has not received any invitation for staffs of the National People's Army to participate in the combined command staff exercise, which is to take place under your command in the ČSSR. [...] I regret this fact and fail to understand it."[27] As the GDR leadership under Walter Ulbricht knew such exercises were intended to disguise the buildup plans, they wanted to demonstrate clearly to the USSR their readiness to be on the "correct side" at all times. The NVA was subsequently included in all the exercises and maneuvers of the Pact conducted in advance of the military intervention against the ČSSR.

The Soviet general staff had prepared operation "Danube" (Dunaj) for the immediate invasion of the ČSSR.[28] It began under the strictest secrecy as an exercise scenario in late July 1968 and this time directly included forces of the East German army. Upon request of the Supreme Commander of the Warsaw Pact's Unified Armed Forces, an operational group of NVA officers joined the forces' headquarters in Legnica, Poland, on July 25, 1968. Marshal

---

26 Rüdiger Wenzke, „Die Nationale Volksarmee (1956-1990)," in *Im Dienste der Partei. Handbuch der bewaffneten Organe der DDR*, ed. Torsten Diedrich, Hans Ehlert and Rüdiger Wenzke, 2nd ed. (Berlin, 1998) 423–535.

27 BA-MA, AZN Strausberg 28044, p. 108, teletype message from Army General Hoffmann to Marshal Yakubovsky, 10.6.1968.

28 On Operation "Danube," inter alia. Valerij Vartanov, „Die militärische Niederschlagung des "Prager Frühlings", in *Prager Frühling. Das internationale Krisenjahr 1968*, 661–71; Antonín Benčik, "*Operace "Dunaj". Vojaci a Pražské jaro 1968. Studie a dokumenty* (Prague, 1994); Feliks Tych, „Polens Teilnahme an der Invasion in der Tschechoslowakei," in *Aus Politik und Zeitgeschichte*. Supplement to the weekly *Das Parlament*, B 36/1992, 18–25; Wenzke, *Die NVA und der Prager Frühling 1968*, 86–98.

Yakubovsky received the small delegation and explained that the main task of the imminent exercise was to "protect the working class of the ČSSR from open counter-revolution since all the signs were that it would not be able to master the situation on its own."[29]

Also, the Supreme Commander provided the East German "brothers in arms" with details regarding the envisaged role of the NVA. Besides undertaking extensive logistical tasks in support of the Soviet troops, two NVA divisions—the 7th Armored Division Dresden and the 11th Motorized Rifle Division Halle—were to be included in the military operation. Yakubovky's explanations did not leave any doubt that the NVA would also advance into Czechoslovak territory. Neither the SED leadership nor the NVA leadership offered resistance or refused. As a consequence, the two divisions were deployed to the assigned areas and achieved operational and combat readiness on July 29, 1968. Strictest secrecy and a mail embargo were imposed. The vehicles were armed and supplied with ammunition, all the troops' supplies were loaded up, and the issuance of live ammunition to the soldiers was prepared. Several units were even briefed on specific tasks to be fulfilled on Czechoslovak soil.[30]

On the same day, July 29, the supreme official institution for all security and national defense matters of the GDR, the National Defense Council, convened in Strausberg (near Berlin), the seat of the GDR Ministry of Defense, for a three-hour meeting. A brief outline of the actions to be taken by the GDR armed forces and the Ministry of State Security in direct connection with the expected military action against the ČSSR was given, without going into operational details. The political line of argumentation that was to be communicated to the SED Party organizations was also agreed upon.[31]

No military action took place against the reformers in Prague in late July; rather, in early August, the focus of events again shifted to political issues for a short time. The summits at Čierna nad Tisou and Bratislava at the end of July and beginning of August, and the political agreements reached there only delayed the beginning of military action. During this time, completely

---

29 BA-MA, VA-01/12826, 115 seq., 1. Information report of the NVA operational group in Legnica, July 25, 1968.

30 BStU, HA I, 13239, pp. 6-8; analysis by the Ministry of State Security of the divulgence of military secrets during Operation Danube dated December, 1968.

31 BA-MA, DVW 1/39490, pp. 1–3, Sitzung des Nationalen Verteidigungsrates, July 29, 1968.

in tune with Moscow, the SED leadership also tried to continue its political efforts in parallel with the secret military actions beginning in early August. The media ceased its propaganda against Czechoslovakia. Ulbricht traveled to Karlovy Vary on August 12, for the first official bilateral meeting of both Party leaders in the Dubček era. The intentions behind his journey are not completely understood to this day. Some suggest that Ulbricht's journey was intended to cover up the preparations for the intervention. A different view is that Ulbricht wanted to appear as a reliable negotiating partner with regard to the West and at this time probably had no information about the exact date of the military invasion. A more realistic reason is that Ulbricht believed, as an experienced "leader of the workers," that he would be able to appeal to the conscience of "young comrade" Dubček and lead him back unto the right path. He, therefore, exhibited a relatively conciliatory attitude in Karlovy Vary. Nevertheless, he praised himself and his politics, and his manner towards the Czechs and Slovaks was one of overbearing arrogance. When asked at a press conference on August 13 about the situation of the students, for instance, he said that in the GDR students did not have time to concern themselves with bourgeois ideology but preferred to "sing happy songs."[32] As to censorship of the press, he replied that "when we learned from the press that you [representatives of the ČSSR] had abolished censorship of the press, we were astonished because we were not familiar with such a thing. We have never had censorship of the press and, as you see, we have progressed very well, even without press censorship."[33] In view of such cynicism it is understandable that Dubček thought the SED leader a "repulsive" person, as he later wrote in his memoirs.[34] At the end of the press conference Ulbricht casually mentioned that it was time for him to "finally go on holiday." This was considered a sign of détente. All were lulled into a false sense of security, especially as the Party newspaper *Neues Deutschland* published photographs in which Walter Ulbricht and Alexander Dubček amicably shook hands.

Meanwhile, the southern part of the GDR already resembled a military camp. In addition to tens of thousands of Soviet soldiers, with more than 2,000 tanks and roughly as many armored personnel carriers, there were some

---

32 Stefan Wolle, *Der Traum von der Revolte. Die DDR 1968* (Berlin, 2008), 145.
33 Quotation according to *Neues Deutschland*, August 14, 1968.
34 Alexander Dubček, *Leben für die Freiheit* (Munich, 1993), 253.

16,500 German soldiers and just under 500 tanks waiting in the woods of Saxony for the order to invade the ČSSR. The GDR military not only considered themselves to be too good to serve as auxiliary troops of the Red Army, they were also prepared, without any historical sensitivity thirty years after the attack on Czechoslovakia by the German Wehrmacht, to invade and co-occupy the neighboring country.

The GDR and Military Intervention— Ulbricht's Forces in the ČSSR?

During the night of August 20–21, 1968, armed forces of the participating Warsaw Pact countries massed along the borders of the ČSSR and invaded the country on a broad front. The "Prague group," consisting mainly of Soviet and Polish divisions, advanced rapidly into the Czechoslovak interior, their advance units reaching the capital in the early morning of August 21. The two NVA divisions that had been prepared for the combat mission were part of this "Prague group." The Dresden-based 7th Armored Division, with a combat strength of 7,500 troops, 1,500 vehicles, and 300 tanks, was to accompany Soviet troops as the 2nd echelon in crossing the border with Czechoslovakia and advancing into the area of Litoměřice—Mimoň and Děčín. The Halle-based 11th Motorized Rifle Division of the NVA, consisting of 9,000 troops, 1,700 vehicles, 349 infantry fighting vehicles and 188 tanks stood ready to conduct military action in the direction of Plzeň. Although all the preparations had been made by the Soviet marshals and the NVA leadership and the East German troops were ready to participate, NVA combat units did not, after all, invade Czechoslovakia or occupy it, either on August 20–21, 1968, or in the days thereafter. Both NVA divisions waited in vain for marching orders. During the entire military action conducted by the allied troops, the NVA troops remained on GDR territory.[35]

For more than two decades there was no doubt either in the East or West that the East German army had actually invaded the ČSSR alongside the other intervention forces on August 21, 1968. Contemporary Western media reports and commentaries on the invasion provided an abundance of ostensible evidence for this. The West German public got the impression that the forces of the National People's Army of the GDR advanced, not only into Bohemia, but also as far as Bratislava. The largest West German mass-circulation daily, the

---

35 Wenzke, *Die NVA und der Prager Frühling*, 115–59.

East German Soldiers waiting to invade Czechoslovakia, Saxony, August, 1968
Photo credit: Courtesy of Rüdiger Wenzke

East German Soldiers waiting to invade Czechoslovakia, Saxony, August, 1968
Photo credit: Courtesy of Rüdiger Wenzke

Bild, announced to its readers that "Almost two full divisions of the 'National People's Army' took part in the invasion. The units are stationed mainly in the areas north of Prague, Karlovy Vary and Bratislava".[36] Although only shortly thereafter it was reported that "zone forces" were no longer to be seen in the

---

36 SAPMO-BArch, DY 30, IV A 2/2.028/141, Documentation of the Central Committee Security Directorate of the SED on articles in the Western press concerning the participation of the NVA in the invasion of the ČSSR, September 9, 1968.

ČSSR because they remained hidden "in the Bohemian forests" or had already withdrawn, the invasion by the NVA and the occupation of the ČSSR by East German forces were taken as an indisputable fact. The image of the GDR army invading and occupying its neighboring country, just as the German Wehrmacht had done before, persisted in the media, in academic and political circles, and within the public at large in the West until the early 1990's. Czechs and Slovaks, too, had no doubt that their country had been occupied by East German troops. The slogan "1938 Hitler—1968 Ulbricht" encapsulated this. While Ulbricht was deemed a particularly "popular" target for ridicule, resentment and contempt by the people in the ČSSR, many slogans, banners, cartoons and leaflets referred explicitly to the, at least, "perceived" historical parallelism of the events of 1938 and 1968.

Surprisingly, the SED did not issue any official information to dispute the Western reports about the role of NVA troops in the invasion of the ČSSR in 1968. On the contrary, for reasons of secrecy and drawing upon ideological premises, a vague legend of the "unswerving brotherhood of arms" and of the NVA overcoming the "challenge" of fighting the so-called Czechoslovak counter-revolution was created. GDR citizens, therefore, were given only general information about the NVA "operation." They were informed in hazy terms about the actions of their own troops in "captured areas" and without the names of any locations. All this served to increase the vagueness and confusion among the population regarding the real activities of the NVA. Thus was born the legend that the NVA participated as an equal partner in the Warsaw Pact operation to "safeguard peace" in the ČSSR.

The GDR continued to uphold this lie as a means of cultivating its own image. An official publication of the East Berlin-based Militärverlag publishing house entitled *Armee für Frieden und Sozialismus. Geschichte der Nationalen Volksarmee der DDR* stated in 1985, for instance, that forces and supporting staffs of the NVA had entered ČSSR territory in August 1968 side-by-side with the "fraternal armies" and assisted the "Czechoslovak working people" in "defeating the counter-revolution, preventing civil war in the country and, thereby, preserving European peace."[37] Until its downfall in 1989, the SED leadership continually scotched any political or academic effort to inquire about or even critically approach the 'Prague Spring' or the role of NVA in it.

---

37   *Armee für Frieden und Sozialismus. Geschichte der Nationalen Volksarmee der DDR* (Berlin [East], 1985), 371.

As a result, we have the strange phenomenon described by historian Stefan Wolle, "Whereas dictatorships usually try to conceal their crimes, we are faced here with a rare if not singular case of a state accusing itself of a breach of international law that it has not committed at all."[38]

Only in the course of the peaceful revolution and the collapse of SED rule in 1989–1990 was more light shed upon this issue. New research on the basis of previously top-secret documents from the recently-opened archives, as well as an interview by *Der Spiegel* newsmagazine with former President of the GDR People's Chamber, Horst Sindermann, brought the issue of NVA participation in the suppression of the 'Prague Spring' into broad public focus. That new research, as well as Sindermann's statement that "no invasion of the ČSSR by GDR troops" had taken place,[39] triggered a very wide range of reactions, not only in the then still extant GDR, but also in Czechoslovakia and the Federal Republic of Germany. For a time, the findings regarding the events of August 1968 attracted considerable interest in the media. Some supporters of the old system in the GDR used them as welcome opportunities to justify their own actions and glorify them as Ulbricht's act of "opposition" against Moscow. Others dismissed them as "lies." Not everything that was said or written helped to clarify the facts. Although the question of the NVA units' participation in the direct invasion of August 1968 has, meanwhile, been clarified from the viewpoint of serious academic research, it is certain that, with the exception of a few officers, a small group of military intelligence personnel, a low number of reconnaissance and supply forces and several members of the border troops, no East German soldiers entered ČSSR territory as NVA combat troops in battalion, regiment or even division strength. There was until recently still no answer to the no less tantalizing question as to why the original Soviet plans with regard to the two NVA units were not implemented and who in the end was responsible for this.

Previous attempts by politicians, military personnel and historians to provide an answer revealed very different perspectives. Valentin Falin, Soviet ambassador to the Federal Republic of Germany from 1971 to 1978, said that the uncertain international legal status of the GDR at the time was one reason.[40] However, the Soviets obviously paid no attention to international

---

38 Stefan Wolle, *Der Traum von der Revolte*, 154.

39 *Der Spiegel*, 19 (May 7, 1990), 62.

40 Pauer, *Prag 1968*, 229.

legal aspects during the invasion. The former chief of the southern NVA military district, Lieutenant General (ret.) Hans Ernst, expressed the view that the GDR government had requested allowing the GDR troops to remain in their concentration areas. This was explained to him by the Supreme Commander of the Warsaw Pact forces, Marshal Yakubovsky, during a walk in the woods.[41] Several other, former high-ranking politicians of the GDR as well as some generals and officers of the NVA still adhere to this view. Contrary to it are statements by former East German officers to the effect that several representatives of the NVA leadership and Ulbricht himself were extremely displeased about the non-participation of the NVA.[42] Yet another explanation was that Dubček opponents surrounding Vasil Biľak and Alois Indra requested Moscow on relatively short notice not to use German forces, which was also very quickly acceded to through Kirill T. Mazurov, the Secret Commissioner of the Soviet Politburo for the intervention.[43]

It was not until 2008, at an international joint project on the 'Prague Spring,' that researchers from the Austrian Ludwig Boltzmann Institute in Graz, from Russian institutes and archives and from other research institutions were able to provide a clear answer. In Moscow they found previously unknown documentary evidence that the decision for the non-participation of the NVA in the invasion was indeed made on short notice by Soviet Party leader Leonid Brezhnev following requests by high-ranking Czechoslovak opponents of Dubček. One document states, for example, that during the negotiations of the Soviet leadership with Ludvík Svoboda in Moscow on August 23, 1968, Brezhnev replied to the question of Czechoslovak delegation member Milan Klusák whether there were East German soldiers on the territory of the ČSSR, as follows: "It is quite certain that no German soldiers were present on the territory of Czechoslovakia. We have withheld them. [...] Speaking among ourselves, the German comrades were offended at being in some way mistrusted."[44] Nikolay V. Podgorny added that "this was done upon

---

41 Hans Ernst, „Der Sommer 1968 im Militärbezirk Leipzig," in *Vom Kalten Krieg zur deutschen Einheit*, 187–91, here, p. 190.

42 Wenzke, *Die NVA und der Prager Frühling*, 144–8.

43 Pauer, *Prag 1968*, 229.

44 Russian State Archive of Contemporary History (RGANI), F. 89, op. 38, d. 57, pp. 1–19, here, p. 13, Shorthand report of the negotiations of Leonid I. Brezhnev, Alexey N. Kosygin and Nikolay V. Podgorny with Ludvík Svoboda and Milan Klusák, August 23, 1968. Printed in *Prager Frühling. Das internationale Krisenjahr 1968. Dokumente*, 827–39, here, p. 835.

your request. We took the situation into consideration, although they also [the GDR forces] should have gone with all the others."[45] Thus, there is no doubt that in the end the decision was made in Moscow and not in East Berlin.[46]

The development of the military situation on August 21, 1968, of course, helped Brezhnev in adhering to his political decision. The rapid advance of the complete Soviet–Polish armed forces group to Prague had rendered the originally planned seizure and wide-area control of the northern Czech territory unnecessary, and the East German 7th Armored Division was consequently able to remain in reserve. But even up to the end of August, the Soviet military allowed their East German "brothers in arms" to believe that troops might still be sent into the ČSSR. Marshal Yakubovsky explained to the GDR Deputy Defense Minister, Colonel General Heinz Keßler, that "depending on the development of the political situation, it is still necessary to fully maintain combat readiness as ordered and that there is the possibility that the 11th Motorized Rifle Division may be employed in the direction of Karlovy Vary, and the 7th Armored Division in the direction of Děčín—Prague, as planned".[47]

Although the two NVA combat units remained on GDR territory from August until late October 1968, many institutions and bodies of the GDR contributed to the invasion of Czechoslovakia. All persons bearing arms in the GDR had been alerted on August 21 and had established combat readiness.[48] This occurred without any problems since most of the agencies of the Ministry of the Interior, Ministry of State Security and Ministry of Defense had been prepared for day "X" since late July. Under their direction, beginning at 1:30 a.m. on August 21, all border crossing points were closed to civilian transport, and all other civilian contacts, such as telephone and mail, between the GDR and ČSSR were discontinued. Preparations had even been made to set up NVA military garrison headquarters in the northern Czech territory.

NVA units and staffs additionally provided logistical support to the Soviet forces. The People's Police secured the marching routes and holding areas of the units, while State Security was responsible for monitoring the restricted and

---

45   Ibid.
46   Rüdiger Wenzke, „Die Nationale Volksarmee der DDR. Kein Einsatz in Prag," in *Prager Frühling. Das internationale Krisenjahr 1968, Beiträge*, 673–686.
47   BA-MA, AZN Strausberg 23454, p. 147, Communication from Colonel General Heinz Keßler to Erich Honecker, August 31, 1968.
48   Wenzke, *Die NVA und der Prager Frühling*, 115–26.

off-limits areas. An NVA border brigade was also set up, to ensure as near-complete control of the border region with Czechoslovakia as possible and, above all, the problem-free crossing of Soviet units from the GDR into the neighboring country. The SED regime's *"Aktion Sperrmauer"* (Operation Dam Wall), therefore, played a not insignificant role in the success of the intervention.

On September 11, 1968, the Supreme Commander of the Unified Armed Forces gave his permission to "downgrade the increased combat readiness for the National People's Army, with the exception of the 7th Armored Division and the 11th Motorized Rifle Division."[49] Yet it was not until a month later that the military operation to occupy the ČSSR, which had begun in July 1968, was completed with the gradual redeployment of the forces. Although some 75,000 Soviet soldiers and their combat equipment remained in Czechoslovakia for the long term, around 20 divisions had now to be redeployed to their home garrisons.

The redeployment was to occur, in the words of Soviet Marshal Andrei A. Grechko, just as smoothly as the invasion.[50] Once again the active support and assistance of the GDR, was requested. Army General Hoffmann assured the allies in Moscow that "on the part of the German Democratic Republic, all measures will be taken to assist the redeployment of the forces in every respect."[51] Of the 600 trains required for the redeployment, the GDR Reichsbahn alone provided 240. The East German authorities kept twelve roads through the Erz Mountains completely clear for around three to four days. The Soviet forces, as well as those belonging to the two NVA divisions originally earmarked for the invasion, were welcomed in their home garrisons with a large amount of propaganda. In some garrison towns "victory parades" took place.[52] Allowing the population to believe that the NVA forces came directly from the ČSSR was part of the pernicious web of lies promoted by Party officials and NVA generals in order to further conceal the actual role of the East German army.

---

49   BA-MA, DVW 1/12826, p. 40, letter from Army General Hoffmann to Honecker, September 11,1968.

50   Ibid., AZN Strausberg 32624, p. 113, report from Army General Hoffmann to Honecker, September 25, 1968.

51   Ibid., p.117.

52   Rüdiger Wenzke, „Sachsen als militärischer Aufmarsch- und Handlungsraum von NVA und Sowjetarmee im Sommer 1968," in *Sachsen und der "Prager Frühling,"* 89–126, here, p. 124 seq.

In summary, it is fair to state that the NVA was included from an early stage in the preparation, field security and conduct of the Warsaw Pact intervention, although in the end no combat troops of the GDR National People's Army directly invaded the ČSSR. Ready in 1968 to unconditionally fulfill any order issued by Moscow, the East German leadership planned, prepared and implemented all security, transport, supply and support measures for the military operation in the GDR on behalf of the Soviet authorities. The activities of the civilian GDR bodies and of the military were thus, without a doubt, more than just a symbolic participation in the intervention; they afforded, in breach of international law, an important contribution to the quelling of the Czechoslovak democratic movement. In this respect, the confession made by the GDR's first freely elected parliamentarians on April 12, 1990, being co-responsible for the suppression of the 'Prague Spring' was more than justified.

Response and Reactions of the GDR Population to the 'Prague Spring'

To once again take up this moral assessment, it was mainly the leadership and many officials at various levels of the Party, state and army who were guilty of wishing to invade Czechoslovakia in 1968. Many ordinary GDR citizens, by contrast, had associated the political signs from Prague and the name of Dubček with the hope of change. They could certainly look forward to the replacement of their own "old" GDR socialism with its thousands of deficiencies by the new "ČSSR version." Hardly anybody thought in earnest about the complete abolition of socialism, but there was at least initial reflection about some obvious "faults and mistakes" of the Ulbricht regime. "A lot in our country is too rigid and restricted," is how a young worker from a large East Berlin company summarized things in the summer of 1968, wishing that everything were "more free."[53]

It was above all the young and middle-aged who sympathized with the ČSSR experiment. Ideas of a "marriage" between freedom and socialism, of real democracy or, simply, just the desire to experience beat music and Western

---

53 SAPMO-BArch, DY 30 IV A 2/2028/141, Information from the Central Committee Party Organ Directorate concerning moods within the population, July 18, 1968.

flair drew tens of thousands of young East Germans to Prague prior to August 21, 1968. Upon returning home they discussed their experiences at their universities, workplaces, schools, and even in some SED Party groups.[54]

The NVA leadership, too, was confronted with ideas from the Czechoslovak reform movement in the spring of 1968. However, those who made their criticism and questions too public were punished immediately. When, for example, a member of a military district command described the official GDR information about the ČSSR as untrue and the SED politics as wrong, he was expelled from the Party.[55] In general, GDR propaganda endeavored to keep quiet about what was actually happening in the ČSSR and to commit the people to the SED's line of a "necessary fight against counter-revolution".

As the news of the invasion of the ČSSR by Warsaw Pact forces spread throughout the media in the wee hours of the morning of August 21, 1968, the Party also quickly laid down the official line. The occupation of Czechoslovak territory, it was stated, was legal since it was conducted in response to a call for help from the ČSSR. The action was taken for peace and socialism which, ostensibly, were also in the interest of GDR citizens. Even though more than a few GDR citizens, in particular SED members, believed initially that it was really necessary to put a stop to the "counter-revolution" in the neighboring country to prevent bloodshed, the SED was soon forced to acknowledge that the "fraternal assistance" was rejected throughout the population and that the workers in the factories and on the construction sites made no secret of their negative views.[56]

In many places in the GDR after August 21, people were shocked about the military action taken against the ČSSR. Mostly young people also expressed their protests openly. In the period from August 21 to September 14, 1968, the Ministry of State Security registered 2,129 protests in East Berlin and the GDR districts as "attacks against the assistance of the five socialist fraternal states to safeguard the socialist state and social order in the ČSSR." There is evidence of sympathy by GDR citizens for democracy in the ČSSR in nearly all major towns

---

54 Monika Tantzscher, „Maßnahme Donau und Einsatz Genesung. Die Niederschlagung des Prager Frühlings 1968/69 im Spiegel der MfS-Akten," in *Analysen und Berichte*, publ. by the Federal Commissioner for the Files of the Former East German State Security Service, series B 1/94, p. 25.

55 BA-MA, VA-P-01/5922, p. 157, Information, Issue 19/68, from the Main Political Directorate of the NVA on the current events of May 31, 1968.

56 Ehrhart Neubert, *Geschichte der Opposition in der DDR 1949-1989* (Bonn, 1997), 165.

and cities in the days after August 21. The main locations were East Berlin, as well as the districts of Dresden, Erfurt, Karl-Marx-Stadt (Chemnitz), Leipzig, Magdeburg and Potsdam.[57] In Berlin alone, a total of 3,528 leaflets were discovered in 389 places, as well as more than 270 slogans such as "Freedom for Dubček," "Vivat Dubček" or "We want Dubček" at more than 200 locations.[58] At the embassy of the ČSSR in East Berlin, protest resolutions on display were signed by hundreds of GDR citizens who knew they were being observed by State Security. The only official institution in the GDR to more or less openly disapprove of invading the ČSSR was the Protestant Church.

Immediately after the invasion became known, opinions considering the military action a breach of international law were also expressed in various NVA units. "In several cases, army members followed the point of view of the class enemy, refused supporting measures, and made slanderous remarks against the Soviet Union and the GDR." One report stated that, "listening to Western broadcasting stations, and the spread of hostile arguments, were manifest in all duty sectors."[59] The view that the actions of the Warsaw Pact states constituted an intervention in the domestic affairs of the ČSSR also spread quickly.[60] Conscripts of the Christian faith openly declared that if their units were employed in operations against the ČSSR, they would not use firearms. A young NCO compared the invasion of 1968 to the German occupation of Bohemia-Moravia by the Wehrmacht. "I will not fire a shot because I do not want to be hanged as a war criminal like others after the Second World War."[61] The attitudes of soldiers who deliberately ignored or refused to go along with increased or full combat readiness can also be considered as a kind of protest. A private and an NCO in a reconnaissance battalion, for instance, were unwilling to carry out the orders issued. They were promptly removed from the unit. Tampering with equipment and weapons, as well as

---

57 Bernd Eisenfeld, „Hoffnung, Widerstand, Resignation. Die Auswirkungen des Prager Frühlings und seiner Zerstörung in der DDR," in *Deutschland Archiv*, 36 (2003), 789–807.

58 Wolle, *Der Traum von der Revolte*, 160–72.

59 BA-MA, VA-P-01/5921, p. 131, Information Report No.8/68 from the Chief of the Main Political Directorate of the NVA, September 9, 1968.

60 Ibid., VA-P-01/5975, pp. 20–27, 30–32, 35–37, Information S/1-S/4 from the Main Political Directorate, August 21–22, 1968.

61 Ibid., VA-P-01/1142, p. 146, teletype message from the Head of the Political Administration of the Leipzig Military District to the Main Political Directorate of the NVA, no date (August, 1968).

sabotage directed against the combat and operational readiness of the armed forces, tended to remain isolated. On August 22, for example, the wire connection between a battalion and the headquarters of the 7th Armored Division was interrupted. A repair party established that the cable had twice been deliberately short-circuited.[62]

Discussions with political and ideological deviationists had to be conducted even within the SED itself. By the autumn of 1968, a total of 3,358 Party comrades and candidates were disciplined by the Party for non-conformist remarks, and, although affecting only some 0.2 percent of the total Party membership, action taken by the Party nevertheless resulted in 278 expulsions and cancellations of Party memberships.[63]

There is no doubt that the fascination with the 'Prague Spring' and the rejection of the brutal action taken against the ČSSR occupied representatives of all the social classes, even among the SED ruling Party. Admittedly, the protests and resistance mostly remained restricted to spontaneous individual actions or to those of smaller groups.

Nevertheless, even the smallest public protest and every open demonstration of disapproval was a signal for the surveillance machinery and apparatus of power of the SED regime to become active. State Security and the People's Police stood ready to intervene. The political criminal justice system of the GDR faced its first major test after the adoption of new laws in the spring of 1968.

The GDR's Attorney-General, in statistics compiled in October 1968, noted the names of 1,189 persons who, as opponents of the invasion, had been turned into criminals. Nearly half of them were young people up to 21 years of age. According to their social status, the majority of the identified "criminals" were blue- and white-collar workers, often without any vocational training, as well as apprentices and students.[64]

---

62 Ibid., VA-P 03/7460, p. 73, latest information from the Political Representative of Reconnaissance Battalion 7, August 23, 1968.

63 SAPMO-BArch, DY 30 IV A 2/4/5, Information from the Central Party Control Commission of the SED concerning disputes with members and candidates in connection with the events of August 1968.

64 Wilhelm Schröder and Jürgen Wilke, „Politische Gefangene in der DDR. Eine quantitative Analyse," in *Materialien der Enquete-Kommission „Überwindung der Folgen der SED-Diktatur im Prozeß der deutschen Einheit (13. Wahlperiode des Deutschen Bundestages)*, pub. by Deutscher Bundestag, vol. VI, Baden-Baden (Frankfurt a.M., 1999), 1250 and 1258.

Where the military was concerned, the issue was how the generals and officers conducted themselves in a crisis situation. Most of the regular soldiers supported the actions of the Warsaw Pact by virtue of their subjective convictions. But even though the vast majority of the NVA officer corps agreed with the policies of the SED, there were officers who apparently had mixed feelings, especially regarding the actions against the ČSSR. They expressed their questions and concerns only within their personal environment. However, the army leadership took extremely harsh measures to counter any political criticism and deviation from the official Party line, in particular within the officer corps.

Only a few days after the invasion, the Chief of the Political Main Administration of the NVA, Admiral Waldemar Verner, was forced to acknowledge at a commanders' conference that five officers, all members of the SED, had openly opposed the military action.[65] What the admiral in his speech then referred to as "cowardice" was in reality a brave personal act and a sense of responsibility on the part of individual army members.

In August of 1968 Captain Joachim Rau became the first NVA officer to be called to account, not only by the Party, but also by the Minister of National Defense for his opposition to the invasion. He received the "maximum penalty" in both cases. After Rau was expelled from the SED, he was demoted by order of the Minister to the rank of private for "lack of willingness to defend the socialist achievements" and discharged from the NVA without notice on August 22, 1968.[66] Staff officer Lieutenant Colonel Werner Mantzsch of the 7th Armored Division had sympathized with the Prague reform policies for some time and, in this connection, had stated opinions deviating from the official SED line. This was enough to expel him from the SED for "political unreliability," to deprive him of his commissioned grade and to discharge him without notice as a simple soldier from active military service.[67] All the persons concerned were subjected to diverse kinds of social and moral discrimination

---

65   BA-MA, DVW 1/55541, p. 131, Niederschrift über die Kommandeursberatung beim Minister für Nationale Verteidigung, August 24, 1968.

66   Ibid., VA-P-01/5667, pp. 254 seq., Befehl Nr. 121/68 des Ministers für Nationale Verteidigung der DDR über Kader, August 22, 1968.

67   Ibid., p. 262, Befehl des Ministers für Nationale Verteidigung über Kader Nr. 123/68, August 24, 1968.

in addition to considerable material and social restrictions and disadvantages in the years thereafter. It was not until 1990 that they were rehabilitated by the GDR Ministry of Disarmament and Defense.[68]

From 1968 to 1970 some 20 NVA members received prison sentences with reference to the ČSSR events. The first proceedings against a non-rated serviceman of the NVA before a military court took place in Leipzig in late November 1968. Among the accused was an engineer.[69] In the evening of August 21, 1968, he and three friends had written in chalk "Freedom for the ČSSR—Long live Dubček—Russians out of the ČSSR" at seventeen locations in the town of Köthen (Saxony Anhalt). Only a few days afterwards the group was arrested. Despite their youth, the four accused received prison sentences of up to two years and nine months without probation.

Today it is no longer possible to determine the exact number of all the disciplinary measures taken against military personnel or civilian employees of the NVA in connection with the events in the ČSSR. So far there has been evidence of several hundred persons who were subjected to long-term repression because of their political opinions. The number of protests by GDR citizens in 1968, both in the civilian and military domains, generally exceeded anything that had been known up to then.[70] Therefore, they occupy an outstanding place in the history of resistance in the GDR. The year 1968 eventually became a turning point in the personal development of many GDR citizens. The "68ers" of the GDR co-founded an opposition movement which, in the course of its development in the 1970's and 1980's, produced those political leaders who initiated and helped push through the downfall of the SED rule in the autumn of 1989.[71]

---

68 Rüdiger Wenzke, „Zwischen "Prager Frühling" 1968 und Herbst 1989. Protestverhalten, Verweigerungsmuster und politische Verfolgung in der NVA der siebziger und achtziger Jahre," in *Staatsfeinde in Uniform? Widerständiges Verhalten und politische Verfolgung in der NVA*, ed. Rüdiger Wenzke (Berlin, 2005), 199–428, here, pp. 216–24.

69 BA-MA, VA-11/27631, Urteil des Militärobergerichts Leipzig S 39/68 dated August 29, 1968.

70 SAPMO-BArch, DY 30 IV A 2/12/25, Lagebeurteilung des Ministeriums des Innern, August 29, 1968.

71 Ilko-Sascha Kowalczuk, „,Wer sich nicht in Gefahr begibt...' Protestaktionen gegen die Intervention in Prag 1968 und die Folgen von 1968 für die DDR-Opposition," in *Widerstand und Opposition in der DDR*, ed. Klaus-Dietmar Henke, Peter Steinbach and Johannes Tuchel (Cologne, Weimar, Vienna 1999), 257–74, here, p. 273; Neubert, *Geschichte der Opposition*, 164–8.

Finally, it remains to be said that the crisis triggered in the Eastern Bloc by the 'Prague Spring' had a rather mixed outcome for the Party, state and army leaderships in the GDR. In the spring and summer of 1968 the GDR followed the USSR as the leading power while it expressed its own interests and also tried to assert them among its allies. Walter Ulbricht embodied the Party oligarchy's unlimited claim to power. His understanding of politics formed the key to fighting the reforms in the ČSSR, and he also made the SED an active champion of a strong stand against the ČSSR. Although Ulbricht was able to prove to his allies and opponents that he was a loyal vassal of Moscow, and able to enforce peace and order in his own country, his regime nevertheless suffered severe damage to its image both among the people in the GDR and the international public. The broad sympathy of the East Germans for the 'Prague Spring' and their great embitterment at its suppression were difficult to overlook. Even though the NVA's participation in the military action was celebrated outwardly as if the East German military had passed a "major test," the subordinate position of the GDR army in the invasion, as ordered by Moscow, deeply affected the self-assuredness of the SED leadership and its military. This eventually led to the formulation of a huge propaganda lie. An exaggerated opinion of himself and political individualism soon caused Ulbricht's star to decline in the Soviet bloc. Almost three years after the quelling of the 'Prague Spring,' the rule of one of the fiercest opponents of the Czechoslovak reform also ended.

10

Commentary on the "Role and Activities of the SED, the East German State, and Its Military during the 'Prague Spring' of 1968"

Gary Bruce

One of the key points raised in Rüdiger Wenzke's contribution is the role of personality on the German side during the 'Prague Spring.' Walter Ulbricht is the key figure here, one of the *alte Kämpfer*, the old fighters who lived through the street battles of Weimar and who opposed National Socialism at a time when, it must be said, few dared to. He worked underground against the Nazis before he left for Paris and then Moscow, where he authored pamphlets intended to cause Wehrmacht soldiers to join the Red Army.[1] Perhaps his commitment to socialism originated in his childhood home as the son of two tailors, but certainly no later than the start of his political career in earnest as a co-founder of the Communist Party of Germany in Leipzig in 1919. At the time of the 'Prague Spring,' as a seventy-five year old with a great deal of "revolutionary authority" from his Weimar days, Ulbricht was one of the elder statesmen of Europe, and one of the elder statesmen of the socialist cause. He had survived challenges to his leadership in 1953[2] and most

---

1 An excellent biography of Ulbricht is Mario Frank, *Walter Ulbricht: Eine deutsche Biografie* (Berlin, 2001).

2 See in particular Peter Grieder, *The East German Leadership, 1946–73* (Manchester, 1999) and Nadja Stulz-Herrnstadt, *Das Herrnstadt-Dokument: Das Politbüro der SED und die Geschichte des 17. Juni 1953* (Reinbek, 1990).

recently in 1956 from Karl Schirdewan,[3] who, as a somewhat newer generation of communists, evokes certain parallels to Alexander Dubček. Ulbricht still possessed that revolutionary zeal of his days at the barricades, as did others in key positions of the East German government—Erich Honecker, at the time of the 'Prague Spring' secretary of the National Defense Council, and Erich Mielke, Minister for State Security. These were individuals who believed to their core in the very rightness of the Cause. Even in the late 1940's, when the prospect of German unity was bleak, Ulbricht still believed that an imminent West German economic collapse would pave the way for German unification under the Socialist Unity Party of Germany.[4] In the years prior to the collapse of the GDR, Erich Honecker still continued to believe in the ultimate triumph of the socialist system—this in spite of the fact that the East German debt had become so unwieldy that the country began bartering, not only its prisoners to the West, but also cobblestones from streets in Weimar, artwork, and even blood that had been donated by East Germans.[5]

Much of the explanation for this heady optimism relates to the feeling of superiority earned by rising from under the boot of the Nazis and stems from a profound belief in the "scientifically proven" rightness of their cause, making it plain that individual biographies remain an important tool for understanding this era.[6] It is, then, understandable that Ulbricht would be gravely concerned about destabilization, not only in East Germany, but also in the cause of socialism, occasioned by Dubček's reforms. Having seen it so often, historians can dismiss communist rhetoric as just that, but the fact that Ulbricht constantly referred to the Dubček reforms as the "counter-revolution" was not just political hyperbole. Encountering typical communist vocabulary, such as "anti-fascist" or "imperialist," that East German authorities overused, we should not be too quick to discount the mindset behind the rhetoric. For Ulbricht, the 'Prague Spring' was indeed an act against the revolution to which he had dedicated his life.

---

3   Karl Schirdewan, *Aufstand gegen Ulbricht* (Berlin, 1994).

4   Dirk Spilker, *The East German Leadership and the Division of Germany: Patriotism and Propaganda 1945–53* (Oxford, 2006), 247–8.

5   Jonathan Zatlin, *The Currency of Socialism: Money and Political Culture in East Germany* (Cambridge, 2007), 93.

6   One of the finest examples of this approach is Catherine Epstein, *The Last Revolutionaries: German Communists and Their Century* (Cambridge, MA, 2003).

The crux of Wenzke's paper is Soviet–East German relations during and after the 'Prague Spring.'[7] He shows that "the GDR, and especially its leader Walter Ulbricht, were without a doubt among those who politically and ideologically paved the way for the quelling of the 'Prague Spring.'" But he adds, "The basic decisions, however, were still taken in Moscow." Illustrative of this latter point is the fact that Leonid Brezhnev decided not to have East Germany join in the Warsaw Pact invasion of the ČSSR. This paper offers another perspective on the debate regarding the extent to which the satellite East Germany was able to have its Soviet master do its bidding. Hope Harrison has concluded that the East German "tail" wagged the Soviet "dog" during the Berlin crisis of 1958–1962 which led to the construction of the Berlin Wall,[8] opening up for historians the possibility that the smaller powers of the Soviet Bloc held more weight in the relationship than was previously thought. Even in this paper, we learn that Brezhnev was reacting to requests of high-ranking Czechoslovak opponents of Dubček to halt East Germany's impending invasion. Clearly, the Soviet Union engaged in a certain amount of diplomacy with its satellites. However, as Wenzke shows, the decisions were still made in Moscow, and it is difficult to imagine a scenario in which the Soviet Union could be *cornered* into a decision not of its choosing. In many ways, this paper demonstrates the limits of a satellite's room to maneuver, for Moscow prevented East Germany from participating in the invasion despite Ulbricht's pleading. It is in this context that the GDR's propaganda line that it had, in fact, taken part in the invasion, when we now know that it had not, is particularly striking. It was more important for the GDR to sacrifice its image abroad—given that only twelve countries recognized East Germany in 1968, it desperately sought international recognition—and to weather an internal storm, than to publicly admit to the humiliation of having been denied participation by Moscow. For Ulbricht, this snub must have been especially galling given his legendary egotism.

If Harrison's thesis holds for the Berlin Crisis of 1958 to 1962—and that debate is one to be had another day—we should be careful in seeing a general pattern whereby the East German tail wagged the Soviet dog at will. That

---

7 A useful introduction to the historiography of East Germany's foreign relations is Joachim Sholtyseck, *Die Aussenpolitik der DDR* (Munich, 2003).

8 Hope Harrison, *Driving the Soviets up the Wall: Soviet-East German Relations, 1953-1961* (Princeton, 2005).

was not the case in 1968, as this paper so clearly shows, nor was it the case in confronting Poland's "Solidarity" when East Germany urged Soviet military intervention, nor again in 1989, when East Germany found itself at odds with the Soviet leadership over the path of reform, and once more found the Soviet Union unwilling to adopt an alternative course.[9]

One of the most fascinating sections of this paper is the reaction in East Germany to the crushing of the 'Prague Spring.' Wenzke offers wonderful material on the protests that took place throughout the GDR and, perhaps even more eye-opening, on the opposition within the Socialist Unity Party and within the National People's Army (*Nationale Volksarmee*—NVA). Even a handful of high-ranking officers opposed the actions taken against a fellow Warsaw Pact member.

This information raises two issues. First, one might reasonably ask the extent to which this experience colored the East German leadership's views toward future deployment of the NVA, particularly in the fall of 1989. If the NVA showed signs of disloyalty in an action involving another country, the Party may have been legitimately concerned about the army's reliability against its own people. We know that the NVA was deployed to Leipzig in the fall of 1989 but was not employed against the crowds outside St. Nicholas Church. The accepted reason is that the emerging Party leadership under Egon Krenz had little desire to be an internationally isolated police state,[10] but another part of the explanation may well lie in the events of twenty-one years earlier.

Second, the individual nature of protest by East Germans following the invasion is striking. Although there were over two thousand of acts of protest, indeed, acts that exceeded those following the erection of the Berlin Wall, there was no *coordination* of this protest. In many of the current debates regarding the nature of the GDR, the term "totalitarian" has fallen out of favor, with terms such as "welfare dictatorship," "participatory dictatorship," and "consensual dictatorship" on the ascendance.[11] But the term "totalitarian" still serves a very useful function in explaining how society was "atomized."

---

9   See Peter Grieder, "'To Learn from the Soviet Union is to Learn How to Win,': The East German Revolution, 1989–90," in *Revolution and Resistance in Eastern Europe: Challenges to Communist Rule* ed. Kevin McDermott and Matthew Stibbe (Oxford and New York, 2006), 157–74.

10 See Hans-Hermann Hertle, "Der Mauerfall," in *Mauerbau und Mauerfall: Ursachen—Verlauf—Auswirkungen* ed. Hans-Hermann Hertle (Berlin, 2002).

11 The most recent work in this vein is Mary Fulbrook, *The People's State: East German Society from Hitler to Honecker* (New Haven, 2005).

Following the 'Prague Spring,' despite their numbers, opponents were not able to coordinate their protests, because of a refined secret police. Only at the very end of the regime, when the Party had lost its political will, rather than its ability to control society, were like-minded individuals able to come together in a semblance of organized opposition. However, if one looks at the growth of the Stasi (the secret police), the events of the 'Prague Spring' did not have a noticeable effect. The number of full-time workers for the Stasi increased by ten percent in 1969, but this was actually less than the eleven percent increase between 1967 and 1968. And the growth of the Stasi in 1970 and 1971 slowed even further.[12] It appears, then, that the Party believed it had any opposition emanating from the 'Prague Spring' well under control.

Wenzke's paper makes clear that 1968 was a Pyrrhic victory for hard-line communists in East Germany. They won the day but the price they paid was great—international condemnation (due, in large part, to the GDR's own propaganda about its phantom role in the invasion), the hastened demise of Walter Ulbricht, and mounting potential for resistance among East Germans.

---

12   Jens Gieseke, *Die hauptamtlichen Mitarbeiter der Staatssicherheit: Personalstruktur und Lebenswelt 1950–1989/90* (Berlin, 2000), 556–7.

11

Bulgarian Participation in Suppressing the 'Prague Spring' in August of 1968

Ivana Skálová

Bulgaria was never a significant player in world affairs or even within the former socialist order. However, Bulgaria did play a role in European history and also participated in suppressing the 'Prague Spring.' If its activities in the latter were overlooked, we would fall short of a full explanation of the Dubček era in Czechoslovakia. Even seemingly marginal elements can contribute to a complex evaluation of this period.

The Initial Reaction to the Poltical Changes in Czechoslovakia

What concrete role did the Bulgarian political leadership play in the events of the 'Prague Spring' of 1968? On March 6–7, 1968, a few weeks after the January meeting of the plenum of the Central Committee of the Communist Party of Czechoslovakia (CC CPCs), a meeting of the Political Advisory Committee of the Warsaw Pact took place in Sofia. During this meeting Todor Zhivkov, the First Secretary of the Bulgarian Communist Party, not only expressed feelings of great unease with the situation in Czechoslovakia during a private conversation with Soviet leader Leonid Brezhnev and Premier Alexei Kosygin but referred to the situation as "counter-revolutionary." According to Zhivkov, Czechoslovakia was a very politically and economically important country for the whole socialist camp, and its maintenance was essential for the entire socialist system. Therefore, it would be necessary to take a risk and "we must be prepared to use our armies as well."[1] Brezhnev's announcement at the plenum of the Central Committee of the Communist Party of the Soviet Union (CC CPSU) on March, 21, 1968, consequently said that "comrades Zhivkov, Gomułka, and Kádár turned to us in Sofia with a request to take certain steps in order to solve the problem in Czechoslovakia."[2] Bulgaria's minister of foreign affairs Petur Mladenov, at a meeting of the plenum of the Central Committee of the Bulgarian Communist Party (CC BCP), confirmed that Zhivkov was "the first among the leaders of our brotherly parties who labeled the situation as being counter-revolutionary and suggested the solution that today we consider to be the only possible and correct one."[3] It is, therefore, obvious that before the developing situation could be labeled a crisis, the Bulgarian leader was suggesting the most radical of all possible solutions. However, the first secretary was not the only one in the Bulgarian Party leadership who was convinced that greater attention should be paid to developments in Czechoslovakia.

Alarming reports also came from Prague. Stajko Nedelchev, the Bulgarian ambassador to the Czechoslovak Socialist Republic (ČSSR), considered the situation markedly confusing. According to him, members of the CC CPCs's Presidium, with Alexander Dubček at the head, were trying to create the impression that the situation was firmly under control and that all processes and changes were happening in accordance with the Party's tactics. However, he reported, many of these processes were of an "uncontrolled nature" and were often "antisocialist and anti-Soviet."[4] Discussions about the development of the political situation in Czechoslovakia took place in closed meetings of the top members of the Communist Party of Bulgaria (CPB) and had yet to reach the Bulgarian public.

---

1   Баева И., *България и Източна Европа* (София, 2001), 133 [I. Baeva, *Bulgaria and Eastern Europe* (Sofia, 2001), 133].

2   J. Baev, "Bulgaria and the Political Crises in Czechoslovakia (1968) and Poland (1980/81)," in *Cold War International History Project Bulletin*, 11/1998, 96.

3   M. Kramer, "The Prague Spring and the Soviet Invasion of Czechoslovakia," in *Cold War International History Project Bulletin*, 3/1993, 4.

4   Архив на Министерството на външните работи на Република България, Дипломатичен архив, a.e. 2988, стр. 51 (Archives of the Ministry of Foreign Affairs of the Republic of Bulgaria, Diplomacy Archives, inventory no. 2988, p. 51).

The Dresden Meeting and its Refelection Among the Bulgarian Political Elite

At the end of March the heads of six socialist countries, including Czechoslovakia, meet in Dresden to deal with the situation. Originally Bulgarian representatives were not supposed to attend; however, at the insistence of Todor Zhivkov, they were in the end invited.[5] Zhivkov himself could not attend because of an earlier planned state visit to Turkey. Instead, Stanko Todorov, a member of the Politburo and secretary of the CC CPB, led the Bulgarian delegation. In his relatively short speech, Todorov expressed agreement with the speeches of those who had preceded him, especially that of Leonid Brezhnev, but here, for the first time, he compared the situation in Czechoslovakia to the crisis in Bulgaria in 1956, which the Bulgarian leadership had managed to defuse, suggesting that the Bulgarians could offer words of advice to their Czech and Slovak comrades.[6] This opinion would later be repeated.

In contrast to this relatively moderate speech at the international plenum was the hostility aimed at a problem back home. Stanko Todorov reported on the Dresden meeting to a session of the plenum of the CC CPB on March 29, 1968. Among other things, he drew attention to the spontaneity of the processes underway in the ČSSR and directed most of his criticism at the mass media, which "was publishing articles aimed against the leading role of the Party, and coming forth with ideas about founding an opposition party and ideas about absolute freedom, etc." In his opinion, the events of the previous few days had proven the evaluations presented by leaders of various Communist Parties at the Dresden meeting as being absolutely correct.[7]

Other members of the CC CPB also appraised the situation as dangerous and counter-revolutionary; in their opinion the Czechoslovak leadership was no longer able to maintain control. One member of the CC CPB, Delcho Cholakov, stated: "We should not avoid any drastic measures, as were taken

---

5   Пихоя Р. Г., Чехословакия, 1968 год. Взгляд из Москвы. По документам ЦК КПСС, in: Новая и новейшая история, 6/1994, 15 [R.G. Pikhoia, "Czechoslovakia, 1968: The View from Moscow," in *New and Newest History*, 6/1994, 15].

6   J. Vondrová, J. Navrátil, a kol., *Mezinárodní souvislosti československé krize 1967–1970*, díl I, (Prague, 1995) document 24, p.104.

7   Централен държавен архив BR, ф. 1, оп. 58, а.е. 4, Протокол от заседанието на Пленума на ЦК БКП z 29. 3. 1968, str. 52 [Central State Archives of the Republic of Bulgaria, collection 1, volume 58, inventory number 4, Session Record of the Plenum of the Central Comittee of the BKP, March 29, 1968, p.52].

in Hungary, but only so that they do not write, and speak about it in the West. They will bark, but then be silent and we shall not lose Czechoslovakia. The truth is we will damage the international communist movement a little, but the damage will definitely be less."[8]

Todor Zhivkov spoke at the conclusion of the meeting, and his proclamation can be considered the standpoint of the Bulgarian political leadership from which other steps would follow. In his opening words Zhivkov declared: "If only we could not go to extremes, but you certainly understand that, if it is necessary, our armies will act. We must openly say that there is a pre-counter-revolutionary situation there. They have yet to have an armed rising, but where is our guarantee that there will not be a rising tomorrow?"[9] The meeting's conclusions and the Party line soon began to appear in the actions of the Bulgarian political leadership and government bodies and in the media.

Fears of a "spring infection" activated all units of the Party and government apparatus. In the name of prevention, private and official trips to Czechoslovakia were limited and scrutinized more closely.[10] Whereas Stanko Todorov mentioned that the Bulgarian "intelligentsia maintains a healthy ideological position and is united with our party and socialist establishment," others admitted that the intelligentsia was heading towards sympathizing with the opposition.

Therefore, measures were taken to coordinate methods of informing the public. The Bulgarian press agency and the daily newspaper *Rabotnichesko delo* were to work up all information for the media about the events in Czechoslovakia under the direct control of the Propaganda and Agitation Department and the Foreign Policy and International Relations Department of the CC CPB. Editors-in-chief of several media outlets already had received special instructions on the situation in Czechoslovakia immediately after the delegation returned from Dresden. The activities of the Czechoslovak embassy and Czechoslovak citizens in Bulgaria were more closely monitored.[11] A political campaign was also undertaken to label the situation in Czechoslovakia

---

8   Ibid.

9   Ibid.

10 Archiv Ministerstva zahraničních věcí ČR [Archives of the Ministry of Foreign Affairs of the Czech Republic, hereafter AMZV CR], Telegramy došlé, 1968, šifrovka č. 3140 z 28. 3. 1968.

11 Централен държавен архив BR, ф. 1, оп. 58, а.е. 4, стр. 56 [Central State Archives of the Republic of Bulgaria, collection 1, volume 58, inventory number 4, p. 56].

revisionist and dangerous.[12] Simultaneously considerations about possible military intervention in case the ČSSR separated itself from the socialist camp no longer remained behind the closed doors of the chief members of the Party apparatus. Jozef Chabada, the Czechoslovak *chargé d'affaires* in Hungary, in his dispatch of March 6, cited the official advice of Vasil Pangelov, Bulgarian political secretary in Budapest: "In an extreme situation, if it came to Czechoslovakia breaking away from the socialist camp, the countries of the socialist camp would supposedly not hesitate to use armed force against the ČSSR." Pangelov's statement was considered one of the first open expressions of this kind.[13] Subsequently, during April of 1968, mentioning the possible occupation of Czechoslovakia by Warsaw Pact troops was no longer unusual in diplomatic circles or in Party meetings.[14]

Little information on the reform process in the ČSSR made it to the public, even though there was marked interest in it, especially among the Bulgarian intelligentsia. Among them, only the most well-informed circles were expressing the opinion that Bulgaria also needed it own Dubček. In the Party halls, where the level of information was not much greater, many feared the bad influence of the 'Prague Spring' on Bulgarian society could bring extensive changes in the Party cadre. Czechoslovak diplomats were already confronted with hostile attitudes from the Soviet embassy in Bulgaria.[15] Reports that contact with the Czechoslovak embassy in Sofia could have unfortunate results for those involved led to canceling events at Czechoslovakia's cultural center.[16]

Outside the Bulgarian People's Republic (BPR), Bulgarian state security agents in Czechoslovakia were monitoring the situation. Opinions on the processes underway were collected from their colleagues as well as from the families of their unsuspecting friends and acquaintances and relayed back to headquarters in Sofia.[17] Bulgarian counter-intelligence, in cooperation with the Bulgarian embassy in Prague, also screened the opinions of Bulgarian

---

12   J. Vondrová, J. Navrátil, a kol., *Mezinárodní souvislosti československé krize 1967–1970*, díl I., dokument 31, pozn. 2, str. 127.

13   Ibid., 128.

14   Ibid., dokument 46, str. 155.

15   AMZV ČR, Telegramy došlé, 1968, šifrovka č. 3463, z 5. 4. 1968.

16   AMZV ČR, Telegramy došlé, 1968, šifrovka č. 3599 z 10. 4. 1968.

17   Ústav pro soudobé dějiny, Praha, sb. KV ČSFR, Z/BB, 1-10-449 [Institute of Contemporary History, Prague, col. KV CSFR, Z/BB, 1-10-449].

students in Czechoslovakia. Those who sympathized with the reform process were threatened with having to return home.[18] After the Czechoslovak government protested to the Bulgarian embassy, the agents had to limit their activities in the interest of an upcoming state visit in April of a Bulgarian delegation to Czechoslovakia. Fears arose that pressure on Bulgarian students could eventually result in student protests.

The April Czechoslovak-Bulgarian Meeting in Prague and Its Results

Both countries' delegations met in Prague at the end of April 1968 to sign a new Czechoslovak-Bulgarian Friendship, Cooperation and Mutual Aid Treaty. During the Bulgarian delegation's stay in Czechoslovakia, a special *Bulletin* was distributed among active Party members, which informed them of the dangerous process underway in Czechoslovakia and about the existence of four inter-Party groups.[19] The essence of the reform process was accurately described in the *Bulletin*, along with past mistakes, widespread rehabilitation, and cadre changes. In addition, the process of activating society, the development of new social organizations and clubs, the attempt to have political pluralism and calls for freedom of speech were described. However, the text's authors did not refrain from including their own commentary, alleging "petit-bourgeois" spontaneity, the weakening role of the Party, the workings of anti-socialist forces and the discrediting of Party cadres: "The former bourgeois organization Sokol is coming back to life;" "mysterious disappearances and suicides continue;" "attacks against socialism in the ČSSR now overlap with talk about some kind of 'new way' and of 'a wonderful experiment.'" The Czechoslovak media was attacked for "creating chaos, political nihilism and unleashing passion."[20]

Although Todor Zhivkov publicly voiced fears about further developments in Czechoslovakia after his return home, he again expressed faith in Dubček's leadership, which while corresponding with the official Soviet line was, of course, completely at odds with the internal evaluation of the situation by the Bulgarian Party leadership. At the same time, Zhivkov sent letters to the heads of the four "brotherly" Parties calling the situation in the ČSSR dangerous and

---

18 AMZV ČR, Telegramy došlé, 1968, šifrovka č. 3653 z 11. 4. 1968.
19 AMZV ČR, Teritoriální odbory – tajné (TO-T), Bulharsko 1965-69, 013/117, kt 3.
20 AMZV ČR, TO-T, Bulharsko 1965-69, 013/117, kt 3.

suggesting they meet immediately.[21] Having a group meeting appeared even more urgent after Drahomír Kolder, who represented the "healthy" forces in the CPCs, warned that, "without determined assistance from without, healthy forces will not be able to get the situation under control. Implementing some kind of measures, maneuvers or otherwise, will be unavoidable—however, we will not get by without the requested assistance."[22]

The Czechoslovak minister of foreign affairs Jiří Hájek confirmed in his recollections that Zhivkov acted as an observer during his visit to the ČSSR and did not have in mind expressing his opinion nor influencing the thinking of Czechoslovak politicians. The foreign minister, along with František Kriegel, the president of the National Front, escorted the Bulgarian delegation to Bratislava. "During the flight we attempted to converse with our guest, in order to discover his views on our developments. He remained reserved, however, and limited himself to obligatory courtesy, repeating dogmatic stereotypes about socialism, the leading role of the Party, the need for ideological vigilance and decisiveness." It was hardly likely that Zhivkov would change his mind, and it was even less likely following the assurances of these Czech politicians.

As the situation in Czechoslovakia grew ever more disconcerting to the political leadership of "brotherly" countries, it came up more often within various Communist Parties. Zhivkov's letter, which urgently recommended calling a meeting in order to deal with the situation, definitely contributed to the mounting tension. After the CC CPSU Politburo's meeting on May 6, 1968, when it was decided to conduct "warning" military exercises on Czechoslovak territory, convening the other four leaders of the Warsaw five was accelerated.[23] Zhivkov spoke about three political problems at the Moscow meeting: open counter-revolution, clandestine counter-revolution within the Central Committee itself, and healthy forces. Alexander Dubček was considered a separate problem. In Zhivkov's opinion, Dubček did not belong to any group but was just being pulled along by the stream of events; completely helpless, he did not have the situation under control.[24] Zhivkov focused mostly on the "second center," which he assumed was being led by František Kriegel:

---

21   J. Vondrová, J. Navrátil, a kol., *Mezinárodní souvislosti československé krize 1967-1970*, díl I., dokument 49, pozn. 3, str. 158.

22   K. Pacner, *Osudové okamžiky Československa* (Prague, 2001), 330.

23   A. Benčík, *Rekviem za Pražské jaro* (Třebíč, 1998) 43.

24   AMZV ČR, TO–T, Bulharsko 1965-69, 013/117, kt 3.

When we came to Prague we felt that we were in a place where this center was at work. Kriegel, whom I did not know, grabbed me by the arm, took me aside and started to work me over. The other Czechoslovak comrades, who had been assigned to our delegation, started to work over other members of our delegation. Based on this situation, we decided to stay together. One of the Bulgarian comrades, a member of our delegation, managed to make contact with a representative of this center. From him we received daily information about the itinerary of our delegation's stay and about how they were planning to manipulate us. This information was confirmed. . . I assume this previously mentioned center plans to court comrade Dubček, flatter him, tell him he is an innovator who is creating a new model of a socialist state. . . Therefore, there were some objective shortcomings in Czechoslovakia. But that is just one side of the coin. It is important to correctly appraise the situation which has arisen, and this situation is essentially counter-revolutionary. Although these forces against the people have yet to take up arms—and we know why—then if they could do to it tomorrow they would… We have experience and we take full responsibility for the fate of the revolution. It is necessary to help the healthy forces in Czechoslovakia; otherwise we will not have the situation under control. It is necessary to bring in troops. Another question is how to get them there. It would be best, if we could get them there under the auspices of military training. Further, it is crucial to organize a group within the Czechoslovak leadership with comrade Kolder or comrade Biľak at the head, a group that would be able to manage the situation and whom we could help. Comrade Dubček is incapable of this as he is completely clueless. I spoke with him for three hours and I could sense it. I am convinced that comrade Dubček cannot lead anyone and that he is egoistical and politically short-sighted. He cannot see what is going on around him, and cannot see how the enemy is working against the CPCs.[25]

---

25 J. Vondrová, J. Navrátil a kol., *Mezinárodní souvislosti československé krize 1967–1970*, díl I., dokument 55, str. 206.

The harshness of Zhivkov's condemnation was in complete accordance with the threatening tone of the meeting. Leonid Brezhnev and all the other participants save János Kádár severely criticized the developments in Czechoslovakia. They agreed that it was necessary to take decisive steps against the reformers in the CPCs through the support of "healthy forces" within the CPCs and with unplanned military exercises by Warsaw Pact troops in Czechoslovakia.[26] At the end of May preparations for these military exercises began under the codename "Šumava." When they actually took place between June 20 and 30, 1968, army units from countries neighboring the ČSSR participated in the exercises, but only observers were invited from Bulgaria.

Increased Politcal Activity in Connection with the Warsaw Meeting

In the first days of June the Bulgarian party leadership sent their Czechoslovak counterparts a letter expressing "the growing discontent of Bulgarian communists and our entire public, brought forth by the dangerous developments in the ČSSR recently."[27] One of five similar letters which the Czechoslovak comrades received from the Communist Parties of the Soviet Union, Poland, Hungary, the DDR, and Bulgaria was delivered to the Central Committee on July 5, 1968, by the economic advisor of the Bulgarian embassy.

This letter, just like the others, contained a decisive condemnation of the "Two Thousand Words" manifesto by the Czech writer Ludvík Vaculík on June 27, 1968, and criticism of the both the Party's and the government's inability to prevent such ideas from spreading. The Bulgarian letter further discussed media abuse by anti-socialist forces and the existence of a subversive right-wing center within the CPCs, but it was less pointed and detailed than the letters from the other Central Committees.

These letters were followed by a meeting of select representatives from the various countries of the Warsaw Pact held in Warsaw on July 14–15, 1968, where the only topic was the situation in Czechoslovakia. Todor Zhivkov stood behind the ideas of Władysław Gomułka (Poland) and Walter Ulbricht (DDR) and considered János Kádár's (Hungary) evaluation as incorrect, as did the other participants. In his speech Zhivkov briefly evaluated the situation in

---

26   A. Benčík, *Rekviem za Pražské jaro* (Třebíč, 1998), 47.
27   Národní archiv, Archiv Ústředního výboru KSČ, fond 02/1, sv. 75, a.j. 102 [National Archives, Archives of CC CPCs].

Czechoslovakia and offered just one suggestion to solve the problem. Whereas Brezhnev spoke about "completely different forces," Ulbricht discussed "the united effect of all brotherly parties," and Gomułka mentioned using "moral force," Zhivkov was more direct:

> Unfortunately all the possibilities comrade Kádár spoke about have already been exhausted… We can speak again with comrade Dubček or comrade Černík, but they do not make the decisions… We have just one recourse and that is to offer decisive assistance to the ČSSR… and to no longer depend on inner forces… Socialist countries and their Communist Parties must help Czechoslovakia, along with the Warsaw Pact, especially its armed forces.

He then laid out what he expected from the offered assistance:

> Above all the dictatorship of the proletariat must be reinstated as soon as possible… The Party Congress cannot take place in September, and it needs to be postponed to a later date… All counter-revolutionary and revisionist organizations must be disbanded in accordance with appropriate laws…

In regards to possible outcomes of this help, Zhivkov stated: "We realize that this will have completely negative effects, as well, that it will be taken advantage of in the international response… However, the positive results will definitely be greater, firmer and longer-lasting."[28] His speech was the sharpest at this meeting.

A joint letter written by all participants was addressed to their Czechoslovak comrades. Although Walter Ulbricht originally suggested that only representatives from countries bordering Czechoslovakia sign it, Todor Zhivkov signed it as well.[29] The Warsaw letter was delivered to Alexander Dubček the next day, July 16, 1968, by Soviet ambassador Chervonenko. After the events of the Warsaw meeting were reported to the CC BCP at a plenary meeting, also on July 16, 1968, a motion was passed unanimously supporting the efforts of the involved parties and their final verdict and criticizing the

---

28 J. Vondrová, J. Navrátil ,a kol., *Mezinárodní souvislosti československé krize 1967-1970*, díl I., dokument 92, str. 286.

29 Ibid., 285.

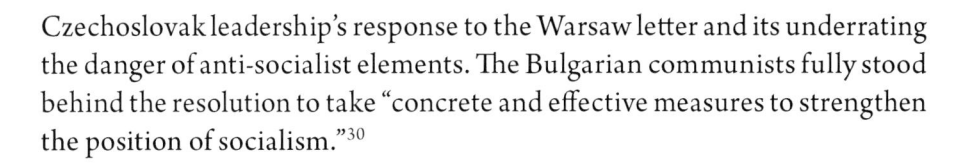

Czechoslovak leadership's response to the Warsaw letter and its underrating the danger of anti-socialist elements. The Bulgarian communists fully stood behind the resolution to take "concrete and effective measures to strengthen the position of socialism."[30]

August – the Solution to the Czechoslovak Question

Bulgarian politicians maintained their unwavering attitude toward the developments in Czechoslovakia during the period of feverish negotiations, when feelings of optimism were aroused in other observers. In the first days of August, in connection with the Czechoslovak-Soviet negotiations at Čierná nad Tisou, Todor Zhivkov reiterated his conviction that the developments in Czechoslovakia were irreversible and that the current leadership was no longer able to handle the situation. "Dubček, Černík and Smrkovský have given us no guarantee that they will turn the events around. They are nationalists and revisionists. They do not like the Soviet Union." He continued to hold to the idea that the only way to change the situation was to use all possible and essential measures if need be, including using the Warsaw Pact's armed forces.[31] Although he considered the meeting in Bratislava more of a tactical maneuver, which would not have any significant influence, he came to the Slovak capital on August 2 with the idea that the only possible solution was "to force them to capitulate. If they will not, then we will take more extreme measures."[32] At the Bratislava meeting comrades Stanko Todorov and Pencho Kubadinski seconded Zhivkov. It is obvious from the concluding remarks of the meeting, in which the Czechoslovak question was not directly mentioned, that all participating parties were agreed upon further strengthening socialist unity and on evaluating the international situation as well. It was emphasized that defending the attainment of socialist systems was the responsibility of all socialist countries. Thus the connection to the Warsaw Pact was increased.[33]

---

30   Централен държавен архив BR, ф. 1, оп. 58, а.е. 12 [Central State Archives of the Bulgarian Republic, collection 1, volume 58, inventory number 12].

31   J. Vondrová, J. Navrátil, a kol., Mezinárodní souvislosti československé krize 1967–1970, díl II., dokument 122, str. 150.

32   Ibid., 151.

33   Ibid., 151.

It was at this meeting that, according to historians, Zhivkov did not show himself in the best light:

> The Bulgarian leader Zhivkov tried to support Brezhnev's viewpoint from time to time… in reality his "help" further complicated the role of Leonid Brezhnev as he was willing to compromise on some points. Although he had good intentions, he did not understand that Brezhnev changed his tactics from time to time, and therefore unwaveringly supporting the original hard-line to Brezhnev's discontent. He ignored Zhivkov's input two or three times and then began to show with hand gestures that Zhivkov should not have been involved in the discussions.[34]

The results of the negotiations at Čierná nad Tisou and Bratislava could have given the false impression that conflict had been avoided. However, only fifteen days later the heads of the brother socialist states determined that the Czechoslovak Communist Party was not filling its promises and that the situation needed to be resolved.

On August 18 Leonid Brezhnev, Władysław Gomułka, Walter Ulbricht, János Kádár and Todor Zhivkov met again in Moscow in order to "crack the whip" over Czechoslovakia. This joint meeting followed a meeting of the Politburo and Secretariat of the CC CPSU, where a resolution was passed on August 17 on military intervention against "counter-revolutionary" forces in the ČSSR. Here Zhivkov limited himself to briefly expressing agreement with all of the proposals and assuring all the other attendees that these measures would meet with understanding from the Bulgarian Party base. At the same time, he thanked the Soviet leadership for having prepared this "courageous, decisive, international project."[35]

The Moscow meeting ended all diplomatic activity connected with the post-January developments in Czechoslovakia. Forces of the Warsaw Pact received the green light to suppress the attempts of the Czechs and Slovaks to democratize their country.

---

34 J. Valenta, *Sovětská intervence v Československu 1968* (Prague, 1991), 79.

35 J. Vondrová, J. Navrátil, a kol., *Mezinárodní souvislosti československé krize 1967–1970*, díl II., dokument 135, str. 202.

Preparations for the Military Suppression of the 'Prague Spring'

The main political administration of the Bulgarian People's Army (BPA) had started a propaganda campaign against the events in the ČSSR as early as May of 1968, when the leaders of the command staff of the BPA began to make more trips abroad. Direct military preparation of Bulgarian units had been underway since the beginning of July. Two Bulgarian regiments were to be included among the allied troops of the Warsaw Pact on orders of the Minister of National Defense—the 12th artillery regiment from the Elchovo garrison under the command of Colonel Alexendar Gencheva and the 22nd artillery regiment from the Charmanli garrison under the command of Colonel Ivan Chavdarov. However, the Bulgarian military did not take part in preparing or in leading the military action. As opposed to other participating armies, the Bulgarian army was completely under the leadership of the Soviet military. By the end of July preparations were made in Bulgaria under the supervision of Soviet officers, and then both regiments were transported to the Soviet Union.

The Charmanli regiment of 962 men was transported to the Kolomyja airport in the Ivano-Frankov oblast of the Ukrainian Soviet Socialist Republic by two Soviet aircraft. They camped there until the red alert was sounded on August 20.[36] The Elchovo regiment of 1206 soldiers was transported across the Black Sea on Soviet ships and stationed in the village of Zhnatino in the Mukachevski region of Ukraine near the Czechoslovak border. Both regiments were incorporated into the Soviet military under the command of General Pavlovsky.[37]

The results of a questionnaire taken by the 22nd regiment on August 1 provide an interesting look into the military situation. The answers to the question "What are you thinking about most often these days?" show why these young men thought they were in the Soviet Union: 43 percent were thinking about the upcoming "exercises;" 33 percent were thinking about the events and the situation in Czechoslovakia and about the meeting between the CPSU and the CPCs and its results; 12 percent considered themselves to be living

---

36 Централен военен архив BR, ф. 24, оп. Xa, a.e.21 [Central Military Archives of the Republic of Bulgaria, coll. 24, vol. Xa, n.i. 21].

37 *Bulharsko a československá krize 1968* (ÚSD, Prague, 1995), 14.

temporarily in the Soviet Union; 8 percent were thinking about the youth festival in Sofia; and 4 percent were thinking about personal problems such as university entrance exams and not being in touch with their parents.[38]

General preparation of the Bulgarian troops in the USSR was completed on August 20, by Decree No. 39 of the BPR's Council of Ministers: "The Bulgarian People's Republic and its armed forces will take part in offering help to the Czechoslovak people in their fight against counter-revolution alongside the USSR and the other countries of the Warsaw Pact."[39] Thirty-three top Bulgarian political figures signed this document. At the same time, battle orders were given to the regiments, signed by the defense minister General Dobri Dzhurov and the chief of staff Atanas Semerdzhiev. Battalion leaders had been informed of these aims and specific orders one day earlier, but company commanders were informed just several hours beforehand. Before that only the Chief of Staff, the regimental commanders, and the representatives for political questions had known the plans. For the sake of secrecy, exact maps and concrete orders were prohibited as well.[40]

The Participation of Bulgarian Artillery Regiments

The 12th artillery regiment started to move from Ukraine to Czechoslovakia on August 20. The entire convoy under the command of the operative group of the Sub-Carpathian military region crossed the Czechoslovak border on August 21 around 4 a.m. at the village of Maťovce. The gate at the border was not lifted; instead the first vehicle simply crashed through it. According to records from those who participated, the troops met with many difficulties along the way as Slovak citizens openly resisted. For example, the citizens of Košice took to the streets and began to shout at the troops and throw cobblestones, rocks and other objects at them. Several Bulgarian soldiers were injured, but most of the damage was inflicted on the convoy's technical equipment. Car windows and antennas were broken and gas tanks set on fire.[41] "They drew

---

38   Ústav pro soudobé dějiny, Praha, sb. KV ČSFR, Z/BB, mikrofiš č. 1 [Institute of Contemporary History, Prague, col. KV CSFR, Z/BB, microfiche no. 1].

39   ÚSD, sb. KV ČSFR, Z/BB, překlad Výnosu č. 39 z deníku Демокрация, 22. 6. 1992; Institute of Contemporary History, coll. KV CSFR, Z/BB (from the *Demokracia* newspaper, June 22, 1992).

40   ÚSD, sb. KV ČSFR, Z/BB, mikrofiš č. 5 a 6, str. 4.

41   ÚSD, sb. KV ČSFR, Z/BB, mikrofiše č. 5 a 6, str. 7.

five-pointed stars and swastikas on our hoods and doors," recalled one participant.[42] The convoy met with the most resistance in the city of Rožňava. The local inhabitants did not limit themselves to throwing rocks, but built barricades with buses, combine harvesters and cranes on the road. They also tried to block the soldiers from passing with their own bodies. Not even after the local Party official called for them to stop did the people leave. After shots rang out, two companies received orders to fire warning shots into the air. Unarmed Czechoslovak soldiers were imprisoned in their barracks and expressed their protest by banging spoons on aluminum trays.[43]

Upon arrival in the central Slovak town of Banská Bystrica in the afternoon of August 22, the soldiers already had 414 long kilometers behind them, which they had traveled over the course of 38 hours. Individual groups took over the barracks, police stations, radio stations, the post office and the office of the *Sme* newspaper. The battalion, led by Lieutenant Colonel Petkov, took control of the SNP Sliač (Tri Duby) airport near Zvolen, which was to be at the disposal of the Soviet air force. At the same time gasoline and kerosene sources were acquired for the troops in the surrounding area. The first phase of the military operation was completed on August 25, when Brezno and the local military garrison were occupied, and important institutions and administrative buildings came under the control of Bulgarian units. The second stage, or the "ideological battle," turned out to be much tougher. "The expectation that in the first few days our commanders and political workers would succeed in making contact with the locals was not met. It turned out that a large part of the nation was misinformed and enchanted by thoughts of 'liberalism,' 'freedom,' 'democracy,' and 'humane socialism'" reported one of the soldiers.[44]

On August 20 at 6 p.m. the 22nd artillery regiment, which formed a part of the 7th airborne division of the Soviet army, received orders to relocate to Czechoslovakia, and gain control of Ruzyně airport near Prague and Vodochody airport. That night the technical equipment was loaded, and on August 21 the Bulgarian contingent landed on Czechoslovak soil in two stages. The locations the Bulgarians had to control were already occupied by Soviet troops and were then handed over.

---

42   *Репортер* 7, 8. 8. 1991, ze vzpomínek Bogdana Chadžijského [*Reporter* magazine, August 8, 1991, from the memories of Bogdan Khadzhiyski].

43   Ibid.

44   ÚSD, sb. KV ČSFR, Z/BB, mikrofiše č. 5 a 6, str. 14.

From August 21 to September 11, Ruzyně airport was prepared for military defense. On-duty soldiers were entrenched,[45] and the other parts of the regiment were accommodated in tents on the fields around the airport.[46]

Bulgarian soldier guarding the Prague airport, August, 1968
Photo Credit: *Courtesy of Ivana Skálová*

One of the first tasks of the Bulgarian soldiers was to transport their fellow countrymen temporarily living in Czechoslovakia back to their home country. On the third day, all of them were gathered at the airport, where they then spent night, and the following day they were flown to Bulgaria. Other tasks included ensuring that the return of the Czechoslovak delegation from the Moscow negotiations went smoothly during landing and on the way to central Prague.

On September 11 the regiment left the airport and set up camp about two kilometers northeast of the airport, where they stayed until they left.[47] Both Bulgarian units met with expressions of contempt from the locals. "They told us the Czech nation would greet us as liberators and would shower us with

---

45   *Bulharsko a československá krize 1968*, 45.

46   *Homo Bohemicus*, 3/1994, p. 21.

47   Централен военен архив BR, ф. 24, оп. Xa, a.e.21 [Central Military Archives, coll. 24, vol. Xa, n.i. 21].

flowers. Nothing like that happened. They spat on us, shouted 'Occupiers, go home—this isn't your country,' and threw eggs and burning containers of gasoline at us."[48] These manifestations by Czechoslovak citizens where viewed as proof of counter-revolutionary elements by the occupying countries.

Afterwards, when the residents of the surrounding area became used to the presence of the occupying forces, the Bulgarian soldiers went into a relatively normal routine. This "calm" was interrupted by the disappearance of one of them: petty officer Nikolai Cekov Nikolov. He was not the victim of an act of military protest, but of a criminal act. Attempting to desert, he met three men who shot him while they were trying to take his gun away from him. According to available information, the Bulgarian troops did not kill any Czechoslovak citizens.

On September 13 the Minister of Foreign Affairs of the ČSSR sent a verbal message to the Bulgarian government that suggested expediting discussions about pulling Bulgarian troops out of Czechoslovakia.[49] However, this withdrawal was to be conditioned on the results of Czechoslovak-Soviet negotiations. On October 16 a bilateral treaty was signed concerning the conditions of the Soviet army's "temporary" stay in Czechoslovakia, as well as the troops from other countries. They were to leave Czechoslovakia within two months of the treaty's ratification.[50] On October 22 the Bulgarian troops in Czechoslovakia received orders to return home.

The soldiers of the 22nd artillery regiment started their return on October 23 in the first of two phases. They were transported by rail to the Soviet Union and then by ship from Odessa to Burgas.[51] Units stationed in Slovakia were also transported to the USSR by rail, traveling in cargo trains until they reached the border and were transferred to sleeper cars. In Odessa, barracks were even vacated for the Bulgarian soldiers. As veteran Isak Gosev said: "Over the Soviet border we were no longer occupying forces, but internationalist heroes." The return to Bulgaria took ten days.

---

48   *Bulharsko a československá krize 1968*, 7.

49   The governments of Hungary, East Germany, Poland and the Soviet Union received the same notes.

50   J. Vondrová, J. Navrátil, a kol., *Mezinárodní souvislosti československé krize 1967-1970*, díl III., dokument 202, str. 157.

51   Централен военен архив BR, ф. 24, оп. Xa, a.e.21 [Central Military Archives, coll. 24, vol. Xa, n.i. 21].

The journey from Burgas to Elchovo and Charmanli turned into ceremonies of triumph for returning heroes. At every stop, excited crowds showered them with flowers and gifts. These "heroes" received a special reward from the head of state; all troops who had applied to university were accepted automatically with the grade of excellent.[52]

Bulgarian officer decorating one of his soldiers who invaded Czechoslovakia, Elchovo, Bulgaria, November, 1968. *Photo Credit: Courtesy of Ivana Skálová*

The Reaction of Bulgarian Society

An organized dissident movement never really developed in Bulgaria, and the reaction to the August intervention was insignificant. Nevertheless, there were several demonstrations of disagreement with the regime over Bulgarian participation in the Czechoslovak occupation. Although condemnations were generally confided only among groups of friends, there were some open reactions as well. As a result, in the second half of 1968 dozens of people were expelled from the youth movement for introducing "enemy and anti-Soviet" propaganda against the suppression of the 'Prague Spring.' Assistant

---

52   *Homo Bohemicus*, 3/1994, p. 23.

Professor Christo Nestorov of the University of Sofia's history faculty was prohibited from teaching as punishment for condemning the intervention to a lecture hall full of students.[53]

This entire faculty was the center of opposition-minded individuals known as "little Czechoslovakia." Eduard Genov, Alexandar Dimitrov and Valentin Radev, three history students who made the most public display of criticism, came from this "hatchery," and each spent several years in jail for producing and distributing flyers critical of the August intervention.

The most comprehensive and famous display of disagreement with the violent suppression of the 'Prague Spring' and resulting "normalization" was the *Czech Cycle* by the author and playwright Georgi Markov. It was not, however, performed in Bulgaria, as Markov fled his country to Great Britain as a protest against the events of August. His essay "21.8.1968" was first broadcast by the BBC in 1970. Until he was killed in 1978 by the Bulgarian secret service, he wrote six essays in this cycle, which regularly returned to the tragic events of August.

Reflections on 1968 After the Political Changes of 1989

In 1989 the Bulgarian Parliament condemned the invasion of 1968, as did other segments of society.[54] In the 1990's the question of the Bulgarian army's participation in the August invasion of the ČSSR became a controversial topic, especially in the media. In the newspapers many participants shared their recollections and stories, while journalists and historians looked through previously closed archives in an attempt to determine the facts.

In addition, the ethical question of moral guilt and innocence received front-page coverage in the public discourse. Bojan Nichev, the former Bulgarian ambassador in Prague, stated:

> ...guilt does not fall on those who were young and who were sent there without knowing why... In regards to moral guilt—our intelligentsia has been living with it for 23 years. Georgi Markov attempted to redeem it through the microphones of the BBC and

---

53 Баева И., България и Източна Европа (София, 2001), 142 [I. Baeva, *Bulgaria and Eastern Europe* (Sofia, 2001), 142].

54 "Bulgarian Leadership Condemns 1968 Invasion of Czechoslovakia," Associated Press, December 2, 1989.

Deutsche Welle in his critical annual reports on the Czechoslovak tragedy of 1968. 23 years later we have a period of moral and political sensitivity, and political hygiene…[55]

Iskra Baeva, an assistant professor of history at the University of Sofia, does not quite agree with this view:

> A part of the Bulgarian intelligentsia was still thinking and acting according to its own thoughts… Therefore I can hardly agree with this thesis of complete compliance and agreement from the Bulgarians. I am against identifying the political leaders who had social concerns and emotions at that time, a time which we now consider to be the darkest era of totalitarianism. There have always been people who have expressed their opinion without regard to which way the wind was blowing.[56]

Information from the Czechoslovak embassy in Sofia confirms that many letters arrived expressing support and sympathy for the citizens of Czechoslovakia, and diplomats at the embassy heard many personal conversations in which the military intervention was condemned, even by Party functionaries.[57]

In conclusion, it must be stated that in 1968 Bulgarian society was completely paralyzed, and the people were prevented from expressing verbal resistance by the repressive political system. It can be said without irony, that the attitude of Bulgarian society was represented by the silent majority.

Conclusion

Contrary to the opinion of many historians that the developments in Czechoslovakia in 1968 did not at first have much influence on the political situation in Bulgaria and that the Bulgarian Party leadership at first did not get involved in international political activities, we must conclude that Todor Zhivkov opposed the reforms in Czechoslovakia from the start and favored taking the most drastic measures. His stance during the whole period was coherent, although he did not make it public and his opinions were never given much attention, creating a false impression of Zhivkov's moderation.

---

55 *Репортер 7*, 15. 8. 1991 [*Reporter 7* magazine, August 15, 1991].
56 *Bulharsko a československá krize 1968*, 16.
57 Ibid., 41.

Indeed, Zhivkov tried to use the prevailing opinion about Bulgarian political passivity in his own defense when he was arrested and sentenced for abusing authority at the beginning of the 1990's. For example, in his 1993 book *Срещу някои лъжи* (*Against Some Lies*) he wrote:

> Bulgaria did not participate in any preparations, political, ideological, pre-organizational, military, nor tactical preparations for inputs. I discovered their contents only when they were investigated. We agreed with a signature, just like everyone else, who took part in the negotiations. I think that no-one had the illusion that this agreement was more than a formality. The occasional disagreement or personal opinion would have resulted in real, long-term, and boundless isolation. Not for the leader who dared to express it, but for his country and people.[58]

A final question remains about the decision to take the lead in suggesting the elimination of Czechoslovak attempts at reform. Facts suggest it arose from a combination of circumstances and individuals.

Bulgaria was the only country involved that did not share a border with Czechoslovakia and faced no direct threat if the ČSSR were to remove itself from the Eastern Bloc, or if it were occupied by NATO forces (as was speculated). As we have seen, the Bulgarian leadership was not supposed to have been involved in this case, in spite of the professed unity of the Warsaw Pact. It was, therefore, evident that Bulgaria's active participation was a result of its free political will. Todor Zhivkov sought an influential supporter in Leonid Brezhnev, whose voice counted for two in case of a stalemate. One of the aims of the Bulgarian leader was to show the Soviet leader his conviction, and thus to assure further subsidies and military support at a time when the conflict line between the East and West had shifted away from the Balkans and into Central Europe, decreasing Bulgaria's significance to the Soviet Union.[59]

---

58 Живков Т., *Срещу някои лъжи*, София 1993, str. 17 [T. Zhivkov, *Against Some Lies* (Sofia, 1993), 17].

59 Баев Й., *Изграждане на военната структура на Организацията на Варшавския договор 1955–1969 г.*, in: *Военноисторически сборник*, 5/1997 [J. Baev, "The Building of the Military Structure of the Warsaw Treaty Organization 1955–1969," in: *Military-historical textbook*, 5/1997].

Another of the important factors in the decision to participate in the suppression of the 'Prague Spring' was Todor Zhivkov's personality. Unfulfilled ambition made him try to get into high politics, top-level negotiations and important decision-making, for his low prestige in the eyes of other statesmen and his position as a mere satrap of the Kremlin, spurred him to behave the way he did in order to maintain his significance. However, the lesser status of Bulgaria was underscored by the small Bulgarian contingent of troops and its lack of independence within the Warsaw Pact's command structure.

Last, but not least, fears that Bulgarian society would be infected by reformist thinking also influenced the Communist Party of Bulgaria, even though signs of opposition were nearly negligible.

The events I have covered took place forty years ago, and views on what happened have since changed. As to the principle of collective guilt, we can only agree with the words of witness Konstantin Uzunov: "Could Bulgarian soldiers, petty officers and officers have refused to follow orders? I repeat with complete responsibility for this statement: the epaulettes of the Bulgarian army are not stained with blood. Every army in every society fulfills the orders of the head of state." That current developments in both countries and their mutual relationship indicate that today this question is closed, does not take away the right and responsibility of historians to look for and present the facts openly, freely and objectively.

12

Bulgaria, the 'Prague Spring' and the Invasion of Czechoslovakia: A Commentary

Mark Kramer

My task in this brief commentary is somewhat complicated because I do not disagree with any major point in Ivana Skálová's paper. Her findings and argument are cogent and sensible. In my commentary, therefore, I will expand on some of the points she raises and offer my own perspective, which at times differs from hers.

I should note at the outset that the range of declassified documents now available concerning Bulgarian policy during the 'Prague Spring' and the Soviet-led invasion is immense—not only in Bulgaria itself but also in most of the other former Warsaw Pact countries. In addition to the huge group of records of the Bulgarian Communist Party (*Bulgarska Komunisticheska Partiya*, or BKP) at the Central State Archive (TsDA) in Sofia, vast quantities of materials pertaining to Bulgaria's role in the 1968 crisis are stored at the Archive of the Ministry of Foreign Affairs (AMVunR), the Central Military Archive (TsVA), and the Archive of the Ministry of Internal Affairs (AMVutR). Although working conditions at the ministerial archives are not always ideal, the records from 1968 are almost all accessible. Even researchers who are unable to spend much time in these archives can now avail themselves of a first-rate website, "*Sofiisko lyato, Prazhska prolet 1968*" (Sofia Summer, Prague Spring 1968), which was set up in 2008 at <http://1968bg.com> with financial support from the Open Society Institute in Sofia, the Trust for Civil Society in Central and Eastern Europe, and the Razum (Reason) Institute. The website features a large, well-organized collection of scanned images of formerly secret documents from all of the major archives. The materials are thoroughly indexed and are supplemented by exceptionally useful information resources. The military documents, including handwritten directives pertaining to the Bulgarian army's role in the August 1968 invasion of Czechoslovakia, are especially worthwhile and are a valuable supplement to a brief compilation of archival materials about this topic that was published by the Czech Republic's Institute of Contemporary History in 1995.[1]

The huge volume of recently declassified evidence has enabled numerous scholars to reassess Bulgaria's policy toward the 'Prague Spring.' Skálová herself produced a very useful, short monograph on this topic in 2005, which is the basis for her paper here.[2] Several Bulgarian scholars have also been publishing insightful analyses in recent years. Vladimir Migev's book, published in 2005, is based on exhaustive research in the TsDA and the State Archive (though not in other Bulgarian or foreign archives) and provides the most comprehensive assessment currently available.[3] His discussion of Bulgarian officials' determination "not to let something similar to the Czech events happen in Bulgaria" (*da ne dopusnem v Bulgariya cheshkite subitiya!*) is particularly intriguing. Perceptive, though much briefer, analyses of Bulgaria's policy toward the 'Prague Spring' have been published by Iskra Baeva and Jordan Baev, both of whom place this issue into the larger context of Bulgaria's relations with the Warsaw Pact countries.[4]

Reassessing Bulgarian Policy

Western scholars had long known that the leaders of Poland and East Germany, Władysław Gomułka and Walter Ulbricht, were vehemently opposed to the 'Prague Spring' from the outset and were among the earliest proponents of military intervention. But, until recently, it was not as clear when Bulgarian leader Todor Zhivkov began expressing similar concerns. Until the early 1990's, most Western analysts surmised that Zhivkov did not clearly join ranks with

---

1   Antonín Benčik et al., eds., *Bulharsko a československá krize, 1968* (Prague, 1995).
2   Ivana Skálová, *Podíl Bulharska na potlačení Pražského jara 1968* (Prague, 2005).
3   Vladimir Migev, *Prazhkata prolet '68 i Bulgariya* (Sofia, 2005).
4   Iskra Baeva, *Bulgariya i Iztochna Evropa* (Sofia, 2001), 131–43; and Jordan Baev, *Voennopoliticheskite konflikti sled Vtorata Svetovna Voina i Bulgariya* (Sofia, 1995), 192–210.

Ulbricht and Gomułka until the Warsaw Meeting in mid-July 1968, which brought together leaders from the USSR, Poland, East Germany, Hungary, and Bulgaria. One of the interpreters at the meeting, Erwin Weit, who later defected to the West, recalled in his memoir published in 1973 that Zhivkov had declared at the meeting that the Warsaw Pact countries must do everything possible to forestall the victory of "counter-revolution" in Czechoslovakia, if necessary by providing direct "military assistance" to the "forces of socialism."[5] For lack of evidence to the contrary, Western scholars had long assumed that until Zhivkov felt the need to issue this stern warning in July 1968, he had "adopted a wait-and-see attitude on the question of military intervention."[6]

Not until the early 1990's, after the collapse of the Soviet bloc, was it possible to check whether Zhivkov really had displayed "belated antagonism" toward the Prague Spring, as H. Gordon Skilling had suggested in his landmark book.[7] Initially, two mutually contradictory interpretations of Bulgaria's position emerged. One implied that Zhivkov's "antagonism" in 1968 was uncompromising from the very start, whereas the other suggested that Zhivkov harbored no "antagonism" at all. The former interpretation was actually enunciated in the early 1970's, but it did not come to light until late 1990, when the transcript of a July 1973 plenum of the BKP Central Committee was declassified. At the plenum the Bulgarian foreign minister, Petur Mladenov, lauded Zhivkov for having been "the first among leaders of the fraternal parties to define the situation [in Czechoslovakia in 1968] as an open counter-revolution and to recommend the measures that all of us now assess as having been the only possible and correct ones."[8] Mladenov's statement would mean that Zhivkov embraced the extreme, hard-line stance of Gomułka and Ulbricht much earlier than Western scholars had assumed.

---

5   Erwin Weit, *Eyewitness: The Autobiography of Gomulka's Interpreter* (London, 1973), 216. The declassified transcript, which I will cite below, fully bears out Weit's recollection.

6   Karen Dawisha, *The Kremlin and the Prague Spring* (Berkeley, 1984), 101. For similar interpretations, see H. Gordon Skilling, *Czechoslovakia's Interrupted Revolution* (Princeton, 1976), 695–8; Jiří Valenta, *Soviet Intervention in Czechoslovakia, 1968: The Anatomy of a Decision*, rev. ed. (Baltimore, 1991), 176; and Fritz Ermarth, *Internationalism, Security, and Legitimacy: The Challenge to Soviet Interests in East Europe, 1964–1968*, RM-5909-PR (Santa Monica, CA, 1969), 81.

7   This is the title of the section on Bulgaria in Skilling, *Czechoslovakia's Interrupted Revolution*, 695–8.

8   "Stenogramata na proslovutiya plenum na TsK na BKP, proveden na 17, 18 i 19 yuli 1973 g.," Stenographic Transcript (Top Secret), July 1973, in Tsentralen Durzhaven Arkhiv (TsDA), Fond (F.) 58, Arkhivna edinitsa (A.e.) 81, Listy (Ll.), 127–8.

The other new explanation of Zhivkov's position came, not surprisingly, from Zhivkov himself. In an interview with several Western newspapers in late 1990, he argued that he had supported the reforms in Czechoslovakia in 1968 and had been extremely reluctant to go along with the "totally unjustified" invasion. Zhivkov insisted that the only reason he ordered the Bulgarian army to take part was that Moscow had threatened to impose economic sanctions otherwise.[9] Throughout the interview, Zhivkov stressed that he, unlike Gomułka and Ulbricht, was never ideologically opposed to the 'Prague Spring.'

Attempts to sort out these three conflicting interpretations—"belated antagonism" versus "early antagonism" versus "no antagonism"—would have been futile before the demise of the Soviet bloc, but the vast amount of declassified evidence that has come to light since 1989 about Zhivkov's role shows that Mladenov was correct. Zhivkov's effort in 1990 (and in his memoirs published in 1997) to rewrite his own role can be dismissed out of hand.[10] The evidence, both in the public record and in recently declassified materials, confirms that Zhivkov displayed profound "antagonism" toward the 'Prague Spring,' and that he did so much earlier than most Western analysts had thought. Indeed, he was the first East-bloc leader to speak openly in favor of military intervention to crush the 'Prague Spring' and ardently supported the invasion in August 1968. In addition, he urged the USSR to impose a harsher occupation regime.

Mladenov's contention that Zhivkov led the way in denouncing the 'Prague Spring' and in calling for military intervention in Czechoslovakia is vindicated by evidence, not only from Bulgaria, but also from other former East-bloc countries. Declassified documents in the former Soviet archives, for example, reveal that Bulgarian leaders reacted "with great anxiety and apprehension" to the removal of Antonín Novotný as the long-time First Secretary of the Communist Party of Czechoslovakia (*Komunistická strana Československa*, hereinafter CPCs), and to the election of Alexander Dubček as his replacement at a CPCs Central Committee plenum in early January

---

9   Chuck Sudetic, "Bulgarian Communist Stalwart Says He'd Do It Differently," *The New York Times*, 28 November 1990, p. A-8.

10 For the relevant portion in Zhivkov's memoirs, see Todor Zhivkov, *Memoari* (Sofia, 1997), 497–500.

1968.[11] Bulgaria was the only Warsaw Pact country in which the newspapers did not feature a lengthy biography and portrait of Dubček supplied by the Czechoslovak Press Agency (ČTK). The only fleeting mention made of Dubček's election in the Bulgarian press was in a brief ČTK news release about the CPCs Central Committee plenum and in some cursory biographical data prepared by the Bulgarian News Agency as an alternative to the full-length ČTK biographical sketch. Furthermore, the congratulatory telegram from the BKP to Dubček was perfunctory and contrary to normal procedures, was not directly addressed to anyone and was not signed by Zhivkov. The coolness of Bulgaria's response to Dubček's election was conspicuous enough that it even drew a protest from Soviet diplomats in Sofia, who called the Bulgarian actions "hasty and basically improper" and urged the Bulgarian authorities "to treat the election [of Dubček] in the same way we have treated changes of leadership in other fraternal parties."[12]

The unease felt by Zhivkov and other Bulgarian officials about Dubček's election was apparently attributable, not only to early forebodings of drastic policy changes to come in Czechoslovakia, but also to the manner in which Novotný was replaced. Normally, such a step would have been "recommended" by the CPCs Presidium and then obediently ratified by the CPCs Central Committee, but in late 1967 and early 1968 the CPCs Presidium was deadlocked. Consequently, Novotný's fate was determined by a vote of the full CPCs Central Committee, which only gradually achieved a consensus in favor of Dubček. For understandable reasons, this unusual way of ousting the long-time CPCs First Secretary was disconcerting for Zhivkov, who had come to power at around the same time that Novotný did in the early 1950's. Although Zhivkov apparently had genuine concerns about Dubček's "bourgeois nationalism" (a charge leveled by Novotný), the even more important motivation behind Bulgaria's less-than-friendly response to the change in the CPCs in early 1968 was undoubtedly Zhivkov's fear that a similar change could occur in Bulgaria.

---

11   "Zapis' besedy s pervym zamestitelem Ministra inostrannykh del NR Bolgarii tov. Gero Grozevym," Cable No. 40 (Secret), 11 January 1968, from N. V. Maslennikov, counselor at the Soviet embassy in Bulgaria, in Rossiiskii Gosudarstvennyi Arkhiv Noveishei Istorii (RGANI) in Moscow, F. 5, Opis' (Op.) 60, Delo (D.) 279, Ll. 2–3.

12   Ibid., L. 3.

In public, Bulgarian officials were relatively restrained in their comments about events in Czechoslovakia during the first few months of 1968, but in private they began at an early stage to express deep hostility toward the CPCs reformers.[13] As early as 6–7 March 1968, in a private conversation with the General Secretary of the Communist Party of the Soviet Union (CPSU), Leonid Brezhnev, who was in Sofia for a session of the Warsaw Pact's Political Consultative Committee, Zhivkov insisted that a "counter-revolutionary" situation had emerged in Czechoslovakia and that the Soviet Union and its allies "must be ready to use our armies" to put an end to the incipient 'Prague Spring.'[14] Zhivkov was thus the first East-bloc leader to suggest that the use of military force against Czechoslovakia might eventually be necessary.

Zhivkov's "antagonism" toward the 'Prague Spring' is also evident in many other declassified documents from the former Soviet and East European archives. Cables from Soviet diplomats in Bulgaria to Moscow left no doubt that senior BKP and Bulgarian Foreign Ministry officials were increasingly alarmed about events in Czechoslovakia.[15] The once-secret transcripts and

---

13 For public commentaries, see, for example, "Zashchitata na sotsializma v Chekhoslovakiya e nashe obshcho delo: Da bude razgromena kontrarevolyutsiyata!," *Rabotnichesko delo* (Sofia), 18 July 1968, p. 1. The first major attacks in the Bulgarian press appeared about two weeks earlier; see, for example, Dimcho Sokolov, "'Dve khilyadi dumi' ili prizyv kum kontrarevolyutsiya?" *Rabotnichesko delo* (Sofia), 4 July 1968, p. 6.

14 Baeva, *Bulgariya i Iztochna Evropa*, 133.

15 See, for example, "Zapis' besedy s zam. ministra inostrannykh del NR Bolgarii tov. I. Popovym," Cable No. 214 (Top Secret) from N. V. Maslennikov, counselor at Soviet embassy in Bulgaria, 1 April 1968, in RGANI, F. 5, Op. 60, D. 278, Ll. 23-25; "Zapis' besedy s ministrom inostrannykh del NP Bolgarii tov. Ivanom Bazhevym," Cable No. 274 (Top Secret) from A. M. Puzanov, Soviet ambassador in Bulgaria, 8 May 1968, in RGANI, F. 5, Op. 60, D. 278, Ll. 97-100; "Zapis' besedy s pervym zamestitelem ministra inostrannykh del NRB tov. G. Grozevym i zamestitelem ministra inostrannykh del NRB tov. I. Popovym," Cable No. 263 (Secret) from A. M. Puzanov, Soviet ambassador in Bulgaria, 4 April 1968, in RGANI, F. 5, Op. 60, D. 278, Ll. 26-29; "Zapis' besedy s ministrom svyazi NR Bolgarii tov. S. Tonchevym," Cable No. 254 (Top Secret), from N. V. Maslennikov, counselor at Soviet embassy in Bulgaria, 12 April 1968, in RGANI, F. 5, Op. 60. D. 279, Ll. 7–11; and "Zapis' besedy s ministrom inostrannykh del NR Bolgarii tov. Ivanom Bashevym," Cable No. 118 (Top Secret) from A. M. Puzanov, Soviet ambassador in Bulgaria, 16 February 1968, in RGANI, F. 5, Op. 60, D. 278, Ll. 4–6. See also the recent memoir by a former agent of the Bulgarian security forces who was stationed in Prague in 1968, Vladimir Kostov, *The Bulgarian Umbrella: The Soviet Direction and Operations of the Bulgarian Secret Service in Europe*, trans. Ben Reynolds (New York, 1988), 124–6.

summaries of the multilateral East-bloc conferences at Dresden and Moscow in the spring of 1968 indicate that Bulgaria took just as harsh a stance as East Germany and Poland in opposing the Czechoslovak reforms. Zhivkov could not attend the Dresden conference in late March 1968 because of a scheduling conflict, but when the Hungarian leader János Kádár proposed that only the countries bordering Czechoslovakia be represented in Dresden, Zhivkov made sure that three other high-ranking Bulgarian officials—Stanko Todorov, Zhivko Zhivkov (no relation to Todor), and Apostol Pashev—would attend in his place to convey his views.[16] The Bulgarian delegates at the Dresden conference joined their Polish and East German counterparts in depicting the events in Czechoslovakia as outright "counter-revolution." Much the same was true of the conference in Moscow in early May, when Todor Zhivkov eagerly joined Ulbricht and Gomułka in denouncing the "counter-revolution" in Czechoslovakia and demanding that immediate action be taken.[17]

In subsequent weeks, Zhivkov continued to push a hard line on Czechoslovakia, mostly behind the scenes. In late May 1968, two weeks after the conference in Moscow, he transmitted a secret "Report Concerning the Situation in Czechoslovakia" and an "information bulletin" on the same topic to the Soviet ambassador in Sofia, Aleksandr Puzanov.[18] The report and the bulletin were prepared by the Bulgarian Ministry of Defense and the Bulgarian State Security (*Durzhaven Sigurnost*) apparatus, respectively, and both items received Zhivkov's official endorsement. The two documents expressed strong opposition to the reforms in Czechoslovakia, often in crudely anti-Semitic terms, and they adverted several times to the desirability of military intervention. To be sure, except for the anti-Semitic remarks, the tone of the two reports was not quite as hysterical as some of the statements that Ulbricht and Gomułka

---

16   "Protokol der Treffen der Ersten Sekretäre der kommunistischen Parteien Bulgariens, der ČSSR, der DDR, Polens, der Sowjetunion und Ungarns," Verbatim Transcript (Top Secret), 23 March 1968, in Stiftung Archiv der Parteien und Massenorganisationen der DDR im Bundesarchiv (SAPMO), Zentrales Parteiarchiv der SED (ZPA), IV 2/201/778.

17   "Zapis' besedy v TsK KPSS s rukovoditelyami bratskikh partii Bolgarii, Vengrii, Germanii, Pol'shi," Verbatim Transcript (Top Secret), 8 May 1968, in Ústav pro Soudobé Dějiny, Sbírka Komise vlády ČSFR pro analyzu událostí let 1967-1970 (ÚSD-SK), Z/S 3, Ll. 151–171.

18   Text reproduced in "Shel avgust 68-go . . .: Dokumenty predany glasnosti," *Pravda* (Moscow), 18 February 1991, pp. 6–7.

had been making. Among other things, Bulgarian officials still expressed confidence that "healthy forces" (i.e., orthodox, pro-Soviet communists) could prevail in Czechoslovakia. Moreover, unlike the strident criticisms voiced by East German and Polish leaders in the mass media, neither of the Bulgarian documents was intended for public consumption. Nevertheless, anyone in Moscow who read the materials from Sofia would have had little doubt that Zhivkov was profoundly hostile to the 'Prague Spring.'

At the Warsaw Meeting in mid-July, Zhivkov went beyond any of the other leaders in openly calling for joint military intervention to "restore the dictatorship of the proletariat" in Czechoslovakia:

> There is only one appropriate way out—through resolute assistance to Czechoslovakia from our parties and the states of the Warsaw Pact. At present, we cannot rely on internal forces in Czechoslovakia. ... Only by relying on the armed forces of the Warsaw Pact can we change the situation.[19]

The transcript amply bears out Erwin Weit's account in his memoir. Zhivkov's appeal was not yet endorsed by the Soviet delegates, but his uncompromising stance was a sign of where things were headed. During a break in the conference, in an informal conversation with Petro Shelest, a member of the CPSU Politburo who favored military intervention in Czechoslovakia, Zhivkov expressed hope that the USSR would act "more decisively" in forcing an end to the 'Prague Spring,' adding: "The sooner troops are sent, the better."[20]

In short, the declassified evidence makes clear that Zhivkov staked out a firm position from the outset, well before he knew where the prevailing sentiment in Moscow would end up. Zhivkov's early stance in favor of military intervention took on a peculiar anti-Semitic twist, perhaps influenced in part by the anti-Semitic campaign under way in Poland at the time. The evidence that has come to light overwhelmingly refutes the claim Zhivkov made in his interview in 1990 about his supposed aversion to using military force in

---

19 "Protokół ze spotkania przywódców partii i rządów krajów socjalistycznych -- Bułgarii, NRD, Polski, Węgier i ZSRR – w Warszawie, 14–15 lipca 1968 r.," Copy No. 5 (Top Secret), 14–15 July 1968, in AAN, Arch. KC PZPR, P. 193, T. 24, Dok. 4, Strona 29.

20 Entry in Shelest's diary, 15 July 1968, "Dnevniki P. E. Shelesta," in Rossiiskii Gosudarstvennyi Arkhiv Sotsial'no-Politicheskoi Istorii, F. 666, Tetrad' 4, Ll. 38–39.

August 1968. His attempt to portray Bulgaria as a reluctant participant in the invasion cannot be taken seriously. The Bulgarian leader's real attitude at the time can be gauged from a secret message he transmitted to the CPSU Politburo in early August 1968, just before the Bratislava meeting:

> Despite the results of the bilateral negotiations at Čierna nad Tisou [which had just concluded], the situation in Czechoslovakia and the entire history and development of events give no reason to believe that the current leadership of the Czechoslovak Communist Party will be able to change things for the better.... To improve the situation in Czechoslovakia and save the Communist Party and socialist achievements, we must use all possible and necessary means, including the Warsaw Pact's armed forces.... If we do not manage to turn events around, it will be a catastrophe—a blow against the Soviet Union, against our socialist countries, against the international communist movement, and against the development of our socialist countries.... The Warsaw Pact forces will be severely weakened, and that will be a grave threat to the GDR, Hungary, and Poland.... Our opinion [in Bulgaria] is: Force the Czechoslovak leadership to capitulate. If they don't give in, then take other extreme measures.[21]

Moreover, when the leaders of the five countries that sent troops into Czechoslovakia gathered in Moscow a few days after the August 1968 invasion to discuss what to do next, Zhivkov expressed disappointment that the occupation forces were not cracking down more vigorously. He called for "the imposition of a military dictatorship in Czechoslovakia" and urged Soviet leaders to embark on a wave of violent repression against the "rightists and counter-revolutionaries" who led the 'Prague Spring.'[22]

Zhivkov remained in power in Bulgaria for another twenty-one years after the August 1968 invasion. His ouster in November 1989 came amid far-reaching political upheavals throughout the Soviet bloc that led to critical

---

21   Zhivkov quoted in top-secret cable from A.M. Puzanov, Soviet ambassador to Bulgaria, to CPSU Secretariat, 1 August 1968, Arkhiv vneshnei politiki Rossiiskoi Federatsii, F. 059, Op. 58, P. 124, D. 573, Ll. 95–96.

22   "Záznam ze schůzek Varšavské pětky v Moskvě ve dnech 24.-27.8.1968," Verbatim Transcript (Top Secret), 24–27 August 1968, in ÚSD-SK, Z/M 21, L. 3.

reassessments of past actions. In early December 1989, just a few weeks after Zhivkov was removed from office, the new leaders in Bulgaria joined the Soviet, Hungarian, Polish, and East German governments in formally condemning the 1968 invasion of Czechoslovakia and in apologizing to "the peoples of Czechoslovakia" for this "act of crude interference in the internal affairs of a sovereign state."[23] That statement put a crimp on Zhivkov's subsequent efforts to rewrite history and aptly summed up Bulgaria's role in 1968.

---

23 "Zayavlenie rukovoditelei Bolgarii, Vengrii, GDR, Pol'shi, i Sovetskogo Soyuza," *Izvestiya* (Moscow), 5 December 1989, p. 2.

13

The 'Prague Spring,' Hungary and the Warsaw Pact Invasion

Csaba Békés

The leadership of most Warsaw Pact countries viewed with reservations and suspicion the unexpected changes in the leadership of the Czechoslovak Communist Party in January of 1968. Hungarian leaders, however, welcomed and supported the reforms in Prague from the outset, as they hoped that the changes would would provide Hungary favorable conditions for introduction of the "new economic mechanism"—the most radical economic reform in the Soviet Bloc—in January of 1968. They believed that Hungary and Czechoslovakia, the two leading reformist countries, would be able to support each other and serve as examples to the other countries of the Warsaw Pact.

The new leadership of the Communist Party of Czechoslovakia (CPCs) also looked upon the Hungarian Socialist Workers Party (HSWP) as a natural ally. De-Stalinization, which had been carried out successfully in Hungary in the early 1960s, and the reformist elan of the leadership, made the Hungarian Party a potential ally of the Prague reformers and one they looked to for support of their policies. On this basis, a virtual alliance between the two leaderships emerged from January of 1968: Alexander Dubček was hoping to get both permanent support for his policies and help in "selling"" the Czechoslovak reforms to Moscow and the other Soviet Bloc countries, while János Kádár did his best to foster the de-Stalinization process and steer developments in Prague in the right direction. Nevertheless, from his experience in

1956, Kádár knew only too well the limits of Soviet tolerance and repeatedly attempted to persuade the Czechoslovak leaders to be cautious, to slow down the pace of reform, to acknowledge realities and not to challenge the Soviets. At the same time, he worked hard up to the middle of July, and even after that, to try to convince the Kremlin and the other Soviet Bloc leaders to be more understanding and patient, since the cause of socialism was not yet critically endangered in Czechoslovakia.

Thus, between January and August of 1968, Kádár played an important mediating role between Prague and Moscow as well as the other Soviet Bloc states. This role stemmed from his own convictions but it was also an assignment from Brezhnev, who saw from the outset that the only leader in the camp who could successfully influence Dubček was Kádár. Between January and August of 1968, Kádár met Dubček on nine occasions: five times bilaterally (three times secretly) and four times at multilateral meetings.[1] The bilateral talks were held in: Topol'čianky, January 20–21; Komárno, February 4; Budapest, June, 13–15; Komárom, July 13; and Komárno, August 17. The two leaders also met at the following multilateral meetings: celebrations of the twentieth anniversary of the Communist takeover in Czechoslovakia, Prague, February 22–24; the meeting of the Warsaw Pact Political Consultative Committee, Sofia, March, 6–7; the meeting of the "Six" (the WP members without Romania), Dresden, March 23; the meeting of the "Six," Bratislava, August 3.

Initial Hungarian Reactions to the Prague Spring

Alexander Dubček, who was elected First Secretary of the Czechoslovak Communist Party in January 1968, held his first negotiations with János Kádár, leader of the Hungarian Socialist Workers' Party. Having received an official invitation to Moscow on January 10, Dubček confidentially asked Kádár for a secret meeting before his trip to Moscow.[2] The meeting, which also included

---

1   Kádár közvetítő szerepéről bővebben lásd Békés Csaba: Kádár János és a prágai tavasz. [János Kádár and the Prague Spring], Beszélő, 2008, 7-8, 97-115. For a German-language version of the same article, see Csaba Békés, "Ungarn zwischen Prag und Moskau," in Stefan Karner, Natalja Tomilina, Alexander Tschubarjan, Günter Bischof, Viktor Iščenko, Michail Prozumenščikov, Peter Ruggenthaler, Oldřich Tůma, Manfred Wilke (Hg.), Prager Frühling. Das internationale Kriesenjahr 1968. Beitrage (Köln Weimar Wien, 2008), 481–500. For a previous work on this topic, see Tibor Huszár, 1968. Prága, Budapest, Moszkva. Kádár János és a csehszlovákiai intervenció [1968. Prague, Budapest, Moscow. János Kádár and the Intervention of Czechoslovakia.] (Budapest,1998).

2   Magyar Országos Levéltár [Hungarian National Archives] (henceforth MOL), M-KS-288, F. 5/444. ő. e., Minutes of the meeting of the HSWP Politburo, January 23, 1968.

a hunting expedition, took place on January 20–21, 1968, in Palárikovo and Topoľčianky in Slovakia. The two leaders had known each other for a long time, creating an amicable atmosphere. Dubček gave Kádár a detailed report on the causes of the Czechoslovak crisis and put the mistakes that had been made since the 1950's in a historical retrospective.[3] He also spoke about the circumstances of Novotný's removal and his own election. Kádár openly admitted that Brezhnev and he had felt in December that Novotný should have been removed at a later date. Kádár advised restoring unity in the Party leadership and tackling the problems methodically, calmly and patiently.

Kádár also mentioned that he deemed secret meetings inadvisable. It was agreed that the Czechoslovak leaders were to come to Budapest in late March or early April on a friendly visit, which would also be reported in the press. In retrospect, Kádár called the meeting "an open, straightforward private conversation," and Dubček a "sane, sober-minded communist motivated by a sense of responsibility and also struggling with problems."[4]

The next meeting between Dubček and Kádár took place before March as developments picked up momentum, not only in Prague and Moscow, but also in East Berlin and Warsaw, where leaders were becoming increasingly alarmed about the situation in Prague.[5] The Czechoslovak leader's trip to Moscow took place earlier than originally planned, at the end of January. A meeting with Gomułka was arranged for February 10[6] and an invitation to the GDR had also arrived. It became important for Dubček, once he had put his introductory visit to Moscow behind him, to schedule the first official negotiations with one of the countries of the Soviet Bloc. He chose Hungary, which was considered a close ally, a fact that Dubček openly mentioned in his January 27 letter of invitation to Kádár.[7]

---

3   For overviews of the history of the 'Prague Spring,' see H. Gordon Skilling, *Czechoslovakia's Interrupted Revolution* (Princeton 1976); Karen Dawisha, *The Kremlin and the Prague Spring* (Berkeley 1984); Jaromír Navrátil et al., eds., *The Prague Spring 1968* (Budapest, 1998); Kieran Williams, *The Prague Spring and its Aftermath: Czechoslovak Politics 1968–1970* (Cambridge, 1997); Karner et al., op.cit.

4   MOL, M-KS-288 F. 47/743. ő. e.

5   For details, see the articles by Manfred Wilke, "Die DDR in der Interventionskoalition gegen den 'Sozialismus mit menschlichem Antlitz'," and Pawel Piotrowski, "Polen und die Intervention," in Karner et al., op.cit., 421–46 and 447–60, respectively.

6   The meeting was later moved forward to February 8 and finally took place on February 7.

7   MOL, M-KS-288, F. 47/743. ő. e.

In order to underline the official character of this meeting, which took place on February 4 in Komárno,[8] the list of participants included the Central Committee Secretaries for Foreign Affairs of the CPCs and the HSWP, Vladimír Koucký and Zoltán Komócsin, as well as the Hungarian deputy foreign minister Károly Erdélyi. Dubček reported on the "Action Program," which was about to be submitted to the session of the Central Committee scheduled for March, and said that "they did not want to tackle too much at once."[9] For the time being, priority was given to solving the most important problems. Kádár expressed his concerns very diplomatically when he said, "Mark my words: now everyone is at work on their own Action Programs."[10]

At the Politburo session of the HSWP on February 6, the Hungarian leader formulated this concern more pointedly: according to information he had received two days before the meeting in Komárno, things had taken a turn in Czechoslovakia "that made one's hair stand on end. In a number of different areas all kinds of twelve-point programs are formulated and submitted to the Central Committee. Their tenor is not hostile or directed against the Party but the initiative has been taken out of the hands of the Central Committee and some proposals go beyond the CC's presently held position. They contain such issues as whether Novotný could be allowed to continue as President."[11]

At the same meeting in Komárno Dubček painted his visit to Moscow as a great success. He said that Brezhnev and the other Soviet leaders had assured him of their assistance. He underlined that he had explicitly made the point that he wanted to solve all problems in close cooperation with the Soviet Union. Dubček and Kádár agreed in their assessments of the international situation across the board (Middle East, Vietnam, the issue of the Budapest Conference of the Communist and Workers' Parties, etc.).

The most interesting discussion regarded relations with the Federal Republic of Germany. Kádár noted with relief that the Czechoslovak and the Hungarian points of view about the desirability of establishing diplomatic

---

8   At the end of negotiations Dubček and his comrades paid a half-hour visit to Komárom on the Hungarian side of the border at Kádár's request. Komárom was originally one town, located on both sides of the Danube, that was cut in two by the Trianon Peace Treaty of 1920.

9   MOL, M-KS-288, F. 47/743. ő. e., Memorandum of conversation between Kádár and Dubček in Komárno, February 5, 1968.

10 Ibid., F. 5/445. ő. e., Minutes of the session of the HSWP Politburo, February 6, 1968.

11 Ibid.

relations with the FRG were identical and felt certain that he had found allies in the Czechoslovak leadership on a question that was crucially important to the Hungarian economy. The fact that Dubček agreed that they were facing an entirely new situation made Kádár hope that, with help from the Czechoslovak leadership, the time might come for the Warsaw diktat of February 1967 to be reviewed.[12]

The meeting also produced agreement on the continued development of bilateral economic and cultural relations. At Dubček's request, Kádár was willling to consider that the twenty-year friendship treaty between the two countries of February 1949 should be renewed a year before its termination, with a clearly demonstrative purpose, in the summer of 1968.

The Making of the Dresden Meeting

In March news from Czechoslovakia that reached the countries of the Soviet camp became more and more alarming. After the abolition of censorship, ever more radical views were finding their way into the media. The Soviet leaders concluded that a meeting had to be called immediately to enable leaders of the "fraternal countries" to offer Dubček and his comrades assistance in the task of consolidating the situation.

While the general story of the meeting of the "Six" in Dresden on March 23, 1968, is rather well known, less known is that it was the result of a series of intensive communications involving Brezhnev, Gomułka and Kádár, on the one hand, and Dubček, on the other.[13] Dubček himself had proposed at the March meeting of the Warsaw Pact Political Consultative Committee in

---

12 MOL, M-KS-288, F. 5/445. ő. e. The secret protocol that had been endorsed under Polish and East German pressure at the meeting of Warsaw Pact Foreign Ministers in February 1967 made it impossible, after Romania's earlier unilateral move, for Bulgaria, Czechoslovakia and Hungary to enter into diplomatic relations with the FRG, even though the Bonn government had extended this offer to all four countries. For details on the Soviet Bloc's FRG policy, see Csaba Békés, "The Warsaw Pact and the Helsinki Process 1965–1970," in: Wilfried Loth and Georges-Henri Soutou, eds., *The Making of Détente: Eastern and Western Europe in the Cold War 1965–75* (London, New York, 2008), 201–20 and Douglas Selvage, "The Warsaw Pact and the German Question, 1955–1970," in Mary Ann Heiss and S. Victor Papacosma, eds., *NATO and the Warsaw Pact: Intrabloc Conflicts* (Kent, OH., 2008), 178–92.

13 For a detailed account of the preparations for the Dresden meeting, see Csaba Békés, "Ungarn zwichsen Prag und Moskau," in Karner *et al.*, op.cit., 490–93.

Sofia that the members should meet more frequently at the highest level to discuss issues of economic cooperation. Therefore, Brezhnev suggested that this March meeting be disguised as one devoted to economic consultations, which meant that, in addition to the Party heads and Prime Ministers, the leaders of the state planning boards would have to be invited as well. Kádár warned Brezhnev against deceiving Dubček about the true nature of the forthcoming meeting, and suggested that participation should be confined to the Party heads of four countries—the Soviet Union, Czechoslovakia, Poland and Hungary. As Kádár knew the points of view of each of the respective leaders, he concluded that a smaller forum, excluding Bulgaria and the GDR, would provide more opportunities for offering the CPCs genuine constructive advice and assistance and reduce the probability of its ending in outright condemnation of the the Prague leadership's erroneous ways.[14] At the begining of the harmonization process Gomułka was in favor of inviting Novotný as well and suggested Moravská Ostrava as a possible venue for the meeting, but, after learning about Kádár's proposal, he too favored a reduction in the number of participants; he would even have agreed to limiting the invitation to the Soviet Union, Hungary and Czechoslovakia.[15]

Dubček wanted to play for time and raised the idea of visiting Kádár for consultations in Hungary before the planned multilataeral meeting. Dubček, however, changed his mind and informed Brezhnev on March 19 that he was ready for a meeting. Not only was he willling to go to Dresden, a venue he proposed, but he even adopted Brezhnev's idea of disguising the meeting as an "economic forum."[16] Therefore, Dubček was well aware of the situation from the outset, and it was precisely he who did not inform his colleagues in the Czechoslovak delegation who were shocked when they recognized the trap into which they had fallen in Dresden.

---

14 MOL, M-KS-288, F. 47/743. ő.e., Memorandum of a telephone conversation between Kádár and Brezhnev, March 11, 1968.

15 MOL, M-KS-288, F. 47/743. ő.e., Memorandum of a telephone conversation between Kádár and Brezhnev, March 12, 1968.

16 MOL, M-KS-288, F. 47/743. ő.e., Memorandum of a telephone conversation between Kádár and Brezhnev, March 19, 1968.

At the Dresden meeting Kádár attempted to divide his efforts evenly between two goals: to assure the Czechoslovak leaders of his unqualified support and to point out the dangers inherent in their present situation. In his speech he underlined the Hungarian leadership's solidarity with the CPCs and stated that what was happening in Czechoslovakia had to be considered an internal affair in which no outsiders were entitled to infere. He urged solving the problems in a manner that strengthened the socialist system. He also pointed out that the leadership was not unified and that there could be no successful conclusion to the present troubles without unity.

A second precondition for victory, according to Kádár, was recognizing the necessity of waging a two-front war, to correct the mistakes that had been made in Czechoslovakia in the construction of socialism before January 1968 and, at the same time, to fight anti-socialist phenomena and tendencies. Kádár insisted that Czechoslovakia had not yet—contrary to the assertions of Brezhnev and Gomułka—reached the stage of counter-revolution although the present situation resembled in a number of ways the one that preceded the Hungarian "counter-revolution" of 1956. He expressed the hope that the outcome would be different in Czechoslovakia. His most effective argument was that the people who had brought about the Hungarian crisis had not been ardent counter-revolutionaries either:

> In Hungary, comrades, no counter-revolutionary elements of any kind took action openly before October 23, 1956. Those who took action were quite different people. Those were Party members, Party functionaries, and people working in very different fields. And the main slogan—forgive me for this—was the same that is voiced by everybody in your country. The main slogan was this in Hungary: Forward to the implementation of the resolutions of the 20th congress oft the CPSU! And this was so until the evening of the 23rd of October. This must be taken into consideration. You may ask: what kind of people were taking action then? I can bluntly tell you, these were people who were simply confused, who were grabbed by some sort of senseless wave, people who saw some kind of ghosts. I think that these people, without hostile intentions, cause great damage. These people, in a given situation cause greater damage than the openly and expressly anti-communist elements, because those anti-communist elements can take no action openly in such situations. Please, consider this and take it seriously: these people,

of whom I subjectively think that they are not enemies of socialism, they may actually think they represent socialism, but in fact they do exactly the opposite.[17]

In case this was not powerful enough a warning, Kádár added for good measure, "Imre Nagy had not been a conscious counter-revolutionary aiming for regime change; he was carried away by the events of October 25 and 26 and made common cause with the class enemy." Finally Kádár said quite bluntly to the Czechoslovak delegates, "These events can turn any one of you into an Imre Nagy."[18] As Kádár was the only representative of the five parties to support the Dubček leadership openly and to maintain that the solution of the Czechoslovaks' problems was exclusively their own concern, his speech was the most liberal at the meeting in Dresden. Conversely it must be said that his remarks about Nagy were by far the bluntest reference to a worst-case scenario: everyone knew that Nagy had been executed.

In his long speech Kádár, who has been often criticized by historians for his lack of interest in the national issue, presented a remarkable argument concerning the problem of the national minorities. He deplored that, in Czechoslovakia, Hungary had been criticised in the press for its dealing with the Slovak minority. For the first time, he referred to the Trianon syndrome at a Warsaw Pact multilateral meeting, declaring that "thirty per cent of the Hungarians live abroad, in the neighboring countries." Although he offered an "internationalist" solution of the problem by warning that it would be a dangerous path if they were to start dealing with the fate of ethnic minorities living in each other's countries, he also hinted at another possible scenario: "If you ask a Hungarian: what is this actually?—then I can reply: this is not a purely internal matter of Czechoslovakia since we are concerned too." While publicly not much was shown of this Hungarian concern up until the middle of

---

17 For the full text of Kádár's speech, see Stiftung Archive der Parteien und Massenorganisationen im Bubdesarchiv, Zentrales Parteiarchive, Berlin, (SAPMO BArch. ZPA), IV 2/201/778. Minutes of the Dresden Meeting, March 23, 1968. The speech is printed with omissions in Stefan Karner et al., op.cit. vol 2. Dokumente, 451–459. The full text of the speech is published in Hungarian in Csaba Békés "Kádár János és az 1968-as csehszlovákiai válság" [János Kádár and the Czechoslovak Crisis in 1968], in Évkönyv 2008 [Yearbook, 2008]. 1956 Institute. Budapest, 2008,197–208.

18 SAPMO BA, ZPA, IV 2/201/778, Minutes of the Dresden Meeting, March 23, 1968.

the 1980's, Kádár's statement was of historic importance as it was an open break with the ever-existing communist dogma of treating the national minorities as exclusively under the jurisdiction of the states in which they lived.

At the meeting of the "Five" in Moscow in May of 1968, Kádár outlined even more explicitly the potential outcome of this re-evaluation process:

> We did not go any further publicly thus far, but we summoned the Czechoslovak Ambassador because they [journalists] had made God knows what kinds of statements concerning the minority issue. They claimed, for instance, that Hungary conducts a policy aimed at the assimilation of the Slovaks in our country. In connection with this we warned them that, if it continues like this, then, well, we will also devote great attention to the fate of the Hungarian population in Czechoslovakia.[19]

Kádár and the Meeting of the "Five" in Moscow

Despite the warnings of the allies in Dresden, the Czechoslovak leadership failed to halt the process of democratization and attempted to paint it as a renewal of socialism. In a manner that was actually rather naive, the leadership continued to believe that it was not going to endanger the leading role of the Communist Party.

In view of the latest developments, Brezhnev summed up his assessment in a conversation with Kádár on April 16: "We are about to lose Czechoslovakia." He hinted at the necessity for the fraternal parties to meet again in secret very soon, this time without the CPCs. Kádár signalled his readiness to attend this meeting, but he sensed that the handling of the crisis was set to undergo a drastic qualitative change, he demurred that "he could not envisage discussing [the Czechoslovaks'] fate in their absence."[20]

In spite of Kádár's misgivings, at the Moscow meeting on May 8 the only option left to the Hungarian Party leader was to convince his comrades that the present Czechoslovak leadership only needed sufficient support in order to get the situation back under control. In contrast, the representatives of the other Communist Parties had assembled in Moscow saw the situation as

---

19   Ibid.

20   MOL, M-KS-288 F 47/743. ő. e., Memorandum of a telephone conversation between Kádár and Brezhnev, April 16, 1968.

counter-revolutionary and the CPCs leaders as incapable of halting it. From this time onwards, the idea gained ground that consolidation through political means was to be achieved by "healthy forces" seizing power internally. Kádár acknowledged in his statement that there was rampant anarchy in Czechoslovakia and that it was being exploited by anti-socialist forces. The leadership was weak, divided and unable to control state or society.

There was no doubt in Kádár's mind that the CPCs was engaged in a two-front struggle. He called the CPCs's Action Program a "big zero" because it could be interpreted either as a defense of socialism or as its abandonment. So the situation was indeed dangerous, but counter-revolution had not yet gained the upper hand.[21] Kádár, therefore, proposed that in assessing the situation simplistic schemata should "be replaced by societal analyses, by the analysis of necessities." To illustrate, he appeared to caricature the simplifications endemic to the Eastern Bloc: "For instance, if you call Mao Tse-tung and his clique insane, Castro a petty bourgeois, Ceauşescu a nationalist, the Czechoslovaks crazy, you have not actually done anything to deal with the underlying problems."[22] He emphasized that "the way out of what is happening now will be decided *within* the CPCs and the Czechoslovak working class and by the people of Czechoslovakia themselves." In conclusion, Kádár proposed that "we must do everything we can to help the CPCs extricate itself from this difficult situation. And, on the contrary, we must not do anything that could play into the hands of the enemy."[23] As he was certain that there would be those who would advocate a military solution, he said that he, too, was in favor of using military maneuvers to exert pressure on both the Czechoslovak leadership and on the people, yet "the problem cannot be solved by military means alone; the political issues are too complex for that."[24]

---

21 Navrátil, *et al.* op.cit., p. 138.

22 For Kádár's entire speech at the meeting of the CPSU leadership with the leaders of the Communist Parties of Bulgaria, Hungary, the GDR and Poland on May 8 in Moscow, see AdBIK, holding 'Prague Spring,' "Minutes of the Meeting of the Leaders of the CPSU CC with the leaders of the Communist Parties of Bulgaria, Hungary, the GDR and Poland, May 8, 1968," reprinted in Karner *et al.*, op.cit., vol. 2. *Dokumente*, Dokument 77. The quotation, as cited above, is a translation from the report compiled by Károly Erdélyi. MOL, M-KS-288, F. 5/455. ő. e., cited in Huszár, op.cit., 86.

23 Navrátil, *et al.*, op.cit., 139.

24 MOL, M-KS-288, F. 5/455. ő. e.,

The official visit of the Czechoslovak Party and government delegation to Hungary, originally planned for March, finally took place on June 13–14,[25] giving Kádár another opportunity to continue his role of mediator. Brezhnev telephoned Kádár on the eve of the visit and urged him to help Dubček understand "the dangers that are threatening the CPCs, socialism and himself." If they wanted to count on Soviet support, then the least they had to do was to get the mass media under control and detach and distance themselves from the revisionist group.[26] After the Moscow meeting of the "Five," this visit had something of a demonstrative character, which was further enhanced by the renewal for another twenty years of the "Treaty of Friendship, Cooperation and Mutual Assistance between the ČSSR and the People's Republic of Hungary."

Kádár publicly assured the Czechoslovak leadership of his support for their efforts to consolidate the situation; in private he sounded a note of warning. The Hungarian experiences of 1956 showed that it was necessary to curb democratization and to draw an unmistakable line against deviations and hostile tendencies; otherwise the Party was bound to lose control. Dubček replied in a self-confident vein: "If the antisocialist forces were to become so powerful as to endanger the socialist system, they [Dubček and the other leaders] would not hesitate to confront them and neither their hands nor their knees would tremble as they did so. They were powerful enough to call to account those who were scheming against the socialist system, even if there was the threat of external interference."[27]

The Road to Warsaw

To leaders in Moscow, the determination of the Czechoslovak leadership began to sound increasingly hollow, and the news from Prague worried them even more. An article published in *Literární listy* on the tenth anniversary of the execution of former Prime Minister Imre Nagy, which said he was wrongfully executed and a martyr, also caused indignation in Budapest. Kádár considered it sniping aimed at him personally and at his support for the Prague leadership. What he found particularly galling was that the leadership of CPCs did not

---

25 The Czechoslovak delegation consisted of Alexander Dubček, Oldřich Černík, Vasil Biľak and Jiří Hájek.

26 MOL, M-KS-288, F. 47/743. ő.e., Memorandum of a telephone conversation between Kádár and Brezhnev, June 12, 1968.

27 Huszár, op.cit., 117.

react unequivocally to this provocation. The "Two Thousand Words" manifesto, which was published on June 27 in the same newspaper, was counter-revolutionary in the eyes of the Hungarian leadership, and they expected it to draw a number of resolute administrative responses. In a letter to Dubček of July 5, Kádár outlined in detail his utter condemnation of the two articles. Whereas the one on Nagy was also classified as a provocation by Dubček, he defended the CPCs's attitude concerning the "Two Thousand Words" by pointing out that the manifesto had produced no tangible result.[28] It is important to declare that, contrary to previous interpretations, neither the Nagy article nor the "Two Thousand Words" manifesto was a turning point in the policy of the Hungarian leadership, since, as we will see, the HSWP's position remained the avoidance a military solution at all costs, even in the middle of July.

Towards the end of June, Kádár travelled to Moscow at the head of a Party delegation. Brezhnev painted a sombre picture of the ČSSR: Dubček was gradually drifting to the right; the right was growing in strength; Czechoslovakia was getting ever closer to going down the road of Yugoslavia and its further trajectory might even take it into the bourgeois camp.[29] Brezhnev announced that Moscow was planning: first, a letter to the CPCs and, then, another meeting with those of its allies who had been present in Dresden. Kádár agreed in principle but, remembering the negative Czechoslovak echoes of the meeting of the "Five" in Moscow in May, he underlined the crucial importance of allowing Czechoslovakia to participate. The Hungarian leadership itself differed at that time from the Soviet line on a number of issues, such as economic relations with the West in general and relations with the FRG in particular, so it seemed important to maintain the goodwill of the Soviet leadership. Kádár presumably felt that the time had come to make it quite clear that, while the Hungarian Party favored a political solution for the Czechoslovak crisis in principle, it would support a military intervention as a measure of last resort, if a political settlement could not be achieved and the continued existence of the socialist order was in danger. This had been his point of view all along; yet from what he had said so far, the Soviets could not be sure. That is why his "declaration of loyalty" was so important. Kádár did not want to irritate Moscow with aberrations that he was not guilty of. The minutes of the meeting of the Politburo of the CPSU of July 3, 1968, contain Brezhnev's interpretation:

---

28   Ibid., 138.
29   Ibid., 135.

"In expounding his thoughts on the Czechoslovak situation, comrade Kádár said it was obvious that an occupation of Czechoslovakia was inevitable. 'If this should become necessary, we will vote in favor of this move.'"[30] In the version of the report prepared for the Politburo of the HSWP this pledge was not mentioned. Nevertheless, it is very likely that Kádár actually made this statement, and that it was made in the dialectical form outlined above, in which military intervention was seen as a *measure of last resort*.[31]

Kádár also came to play an important role in preparing the meeting of the "Warsaw Five" on July 14–15 in Warsaw. Brezhnev had informed the others on July 9 that the Presidium of the CPCs had on the previous day declined on short notice the invitation to another meeting of the six "Dresden" allies. Kádár was taken aback by the reaction of the CPCs, for during his visit to Budapest, Dubček had voiced his dissatisfaction that in May the "Five" had met for consultations in Moscow without the Czechs and Slovaks. That is why Kádár proposed a meeting between representatives of the CPCs and the CPSU within a day or two, which would be followed in seven to ten days' time by a meeting of the six allies. This would allow the leaders from Prague sufficient time to do their homework. If they were to decline this invitation as well, then the meeting would have to proceed without them.[32]

In this difficult situation, Dubček urgently asked Kádár for a secret meeting that took place on July 13 in Komárom. Here Dubček and his companion Černík were disappointed. Instead of offering assurances of continued support, Kádár and Prime Minister Jenő Fock severely criticized them for declining to take part in the Warsaw meeting. Kádár told them, not only that this had been their worst mistake since January, but that they had also reached a point of no return, which meant "that we haved parted ways and will be fighting on opposite sides."[33]

---

30   Ibid., 145.

31   Ibid.

32   MOL, M-KS-288, F. 47/743. ő. e., Memorandum of a telephone conversation between Kádár and Brezhnev, July 9, 1968. Kádár, therefore, suggested to Brezhnev wording the letter to the CPCs in a tone that would make the Czechoslovaks' participation possible. He added, for tactical reasons, that the topic of the talks had better not be the situation in Czechoslovakia; each Party was to be asked to report on its own situation. Although Kádár's idea was accepted by Brezhnev, as the CPCs delegation did not show up in Warsaw, the meeting's only agenda was the situation in Czechoslovakia. MOL, M-KS-288, F. 47/743.

33   Ibid., F. 4/93. ő. e., Minutes of the meeting of the HSWP CC, August 7, 1968; Huszár, op.cit., 163.

When Kádár set out for the July 14–15 meeting in Warsaw, he did so equipped with a resolution of the HSWP Politburo made on July 12 that continued to call for a political settlement for Czechoslovakia and that was designed to keep the leaders of the "fraternal parties" from opting for a military solution.[34] In Warsaw Kádár stuck to his brief in his first speech. He gave a detailed report on his meeting with Dubček and Černík in Komárom the previous day and underlined the danger inherent in the country's situation, which had, however, not yet reached the stage of counter-revolution.

Following Kádár's speech, the discussion took an unexpected turn: Walter Ulbricht of East Germany and Todor Zhivkov of Bulgaria attacked Kádár's position, something that had never happened before. They not only resolutely and openly condemned Kádár's point of view, but added that Hungary's internal problems might be next in line for a "solution" at a future meeting of the Warsaw Pact countries.[35]

This was evidence of the emergence of a dangerous policy that entitled "fraternal parties" to act as joint trouble-shooters, not only in certain crises, but also in the context of developments or reforms that did not endanger socialism as such, yet were considered undesirable by the others. There was no doubt that Hungary was a case in point at that time. Kádár, therefore, thought it advisable to repeat in front of them the "declaration of loyalty" he had issued two weeks before in Moscow. He unexpectedly rose to his feet a second time and announced: "We unreservedly agree with the explanations and conclusions of our Soviet comrades and are prepared to take part in any joint action."[36] Although this was a serious violation of the HSWP's resolution, taking this step was arguably facilitated for Kádár by Brezhnev's making it clear that, despite pressure from the others, no final decision would be reached at this meeting. Kádár was, therefore, still free to work towards a political settlement, even though he had publicly committed himself to agreeing in principle to a military solution. Yet, the chances for such a political settlement were rapidly dwindling.

---

34 MOL, M-KS-288 5/461. ő.e. Minutes of the meeting of the HSWP Politburo, July 12, 1968.

35 Navrátil et al. op. cit., 218, 220. Kádár's entire speech is reprinted in: Karner et. al., op. cit., vol. 2, document 77.

36 Navrátil et al., 229.

Preparing for the Invasion: Consent and Last Efforts at Averting It

After the Warsaw meeting of the "Five," Kádár concentrated on persuading Brezhnev to make a last-ditch effort at one more Soviet–Czechoslovak meeting. There, the Soviets would make it clear to Dubček and his comrades that, in case they continued to do nothing to stop developments that bore all the hallmarks of total disintegration, there would have to be outside intervention to save the socialist system. Kádár had the impression that he had succeeded in frightening Dubček and Černík in Komárom; at the end of the meeting, when they realized the danger they were in, both men burst out crying.[37] He hoped that a last warning to the leadership by the Soviets would prove effective and trigger, at long last, the administrative measures required for a consolidation of the communist system. The Soviet-Czechoslovak meeting on their common border at Čierná nad Tisou at the end of July was mainly the result of Kádár's tireless efforts at mediation.

At the ensuing meeting of the "Six" in Bratislava at the beginning of August, Kádár confronted Dubček with the alternatives the CPCs had to choose. Either they themselves used force to stop certain tendencies, or force would be applied from outside. He illustrated this with his own example and underlined that in 1956 it had been necessary to use deeply unpopular measures to save the communist system in a context that was much more difficult; yet he had done what had to be done.[38]

At Brezhnev's invitation, Kádár flew to Yalta on August 15. During the ensuing negotiations, everyone knew that a decision in favor of a military solution was in the offing. Kádár now concentrated on the time after the intervention. The situation being as it was, he consented to the military solution, but he emphasized that in the long term only a political settlement could ensure success.[39] The struggle for the correction of the mistakes made before

---

37 Ibid., 216; MOL, M-KS-288, F. 5/462. ő. e., Minutes of the meeting of the HSWP Politburo, July 15, 1968.

38 Huszár, op. cit., 228.

39 It was cold comfort to Kádár that Brezhnev was satisfied with only one Hungarian division's participation in the invasion. For the role of the Hungarian army in the invasion of Czechoslovakia, see Iván Pataky, *A vonakodó szövetséges. A Magyar Népköztársaság és a Magyar Néphadsereg közreműködése Csehszlovákia 1968. évi megszállásában.* [The Wavering Ally. The Participation of the Hungarian People's Republic and the Hungarian People's Army in the Occupation of Czechoslovakia in 1968] (Zrínyi, 1996).

January 1968 had to be continued, and the CPCs must not relinquish its two-front struggle. Kádár felt that the difficult situation the Soviets were in might provide him with an opportunity to criticize the policy of the CPSU in a constructive manner. He said the Soviet leadership had been impatient in its dealings with the Czechoslovak Party and that this impatience had been a key factor in the escalation of the crisis; a more patient approach might have rendered military intervention unnecessary. In this context Kádár formulated a question that rose far above the present context: "When the CPSU is perceived as rigid by the world, by the global communist movement, who is going to play the role of the standard-bearer in the global communist movement?"[40] He praised Soviet policy after 1956—without mentioning Khrushchev's name—and said the Soviet leadership had then shown trust in the Hungarian and Polish Party leaders and had allowed them to seek new solutions that had consolidated the situation in their countries.[41] With these lessons from history Kádár was trying to make sure that post-invasion Czechoslovakia would be allowed to re-establish order with minimum interference from the Soviets and also trying to broaden the maneuvering space of domestic policies within the states of the Soviet Bloc.

At Yalta, Brezhnev entrusted a last mediation mission to Kádár, saying that the Hungarian Party was the only one, in addition to the CPSU, that Dubček might be prepared to heed. The ensuing meeting took place in Komárno on August 17.[42] According to Kádár, Dubček, who in Komárom on July 13 had acknowledged the mistake of not attending the Warsaw meeting, now changed his mind and declared that the CPCs's decision had been correct. Kádár then explained to Dubček that, following his logic, the five other Parties must have been wrong, and the conference in Bratislava was worthless, implying that the compromise achieved there was no longer binding for the five Parties. When Dubček told Kádár that now they were dealing only with the forthcoming Party Congress, Kádár asked about the political character of the Congress— what kind of policy it would follow, how its conveners wanted to maintain the leading role of the Party, how they planned to fight against the right-wing forces—but he got no reply. Kádár then warned Dubček that, in case they disregarded these basic problems and held elections after the Congress without

---

40 MOL, M-KS-288, F. 5/467. ő. e., Minutes of the Meeting of the HSWP Politburo, August 20, 1968.
41 Ibid.
42 Ibid.

a firm political platform, there would be unpredictable consequences, clearly referring to the possibility of a "bourgeois restoration." As a communist, Dubček must have been well aware that such "unpredictable consequences" would not be permitted by Moscow. By the end of the meeting, Kádár was sure that the situation in Czechoslovakia was hopeless and had no illusions about the decision to be taken by the "Five" the following day in Moscow.

Hungarian soldiers in southern Slovakia, August, 1968   *Photo credit: Courtesy of Csaba Békés*

The Aftermath of the Invasion

After the invasion on August 20–21, an unexpected opportunity arose for Kádár to positively influence the course of events. On the first day of the crisis-management negotiations of the "Five," which took place parallel to the Soviet Union's talks with the captive Czechoslovak "delegation" between August 24 and 26 in Moscow, he was a fervent advocate of the need to find a compromise with the legitimate Czechoslovak leadership. In order to emphasize this Hungarian position, he first submitted to the Soviets, in writing, three possible scenarios for settling the crisis in Czechoslovakia.[43] The first was the creation of a new power center consisting of representatives of the

---

43   Huszár, op. cit., 273

left, i.e., the "healthy forces," but the HSWP deemed this plan unrealistic. The second was built on finding a way to cooperate with the existing legitimate Party and goverment leadership. The third was a military administration, which Kádár warned his partners against, because of the "well-known serious consequences." Thus, Kádár clearly suggested that the only realistic option was to work out a compromise with the existing Czechoslovak leadership.

Ulbricht and Zhivkov were pushing for a dictatorial solution, the formation of a revolutionary government of workers and peasants in keeping with the Hungarian model of 1956. Władysław Gomułka of Poland, who was apparently completely out of his depth, went so far as to claim that the situation in Czechoslovakia was much worse than the one in Hungary at the time of the "counter-revolution."[44] Because there were a number of influential supporters of a radical solution among the Soviet leaders, Kádár's plea on behalf of Dubček and his comrades came down clearly on the side of the realistic solution favored by Brezhnev and Kosygin, contributing to a political compromise that involved the legitimate Czechoslovak leaders and culminated in the signing of the Moscow Protocol.

In fact, Kádár may have had an even more important role in bringing about this historic compromise. Without his efforts to convince Brezhnev and Kosygin, most likely the Čierná nad Tisou talks between the Soviet and Czechoslovak leadership would never have occurred. Without those talks, there would not have been the meeting of the "Six" in Bratislava, and without the compromise in Bratislava, there would not have been a chance to negotiate a political settlement with the legitimate leadership following the invasion. Instead, the "revolutionary" option would have been applied, as was favored by most Warsaw Pact allies and quite a few influential members of the CPSU Politburo as well. That "normalitzation" process led by purely orthodox-hardliner leaders would have caused much greater suffering for Czechoslovak society than it actually had to experiencee.

After the 1956 Hungarian Revolution János Kádár had restored order with the help of the Red Army. Although he was in fact a solid anti-Stalinist political leader, the reprisals that occured during the first years of his rule were so wide-scale and irrationally cruel that even today there is no explanation as to

---

44   For details of the negotiations of the "Five" between August 24and 26, 1968, see Navrátil, op. cit., 474–6; MOL, M-KS-288, F. 4/95. ő. e., Minutes of the Meeting on August 27, 1968; Huszár, op.cit., 272–4.

why. Following the crushing of the revolution, 230 individuals were executed, including Prime Minister Imre Nagy and several of his closest associates; over 20,000 were imprisoned; and 13,000 interned.[45] A large number of the victims, including many among the executed, had not participated in any violent actions but were leaders or simple members of revolutionary committees or workers' councils or just were at the wrong place at the wrong time.

A few hours after the return of the Hungrian delegation from Moscow, the HSWP Central Committe was convened on August 27, 1968.[46] Kádár gave a sanitized report on the talks in Moscow and provided the first official Hungarian standpoint on the new situation. He explained to the Central Committee members how embarasing it had been for all the Warsaw Pact leaders to see that the original plan they had agreed to did not work. He harshly criticized the members of the "healthy forces" in the CPCs who had promised to seize power by the time of the invasion but who actually did not even dare to stand up for the intervention. Now the Hungarian leadership simply had no answer to the often asked question: who were the brave men who had invited the allies to come to the rescue of the socialist cause in Czechoslovakia?

For Kádár, it was personal. In 1956 he did take the role of a Quisling when he thought there was no other way of saving the communist regime in Hungary. Now Kádár concluded that with the historic compromise achieved in Moscow, there would be a much greater chance of consolidating the political situation on the basis of communist rule in Czechoslovakia. Prime Minister Jenő Fock addressed the issue from a different perspective, with a surprising twist: he claimed that it was great luck that the plan had not worked out, because now the process of restoring order could be directed by the legitimate leadership, with whom it would be much easier to work, than it would have been with a group of orthodox hardliners.

On September 12 the HSWP Politburo discussed an extensive policy paper evaluating the internal and international effects of the crisis in Czechoslovakia.[47] The most remarkable statement in the position paper was that Hungarian

---

45   On the reprisals following the 1956 Hungarian Revolution, see Attila Szakolczai, „A forradalmat követő megtorlás során kivégzettekről," [On those who were executed during the reprisals following the revolution] in *Évkönyv III*. Bp. 1956-os (Intézet, 1994), 237–57.

46   MOL, M-KS-288, F. 4/95. ő. e., Minutes of the Consultative Meeting of Members of the CC and the Government, August 27, 1968.

47   MOL, M-KS-288, F. 5/471. ő. e., Minutes of the HSWP Politburo, September 13, 1968.

society accepted the invasion and Hungary's participation in it as an unavoidable step, but it did not agree with it. Rather, the basis of this consent was the confidence that the HSWP had been able to generate effective efforts for the improvement of political and economic conditions in the country since 1956.

Indeed, in Hungary there were only isolated negative reactions to the invasion. The philosopher George Lukács and former Pime Minister András Hegedűs, now head of the Reseach Group for Sociology at the Hungarian Academy of Sciences, wrote letters to the HSWP Central Committe condemning the intervention. The Party meeting of the Reseach Group for Sociology unanimously passed a resolution denouncing the HSWP's policy. Five Hungarian philosophers and sociologists (György Márkus, Vilmos Sós, Zádor Tordai, Ágnes Heller and Mária Márkus), attending a conference on the island of Korcula in Yugoslavia, publicly condemned the invasion.[48] A few young writers launched a campaign for signing a letter of condemnation of the Warsaw Pact action but, according to the above-mentioned HSWP position paper, "no serious writer, artist or intellectual" signed the letter. Within the communist establishment the only visible protest was the resignation of András Tömpe, a veteran of the Spanish Civil War, as Hungarian ambassador to East Germany.[49]

The position paper on Czechoslovakia adopted at the September 13 meeting of the HSWP Politburo declared that the political situation in that country was much more favorable than it had been before August 21. It stated that now the most important task was the starting of a process of polarization of the political forces. The consolidation, nevertheless, had to be based on the CPCs's policy conducted since January 1968; that is, a two-front battle was to be fought against the mistakes of the pre-January period and against the antisocialist forces. The "healthy forces" were severely criticized for their lack of courage in openly supporting the intervention. The document emphasized that, in the present situation, great patience had to be shown by the allies concerning developments in Czechoslovakia and that the leadership

---

48 On Hungarian dissident reactions to the invasion of Czechoslovakia in 1968, see János M. Rainer, „Prága-Korcula-Budapest, 1968. augusztus 21," *Élet és Irodalom*, LII. évf. 32. sz, 2008. augusztus 8.

49 Retaliation for these deviant actions was relatively mild: András Hegedűs was replaced as head of the Reseach Group for Sociology, András Tömpe was made director of Corvina Publishing House; three of the Korcula "five," György Márkus, Vilmos Sós, and Zádor Tordai, were expelled from the Party (the other two were not Party members).

had to be given sufficient time to execute the required changes. As for the withdrawal of foreign troops from Czechoslovakia, the HSWP suggested it occur in several stages, the first to be started as soon as possible. As for the troops remaining "temporarily" in the country, only Soviet troops should stay, because the presence of the other Warsaw Pact states' troops would be much more annoying for Czechoslovak society. Moreover, even a symbolic presence should be avoided in the form of allied participation in the general staff of the "allied" troops, the Soviets insisted.

The Politburo also decided that the Soviet, Bulgarian, GDR and Polish leaders should be informed about the Hungarian position in a letter to the fraternal Parties. The letter was sent but no reply came from any of the allies. More importantly, the resolution of the Politburo included a paragraph stating that both the Yugoslav and the Romanian leaders had to be informed confidentially that the rumors about a possible invasion of their countries lacked any foundation.

The Politburo's position was represented by Kádár at a secret summit of the "Five" in Moscow on September 27 that was hastily convened just before the Soviet-Czechoslovak talks at the beginning of October.[50] He emphasized that, concerning the Czechoslovak leadership, the allies should conduct a policy based on principles, rather than focusing on the evaluation of certain persons, as the attitude of the leadership could change either for the better or for the worse during these trying times. He warned that "whenever we voiced our opinion on personnel issues, it always backfired. Whomever we criticized became popular, and whomever we praised became isolated." Reacting to Gomułka's proposal on launching a large-scale propaganda campaign against revisionism by the allies, Kádár stressed that "in the present situation Czechoslovak ears are closed to our arguments." Therefore, it was necessary to find communists in Czechoslovakia who would represent the proper policy line. He also rejected Brezhnev's argument that if Dubček signed the agreement on the stationing of Soviet troops in Czechoslovakia, it would have the additional benefit of compromising Dubček in his own country. Kádár warned the allies against making an agreement with a compromised politician, and in trying to save Dubček from this trap, he noted that in 1958 a similar agreement between the Soviet Union and Hungary was signed by the foreign and

---

50 MOL, M-KS-288, 5/473. ő.e. Minutes of the HSWP Politburo, October 1, 1968.

defense ministers. In order to avoid the complications of directly negotiating with the Czechoslovak government about the withdrawal of the Hungarian troops, he suggested that, at the forthcoming bilateral talks, the Soviets should talk on behalf of all the "Five."

At the end of the meeting, Brezhnev apologized for not responding to the HSWP's recent letter on Czechoslovakia, mentioning that he had been too busy and there was nothing to reply to as the Soviet position was in line with the one outlined in the letter. Prime Minister Jenő Fock commented on Brezhnev's attitude that "… it is likely that when he received the letter this was not yet his opinion, this opinion was formulated by him during the course of a week. This was confirmed by the fact that the other First Secretaries did not mention the letter at all. This has reinforced my view that the Soviets, when formulating their opinions, are considering our position more seriously than that of the other three partners, who keep on pushing them in a nervous, impatient, atmosphere."[51]

During the period of "normalization" in Czechoslovakia, the Hungarian leadership continued to play a mediating role between Moscow and Prague. It hoped that the sobering experience of the violent end of the 'Prague Spring' would eventually result in the emergence of a modestly reform-oriented political course in Czechoslovakia, akin to the Hungarian model. According to this logic, many achievements of the 'Prague Spring' would be preserved, just as the Kádárist regime, in fact, did incorporate several goals of the failed revolution of 1956. Then the two reformist states in the Soviet Bloc would form a virtual alliance that would help them to avoid isolation and, together, fight successfully for the renewal of the communist system on pragmatic grounds.

From a historical perspective it is clear that without intervention the 'Prague Spring' would have led to the restoration of parliamentary democracy, as eventually occurred in 1990. Therefore, the invasion was the only option for Moscow to avoid that unwelcome eventuality. Consequently, the question about a possible alternative course of history is not whether the 'Prague Spring' could have survived under different circumstances, but rather this: if János Kádár, the most hated man right after the bloody suppression of the revolution of 1956 in Hungary, was able to develop a rather liberal version of the communist dictatorship, which could generate even relative popularity within society, why could the same model not be applied to Gustáv Husák's Czechoslovakia?

---

51   Ibid.

14
Comments on "The 'Prague Spring,' Hungary and the Warsaw Pact Invasion"

Peter Pastor

Professor Csaba Békés describes and analyzes the response of the General Secretary of the Hungarian Socialist Workers' Party, János Kádár, to the events of 1968 in Czechoslovakia, making use of recently-available documents from the Hungarian National Archives and other important primary and secondary sources.

Békés reminds us that the political reforms in Prague started in January of 1968, at the same time that the New Economic Mechanism was put into practice in Hungary (p. 1). He argues that because the Hungarian leadership, led by Kádár, hoped that the new domestic program would be supported by the reform process then unfolding in Prague, Kádár's policies towards Czechoslovakia were shaped with Hungary's needs in mind. Thus, twelve years after the Soviets crushed the Hungarian Revolution and put him into power and after years of repression, he wanted to sway Hungarian public opinion over to communism with policies based on the non-Leninist slogan "he who is not against us is with us." Kádár's program sought to entice non-Party members into collaborating with Party goals and with the "market socialism" of the New Economic Mechanism, which was intended to put money into the pockets of average Hungarians. He intended to revitalize his own regime's legitimacy without changing the system. The use of force anywhere in the bloc, therefore, threatened this process, especially if Hungarian troops were involved.

From this perspective, the director of the Budapest 1956 Institute, János Rainer characterized Kádár not as a reformer, "but a pragmatic (communist) politician," explaining that "a pragmatic communist leader is like a chameleon, he will take the color of a reformer, or of a conservative depending on the need. If he has a real color, it is closer to the latter." This two-faced personality, Rainer claims, was reflected in Kádár's handling of the Hungarian economic reforms, as well as "Hungary's participation in the occupation of Czechoslovakia."[1] This interpretation may explain Kádár's seemingly contradictory behavior during the Czechoslovak crisis of 1968.

Békés also stresses some commonality between Kádár and the other Warsaw Pact leaders: the right to intervene if "the continued existence of the socialist order was in danger" (p. 14). For Kádár, however, as Békés points out, intervention was needed only when all attempts at a "political solution" were exhausted and capitalism gained the upper hand.

In his August 23, 1968, report to the Hungarian Central Committee and to the Council of Ministers, however, it is evident that the so-called political solution for Kádár represented the solution offered by the left, "the "healthy forces," represented by Vasil Biľak, and not that of the "center" led by Alexander Dubček, which, according to the "left," was shifting to the "right." At that meeting Kádár was also asked how the intervention should be presented for home consumption. This was a serious concern as the Hungarian public, wooed by the carrot, could have resented the use of the stick against the Prague reformers. He replied: "About military intervention: we do not have to be ashamed, we should not skip over it, we have consciously acted out of internationalist duty. We did not look for this method, but the developments in Czechoslovakia forced our hand."[2] It soon became evident, however, that the Hungarian leader's concern was misplaced, and as we can read from Békés's paper, the public with the exception of a few intellectuals paid little attention to the fate of their neighbors to the north (p. 22).

---

1   János M. Rainer, "Kádár János, a reformer?" [János Kádár, the reformer?], http://www.rev.hu/portal/page/portal/rev/tanulmanyok/kadarrendszer/rainer_kadar_reformer

2   "Jegyzőkönyv a Központi Bizottság és a Minisztertanács 1968. augusztus 23-án megtartott együttes és zárt üléséről" [Minutes of the Combined and Closed Meeting of Central Committee and the Council of Ministers], August 23, 1968, 288 f. 4/94 ő. e., p. 27, Hungarian National Archives, p. 27, http://www.digitarchiv.hu/resources/kepek/mszmp_jgyk/mszmp1/kepek/2880400940/R8804009400001....

Békés identifies Kádár as a mediator who had the trust of both Brezhnev and Dubček. With Dubček, he shared the common interest of establishing diplomatic relations with West Germany. Dubček had the impression that Kádár's "political solution" translated into support for the Prague reforms. Brezhnev, who at first also sought a peaceful outcome, was in regular telephone contact with Kádár. According to Békés, the Soviet Party chief "assigned" the mediator's role to Kádár because he was aware of mutual trust between the Hungarian and Czechoslovak Party leaders. But Kádár's task also "stemmed from his own convictions" (p. 2). A mediator, however, is an impartial third party who seeks to bring about compromises between two adversaries. Therefore, I would rather portray Kádár as a go-between, Brezhnev's messenger, seeking his approval, carrying out his wishes, and thereby betraying Dubček's trust.

According to Békés, Kádár's role as mediator was amply demonstrated at the March 23, 1968, Dresden meeting of the Warsaw Pact when Kádár demonstrated reluctance to go along with the hawks "out of genuine conviction." He acted on the basis of "two goals": "to assure the Czechoslovak leaders of his unqualified support and to point out the dangers inherent in their present situation" (p. 7). In fact, by pointing out the dangers, Kádár *qualified* his support. What I read from Békés's description is that Kádár first rejected outside interference in Czechoslovakia's internal affairs, then he reminded his colleagues from Prague of the fate of Imre Nagy in 1956 if they went too far (p. 9). Since Nagy's fall as the revolutionary prime minister was the direct result of Soviet intervention, Kádár negated his unconditional defense of Czechoslovak sovereignty. His alleged concern about the Hungarian minority in Slovakia, which Békés sees as being of "historic importance" as it broke with the "communist dogma of treating the national minorities as exclusively under the jurisdiction of the state in which they lived" (p. 9), also demonstrates that Kádár was ready to use any pretext to meddle in Czechoslovakia's internal affairs. Thus Kádár was not mediating; rather, he was talking out of both sides of his mouth.

It seems that Kádár during the Prague Spring was as duplicitous as Tito had been during the Hungarian Revolution. The Yugoslav dictator gained the trust of Imre Nagy, when, in a letter of October 29, 1956, he supported the program of the Nagy government, calling for democratic and social reforms and negotiations regarding Soviet troop withdrawals. On November 2, however, Tito told Khrushchev and Malenkov that "the accomplishments of socialism" must be defended, and he backed the Soviet decision on military intervention.[3]

The presentation of Kádár as a biased intermediary was first offered by the historian Miklós Kun.[4] His work is based on Soviet and Hungarian archival sources, at times the same ones Békés uses, as well as on interviews with some of the major participants. A specialist reflecting on Kun's work has made a case that the portrayal of Kádár as a reluctant supporter of the intervention is a myth that was first propagated by Kádár himself.[5] His presentations to his Party's Politburo and Central Committee during the 'Prague Spring' bear this out.

On the tenth anniversary of Imre Nagy's execution on June 16, 1968, the Prague *Literární listy* published a commemorative article. This was followed by the incendiary June 27 "Two Thousand Words" manifesto. As Békés writes, Kádár condemned both, which is not surprising, since the article on Nagy declared that "The text of the death sentence is in the style of the 1949 Comintern decisions 'against Tito and his band of spies.'... Here is a poorly camouflaged action by the Hungarian and Soviet security forces."[6] The truth was much worse. Kádár was personally responsible for the execution of Nagy. Reading the article, Kádár must have seen Banquo's ghost, perhaps re-membering his truculent words to the Party's Central Committee for the initiation of proceedings against Nagy and his associates: "they must be put before the court in a procession, sentenced to death, and executed."[7] Békés claims that "contrary to previous interpretations" these publications from Prague did not represent a turning point in favor of intervention by the Hungarian leaders, as the HSWP continued to oppose a military solution (p. 13). Previous interpretations,

---

3   József Kiss, Zoltán Ripp, and István Vida, eds., *Top Secret. Magyar-Jugoszláv kapcsolatok 1956. Dokumentumok* [Top Secret: Hungarian-Yugoslav Relations 1956] (Budapest, 1995), 18–19.

4   Miklós Kun, *Prágai tavasz-prágai ősz, 1968 fehér foltjai* [Prague Spring, Prague Fall. Blank Spots of 1968] (Budapest, 1998; English transl. 1999). A recent Hungarian edition of the book includes facsimiles of key documents from the Hungarian archives. See Miklós Kun, *A "Prágai Tavasz" titkos története* [The Secret History of the "Prague Spring"] (Budapest, 2008), 127–68, 183, and 347.

5   János Kenedi, "Kismester dalnokok. Egy-két szó Kun Miklós könyve ürügyén" [Minor Meistersingers. A few words using the book of Miklós Kun as an excuse], http://www.rev.hu/portal/rev/tanulm'nyok/kadarrendszer/kismester

6   Quoted in Kun, *A "Prágai Tavasz,"* 81.

7   Quoted in János Rainer, *Nagy Imre 1953–1958. Politikai életrajz* [Imre Nagy, 1953–1958, Political Biography (Budapest: 1956-os Intézet, 1999), 383.

however, refer only to Kádár,[8] and it is difficult not to assume that the attack on his person did not contribute to Kádár's change of heart during his Party delegation's visit to Moscow at the end of June and early July. The fact that Kádár wrote a letter protesting the Nagy article and the "Two Thousand Words," which was handed to Dubček on July 5, indicate, that these had an impact on Kádár.[9] Moreover, even at his last meeting with Dubček on August 17, Kádár again brought up the episode and charged that the Czechoslovak leaders' "reaction to the Imre Nagy article was not [a] communist answer."[10]

Békés's explanation for Kádár's switch is that "The Hungarian leadership itself differed at that time from the Soviet line on a number of issues, such as economic relations with the West in general and relations with the FRG in particular, so it seemed important to maintain the goodwill of the Soviet leadership." According to Békés, for this reason, Kádár made a vague claim that the Hungarian Party "would support a military intervention as a measure of last resort" (p. 14). Even though this visit reflected a keen awareness on the part of Kádár and his delegation that Hungary's road to Bonn was through Moscow, and so they must toe the line, one cannot reject the possibility that the sensitive issue of Nagy pushed Kádár to a stance which went against the will of the Hungarian Party leadership.

This episode was identified by a recent biographer of Kádár, Roger Gough, as "the murkiest incident in Kádár's role in the Czechoslovak crisis."[11] Gough claims that historians are split on explaining what really happened in Moscow. One group argues that throughout the 'Prague Spring' Kádár projected an image of moderation for his Hungarian comrades' consumption at home. Consequently, his report to the Party's Politburo about the Moscow visit did not include the commitment he had made for intervention. The other group claims that Brezhnev's account identifying Kádár as explicitly supporting intervention was mistaken and distorted because military intervention was

---

8   See for example Kun, A *"Prágai Tavasz,"* 81.

9   See a facsimile of the report July 6, 1968, of the Hungarian Consul General in Bratislava concerning the transmission of Kádár's letter in ibid., 140–41.

10 "Jegyzőkönyv a Központi Bizottság és a Minisztertanács 1968. augusztus 23-án megtartott együttes és zárt üléséről," p. 8. The author of a recent Kádár biography also claims that the article on Nagy played a role in making the Hungarian leader "re-examine his position." See Tibor Huszár, *Kádár. A hatalom évei, 1956–1989* [Kádár: The Years of Power, 1956–1989] (Budapest, 2006), 175.

11 Roger Gough, *A Good Comrade: János Kádár. Communism in Hungary* (New York, 2006), 166.

acceptable to the Hungarian leader only when all other options were exhausted. I find the former argument more convincing. For me, Kádár was a "faux bonhomme." Békés, on the other hand, embraces the latter interpretation. For him Kádár was a reluctant ally.

Békés points out that, at the Warsaw meeting of July 14–15, in response to Walter Ulbricht's and Todor Zhivkov's attacks on Czechoslovakia, Kádár thought it advisable to repeat the "declaration of loyalty" he had made two weeks before in Moscow. Békés claims that this was "facilitated for Kádár by Brezhnev, arguably making it clear that, despite pressure from others, no final decision would be reached at this meeting. Kádár was, therefore, still free,…to work towards a political settlement" (p. 16). In fact, at this meeting, following the attack on Kádár by his comrades, Brezhnev pronounced his infamous doctrine of the right of intervention to defend the achievements of socialism.[12] Brezhnev directed these words at Kádár, and it was this apparent dressing down that led Kádár to declare his support for what really was the Soviet proposal favoring preparations for a joint action.[13] Praising Brezhnev's "profound and accurate assessment" of the Czechoslovak crisis, Kádár concluded that "as far as the assessment and conclusion of the Soviet comrades are concerned, we completely agree with them and are prepared to take part in all joint actions."[14] Békés is correct that Kádár's statement violated the HSWP's resolution calling for a political settlement of the Czechoslovak crisis. That Kádár could disregard the will of his Party again clearly confirmed that Hungary's foreign policy was shaped, not in Budapest, but in Moscow. To justify his stance in Warsaw, at the July 23 Politburo meeting, Kádár reiterated the Brezhnev Doctrine when he declared:

> Our principles did not change…that we help and warn the Czechs with political tools, but at the same time we can use all means in order to block the eventuality that Czechoslovakia ceases to be a socialist country. This is our principle and it is on this basis we were active at the past meeting. Naturally this is also valid for Warsaw.

---

12   Iván Pataki, *A vonakodó szövetséges. A Magyar Néphadsereg közreműködése Csehszlovákia 1968. évi megszállásában* [The Reluctant Ally. The Hungarian People's Army's Participation in the Occupation of Czechoslovakia] (Budapest, 2008), 35

13   Kun, *A 'Prágai Tavasz,'* p. 83.

14   Quoted in Gough, *A Good Comrade*, p. 168.

Since he claimed a consistency of policy, Kádár was forced to argue that the change in the Czechoslovak situation altered the Hungarian position and the evaluation of that situation also changed.[15] Kádár clearly engaged in double-speak. At the closed session of the meeting his position became clearer. In response to the July 22 request of the Soviet military planners, Kádár, supported by his comrades, opted for the participation of one reduced division in the "military exercises" in Czechoslovakia.[16] By this time, in the parlance of the Warsaw Pact leaders, "military exercise" meant intervention.

The Soviet-Czechoslovak negotiations at Čierna nad Tisou that started on July 29 were sanctioned by an earlier decision in Warsaw that called for a final attempt at reconciliation. Békés sees it as the "result of Kádár's tireless efforts at meditation" (p. 17). Instead, it was more like the last hope for Kádár that Dubček could be made to accept the will of the Soviets without their resorting to force. For Brezhnev, the concession to meet with Dubček and company was due to the fact that "the healthy forces" were still not ready to take action. Although mobilization was completed and the troops were ready for intervention, the Czechoslovak "invitation" justifying the aggression was still missing.[17] In Hungary the minister of the interior András Benkei issued his order mobilizing the state security services on August 1.[18]

The Hungarian Central Committee went on record in its support for mobilization on August 7. It seems very likely that by then the Hungarians leaders were informed that there would be no resistance to the invasion. Whether this information came from Czech informants, such as Oldřich Švestka,[19] a member of the Czechoslovak CP's Presidium and editor of *Rudé právo*, who was in constant contact with the Hungarian embassy in Prague, or from Soviet sources, is not clear. What is evident is that at the August 23 combined Central Committee and Council of Ministers meeting Kádár informed his comrades that, "three weeks ago an order was issued to the Czechoslovak army

---

15 Jegyzőkönyv a Politikai Bizottság 1968. július 23-án megtartott üléséről [Minutes of the July 23 meeting of the Politburo], M-KS 288 f. 5/463 ő. e, Hungarian National Archives, 28.

16 Ibid. For a facsimile of Kádár's note that became the text of the Politburo's minutes on the intervention, see Pataki, *A vonakodó szövetséges*, 38.

17 Gough, *A Good Comrade*, 169; and Pataky, *A vonakodó szövetséges*, 76.

18 Kenedi, "Kismester dalnokok," op. cit.

19 Miklós Kun, "A prágai bevonulás órái" [The hours of march into Prague], *Magyar Hirlap Online*, Aug. 19, 2008.

in case the Soviet or other allied troops arrive. Its contents: do not resist." Kádár then drew the conclusion that, "The right, therefore does not wish to start bloodshed, but will continue the political war. This means that during their earlier negotiations they were not sincere."[20] This certainly seems like the pot calling the kettle black!

Dubček, in turn, was not aware of Kádár's insincerity. In his memoirs Dubček wrote:

> Kádár seemed to understand and to agree with me, and, we parted in friendly fashion. Later on he disappointed me profoundly, because he lacked the courage to challenge the Russians by supporting reform in my country. And that disappointment turned into bitterness when I learned, after 1968, that, immediately after meeting me, Kádár called Brezhnev and informed him in great detail about our discussion. It now seems probable that the initiative came from Brezhnev, and the Hungarian leader continued tamely on the Kremlin leash until the invasion....In his own way, he was as much the product of 'Leninist morality' as any of the others.[21]

Between August 12 and 15 Kádár was in Yalta. He was accompanied by the deputy minister of foreign affairs Károly Erdélyi, who was also a Central Committee member, a specialist on the Czechoslovak crisis, and a confidant and former private secretary of Kádár. At the Crimean resort they met with Brezhnev, Kosygin, and Podgorny, and the last details of the intervention were worked out. According to Békés, Kádár concentrated on the post-intervention period and continued to stress that "in the long term only a political settlement could ensure success." The term Kádár used, however, was not "settlement," which would indicate compromise, but "political solution." By that he still meant a solution offered by the left, the "healthy forces." Kádár summed up the two-day Soviet-Hungarian discussions in Yalta:

> We stressed that in the fundamental questions we agree and always agreed: it was about the basic questions of Czech society, and foremost that these questions be resolved in the spirit of socialism and

---

20 20 "Jegyzőkönyv a Központi Bizottság és a Minisztertanács 1968. augusztus 23-án megtartott együttes és zárt üléséről," p. 13.

21 Alexander Dubček, *Hope Dies Last* (New York, 1993), 133 and 173.

in favor of it. Also, our position was and is completely similar to the goals of the leaders of the Soviet Communist Party, the government of the Soviet Union, and our aim to the very end was that united we should help the solution of the questions of Czech society within the interest of socialism.[22]

Békés stresses that at Yalta the Hungarian leader "had the opportunity to criticize the policy of the CPSU in a constructive manner" (p. 17). According to Békés, among other criticisms, Kádár told Brezhnev and company that "the Soviet leadership had been impatient in its dealings with the Czechoslovak Party and that this impatience had been a key factor in the escalation of the crisis; a more patient approach might have rendered military intervention unnecessary." The problem with Békés's summary is its method. Evidently there were no minutes written of the bilateral meeting, and Békés uses Kádár's August 20 report to the Hungarian Politburo as incontrovertible truth on what was said in Yalta. One cannot be sure if he really criticized his Soviet hosts the way he claimed. As Gough pointed out, Kádár, in his report to his Politburo following the early July meeting with Brezhnev, omitted the commitment he had made to the Soviet leader about intervention for the sake of appearing to be a moderate at home. Therefore, it is possible that at the August 20 Politburo meeting he continued to play this role in claiming that he criticized the Soviet leaders in Yalta for the way they conducted their business with Czechoslovakia. It is difficult to trust Kádár's words when he also reported that "The Soviet comrades did not reject our position on any of the questions."[23]

Another problem with Békés's description is that in the five-page long minutes of the August 20 Politburo meeting there is no mention that Kádár told his host that "a more patient approach might have rendered military intervention unnecessary." What the minutes say is that in Yalta Kádár noted the uniqueness of the Polish, Hungarian, and Czechoslovak events and stressed that the Czechoslovak situation was closer to the Polish one.

---

22 "Jegyzőkönyv a Központi Bizottság és a Minisztertanács 1968. augusztus 23-án megtartott együttes és zárt üléséről," 2–3.

23 "Jegyzőkönyv a Központi Bizottság és a Minisztertanács 1968. augusztus 23-án megtartott együttes és zárt üléséről," p. 6.

"Still the Soviet comrades followed the Hungarian recipe,"[24] he declared. This statement indicates that, even on the eve of the Warsaw Pact invasion, Kádár was still playing to his Hungarian audience the moderate's role of one who objected to the use of force.

Békés writes that in Yalta, "Brezhnev entrusted a last mediation to Kádár, saying that the Hungarian Party was the only one, in addition to the CPSU, that Dubček might be prepared to heed" (p. 18). But it was also on August 17 that the CPSU's Politburo gave its final blessing and provided a date for the start of the invasion. Therefore, Kádár's mission was not mediation, but as Roger Gough pointed out, Brezhnev's goal was to have Kádár check whether Dubček could be trusted in some future position.[25]

At their meeting, Kádár, who kept mum about the coming invasion, tried to make Dubček accept the Soviet position by saying "But you know them, don't you?"[26] This question, in my opinion, revealed more about Kádár's modus operandi during the 1968 crisis than anything else. For Kádár knew "them," and he always acted in a way that would please "them." His "mediation" should be seen in this light, and his call for a political solution instead of force meant merely that the reformist Czechoslovak leaders should come around peacefully and accept the will of their Soviet masters.

Following the Soviet Politburo's decision, Kádár was ordered by Brezhnev to return to Moscow on August 18 by 10:00 a.m. for a meeting on the Czechoslovak crisis.[27]

On that day, the Warsaw Pact "Five" approved the intervention. As expected, the invasion and occupation of Czechoslovakia proceeded without a hitch, but as Kádár admitted to the Central Committee on August 23, "unfortunately the execution of the political plan suffered a serious break at the very beginning...consequently there is no Czechoslovak authority."[28]

---

24 "Jegyzőkönyv a Politikai Bizottság 1968. augusztus 20-án tartott üléséről" [Minutes of the August 20, 1968, meeting of the Politburo], August 20, 1968, 288 f. 5/467 ő. e., 1R/5, Hungarian National Archives, 1.

25 Gough, A Good Comrade, 171.

26 Dubcek, Hope Dies Last, 173.

27 For a facsimile of Brezhnev's "invitation," see Kun, A "Prágai Tavasz," 145.

28 "Jegyzőkönyv a Központi Bizottság és a Minisztertanács 1968. augusztus 23-án megtartott együttes és zárt üléséről," 12.

Békés gives credit to Kádár for helping to resolve the impasse by supporting a "compromise with the existing Czechoslovak leadership" (p. 19), who were taken to Moscow by force. The Moscow Protocol is seen by him as a historic compromise, although I tend to think that it was a dictate. He argues that, by sidestepping the "orthodox-hardliner leaders," the Czechoslovaks were saved from the kind of reprisals that took place in Hungary following the crushing of the 1956 revolution by Soviet troops (p. 21). This is the kind of counterfactual argumentation that cannot be proven or disproven. It should be remembered, though, that history never repeats itself. Moreover, a case could be made that, in the light of a potential general strike and actual passive resistance in Czechoslovakia, Brezhnev had no other choice but to use the Leninist tactic of one step forward and two steps back. Compromise was favored first, and then "normalization."

Békés concludes by noting that the "'Prague Spring' would have led to the restoration of parliamentary democracy....Therefore the invasion was the only option for Moscow to avoid that unwelcome eventuality" (p. 25). It is evident that the same was true for Kádár. Halfway through his paper, Békés writes that when the Czechoslovak delegation led by Dubček came to Hungary in mid-June, Kádár reminded his visitors that "The Hungarian experiences of 1956 showed that it was necessary to curb democratization and draw an unmistakable line against deviations and hostile tendencies; otherwise the Party was bound to lose control" (p. 12). All this indicates that the means favored were different, but for both Brezhnev and Kádár, the end was the same: the perpetuation of the Party's monopoly on power. And to answer the question, with which Békés closes his essay, Kádár saw his "liberal" approach as the best way to maintain the Party's power in Hungary, while Husák believed that, for Czechoslovakia, his own hard-line policy worked the best. Both were right, and also wrong, since between 1989 and 2000 communist power evaporated with the same speed in both countries.

15

Legitimacy, Nation-Building and Closure: Meanings and Consequences of the Romanian August of 1968

Dragoş Petrescu

The year 1968 was a watershed in the history of communist Romania. Nicolae Ceauşescu's public condemnation of the August 20–21 invasion of Czechoslovakia by Warsaw Pact troops under Soviet command had a major influence on the subsequent development of Romanian national-communism and, therefore, deserves a thorough examination. With regard to the relationship between the Romanian Communist Party (RCP) and Romanian society at large, 1968 had a threefold significance, best described in terms of three concepts: (1) legitimacy; (2) nation-building; and (3) closure. First, this paper argues that the political actions taken by the Romanian communists throughout 1968 resulted in positive actions expressing consent on the part of large segments of society, which ultimately conferred legitimacy on single-party rule. Nicolae Ceauşescu's gesture of defiance brought him broad popular support and silenced domestic criticism of his regime for many years. Second, the paper demonstrates that 1968 marked the transition from a process of "selective community-building" to a comprehensive nation-building project aimed at constructing an ethnically homogenous Romanian "socialist" nation. What is more, this shift from community-building to nation-building had enormous consequences on the further development of Ceauşescu's chauvinistic nationalism. Third, this paper argues that 1968 marked the beginning of the end of the period of relative economic liberalization and closely watched ideological relaxation initiated by Ceauşescu's predecessor, Gheorghe Gheorghiu-Dej, in 1964.

Nicolae Ceaușescu making his balcony speech in Bucharest on August 21, 1968
Photo Credit: Courtesy of Dragoș Petrescu

Ceaușescu and the RCP, March 1965–April 1968: Consolidation of Power and Belated De-Stalinization

How Ceaușescu managed to be named as Gheorghiu-Dej's successor is still a matter of debate. Post-1989 witness accounts by former "nomenklatura" members reveal that Ceaușescu skillfully managed to convince some of the most influential members of Gheorghiu-Dej's inner circle to support him in order to continue the "national line" initiated by Dej.[1] Indeed, like his predecessor, Ceaușescu was fully convinced that independence and industrialization were the fundamental elements of Romania's strategy of building "socialism." In

---

1   The testimony of Ion Gheorghe Maurer, one of the most influential "nomenklatura" members under the late Dej and early Ceaușescu regimes, is telling in this respect. Maurer became a member of the Politburo in 1960 and was a president of the Council of Ministers (1961–1974) and member of the Permanent Presidium of the Central Committee of the RCP (1965–1974). See Lavinia Betea, *Maurer și lumea de ieri: Mărturii despre stalinizarea României* [Maurer and the World of Yesterday: Testimonies on Romania's Stalinization] (Arad, 1995), 172–7. For more on Maurer's political biography, see Florica Dobre et al., eds., *Membrii C.C. al P.C.R., 1945–1989* [Members of the Central Committee of the Romanian Communist Party, 1945–1989] (Bucharest, 2004), 385. Hereafter quoted as *The Members of the CC of the RCP*.

terms of foreign policy and relations with the Soviet bloc countries, Ceauşescu followed the line set forth by the "Declaration of April 1964," one of the most important official documents of Romanian communism in the post-World War II period. Briefly put, the Declaration proclaimed that all Communist Parties were equal within the international communist movement and, therefore, they were free to choose their own path towards communism. The following paragraph is telling:

> It is the exclusive right of each Communist Party to elaborate independently its political line and specific objectives, as well as the ways and methods to reach them, by applying creatively the general truths of Marxism-Leninism and the conclusions it draws from the thorough study of the experience of other Communist and Workers Parties. *There is no "parent" Party and "offspring" Party, "superior" and "subordinated" Parties, but only the large family of Communist and Workers' Parties having equal rights* [emphasis added].[2]

At the same time, Ceauşescu emulated the Khrushchevite strategy of condemning the crimes committed by his predecessor against Party members in order to consolidate his power. After a period of "collective leadership," from March 1965 to April 1968, Ceauşescu staged a Plenum of the Central Committee of the RCP on April 22–25, 1968. There, Ceauşescu was unequivocal in his disapproval of his predecessor's abuses against a number of Party members. The Plenum's agenda was based on six points: (1) the development of the education system in Romania; (2) an analysis of Party membership and the level of instruction of Party members; (3) an appraisal of the activity of the Party and state apparatus in solving citizens' claims and requests; (4) an analysis of the training level of the armed forces and the problems related to their equipping; (5) the international activity of the RCP; and (6) the rehabilitation of a number of RCP activists.[3]

---

2   See *Declaraţie cu privire la poziţia Partidului Muncitoresc Român în problemele mişcării comuniste şi muncitoreşti internaţionale, adoptată de Plenara lărgită a C.C. al P.M.R. din aprilie 1964* [Declaration concerning the position of the Romanian Workers' Party with regard to the problems of the international communist and workers' movement adopted by the enlarged Plenum of the CC of the RWP of April 1964] (Bucharest, 1964), 55.

3   *Plenara Comitetului Central al Partidului Comunist Român din 22–25 aprilie 1968* [The Plenum of the CC of the RCP of 22–25 April 1968] (Bucharest, 1968). Hereafter quoted as *The Plenum of the CC of the RCP of 22–25 April 1968*.

Point six proved to be the key as it entailed issuing an official decision of prime importance with regard to the wrongdoings of the Gheorghiu-Dej regime: the "Decision of the CC of the RCP regarding the rehabilitation of a number of Party activists." This decision represents the essence of Romania's belated and short-lived de-Stalinization, which lasted from April 1968 to July 1971. It is clear by now that the same year he acceded to the supreme position in the Party hierarchy, Ceaușescu decided to employ the Khrushchevite strategy mentioned above. (This also supports the idea that, from a psycho-historical perspective, Ceaușescu was more of a planner than an improviser.) Thus, in November 1965 he had established a Party Commission composed of four members—Gheorghe Stoica, Vasile Patilineț, Nicolae Guină and Ion Popescu-Puțur—to examine the "political situation of a number of Party activists" arrested or condemned "many years ago." The archival sources that came to light after 1989 show that the commission organized a series of hearings, which looked very much like interrogations, with those involved in the purges or executions of Party militants, especially during the period 1944–1954. The transcripts that were preserved reveal, not only the mechanisms of the bloody power struggle that was fought within the ranks of the RCP during that period, but also that the main goal of the Commission was to condemn the misdeeds of the defunct leader, Gheorghiu-Dej, rather than to establish the facts.[4]

The decision of April 1968 comprised six provisions, which were six indictments of Gheorghiu-Dej's policies concerning the Party apparatus: (1) the "post-mortem political rehabilitation" of Lucrețiu Pătrășcanu; (2) the "post-mortem political rehabilitation" of Ștefan Foriș; (3) the "post-mortem political rehabilitation" of nineteen former party activists: Ecaterina Arbore, Imre Aladar, I. Dic-Dicescu, Tudor Diamandescu, Alexandru Dobrogeanu-Gherea, Elena Filipovici, David Fabian Finkelstein, Dumitru Grofu, Jacques Konitz, Elek Koblós, Leon Lichtblau, Marcel Leonin, Gelber Moscovici (Ghiță Moscu), Alexandru Nicolau, Marcel Pauker, Eugen Rozvan, Alter Zalic, Petre Zissu, and Timoteej Marin; (4) the revoking of the Party sanctions issued against eight Party members: Miron Constantinescu, Ion Craiu, Ioan Demeter,

---

4   For the results of the Party Investigation Commission, see Section L: *Rezultatele anchetei din 1967–1968* [Results of the investigation of 1967–1968], Docs. 66 to 73, in Gheorghe Buzatu and Mircea Chirițoiu, eds., *Agresiunea comunismului în România: Documente din arhivele secrete, 1944–1989*, vol. 2 [Communist Aggression in Romania: Documents from the Secret Archives, 1944–1989] (Bucharest, 1998), 86–120.

Constantin Doncea, Mihai Levente, Vasile Modoran, Dumitru Petrescu, and Aurel Vijoli; (5) analysis of similar cases of other old-timers; and (6) the decision to dismiss Alexandru Drăghici [former head of the Securitate] from the CC of the RCP and to establish the responsibility of those involved in "illegal repressive actions" in order to punish them.[5]

Although it did not have a major impact on Romanian society at large, the Plenum of April 1968 showed the Party and the Securitate that the period of "collective leadership" was over and that Ceauşescu had become the undisputed leader of the Party whom the Securitate had to obey. Nonetheless, Ceauşescu's major achievement in terms of domestic support for his rule was yet to come: the "charismatic" moment that conferred almost overnight legitimacy on communist rule in Romania.

On Ceauşescu's Public Support for the 'Prague Spring': Independence as Reform Communism

Ceauşescu's official condemnation of the crushing of the 'Prague Spring' and his subsequent rejection of the "Brezhnev Doctrine" were interpreted as the display of a reformer. That it was not so can be determined by looking at the way Ceauşescu himself and the Party propaganda machine presented to the Romanian public the events that were taking place in Czechoslovakia. Specifically, throughout the period January–August 1968, the reform process in Czechoslovakia was depicted as a version of the independent-path policies of communist Romania. Not a single reference was made to the significance of the reforms introduced by the regime of Alexander Dubček. Furthermore, nothing was said about the way Czecho-Slovak society at large reacted to the reforms initiated from above, i.e., from the top of the Communist Party of Czechoslovakia (CPCs).

On January 26, 1968, Ceauşescu turned fifty. At a "comradely lunch" offered by the CC of the RCP, Ceauşescu delivered a speech in which he referred only to the importance of maintaining the unity of the international working-class movement and stated that Romania had decided "not to participate to any action that would endanger such a unity," but made no reference

---

5 See *Hotărîrea C.C. al P.C.R. cu privire la reabilitarea unor activişti de partid* [The decision of the CC of the RCP regarding the rehabilitation of a number of Party activists], in *The Plenum of the CC of the RCP of 22–25 April 1968*, 64–76.

to the changes that had taken place at the top of the CPCs.[6] The next month representatives of the RCP leadership had a chance to meet the new leaders of the CPCs when an official delegation of the RCP went to Prague and participated in the festivities occasioned by the twentieth anniversary of the February 1948 coup that brought the communists to power in post-World War II Czechoslovakia. In his speech on February 22, Ceaușescu referred to the "unshakable alliance" between the two "socialist states" and spoke of the need to strengthen the "cohesion of the international working-class movement." Ironically enough, Ceaușescu also invoked the term *normalization* when he spoke about the necessity of "normalizing the relationships between Communist Parties on the basis of equality and mutual respect."[7]

Here, one should assess what stood behind the stereotypical phrases rooted in the "wooden language" of the Romanian supreme leader and try to ascertain what the leadership in Bucharest really thought about the political changes in Czechoslovakia. In this respect, eyewitness accounts by former "nomenklatura" members could be useful. Officially, Ceaușescu expressed in Prague his trust in the "Communist Party of Czechoslovakia, headed by its First Secretary, comrade Alexander Dubček." Unofficially, it seems that Ceaușescu had doubts with regard to the person of Dubček, whom he considered far too lenient and "lacking a clear and firm personal stance." At least, this is what Dumitru Popescu, who would become the RCP chief ideologue, remembers.[8]

After the carefully staged Plenum of April, Ceaușescu received the French president, Charles de Gaulle, on an official visit (May 14–18, 1968). Then, on May 27–June 1, Ceaușescu paid another visit to Yugoslavia and held talks with Iosip Broz Tito. In his official speeches, Ceaușescu referred, time and again,

---

6 Ceaușescu's speech is reproduced in Nicolae Ceaușescu, *România pe drumul desăvîrșirii construcției socialiste: Rapoarte, cuvîntări, articole: ianuarie 1968–martie 1969* [Romania on the road towards completing the building of socialism: Reports, speeches, articles: January 1968–March 1969] (Bucharest: 1969), 37–8. Hereafter quoted as *Reports, speeches, articles: January 1968–March 1969*.

7 Ceaușescu, "Cuvînt de salut la festivitățile de la Praga consacrate celei de-a 20-a aniversări a victoriei oamenilor muncii din Cehoslovacia din februarie 1948" [Greeting speech at the festivities dedicated to the 20th anniversary of the victory of the working people of Czechoslovakia of February 1948] in Idem, *Reports, speeches, articles: January 1968–March 1969*, 80–84.

8 See Dumitru Popescu, *Un fost lider comunist se destăinuie: "Am fost și cioplitor de himere"* [A former communist leader confesses: "I was also a carver of chimeras"] (Bucharest, n.d.), 142. For more on the political biography of Dumitru Popescu, nicknamed "Dumnezeu," i.e., "the Almighty," see Florica Dobre et al., eds., *The Members of the CC of the RCP*, 480–81.

to the fact that all Communist Parties were equal within the international communist movement and free to choose their own path toward communism, emphasizing the need to observe the principle of non-intervention in the internal affairs of a "fraternal" party. During his visit to Yugoslavia, for instance, Ceaușescu stressed these ideas in speeches on May 27 and 29.[9] Nonetheless, it was not until mid-July 1968 that he spoke openly about the right of Czech and Slovak communists to pursue their own path towards "socialism."

For ordinary Romanians, it was clear that something was happening in Czechoslovakia and that the Romanian communists were supportive of the CPCs's initiatives. The Party newspaper *Scînteia* wrote constantly about the political changes in Czechoslovakia. However, no reference was made to official documents of paramount importance, such as the Action Program of the Central Committee of the Communist Party of Czechoslovakia (April 10, 1968), which indicated to a large extent the direction of the reforms envisaged by CPCs. Furthermore, nothing was said about the response of Czechoslovak society in general to the reforms introduced from above. For instance, the "Two Thousand Words" manifesto of June 27, 1968, was not commented on by the Romanian press.[10]

Documents from the archive of the Romanian Ministry of Foreign Affairs indicate that the Romanian embassy in Prague was sending to Bucharest timely and comprehensive reports on the pace of changes in Czechoslovakia. Consequently, it is reasonable to argue that Ceaușescu was aware of the real situation in Prague and of the way some segments of the Czechoslovak society—most prominently the students—were responding to the reforms initiated by the CPCs. For instance, a telegram sent to Bucharest on March 23, 1968, mentioned that among Czechoslovak students there were "inappropriate manifestations," such as requests for renouncing the leading role of the CPCs, hostile statements concerning the army or wishes that Czechoslovakia would pursue a policy of neutrality.[11] Such critical stances by students and

---

9   See Ceaușescu's speeches delivered at the official dinner offered by President Tito (27 May 1968) and on the occasion of his visit to the town of Krani (29 May 1968) in Nicolae Ceaușescu, *Reports, speeches, articles: January 1968–March 1969*, esp. pp. 241 and 249.

10   For a collection of documents related to the Prague Spring and its suppression by the Soviet-led intervention, see Jaromír Navrátil et. al., eds, *The Prague Spring 1968* (Budapest, 1998).

11   Mihai Retegan, *1968—Din primăvară pînă în toamnă: Schiță de politică externă românească* [1968—From Spring Until Autumn: An Outline of Romanian Foreign Policy] (Bucharest, 1998), 96–7.

intellectuals in Prague did not escape the notice of Władysław Gomułka of Poland or János Kádár of Hungary, who had learned from the lessons of 1956. Thus, at the Dresden Meeting, held on March 23, 1968, Gomułka stated: "Why shouldn't we draw conclusions from the experience which we acquired in 1956 in Poland? Why not draw conclusions from what happened in Hungary? That all began in a similar way, comrades. In our country and in Hungary everything started with the writers." For his part, Kádár warned: "The Czechoslovak comrades know best, I believe, what is happening in Czechoslovakia today. But the process we observe, what we see and hear, and what we do not yet see—permit me to explain—this process is extremely similar to the prologue of the Hungarian counter-revolution at a time when it had not yet become a counter-revolution. This means that is the process that took place in Hungary from February 1956 to the end of October."[12]

It should be stressed once again that, in his speeches, Ceaușescu presented the situation in Czechoslovakia as mirroring that in Romania. Ordinary Romanians were told that the Czechoslovak communists, largely supported by the population, were determined to pursue their own, independent path towards "socialism" and that the communist parties of Bulgaria, Hungary, East Germany, Poland and the Soviet Union were not happy with that.[13] Beginning in mid-July Ceaușescu referred constantly to the situation in Czechoslovakia and stressed consistently that the CPCs had the right to decide by itself its way of building "socialism." On July 15, during his visit to the Galați Steel Combine, Ceaușescu delivered a speech in which he stated:

> Our people and the RCP do not share the view of those who are worried by the unfolding of events in Czechoslovakia and who consider that one should intervene in the processes of perfecting the socialist society that are taking place in Czechoslovakia. We fully trust the CPCs ... and the Czech and Slovak peoples and we are convinced

---

12 See Document No. 14: "Stenographic Account of the Dresden Meeting, March 23, 1968, (Excerpts)" in Navrátil et al., eds., *The Prague Spring 1968*, 67, 69.

13 For instance, during the month of July 1968, the Party newspaper *Scînteia* published news about the situation in Czechoslovakia in its issues of 2, 3, 4, 5, 6, 10, 11, 12, 13, 14, 16, 17, 18, 19, 20, 21, 22 and 24 July, which amounts to 18 issues. One has to mention that *Scînteia* did not appear on Mondays.

that under the lead of their Communist Party ... they know how to build socialism in Czechoslovakia in accordance with their wishes and aspirations. We wholeheartedly wish them success.[14]

During the month of August, Ceaușescu took every opportunity to display the RCP's support for the CPCs. On August 11, when he delivered a speech on the occasion of Miner's Day (*Ziua minerului*) and the hundredth anniversary of the establishment of the mining industry in the Jiu Valley, Ceaușescu once again stated that the RCP had expressed from the very beginning its conviction that the actions taken by the CPCs were directed towards the "building of socialism" in that country and would "consolidate and develop the revolutionary achievements of the Czech and Slovak peoples."[15] Then, on August 14, Ceaușescu took the graduation ceremonies at the Romanian Military Academy as an opportunity to address the graduates on the national armed forces and their role within the Warsaw Treaty Organization:

> The command of the armed forces cannot be exercised by an institution from abroad; this is the inalienable right of the leadership of our party and our state.... There can be no justification to admit, in any way, the use of armed forces to intervene in the internal affairs of a WTO member country. The solving of domestic problems belongs exclusively to the Party and people of each country and any kind of interference can only do harm to the cause of socialism, friendship and collaboration among the socialist countries.[16]

14　Ceaușescu, "Cuvîntare la mitingul de la Combinatul siderurgic din Galați—15 iulie 1968" [Speech delivered at the meeting at the Galați Steel Combine—15 July 1968] in Idem, *Reports, speeches, articles: January 1968–March 1969*, 327–328.

15　Ceaușescu, "Cuvîntare la sărbătorirea Zilei minerului și a Centenarului industriei carbonifere din Valea Jiului–11 august 1968" [Speech delivered to the celebration of Miner's Day and the Hundredth Anniversary of the establishment of the mining industry in the Jiu Valley] in Idem, *Reports, speeches, articles: January 1968–March 1969*, 353–355.

16　Ceaușescu, "Cuvîntare la Adunarea festivă din Capitală cu prilejul absolvirii promoției 1968 a Academiei Militare Generale și acordării gradului de ofițer absolvenților școlilor militare—14 august 1968" [Speech delivered at the Bucharest festive meeting occasioned by the graduation of the 1968 contingent of the Military Academy and conferring the rank of officer to the graduates of military schools—14 August 1968] in Idem, *Reports, speeches, articles: January 1968—March 1969*, 365–366.

The supreme leader of the Romanian communists also announced that in the near future a RCP delegation would pay an official visit to Czechoslovakia. That delegation, led by Ceauşescu himself, visited Prague during the period August 15–17. On August 16, during a tour of the *Avia* plant, besides praising the collaboration between the Czechoslovak plant and the Braşov Truck Enterprise, he reiterated that the RCP fully supported the CPCs: "As dear friends and comrades, we wish you to completely succeed in your efforts towards the multilateral development of socialist Czechoslovakia and we assure you on this occasion of the solidarity and the fraternal internationalist support of Romanian communists and the entire Romanian people."[17] The same day, when he signed the "Treaty of friendship, cooperation and mutual assistance between the Socialist Republic of Romania and the Czechoslovak Socialist Republic" (*Tratatul de prietenie, colaborare şi asistenţă mutuală dintre Republica Socialistă România şi Republica Socialistă Cehoslovacă*). Ceauşescu again expressed his support of the course pursued by the Czech and Slovak communists.[18]

About his visit to Prague and the alleged wholehearted approval by the RCP of CPCs policies, Ceauşescu spoke in public on August 20, when he inaugurated the Piteşti Automobile Plant (*Uzina de Autoturisme Piteşti*), which would produce the most popular car in Romania, the *Dacia*.

> During our visit, on the occasion of the talks we had, we could observe with complete satisfaction that the CPCs, its leadership, the Czechoslovak government, the working class, the Czechoslovak peasantry, the intellectuals, the entire people are unabatedly putting into practice the Party policy of building socialism and of developing Czechoslovakia on the path of socialism, in order to ensure a bright future for the working people. We have been profoundly impressed. We have returned with an even stronger conviction that the destinies

---

17 Ceauşescu, "Cuvîntare la mitingul de la uzinele Avia din Praga—16 august 1968" [Speech delivered to the rally at the Avia plant in Prague—16 August 1968] in Idem, *Reports, speeches, articles: January 1968–March 1969*, 385–386.

18 Ceauşescu, "Cuvîntare la solemnitatea semnării Tratatului de prietenie, colaborare şi asistenţă mutuală între Republica Socialistă România şi Republica Socialistă Cehoslovacă—16 august 1968" [Speech delivered to the ceremony of signing the Treaty of friendship, cooperation and mutual assistance between the Socialist Republic of Romania and the Czechoslovak Socialist Republic] in Idem, *Reports, speeches, articles: January 1968–March 1969*, 391–395.

of socialism and of the Czechoslovak people are in safe hands, in the hands of the Communist Party and of its leadership, and that the Czechoslovak people is a wonderful friend of ours in our common struggle for socialism.[19]

The fact that the supreme leader of the RCP was ready to bear witness that the "destinies of socialism and the Czechoslovak people" remained firmly in safe hands could not change the decision already taken "from above and abroad." On the night of August 20–21, 1968, Warsaw Pact troops under Soviet command invaded Czechoslovakia and put an end to the 'Prague Spring.'

After the Balcony Scene:
A Discussion on Legitimacy, Nation-Building, and Closure

On August 21, 1968, from the balcony of the building of the CC of the RCP, Nicolae Ceaușescu addressed the crowds gathered before him. His discourse, highly patriotic and with strong anti-Soviet accents, created a particular state of mind among large segments of the population that seemed to forget about the open wounds of the past two decades of single-party rule in Romania:

> The incursion in Czechoslovakia of troops belonging to the five socialist countries represents a big mistake and a serious threat to peace in Europe and for the destiny of socialism in the world. It is inconceivable in the present day world— when peoples rise to defend their national independence and for equal rights—that a socialist state, that socialist states infringe on the liberty and independence of another state. *There can be no excuse, and there can be no reason to accept, even for a single moment, the idea of a military intervention in the domestic affairs of a fraternal socialist state* [emphasis added].[20]

The significance of Ceaușescu's "balcony speech" of August 21, 1968, is analyzed below in terms of the three concepts mentioned above: (1) legitimacy; (2) nation-building; and (3) closure.

---

19   Ceaușescu, "Cuvîntare la mitingul organizat la inaugurarea Uzinei de Autoturisme Pitești—20 august 1968" [Speech delivered at the rally occasioned by the inauguration of the Pitești Automobile Plant] in Idem, *Reports, speeches, articles: January 1968–March 1969*, 411–412.

20   Ceaușescu's speech of 21 August 1968 was published by the Party daily *Scînteia*, no. 7802 (Thursday, 22 august 1968), 1. The speech was also published in Ceaușescu, *Reports, speeches, articles, January 1968– March 1969*, 415–418.

During the period March 1965–August 1968, perceptions of the regime from below improved gradually as a result of Ceaușescu's foreign policy of independence from Moscow and opening up towards the West, and his domestic policies of relative economic and ideological relaxation. The slight improvement in the standard of living of the population found an echo in the hearts and minds of a majority of Romania's population. Thus, in August 1968—ten years after the withdrawal of Soviet troops from Romania—when Ceaușescu gave his famous "balcony speech" condemning the invasion of Czechoslovakia by Warsaw Pact troops, large segments of the population supported him without hesitation. The effect of Ceaușescu's discourse on Romania's population at large was enormous. It represented for many Romanians the "proof" of Ceaușescu's charismatic qualifications.[21] It may be argued that Ceaușescu's "charismatic leadership," to use Reinhard Bendix's concept, emerged in the dramatic conditions of that August 1968.[22] At the same time, this author agrees with David Beetham, who has argued that the use of the Weberian concept of "charismatic authority" is problematic in the sense that it "assigns far too exclusive an importance to the individual, and leads to fruitless, because unresolvable, disputes about whether particular leaders possess the indefinable quality of 'charisma' or not."[23] Rather, in order to understand the mechanism that provided the Ceaușescu regime with unprecedented mobilizing capacity, one should concentrate on Ceaușescu's personality and leadership style and on the particular circumstances in which popular mobilization occurred.

Ceaușescu was far less flexible in adopting various policies than his predecessor, Gheorghiu-Dej. He was also less imaginative, and his ideological commitment to the main tenets of Marxism-Leninism remained strong. Nonetheless, he was only forty-seven when he became secretary general of the RCP and managed to build a positive image of himself as a "man of the people" by proceeding consistently with grassroots consultations. One can easily grasp the extent of the phenomenon from the large number of domestic

---

21 According to Max Weber, charisma is: "A certain quality of an individual personality by virtue of which he is set apart from ordinary men and treated as endowed with supernatural, superhuman, or at least specifically exceptional powers or qualities." Quoted in Reinhard Bendix, "Reflections on Charismatic Leadership," in Reinhard Bendix et. al., eds., *State and Society: A Reader in Comparative Sociology* (Berkeley, 1973), 619.

22 Bendix, "Reflections on Charismatic Leadership," 616–29.

23 David Beetham, *The Legitimation of Power* (London, 1991), 156.

mass rallies analyzed above, just for the period January–August 1968. During the years 1965–1968, Ceauşescu's domestic visits were carefully staged and often took in the most relevant historic monuments in the area, paying respect to the ancestors with an emphasis on the medieval rulers of the Romanian principalities. This was in sharp contrast with the leadership style of Gheorghiu-Dej, who did not champion such staged domestic visits. Furthermore, the launch of his belated and short-lived de-Stalinization—which was intended primarily to unmask the wrongdoings of Gheorghiu-Dej and damage his legacy among the "nomenklatura" members—made Ceauşescu the undisputed leader of the RCP.

Ceauşescu's policy of independence from Moscow and opening toward the West—initiated in fact by Gheorghiu-Dej—contributed decisively to the mass mobilization that followed his speech of August 21. Critical intellectuals, who became fierce political opponents of the supreme leader of the RCP after 1977, such as the writer Paul Goma, the initiator of the 1977 Goma movement for human rights and perhaps the most famous Romanian dissident, wrote about the atmosphere in Bucharest on August 21, 1968. According to Goma, Ceauşescu's appeal to the population to take up arms and defend their country had a tremendous mobilizing force.[24] Writer Dumitru Ţepeneag remembers that Ceauşescu's discourse had an instantaneous effect on him: "For some days, I was a convinced Ceauşescuist."[25] Journalist Neculai Constantin Munteanu, who became one of the most acerbic critics of Ceauşescu's dictatorship as part of the Romanian desk of Radio Free Europe during the 1980's, in 1977 addressed a letter to Ceauşescu explaining his decision to leave Romania forever. In it, Munteanu mentioned that on August 21, 1968, while he was in front of the CC building listening to Ceauşescu's speech, he felt proud of being a Romanian: "The vehemence of your condemnation of the armed aggression of some member countries of the WTO against a friendly and allied country made me feel proud of being a Romanian."[26]

---

24 Paul Goma, *Amnezia la români* [Amnezia to Romanians] (Bucharest, 1992), 54.

25 Dumitru Ţepeneag, *Reîntoarcerea fiului la sînul mamei rătăcite* [The Return of the Son to his Prodigal Mother's Breast] (Iaşi, 1993), 95.

26 See Neculai Constantin Munteanu, *Ultimii şapte ani de-acasă: Un ziarist în dosarele Securităţii* [The Last Seven Years from Home: A Journalist in the Files of the Securitate] (Bucharest, 2007), 120. Hereafter quoted as *A Journalist in the Files of the Securitate*.

There were some simple themes, such as the struggle for independence and return to traditional values that found an echo in the minds and hearts of a majority of the Romanian population. At the same time, there were some things that people could experience on an everyday basis such as: a cautious ideological relaxation, a slight improvement of living standards, and an opening towards the West. In 1968, things seemed to move in the right direction, and many felt that the RCP leadership was truly concerned with improving the general situation of the population. Such a widespread positive perception of the regime permitted the RCP to achieve a "limited legitimation through consent."[27] Moreover, the "balcony speech"—which was generally perceived as "proof" of Ceaușescu's charismatic qualifications—was given at the beginning of his rule. As Max Weber put it, if a charismatic leader "is for long unsuccessful, above all if his leadership fails to benefit his followers, it is likely that his charismatic authority will disappear."[28] It took more than ten years for Ceaușescu's charisma to erode.

Under Ceaușescu's rule, the RCP engaged in a sustained policy of reinforcing the ethnic ties among the Romanian majority and assimilating the ethnic minorities. In this respect, 1968 was also a watershed. Again, it was Gheorghiu-Dej who initiated a return to the local traditions and thus to an ethnic understanding of the nation. However, Ceaușescu's predecessor applied random terror in order to Sovietize the country and only managed to engage in "selective community-building." As Kenneth Jowitt aptly observed, such a process was aimed at building a political consensus to give a new meaning to the relations between the communist elite and the population at large.[29] This initiative was triggered by Nikita Khrushchev's condemnation, at the 20th Congress of the CPSU, of the crimes perpetrated by Stalin. In its wake, the Stalinist elite in Bucharest, headed by Gheorghiu-Dej, feared a Soviet-backed party coup would replace them with a Khrushchevite faction just as they were close to the Party-State fusion.

The Romanian communist elite used national identity to ensure its political survival. The Romanian Stalinists, however, were not familiar with the language of nationalism and took some eight years (1956–1964) to fully

---

27 Beetham, *The Legitimation of Power*, 117.

28 Quoted in Bendix, "Reflections on Charismatic Leadership," 620.

29 See Kenneth Jowitt, *Revolutionary Breakthroughs and National Development: The Case of Romania, 1944–1965* (Berkeley, 1971), 74.

understand its extraordinary force as an instrument for preserving their absolute power. It was only from 1964 onwards that the process of building selectively a political community was turned into an all-encompassing nation-building process. In 1964, when political prisoners were liberated it seemed no major segments of the population were left out anymore, and the preconditions for engaging in a comprehensive, "socialist" nation-building project were set. But one thing was still missing: the consent of the ruled. Gheorghiu-Dej tamed society through random terror, then distanced himself from Moscow and returned to traditional values in order to avoid de-Stalinization. He thus left the RCP with a legitimacy problem, which was solved only in August of 1968.

As John Breuilly perceptively points out: "Nationalism is, above and beyond all else, about politics and ... politics is about power. Power, in the modern world, is principally about control of the state."[30] The societal response to Ceauşescu's speech of August 21, 1968, made clear that nationalism was a most powerful political principle, able to confer legitimacy on RCP rule in Romania. From that moment on, the RCP propaganda machine emphasized the ancestors' struggles for independence and their heroic deeds. According to George Schöpflin: "Mythic and symbolic discourses can ... be employed to assert legitimacy and strengthen authority. They mobilize emotions and enthusiasm. They are a primary means by which people make sense of the political process, which is understood in a symbolic form."[31] In Ceauşescu's Romania, historians co-opted by the propaganda machine devised a "national" history centered on the four fundamental historical myths of the Romanians: (1) ancient roots, (2) continuity on the present day territory, (3) unity, and (4) struggle for independence.

Ancient roots and *continuity* had to do with the ethnic origins of the nation and with Transylvania, considered a cradle of their nation by both Romanians and Hungarians. *Unity* and *independence* were intrinsically linked to the RCP policies from 1956 onwards. It was the unity of the Party and its independence from Moscow that permitted the Stalinist elite in Romania to survive de-Stalinization. The transfer of such a vision to the Party-State level came almost naturally and was very effective as a propaganda instrument. The medieval rulers of the Romanian principalities had to defend their

---

30 John Breuilly, *Nationalism and the State*, 2nd ed. (Chicago, 1994), 1.
31 George Schöpflin, *Nations, Identity, Power: The New Politics of Europe* (London, 2000), 89.

independence by fighting against the Ottomans; the rulers of communist Romania had to oppose the Soviets in order to preserve the independence of their "socialist" nation-state.

Because Ceaușescu wanted to win a place for himself in the heroic tradition of the medieval rulers of the three Romanian Principalities (Wallachia, Moldavia and Transylvania), from the very beginnings of his rule he manifested his appreciation for the heroic deeds of those medieval rulers and based his leadership style on a systematic program of domestic visits.[32] Under Ceaușescu the myth of Michael the Brave (*Mihai Viteazul*)—the *condottiere* who realized a short-lived unification of the three principalities under his scepter in 1600—was revived. In 1969 Sergiu Nicolaescu started production of the movie *Mihai Viteazul*. Released in 1971, it became the third most watched Romanian film of all time. While *Mihai Viteazul* epitomized the historical myths of *unity* and *independence*, Nicolaescu's *Dacii* (The Dacians), released in 1967, concentrated on *ancient roots* and *continuity*, alluding to the Roman conquest of the Dacian kingdom and the formation of the Romanian people as a Dacian-Roman synthesis. *Dacii* ranks second after *Mihai Viteazul* in the hierarchy of the most watched Romanian historical movies and fourth in the national rankings of the most watched movies of all time.[33]

In the aftermath of the Warsaw Pact invasion of Czechoslovakia, Ceaușescu began what might be termed "itineraries of national cohesion," meant to provide popular backing to the independent policies of the RCP. The day after his famous "balcony speech," August 22, 1968, the Romanian Grand National Assembly—GNA (*Marea Adunare Națională*)—was convened for an

---

32 For more on this, see Cristina Petrescu, "Vizitele de lucru, un ritual al Epocii de aur" [Domestic Visits, a Ritual of the Golden Epoch], in Lucian Boia, ed., *Miturile comunismului românesc* [Myths of Romanian Communism] (Bucharest, 1998), 229–38.

33 For details regarding the movies *Dacii* and *Mihai Viteazul*, see Grid Modorcea, ed., *Dicționarul filmului românesc de ficțiune* [Dictionary of the Romanian Feature Film] (Bucharest, 2004), 164–5 and, respectively, 198–9. For a conceptual framework concerning the process of nation-building in communist Romania, see Dragoș Petrescu, "Communist Legacies in the 'New Europe.' History, Ethnicity, and the Creation of a 'Socialist' Nation in Romania, 1945–1989," in Konrad H. Jarausch and Thomas Lindenberger, eds., *Conflicted Memories: Europeanizing Contemporary Histories* (New York, 2007), 37–54. On the rankings devised by the National Centre of Cinematography regarding the most watched Romanian movies of all times, see "Cele mai vizionate filme românești din toate timpurile" [The most watched Romanian movies of all time] in *Cotidianul* (Bucharest), 23 August 2005; Internet; http://cotidianul.ro/cele_mai_vizionate_filme_romanesti_din_toate_timpurile-2116.html; accessed 29 July 2008. *Mihai Viteazul* was watched by 13,330,000 persons; *Dacii* was watched by 13,112,000.

extraordinary session. In his speech there Ceaușescu stated: "In our opinion, a big and tragic mistake, with heavy consequences upon the fate of the unity of the socialist system and the international communist and workers' movement, occurred."[34] Two days later, Ceaușescu paid another visit to Yugoslavia and again held talks with Tito.[35]

Then, on August 26, 1968, Ceaușescu embarked on an ample program of domestic visits. Transylvania was the prime target of regime's propaganda, where he visited three counties, Brașov, Harghita and Covasna, and took part in four mass rallies in the towns of Brașov, Sfîntu Gheorghe, Miercurea Ciuc and Odorheiul Secuiesc. In two of the counties visited, Harghita and Covasna, the majority of the population is ethnic Hungarian. It seems that, recalling the 1956 Hungarian Revolution, Ceaușescu feared that invasion of Czechoslovakia would stir unrest among the Hungarian-speaking population of Romania. It should be added here that in February 1968 the RCP re-organized the country's territory by, renouncing the Soviet-type organization into regions (*regiuni*) and districts (*raioane*) in favor of the traditional organization into counties (*județe*) and communes (*comune*), and more importantly, replacing the Hungarian Autonomous Region (*Regiunea Autonomă Maghiară*) with three counties, Covasna, Harghita, and Mureș,[36] a situation that angered the ethnic Hungarian population. Consequently, Ceaușescu had good reasons to fear that the Hungarian minority in Romania would take advantage of the international context to fight for its rights.

---

34 The same day, the GNA adopted a document whose importance was equaled only by that of the "Declaration of April 1964": *Declarația Marii Adunări Naționale a R.S.R. cu privire la principiile de bază ale politicii externe a României* [Declaration of the Grand National Assembly of the Socialist Republic of Romania Regarding the Fundamental Principles of Romania's Foreign Policy]. See *Principiile de bază ale politicii externe a României* [The Fundamental Principles of Romania's Foreign Policy] (Bucharest, 1968).

35 Florin Constantiniu, *O istorie sinceră a poporului român* [A Sincere History of the Romanian People] (Bucharest, 1997), 509–10.

36 The Hungarian Autonomous Region was established through *Decree No. 12 of 10 January 1956* and reconfirmed by the *Law for the Modification of the Constitution of 27 December 1960*. The 1968 administrative organization was established by the *Law Concerning the Administrative Organization of the Territory of the Socialist Republic of Romania of 16 February 1968*. For more on this, see Ioan Silviu Nistor, *Comuna și județul, factori ai civilizației românești unitare: Evoluția istorică* [The Commune and the County, Factors of Unitary Development of Romanian Civilization: The Historical Evolution] (Cluj, 2000), 131–7 and Ioniță Anghel et al., *Județele României Socialiste* [Counties of Socialist Romania] (Bucharest, 1969).

At the mass rallies in Sfîntu Gheorghe, Miercurea Ciuc, and Odorheiul Secuiesc, Ceaușescu ended his speeches with a few words in Hungarian, the only occasions when Ceaușescu strove to speak in the Hungarian language.[37] With regard to the revival of historical myths in order to stir popular support for the RCP's policies, one mass rally was of paramount importance: the one on August 30, 1968, in the Transylvanian city of Cluj. In a flamboyant speech to a large audience, Ceaușescu referred for the first time to the RCP as the direct descendant of the heroic deeds of the Romanian medieval rulers *Ștefan cel Mare* (Stephen the Great), *Mircea cel Bătrîn* (Mircea the Old) and *Mihai Viteazul* (Michael the Brave).[38]

It should be stressed once again that Ceaușescu made appreciable efforts to convince Romania's national minorities that the RCP policy was not aimed at their assimilation. In a new series of domestic visits during the period September 20–21, 1968, in another ethnically mixed region of Romania, the Banat, Ceaușescu visited another three counties, Caraș-Severin, Timiș, and Arad, and spoke at at mass rallies in the cities of Reșița, Timișoara, and Arad.[39] Nevertheless, from September 1968 onwards, the emphasis on independence and unity, as well as the cult of ancestors and the manipulation of national symbols became the main ingredients of "Ceaușescuism."

Another proof of Ceaușescu's commitment to pursuing independent policies within the Soviet bloc was his public rejection of the "Brezhnev Doctrine." On November 29, 1968, in front of the GNA a special session

---

37 See Ceaușescu, "Cuvîntare la mitingul din municipiul Brașov—26 august 1968" [Speech Delivered at the Mass Rally in the city of Brașov—26 August 1968); "Cuvîntare la mitingul din orașul Sfîntu Gheorghe-—26 august 1968" [Speech Delivered at the Mass Rally in the Town of Sfîntu Gheorghe—26 August 1968]; "Cuvîntare la mitingul din orașul Miercurea Ciuc—26 august 1968" [Speech Delivered at the Mass Rally in the Town of Miercurea Ciuc—26 August 1968]; and "Cuvîntare la mitingul din municipiul Odorheiul Secuiesc—26 august 1968" [Speech Delivered at the Mass Rally in the Town of Odorheiul Secuiesc—26 August 1968], in Idem, *Reports, speeches, articles: January 1968–March 1969*, 422–30, 431–38, 439–48, and 449–54.

38 Ceaușescu, "Cuvîntare la marea adunare populară din municipiul Cluj—30 august 1968" [Speech Delivered at the Mass Rally in the City of Cluj—30 August 1968], in Idem, *Reports, speeches, articles: January 1968–March 1969*, 478.

39 Ceaușescu, "Cuvîntare la mitingul de la Reșița—20 septembrie 1968" [Speech Delivered at the Mass Rally in the City of Reșița—20 September 1968]; "Cuvîntare la mitingul de la Timișoara—20 septembrie 1968" [Speech Delivered at the Mass Rally in the City of Timișoara—20 September 1968]; and "Cuvîntare la mitingul de la Arad—21 septembrie 1968" [Speech Delivered at the Mass Rally in the City of Arad—21 September 1968], in Idem, *Reports, speeches, articles: January 1968–March 1969*, 506–516; 517–21, and 521–31.

celebrating fifty years of the union of Transylvania with Romania, Ceauşescu resolutely criticized the concept of "limited sovereignty" applied to the relations between communist countries:

> The thesis that one tries to validate lately, according to which the common defense of the socialist countries against an imperialistic attack presupposes the limitation or renunciation to the sovereignty of a state participating to the [Warsaw] Treaty, does not correspond to the principles characterizing the relations between socialist states and under no circumstances may be accepted. The affiliation to the Warsaw Treaty Organization not only does not question the sovereignty of the member states, but does not "limit" in one way or another their state independence, but, on the contrary, as the Treaty stipulates, is a means of strengthening the national independence and sovereignty of each participating state.[40]

Thus, Romanian national-communism reached its full development only in the aftermath of Ceauşescu's "balcony speech" of August 21, 1968. This was due to the fact that in those days the RCP could safely claim that it was continuing the political traditions of the three Romanian principalities and, what is more, it was perceived as such by large segments of the population.

At the end of August no one imagined that from the mid-1970's on the situation in Romania would decline so rapidly and that by the mid-1980's its standard of living would rank among the lowest in Sovietized Europe. On the contrary, it was widely believed that 1968 was only the beginning of a period of even greater economic liberalization and ideological relaxation. Mobilized by Ceauşescu's bold condemnation of the repression of the 'Prague Spring,' many overlooked the ideological orthodoxy that the Secretary General of the RCP had publicly expressed on numerous occasions even before August 21, 1968.

Apart from the special emphasis on independence, there were not many signs of reform communism in the political thought of Ceauşescu. Instead, Ceauşescu consistently followed the principles enunciated in his Report to

---

40 Ceauşescu, "Expunere la şedinţa jubiliară a Marii Adunări Naţionale consacrată sărbătoririi semicentenarului unirii Transilvaniei cu România—29 noiembrie 1968" [Speech Delivered at the Special Session of the Grand National Assembly Dedicated to the Celebration of Fifty Years since the Unification of Transylvania with Romania—29 November 1968], in Idem, *Reports, speeches, articles: January 1968–March 1969*, 745–746.

the Ninth Congress of the RCP (July 19, 1965). A phrase from Ceaușescu's discourse epitomizes his political credo: "Free and master of its fate, following unabatedly its well-versed shepherd, the Party of the Communists, of the Romanian people, raises its motherland higher and higher to the peaks of socialism, well-being and happiness."[41] One can argue that the underlying meaning of Ceaușescu's statement was that the RCP should be left to lead the country according to its wish, without any external interference. Nevertheless, there was one principle in Ceaușescu's 1965 Report which the Secretary General renounced after 1968, that of "collective leadership and labor." In addition, the idea of "abandoning any tendency of subjectivism in evaluating the cadre," emphasized by Ceaușescu in 1965, also was renounced gradually after 1968, when he started to rely increasingly on his relatives.[42]

References to Stalinist methods of mass mobilization, "systemization" of the national territory, and return to autochthonous values in the sphere of culture were all present in the discourses of the general secretary of the RCP throughout 1968. The same year, the RCP proceeded with the reorganization of the secret police, the infamous Securitate, which was ordered to emphasize the recruitment of intellectuals as informal collaborators. On February 10, 1968, in a speech at the National Meeting of the Union of Communist Youth (*Uniunea Tineretului Comunist*—UTC), Ceaușescu proposed reviving the "traditions of voluntary labor" and re-opening the "national youth worksites," characteristic of the early Stalinist period, as a means of "revolutionary" education of the younger generation.[43] On February 15, the GNA held an extraordinary session to which Ceaușescu presented the project of administrative reorganization of the territory.[44] Then, on February 17, Ceaușescu visited Prahova county, which, in the new administrative organization, was one of the largest. On that occasion Ceaușescu spoke about making rational use of the

---

41 Ceaușescu, *Raport la cel de-al IX-lea Congres al Partidului Comunist Român—19 iulie 1965* [Report to the Ninth Congress of the RCP—19 July 1965] (Bucharest, 1965), 6.

42 Ceaușescu, *Report to the Ninth Congress*, 72, 74.

43 Ceaușescu, *Reports, speeches, articles: January 1968–March 1969*, 50–53.

44 Ceaușescu, "Expunere cu privire la îmbunătățirea organizării administrative a teritoriului Republicii Socialiste România—15 februarie 1968" [Exposé Concerning the Improvement of the Administrative Organization of the Territory of the Socialist Republic of Romania—15 February 1968], in Idem, *Reports, speeches, articles: January 1968–March 1969*, 5-19.

arable land and reducing the built-up areas of towns and villages.[45] By then, the RCP supreme leader already had in mind a plan to "systematize" the territory of the country. Regarding the cultural sphere, on April 19, 1968, Ceaușescu told the National Conference of the Union of Fine Artists in Romania: "During the conference it has been stressed that artists must be devoted body and soul to serving the interests of their socialist motherland, that their highest ideal is to create an art of this country, of this people, an art that responds to the necessities of this glorious moment that Romania experiences."[46]

Last, but not least, one should discuss the reorganization of the Securitate after the Plenum of April 1968. As shown above, the Plenum was carefully staged and represented a frontal attack on the legacy of the previous supreme leader of the party. When Ceaușescu accused Gheorghiu-Dej of wrongdoings with regard to a number of actions taken against Party members, he meant the way Gheorghiu-Dej got rid of his rivals from within the Party. Of course, being part of the "group from prisons" Ceaușescu knew perfectly well what had happened at the time. Another target of the April 1968 Plenum was Alexandru Drăghici, former head of the Securitate, whom Ceaușescu hated. As recent research has shown, beginning in 1967 the Securitate underwent a transformation which culminated with the appointment of Ion Stănescu—a Party activist quite close to Ceaușescu—as its head (May 1968–April 1972). At the same time, the reorganization of the Securitate led to the promotion of officers with higher education, as well as the inclusion of intellectuals among its informal collaborators.[47] Although the methods of the Securitate shifted from sheer repression to prevention, its scope never changed.

To conclude, it is worth citing the bitter words of Neculai Constantin Munteanu: "Back then, in August 1968, in my patriotic euphoria, I did not pay much attention to the placards with slogans that read: 'Ceaușescu—RCP,'

---

45 Ceaușescu, "Cuvîntare la adunarea activului de partid din județul Prahova—17 februarie 1968" [Speech Delivered at the Meeting of the Party Cadre from Prahova County—17 February 1968] in Idem, *Reports, speeches, articles: January 1968–March 1969*, 67.

46 Ceaușescu, "Cuvîntare la Conferința pe țară a Uniunii Artiștilor Plastici—19 aprilie 1968" [Speech at the National Conference of the Union of the Plastic Artists], in Idem, *Reports, speeches, articles: January 1968–March 1969*, 153.

47 For more on this, see Elis Neagoe-Pleșa, "1968—Anul reformării agenturii Securității" [1968—The Year of Reorganizing the Securitate], in *Caietele CNSAS* (Bucharest), no. 1 (2008): esp. pp. 19–22. On the political biographies of Alexandru Drăghici and Ion Stănescu, see Dobre et al., eds., *The Members of the CC of the RCP*, 231 and, respectively, 545.

'Ceaușescu—Romania,' 'Ceaușescu and the people.' Very few could have imagined at the time that those placards were only the prelude to a future and violent recrudescence of the personality cult."[48] Unfortunately, that August in 1968 a majority of the population, including former political prisoners, were misled by Ceaușescu's stance.

This paper has demonstrated that the political actions taken by the Romanian communists throughout 1968, which culminated with Ceaușescu's public condemnation of the Soviet-led invasion of Czechoslovakia, ultimately conferred legitimacy on single-Party rule. Furthermore, Ceaușescu's gesture of defiance not only brought him broad popular support, but also permitted him to portray himself as a "dissenter" within the Soviet bloc, which undermined domestic critical stances towards the regime for many years. In 1968, people in the street could see and feel that something had changed in Romania: the country was opening towards the West; a cautious ideological relaxation was under way as was a slight improvement of the living standard, while the Party was distancing itself from the Kremlin. All in all, a rather positive perception of the regime permitted the RCP to achieve a "limited legitimation through consent."[49]

Second, this paper has demonstrated that 1968 marked the transition from a process of "selective community-building" to a comprehensive nation-building project aimed at constructing an ethnically homogenous Romanian "socialist" nation. As its result, Romanian national-communism reached full development in the aftermath of Ceaușescu's "balcony speech" of August 21, 1968. In those days the RCP could claim that it was the heir of the political traditions of the three historic Romanian principalities, and it was perceived as such by large segments of the population. In order to convince the population of its commitment to traditional values, the RCP propaganda machine made full use of the four fundamental historical myths on which modern Romania was created in the second half of the nineteenth century: ancient roots, continuity, unity, and struggle for independence.

Third, the present analysis has shown that 1968 actually marked the beginning of the end of the period of relative economic liberalization and timid ideological relaxation initiated by Ceaușescu's predecessor, Gheorghe Gheorghiu-Dej, in 1964. Ceaușescu's support for the 'Prague Spring' did not

---

48 Neculai Constantin Munteanu, *A Journalist in the Files of the Securitate*, 121.

49 As defined by Beetham, 117.

derive from his commitment to reform communism. On the contrary, there were no similarities between the RCP's domestic policies and the reform program of the CPCs. On the contrary, apart from the special emphasis put on independence and non-interference in the internal affairs of a "fraternal" party, there were not many signs of reform communism in the political thought of Ceaușescu. From January to August 1968, Ceaușescu constantly referred in his speeches to Stalinist methods of mass mobilization, "systemization" of the national territory and the return to autochthonous values in the sphere of culture. Moreover, in the same year the RCP proceeded with the reorganization of the infamous Securitate to put a stronger emphasis on the promotion of officers with higher education and the recruitment of intellectuals as informal collaborators. This was the true legacy of 1968 for Romania.

16

Commentary on "Legitimacy, Nation-Building and Closure: Meanings and Consequences of the Romanian August of 1968"

Monica Ciobanu

Nineteen sixty-eight remains a decisive year in the history of communism. The failed attempt of the reformist faction of the Czechoslovak Communist Party to build "socialism with a human face," based on a more flexible interpretation of Marxist ideology which departed from the Leninist Soviet model, signaled the future evolution of socialist regimes as well as their eventual demise. To an important degree, it shaped the evolving relationship between the regimes of satellite countries in the communist bloc including—besides Czechoslovakia—Bulgaria, East Germany, Hungary, Poland, and Romania and their respective societies. For the next twenty-one years, this state-society dynamic was characterized by a mixture of coercion, compromise and tacit consent. In exchange for a ritualistic participation in the political process, these regimes offered citizens limited freedoms as well as some social and economic benefits.

After the repression of the Hungarian revolution in 1956, the 1968 invasion of Czechoslovakia by countries of the Warsaw Pact led by the Soviet Union taught the reformist and dissident movements from East and Central Europe two important lessons. In the first place, East European communist parties learned to exercise restraint in their relationship with Moscow. Second, the reformist elements of the communist parties understood that any departure from the Soviet model was acceptable only insofar as it did not question the hegemony of the Party-state. Dissident movements themselves saw the necessity of engaging in limited opposition. In some cases, the lessons of 1968 resulted in either the development of more liberalized regimes or in opposition movements from below. János Kádár's communist regime in Hungary, which promoted a type of consumerist socialism under the slogan "Who is not against us is with us!" became at the time the most economically open socialist regime. The workers' opposition in Poland, represented by the Solidarity movement, adopted the evolutionary model of change based on a gradual democratization of society.[1]

In respect to Romania, the 1968 events in Czechoslovakia brought the fundamental and definitive transformation of the regime into a nationalist-dynastic version of the Soviet model. This regime became the most repressive in Eastern Europe and, unlike its other socialist counterparts, remained autarkic and unchallenged under the authority of its leader Nicolae Ceaușescu until December 1989. Dragoș Petrescu's empirical and conceptual analysis of the three basic levels that determined the relationship between the Romanian Communist Party (RCP) and the Romanian society—legitimacy, nation-building, and closure—vigorously demonstrates this thesis. Ceaușescu's patriotic speech of non-interference in the internal affairs of another socialist state delivered from the balcony of the Central Committee headquarters of the Communist Party in 1968 had a twofold meaning. It symbolized the end of a very brief period of liberalization of the regime initiated in 1958 by the former Party leader Gheorghe Gheorghiu-Dej, which had culminated with Dej's 1964 "Declaration of Independence" criticicizing Russia's hegemony in the Soviet bloc as well as its permanent capacity to threaten the national independence of Romania.[2] Ceaușescu's speech also marked the beginning of an ideological

---

1   For an analysis of Hungarian communism under Kádár, see Ferenc Feher, Agnes Heller & Gyorgy Markus, *Dictatorship Over Needs* (New York, 1983) and Ferenc Feher, "Paternalism as a Mode of Legitimation in Soviet-Type Societies," in T.H. Rigby & Ferenc Feher, eds., *Political Legitimation in Communist States* (New York, 1982), 53–72. For the Polish Solidarity, see Michael Bernhard, *The Origins of Democratization in Poland: Workers, Intellectuals, and Oppositional Politics* (New York, 1993) and Laba Roman *The Roots of Solidarity: A Political Sociology of Poland's Working Class Democratization* (Princeton, 1991).

2   Regarding the conflict between the RCP and the Soviet Union, I agree with Vladimir Tismaneanu's interpretation that this was not rooted in the tension between center and periphery, but rather in the inability of Romanian communists to cope with the Stalinist legacy. Vladimir Tismaneanu, "The Tragicomedy of Romanian Communism," *East European Constitutional Review*, 3, no. 2, (1989), pp. 55–83.

reconstruction that was finalized in the 1970's. This shift relates to the development of Ceaușescu's cult of personality linked to the myths of heroic historical figures that had fought for Romanian national unity and independence since ancient and medieval times. Eventually, this personality cult resulted in a total ideological identification between the leader, the party, and the nation.[3]

The tendency to combine the cult of personality with nationalist propaganda was initiated by Gheorghiu-Dej. After 1958, when the Soviet Union withdrew its troops from Romania, a new era of national communism seemed to take shape. The ethnic Romanian faction of the party led by Gheorghiu-Dej managed to ensure its supremacy over a foreign faction, led by Anna Pauker, consisting of non-ethnic Romanians who had been trained and sent by the Soviet Union. Consequently, the early 1960's history began to be rewritten while some "bourgeois" intellectuals and professional cadres willing to serve the country on the road to socialism were rehabilitated.[4] Russian-language studies as an educational requirement were abolished, as was the Maxim Gorki Institute of History in Bucharest. As Petrescu shows, this effort of the RCP to identify itself with the cause of national independence was by no means a genuine attempt to reform the system, but rather a reflection of the desperate need of Romanian communists to break with the anti-national history of Soviet ideology.[5] It is appropriate that Ceaușescu's historic speech from 1968 be examined in this context of the problematic history of Romanian communism. This history has always been rooted in an ongoing problem of credibility that the RCP faced after it took power in 1947, but the need to modify or add to the slavish imitation of Soviet ideology and indigenous sources of legitimacy became even more evident after Khruschev's denunciation of Stalin and his cult in 1956.

Ceaușescu's own cult of personality, which emerged in 1968 and then reached levels of Orwellian absurdity, differentiated him from his predecessor. In this respect, Petrescu's use of the concept of charisma, as developed by Max Weber within the framework of his classical theory of legitimacy

---

[3] Mary Ellen Fischer provides an insightful analysis of Ceaușescu's cult of personality in *Nicolae Ceaușescu: A Study in Political Leadership* (Boulder, CO, 1989).

[4] For a thorough examination of Dej's era see Stelian Tanase, *Elites and Society: Gheorghe Gheorghiu-Dej's Government 1948–1965* (Bucharest, 1988).

[5] At its third congress, the RCP expressed its approval of the return of Bessarabia (the northern part of Romania that was acquired in 1917) to the Soviet Union. For a detailed and objective history of the RCP, see Robert R. King, *A History of the Romanian Communist Party* (Stanford, CA, 1980).

and domination, needs further analysis. According to Weber, any system of domination exerts its authority through a belief in its legitimacy and obtains as a consequence the desired outcome of obedience. He distinguishes three pure types of authority on which legitimate domination establishes its claims. The first is legal authority based on rational grounds and principles of legality embodied in it. The second is traditional authority, where obedience is seen as a matter of personal loyalty to the chief, who by virtue of his position is bound to specific traditions of rule or governance. The third type of authority, charisma, is characterized by the existence of a leader, who, through the recognition of his virtue or exceptional qualities, claims and gains obedience from his followers and disciples.[6]

Ceaușescu's speech provided him the opportunity to present himself as a patriotic and heroic leader who put the national interest ahead of Soviet ideology. In the eyes of many he became—even if for a brief period—a charismatic leader. The speech made him popular and raised hopes even among former political prisoners. In it, he condemned the invasion of Czechoslovakia, criticized any foreign intervention in the internal affairs of a sovereign state, and reaffirmed that he and the RCP would never tolerate such an attack on Romania, suggesting that Romania might be in danger of Soviet invasion. Such was its power that some intellectuals were persuaded to join the RCP. These reactions are not surprising given that Romanian society was awakening from a long and painful period of Gulag-style repression. The reference to national independence would resonate very strongly in Romania, and also shape Ceaușescu's image in the Western world into the early 1980's. In this context, there is a strong connection between national and international legitimacy that the paper does not explicitly address.[7] For a brief period, Ceaușescu was to become a highly popular leader in the West. His foreign policy actions—refusing to break diplomatic relations with Tel Aviv in 1967 and visiting the United States in 1970 and China in 1971—conferred on him a reputation as an independent communist leader somewhat like Tito in Yugoslavia.

---

6   Max Weber, *Economy and Society*, vol. 1, ed. by Guenther Roth & Claus Wittich (Los Angeles, 1978).

7   For the significance of the international dimension in the process of legitimation undertaken by communist regimes, see Arthur Vidich, "Legitimation of Regimes in World Perspectives," in Arthur Vidich & Ronald Glassman, eds., *Conflict and Control to Legitimacy of Modern Government* (Beverly Hills, CA, 1979), 501–74.

Weber's interpretation of the problematic and temporary nature of charisma also gives us an important historical and theoretical insight into the evolution of Ceaușescu's regime towards a nationalist-communist and dynastic system. Weber's argument that for charisma to become stabilized it needs to be routinized, in either a traditional or a rational-legal (democratic) direction, is of particular relevance. That Ceaușescu chose the former is evident from Petrescu's analysis of the nation-building process and Ceaușescu's own propaganda machinery, which presented him as a patriotic leader. Because Ceaușescu's manipulation of nationalist symbols in the context of the RCP's problematic history and its relationship to the cult of personality is important here, it is also important to emphasize the contribution of a sector of the humanist intelligentsia in constructing this extreme brand of nationalist-communist ideology that incorporated elements of a pre-communist intellectual tradition. This group of novelists, poets, painters, and dramatists initiated a distinctive literary fashion whose guiding ideology—*protochronism*—promoted a nationalist vision of Romanian history that denied any foreign influence on national culture.[8] In their various works they exalted the cult of the nation and glorified the communist leader at the same time.[9]

The cult of personality enhanced the traditional nature of the regime to the extent that it became very similar to what Weber describes as "sultanism," defined as an extreme form of paternalism (a type of traditional legitimacy) that tends to subordinate the power of tradition and administrative apparatus to the discretionary power of the master.[10] The most important elements of the administrative staff that sustained Ceaușescu's personal rule were the secret services (*Securitate*) and the upper echelons of the RCP, both of which were entirely subordinate to Ceaușescu himself. Dragoș Petrescu addresses the importance of the reorganization of the secret services after 1968 in establishing

---

8   The word "protochronism" comes from the ancient Greek and means "before in time." Initially, protochronism referred to the major role played by the original Dacian population that inhabited what the current territory of today's Romania and its contribution to world civilization before colonization by the Roman Empire. Before World War II the fascist movement of the Iron Guard developed a fascist-nationalist ideology that also incorporated elements of the Christian-Orthodox religion.

9   See Katherine Verdery, *Identity and Cultural Politics in Ceaușescu's Romania* (Berkeley, 1991). For the role of intellectuals, see also Michael Shafir, "Political Culture, Intellectual Dissent, and Intellectual Consent: The Case of Romania," *Orbis*, 27, no. 2 (1983), pp. 393–420.

10 Max Weber, op. cit., 231–2.

a closed and autarkic communist regime. Unlike the Stalinist era, in which the secret police overtly engaged in brutal physical repression, under nationalist-communism the Securitate exercised widespread control over the population and prevented any attempt at revolt or opposition by using more subtle methods. Among these methods, Dennis Deletant shows, were the coexistence of physical and psychological terror as well as the practice of spreading rumors.[11]

The upper echelon of the RCP was, like the Securitate, quite small and consisted primarily of "apparatchicks" of rural or working class background educated at the Party academy. Ceaușescu's practice of placing close members of his family in key positions in the RCP, and within the main institutions of power, made any attempts at reformation from within the state apparatus impossible. Despite the appearance of independence that he created for himself in 1968, Ceaușescu never intended to reform the communist system. Petrescu's detailed analysis of the distorted manner in which Ceaușescu presented the reformist character of 1968 in Czechoslovakia sustains this argument as well. Ultimately, by appearing to combine the project of institutional and economic reforms simultaneously with the creation of an indigenous communist ideology, Ceaușescu consolidated his personal rule. This process is well captured by Michael Shafir's conceptual characterization of "simulated change." Analyzing the leadership, cadres, and organization of the RCP, Shafir catalogues Ceaușescu's endless list of official titles that conferred on him sultanistic powers.[12] Meanwhile, his cult of personality was extended to his wife, Elena Ceausescu, whose position within the RCP was substantially enhanced by this halo effect.

The final section of Petrescu's paper connects the events of 1968 to the final stage of Ceaușescu's regime. This is an important argument since many analysts of the communist regime still make a sharp distinction between the so-called period of liberalization initiated in 1968 and abruptly ended in the early 1970's and the late stage of the regime in the 1980's that was characterized by a severe economy of shortages, low standards of living, and extreme repression. Based on the examination of Ceausescu's public statements, Petrescu concludes that "apart from the special emphasis put on independence

---

11   Dennis Deletant, *Ceaușescu and the Secret Services: Constraints and Dissidence in Romania during 1965–1989* (Bucharest, 1998).

12   Michael Shafir, *Romania: Politics, Economics and Society. Political Stagnation and Simulated Change* (Boulder, CO, 1985), 80.

there were not many signs of reform communism in the political thought of Ceaușescu." I believe that this is an important and accurate interpretation. The last ten to fifteen years of the dynastic-nationalist communist regime in Romania, including its violent and abrupt end in December 1989, demonstrate that what seemed unthinkable for many in 1968 ultimately became a reality. In attempting to challenge Soviet hegemony, Romanian communism had essentially reproduced its worst characteristics.

By the late 1980's, Romania was completely isolated from both East and West, and the leadership refused to acknowledge the policies of economic and political decentralization taking place in the Soviet Union under Mikhail Gorbachev. When peaceful negotiations were undertaken between former communist parties and opposition movements in Bulgaria, Hungary and Poland, and the "Velvet Revolution" was unfolding in Czechoslovakia, the RCP was so closely intertwined with Ceaușescu's clan that there was no possibility for agreements, compromise or negotiation. After the execution of the Ceaușescus on December 24, 1989, the RCP disappeared entirely from the political scene.

I would also argue that the false legacy of an "independent foreign policy" initiated in 1968 persisted after 1989. During the first decade of the political transition to democracy, the democratic process was constrained several times by a similar nationalist and xenophobic rhetoric propagated by both former communists and extreme nationalists.[13] Their condemnation of ethnic minorities and of the West, represented by the European Union, NATO, and other international organizations, appealed for a while to disenchanted or marginalized groups. Given that an important segment of the mass-media is still inclined to interpret the events of 1968 as an example of patriotism, it is important that their real significance be properly presented to the public.[14]

---

13   I am mainly referring to the xenophobic rhetoric practiced by the extreme nationalist Party of Great Romania and its leader Corneliu Vadim Tudor. After the 2000 elections it became the most important opposition party. Also, the former communists represented in the 1990's by the Party of Social Democracy and led by Ion Iliescu employed, although to a lesser extent, a nationalist discourse.

14   Rodica Culcer, "1968: promises, illusions and utopias," 22 (a weekly published in Romania), November 25, 2008.

NOTES ON CONTRIBUTORS

CSABA BÉKÉS is a senior research fellow at the Institute for the History of the 1956 Hungarian Revolution and the founding director of the Cold War History Research Center, both in Budapest. He received a Ph.D. in 1989 from Szeged University, where he was a visiting lecturer on post-World War II Hungarian foreign policy from 1990 to 1992. Békés also received a visiting fellowship from the Cold War International History Project, which enabled him to conduct research in American archives. His publications include *The 1956 Hungarian Revolution and World Politics* in the Cold War International History Project Series and *Cold War, Détente and the 1956 Hungarian Revolution*. He was an editor of *Political Transition in Hungary, 1989–1990: A Compendium of Declassified Documents and Chronology of Events* and *The 1956 Hungarian Revolution: A history in documents*. Békés is a visiting scholar of history at Janus Pannonius University, Pécs, Hungary.

GARY BRUCE, Associate Professor of History at the University of Waterloo, holds a Ph.D. from McGill University. His book *Resistance with the People* appeared in 2003 in the Harvard Cold War Project Book Series. He has published numerous book chapters and scholarly articles in the *Journal of Cold War Studies*, *Intelligence and National Security*, and *Contemporary European History*. He has also been an invited participant at workshops hosted by the Federal Commission for the Stasi Files and has presented his work at conferences in Poland, Romania, Germany, Britain, the USA, and Canada. His book on the Stasi at a grassroots level is scheduled to appear in 2010.

MONICA CIOBANU recently received her Ph.D. in Sociology from the New School for Social Research in New York. Her dissertation was entitled "Problems of Political Legitimacy and Democratic Consolidation in Post-Communism: The Case of Romania in Comparative Perspective." As a graduate student, she participated in international seminars on democratization in Hungary and Poland, and she has been affiliated with the Transregional Center for Democratic Studies at the Graduate Faculty at the New School for Social Research. Before she came to SUNY Plattsburgh as an Assistant Professor, Dr. Ciobanu had been teaching courses in the areas of social theory, international criminal justice, and gender at John Jay College of Criminal Justice of the City University of New York.

ŁUKASZ KAMIŃSKI received his doctorate in modern Polish history from the University of Wrocław, where he also teaches in the history department. From 2006–2009 he was Deputy Director (in 2009 he became Director) of the Office of Public Education of the Polish Institute of National Remembrance in Warsaw. He is the co-editor of "Pamięć I Sprawiedliwość" (Warsaw) and author, editor or co-editor of several books, including *Polacy wobec nowej rzeczywistości* (Torún, 2000), *Wokół Praskiej Wiosny. Polska i Czechoslowacja w 1968 roku* (Warsaw, 2004), *Przed I po 13 grudina. Państwa bloku wschodniego wobec kryzysu w PRL 1980–1982, II Vols.* (Warsaw, 2006–2007), and *A Handbook of the Communist Security Apparatus in East Central Europe* (Warsaw, 2005).

STANISLAV J. KIRSCHBAUM graduated from the Universities of Ottawa (B.Sc.Soc.), Toronto (M.A.) and Paris (Drech) and is Professor of International Studies and Political Science at Glendon College, York University, in Toronto. In 1969–1970 he taught at Queen's University in Kingston, Ontario. He has also held visiting professorships at the Université de Montréal and Université Laval in Quebec City and at Trnavská univerzita in Trnava, Slovakia. He has published more than 70 scholarly articles, and edited 14 books and is the author of *Slovaques et Tchèques. Essai sur un nouvel aperçu de leur histoire politique* (1987), *A History of Slovakia: The Struggle for Survival*, 2nd edition (2005), and a *Historical Dictionary of Slovakia*, 2nd edition (2007). He was made a Chevalier des Palmes académiques de France in 1994, received the Commemorative Medal from Matica slovenská in Slovakia in 1995, and the Jubilee Medal from Trnavská univerzita in 2008, and was elected a Fellow of the Royal Society of Canada in 2002.

MARK KRAMER is the Director of the Harvard Project on Cold War Studies and a Senior Fellow of the Davis Center for Russian and Eurasian Studies, Harvard University. He has taught at Harvard, Yale, and Brown Universities and was formerly an Academy Scholar in Harvard's Academy of International and Area Studies and a Rhodes Scholar at Oxford University. Professor Kramer's recent publications include, *The Dynamics of the Soviet-Czechoslovak Crisis, 1968: The Prague Spring and the August Invasion*. He is completing two other books–*Crisis, Compromise, and Rebellion in the Soviet Bloc, 1956* (Stanford University Press, forthcoming) and *From Dominance to Hegemony to Collapse: Soviet Policy in East-Central Europe, 1945–1991* (Oxford University Press, forthcoming).

MICHAEL KRAUS, Frederick C. Dirks Professor of Political Science, directs Russian and East European studies at Middlebury College, Vermont. His publications include *Irreconcilable Differences? Explaining Czechoslovakia's Dissolution* and *Russia and Eastern Europe After Communism: The Search for New Political, Economic, and Security Systems*, as well as articles in the *Journal of Democracy, Current History, Foreign Policy, Politique Internationale, New England Review, European Affairs,* and elsewhere. He has held research and teaching appointments at Harvard's Kennedy School of Government, Columbia University, George Washington University and Charles University (in Prague).

MIKHAIL LATYSH graduated from Moscow State University in 1979. In 1985 he earned the degree of Candidate in Science (CSc.) in history. For many years Dr. Latysh was employed as a researcher at the Institute of Slavonic Studies, within the Russian Academy of Sciences in Moscow. At the moment he is loosely affiliated with the Moscow State University history department. He was a Fulbright Fellow and a Woodrow Wilson Fellow and received a grant from the American Council for Learned Societies. Latysh is the author of *The Prague Spring of 1968 and the Kremlin's Reaction*, published in 1998 in Russian. He has also written another volume on "The Czechoslovak Crisis in the Context of Soviet Geopolitics" based on recently-discovered original documents. It awaits publication.

SLAVOMÍR MICHÁLEK is Director of the Historical Institute of the Slovak Academy of Sciences in Bratislava. He is a graduate of Comenius University and received a Doctor of Science degree from the Slovak Academy of Sciences. Michálek specializes in the history of Slovakia in the twentieth century, especially in diplomatic contacts between the USA and Slovakia, Czechoslovakia and Slovaks abroad. He has published or edited a dozen monographs on Slovak diplomatic personalities abroad, as well as dozens of articles. His latest book is *Rok 1968 a Československo: Postoj USA, Západu a OSN* [1968 and Czechoslovakia: The Reaction of the USA, the West and the United Nations] (Bratislava, 2008).

MATTHEW J. OUIMET is Director of Analytic Effectiveness in the U.S. Department of State's Bureau of Intelligence and Research (INR). He has been an analyst of Russian foreign policy in INR's Office of Analysis for Russia and Eurasia for nearly seven years. Before that he was a lecturer in Russian History and International Affairs at the University of Washington in Seattle and at Columbia College. He is the author of *The Rise and Fall of the Brezhnev Doctrine in Soviet Foreign Policy*, published by the University of North Carolina Press. He holds a Master's Degree in International Affairs and a Ph.D. in Modern Russian History from the University of Washington.

PETER PASTOR was educated in Hungary and the United States and received his Ph.D. from New York University. He is Professor of History at Montclair State University, New Jersey. His publications include a monograph, *Hungary Between Wilson and Lenin: The Hungarian Revolution of 1918–1919*. He also edited or co-edited five books including an annotated collection of diplomatic documents sent by the Hungarian ministers in Moscow to Hungary between 1935 and 1941. His articles have appeared in edited books and in various academic journals, including *Slavic Review* and *Europe-Asia Studies*. His recent articles on various aspects of the 1956 Hungarian Revolutions were published in a number of Hungarian journals. For his academic contributions, in 2003 he was awarded the Commander's Cross of the Hungarian Republic.

DRAGOȘ PETRESCU, Ph.D., is Lecturer in Comparative Politics and Recent History in the Department of Political Science, University of Bucharest and a Member of the Board of the National Council for the Study of Securitate Archives (CNSAS) in Bucharest. He co-authored the *Raport Final al Comisiei Prezidențiale pentru Analiza Dictaturii Comuniste în România* [Final Report of the Presidential Commission for the Analysis of the Communist Dictatorship in Romania] (Bucharest, 2007) and co-edited the volume *Nation-Building and Conflicting Identities: Romanian and Hungarian Case Studies* (Budapest, 2001).

JAN RYCHLÍK studied history and ethnology at Charles University in Prague and at St. Kliment Ohridski University in Bulgaria, where he obtained his Ph.D. in 1985. He is a professor of modern Czech, Slovak and Balkan history at Charles University in Prague and professor of modern history at Sts. Cyril and Methodius University in Trnava, Slovakia. He is also a senior researcher at the Masaryk Institute of the Academy of Sciences of the Czech Republic. His main publications are: *The Czechs and Slovaks in the 20th Century* (in Czech and in Slovak); *R. W. Seton-Watson and His Relations with Czechs and Slovaks, 1906–1951: Documents*; *A History of Bulgaria* (in Czech); *A History of Macedonia* (in Czech); and *A History of Croatia* (in Czech).

STANISLAV SIKORA is a graduate of Comenius University in Bratislava and holds the Candidate in Science degree from the Historical Institute of the Slovak Academy of Sciences, where he is employed as an historical researcher. He is a specialist on the Social Democratic movement in Slovakia, as well as on the political history of Slovakia in the 1950's and 1960's. He has published dozens of articles and many monographs on these subjects, including *Predjarie. Politický, ekonomický a kultúrny vývoj na Slovensku v rokoch 1960–1967* [Prelude to the Spring: Political, Economic and Cultural Developments in Slovakia in 1960–1967] (2002) and *Rok 1968 a politický vývoj na Slovensku* [1968 and Political Developments in Slovakia] (2008).

IVANA SKÁLOVÁ, PhDr., is a history graduate of Charles University in Prague and the author of *Podíl Bulharska na potlačení Pražského jara 1968* [The Role of Bulgaria in the Suppressing of the Prague Spring of 1968] (Prague, 2005). She is a professional archivist and is currently Deputy Chief of the Reading Room, Regional State Archives in Prague. She is also editor-in-chief of the *Navýchod* magazine, which focuses on the countries of East Central Europe, the Balkans, the Baltics, the Caucasus, and Central Asia. She also serves on the Archival Science Board, an advisory body to the Minister of the Interior of the Czech Republic.

MARIÁN MARK STOLÁRIK, Ph.D. (Minnesota), is Professor of History and holder of the Chair in Slovak History and Culture at the University of Ottawa. From 1979 to 1991 he was President and CEO of the Balch Institute for Ethnic Studies in Philadelphia. He has published eight books and over 60 articles, including *Slovaks in Bethlehem, Pennsylvania, 1880-1976* (1985); *The Slovak Americans* (1988) and *Immigration and Urbanization: The Slovak Experience, 1870–1918* (1989). He recently edited *The Slovak Republic: A Decade of Independence* (2004). Stolárik was also a consultant and contributor to the *Harvard Encyclopedia of American Ethnic Groups* (1980); to *The Encyclopedia of Canada's Peoples* (1999) and to *The Encyclopedia of American Catholic History* (1997). Currently, he is finishing the manuscript *Where is my Home? A Slovak Odyssey Through the 20th Century.*

Dr. RÜDIGER WENZKE graduated in history from the University of Leipzig. From 1981 to 1990 he was a researcher at the Military History Institute of the GDR. Since 1990/91 he has been a historian at the Military History Research Institute in Potsdam. His main field of research is the military history of the former GDR with a focus on the history of the National Peoples Army and the Warsaw Pact. His most important publications are: *Die NVA und der Prager Frühling 1968* (Berlin, 1995); *Handbuch der bewaffneten Organe der DDR* (Berlin, 1998) (co-author); *Die Generale und Admirale der NVA. Ein biographisches Handbuch* (Berlin, 2000) (co-author); *Die getarnte Armee. Geschichte der Kasernierte Volkspolizei der DDR 1952–1956* (Berlin, 2001) (co-author); and *Staatsfeinde in Uniform? Widerständiges Verhalten und politische Verfolgung in der NVA* (Berlin, 2005).

PIOTR J. WRÓBEL, Ph.D. (Warsaw), holds the Konstanty Reynert Chair of Polish Studies at the University of Toronto. Previously he taught at the Universities of Warsaw, Michigan, Michigan State and at the University of California at Davis. He has authored or co-authored about 50 scholarly articles and nine books, including *The Historical Dictionary of Poland, 1945–1996*, published by Greenwood Press (1998) and *Nation and History: Polish Historians from the Enlightenment to the Second World War*, co-edited with Peter Brock and John Stanley (Toronto, 2006). He serves on the Advisory Board of *Polin: A Journal of Polish-Jewish Studies*, on the Board of Directors of the Polish-Jewish Heritage Foundation of Canada and on the Governing Council of the American Association for Polish-Jewish Studies.

INDEX

A
"Achilles heel," 29
Adams, Sean, v
Afghanistan, 26
Aladar, Imre, 240
Albania, 99, 107, 133
Alexandrov, V., 9, note 28
American, administration, 52
    scholars, xvii
American Association for Polish-Jewish Studies, 275
American Council for Learned Societies, 272
Andrew, Christopher, 25, note 11
Andropov, Juri, colleagues of, 21
    KGB Chairman, proposed use of military, 20
Andrzejewski, Jerzy, 116
Anghel, Ioniță, 253, note 36
Arab-Israeli war of 1967, xxvii
Arad, 254
Arbore, Ecaterina, 240
Ash, Timothy Garton, xviii, note 25
Association of Composers in Prague and Bratislava, 115
Association of Czechoslovak Writers, 116
Association of Polish Writers (ZLP), 96, 115
Austria, xv, 32
Austrian Ludwig Boltzmann Institute, 155
Avia plant, 246
Axen, Hermann, 142

B
Baczko, Bronisław, 98
Baev, Jordan, 172, note 2; 194
Baeva, Iskra, 190, 194; 198, note 14
Balch Institute for Ethnic Studies, 274
Balkans, the, 274
Baltics, the, 274
Banat, 254
Banská Bystrica, 185
Barbírek, František
    denounced the invasion, 48
    mild conservative, 49
    signed Moscow Protocol, 50, note 67
Barela, Stefan, 122
Barnovský, Michal, 62, note 3
Bauman, Zygmunt, 98
Bata, Thomas J., v

BBC, xxviii, 189
Beetham, David, 248 and note 23; 250, note 27; 258, note 49
Békés, Csaba, xxix, xxx, 203, 204, note 1; 207, notes 12 and 13; 210, note 17; 219, 225–8, 231–5, 269
Bednorz, Herbert, 122
Benkei, András, 231
Benz, Wolfgang, 137, note 1
Beneš, Edvard, 61
Benčík, Antonín, 49, note 64; 78, note 28; 99, note 7; 147, note 24; 148, note 28; 194, note 1
Bendix, Reinhard, 248, and notes 21 and 22; 250, note 28
Benkovská, Melánia, xiii
Betea, Lavinia, 238, note 1
Bernhard, Michael, 262, note 1
Berlin
   Crisis, 16, 167
   Greater Berlin, 137
   Wall, 167–8
   West Berlin, 145;
Bieniek, Juliusz, 122
Biľak, Vasil
   anti-Novotný, 66
   approved of Soviet pressure, 8, 52, 74, 81
   conservative (dogmatic) communist, 40, 49, 75, 80
   criticized Dubček, 42, 46
   enemy of Husák, 77
   favored press censorship, 75
   First Secretary of the Slovak Communist Party, 26, 37, 66, 69, 74, 90
   Ideological Secretary of the Slovak Communist Party, 52, 69
   neo-conservative, 75
   opposed use of East German troops, 155
   signed letter of invitation to Brezhnev, 11, 47, 81, 231
   signed Moscow Protocol, 50, note 67
   spy for the Soviet Union, 5, 43, 50, 75
   supporter of Dubček, 69
   welcomed the Warsaw Pact invasion, xiii, xix, xxii, 48, 226
Bild, 152
Bipolar world, 73
Bishop of Częstochowa, xxv
Black Book, The, xvi
Blajfer, Bogusława, 127
Blatov, A., 9
Blazek, P., 98, note 6
Bohemian forests, 153
Bohlen, Charles, 9
Bonn, 4, 25, 134, 145
Bosák
   bank, x
   Martin, Michal, Rudolf, x, note 9;
Branch 63 (Ottawa), Canadian Slovak League, v
Brandt, Willy, Grand Coalition Government of, 134
Braşov Truck Enterprise, 246
Bratislava, xiv
   Bratislava Declaration, 24, 47, 81
   "Bratislava Spring," xv, note 19
   capital of Slovakia, 64
   Extraordinary Congress of Slovak Communist Party meets in, 50
   graffiti in, xv
   occupied, 151
   Party organization, 38
   political situation in, 90
   regional Party committee in, 44
   student demonstrations, 15
   Summit, 9, 47–48, 80, 149, 181, 204, 217, 220
Breuilly, John, 251 and note 30
Brezhnev, Leonid
   accompanied by Bilak, 16
   came to power, 1
   censored Dubček, 57
   condemned by Husák, 12
   criticized developments in Czechoslovakia, 179, 214
   demanded coup in ČSSR leadership, 79

Index

Doctrine of limited sovereignty, 25, 47, 9, 81, 230, 241, 254
Dresden meeting, 173
equated Soviet with Czechoslovak borders, 25
General Secretary of the Communist Party of the Soviet Union, xiii, note 11, xvii
invited "the five" to Moscow, 10, 182
justified invasion of Czechoslovakia, 13
Kádár moderated with, xxx, 224
letter from Biľak, xiii, note 11
meeting at Čierna nad Tisou, 6, 46, 80
meeting with Hungarians in Crimea, 232
meeting with Zhivkov, xxix, 171, 182, 197
met in secret with Husák, 50
misinterpreted support in Czechoslovakia, 7, 27, 77
opposed creation of Czech Communist Party, xx, 15
perpetuation of Party rule, 235
Polish questions about, 110
sabre-rattling, 21, 23
strained relations with Novotný, xvii, 2, 32, 34
supporters in Prague, 42, 44–46
Stalinist, 73
Svoboda negotiates with, 49
telephoned Dubček, 5, 79
telephoned Kádár, 211, 213
upbraided Dubček, 3
vacationed in Crimea, 9
vetoed use of East German army, 155, 167
Brezno, 185
Brno, 44
Brock, Peter, 275
Brown, J. F., 133, note 15
Bruce, Gary, xxvii, 165, 269–70
Bucharest
capital of Romania, xxx
Romanian embassy in Prague sends reports to, 243
Stalinist elite in, 250

Budapest, 204–5
Bukovskii, Vladimir, 26, note 17
Bulletin, 176
Bulgaria, Bulgarians
ambassador (embassy) to Prague, 172, 176
anti-Semitic, 199
apologized to Czechoslovakia for the invasion, 202
archives of, xxix, 193
army, 48, 82, 183, 187, 189, 194
12th artillery regiment (Gencheva),
22nd artillery regiment (Charmanli), 183–5
bad influence of Prague Spring, 175
Czechoslovak embassy, 174
Decree No. 39, 184
delegation to Czechoslovakia, 176
dissident movement, 188
Dresden meeting, 173
"healthy forces," 200
intelligentsia, 174–5, 189–90
invited to meeting in Warsaw, 44
military exercises, 183
military intervention, viii, xxviii, 174–5
News Agency, 197
political secretary in Budapest, 175
Parliament, 189
Propaganda and Agitation Department, 174
secret service, state security agents, xxviii, 175, 189, 199
society paralyzed, 190
students in Czechoslovakia, 175
suppressing Prague Spring, 171
totalitarianism, 190
Bulgarian Communist Party, 172, 193
Central Committee of (CC BCP), 172
First Secretary of, xxviii
Brașov, 253
Brown University, 271
Brusilov, General Aleksei, ix, note 7
Burgas, 188
Bydgoszcz, 106
Bystrický, Valerián, 74 note 20

C

Čaplovič, Miroslav, vii, note 2
Caraş-Severin, 254
Caucasus, 274
Ceauşescu, Elena, 266
Ceauşescu, Nicolae
  balcony speech, xxx, 238, 247–8, 250, 252, 255, 258, 264
  charismatic leadership, 248, 250, 264
  chauvinistic nationalism, 237
  comparison with Czechoslovakia, 244
  condemnation of the invasion of Czechoslovakia, 237, 241, 247–8, 255, 264
  condemnation of his predecessor, 239
  cult of personality, xxxi, 263, 265
  execution of, 267
  independence from Moscow, 248
  legitimacy, 258
  "man of the people," 248
  nationalist-communist, 265
  personality cult, 258
  popular support of, 248
  popular in the West, 264
  reform communism, 259
  rejection of the Brezhnev Doctrine, 241, 254
  Secretary General of the Romanian Communist Party, 241, 247, 262
  speaks Hungarian, 254
  staged visits, 249
  sultanism, 265–6
  supported Czech and Slovak communists, 243, 246, 258
  talks with Tito, 253
  visited Yugoslavia, 242–3, 253
Central Asia, 274
Central Intelligence Agency (CIA), 37
Černík, Oldřich
  meeting with Warsaw Pact in Dresden, 3
  met Soviet Politburo in Moscow, 12, 14, 15, note 48
  opponent of Novotný, 35
  government of (Prime Minister of Czechoslovakia), 39
  defended democratization, 42
  denounced the invasion, 48
  interned in Moscow, 50
  defended reform policies in Moscow, 74
  met with Soviet Politburo at Čierna nad Tisou, 80
  met with János Kádár in Komárom, 215
  signed the Moscow Protocol, 50, note 67
Černý, Václav, 8
Chabada, Jozef, 175
Chair in Slovak History and Culture, v, 274
Charmanli, 183, 188
Chavdarov, Colonel Ivan, 183
Charles University, xix, 271, 273–4
Charter of Human Rights, 123
Chevalier des Palmes académiques de France, 271
Chervonenko, S.V. 5, 8–9, 14, 23, 25, 49, 180
Chief Archivist of the Russian Federation, xviii, 19
China, xxxi, 99, 264
Chňoupek, Bohuslav
  conservative communist, 77
  managing editor of *Predvoj* 7
Cholakov, Delcho, 173
Chovanec, Jaroslav, xxiii, note 29
Chudík, Michal, 35, 38, 71
Chwalko, E., 115, note 28
Čierna nad Tisou
  summit meeting in, xxviii, 6, 10, 25, 28, 46, 48, 80, 110, 149, 181, 217, 220, 231
Císař, Čestimír
  radical reformer, 14
  member of "second center," 75
Cieszyn (Těšín), 132
Ciobanu, Monica, xxx–i, 261, 270
Civic society, 28, 40, 56–7

Cluj, 254
Cold War, 26, 28, 138, 140
Cold War History Research Center, xxix, 269
Cold War International History Project, 269
Collective Farm Union (JRD), 7th session, 69
Collective guilt, principle of, 192
Columbia College, 272
Columbia University, 271
Comenius Institute of Montreal, v
Comenius University, 272, 274
Comintern, The, xxiii, 228
Commander's Cross of the Hungarian Republic, 273
Commander's Cross of Polonia Restituta, 122
Communist International, 107
Communist Party of Czechoslovakia (CPCs)
  "Action Program" of, xix, xxi, xxii, 22, 36, 38–9, 56–9, 69, 77, 83, 206, 212, 243
  all-national, xxiii
  apparatus, 55
  archives of, 91
  arrogance, inefficiency of, vii
  cadre appointments, 14
  centralists, 36, 55
  Central Committee of, xvi, xviii, xix, xxiv, 11, 15, 26, 31–2, 34–6, 38–9, 41, 44, 49, 51–2, 55, 77, 197
  centralization, 62
  change initiated by, 54
  12th Congress of 1960, 31
  13th Congress of 1966, 32, 40
  Czech domination of, xx
  Extraordinary (Vysočany) 14th Congress, 1968, xx, xxi, xxii, 12, 15, 40, 42–3, 48–52, 55, 77, 218
  conservative wing (dogmatists), xiii, note 11; 36–37, 40, 42, 47, 55–7, 71, 77
  counter-revolution of, xxiv, xxvi, xxvii, xxviii, 3, 7–8, 13, 21–22, 24–25, 28–29, 41, 43, 46, 48, 52, 57, 74, 79, 99, 133, 143, 149, 212, 214

  Czech leadership of, 91
  "democratic centralism," 91
  dressed down in Moscow, 73
  federalists, 36–7, 55
  "fifth column," 42, 46, 55
  First Secretary of, xiv, note 14, xix, xxi, xxix, xxx, 21, 31, 34–35, 41, 51, 55, 64, 95
  "healthy forces," 10, 14, 23, 45, 55, 58, 75, 177, 212, 220–1, 226, 231–2
  intra-Party coup, 66
  International Department, 14
  January silence, 66
  leadership of, xxii, 61
  letter of invitation to invade Czechoslovakia, 81
  monopoly on political power, 23, 28–9
  Marxist-Leninist, 41, 52, 57–8, 261
  main ideologist, 52
  neo-conservative wing, 74, 76
  neo-Stalinists, 33, 37, 40, 43
  new era, 95
  "normalizers," 12, 16
  orthodox communist leaders, 2–4, 11, 13, 23, 29
  "Party of the Leninist type," 44
  Party purges, 16
  Presidium of, xvii, xx–xxii, xxvii, 1, 5, 8, 10, 11, 21, 27, 33–5, 38, 40–1, 44–52, 55, 63, 197
  purges of, 32, 51
  reformist (radical) wing of, 2, 6, 8, 32, 34, 36–8, 40–3, 51, 55, 57, 81, 241
  regional conferences, 41
  "revisionism," 41
  "rightist elements," 41, 43, 47, 52
  resolution denouncing the invasion, 48
  "second center" in Prague, 26–27, 75, 177
  "socialism with a human face," xxi, 57, 83, 92, 261
Communist Party of the Czech Lands, xx; 15; 34, note 8; 39

Communist Party of Slovakia
　Central Committee, xxii, 37–38
　Central Supervisory and Auditing
　　Commission, 70
　"changing of the guard," 66
　communist elite, 90
　Congress of, 42, note 34, 43
　dogmatists of, 66, 71
　Extraordinary Congress, 50–51, 77
　First Secretary of, xv, note 19, xix,
　　xxii, 21, 26, 34, 37, 51, 63, 77
　fortuitous existence of, xxiii
　machinations in, xxii
　middle-of-the-roaders, 66, 71
　neo-conservatives, 75–7
　new concept of national economic
　　management, 70, 72
　Presidium, 12, 21
　purged, xxiv
　reformers, 66, 69, 77
　rehabilitation, 89
Communist Party of the Soviet Union
　(CPSU)
　ideological conviction of, 28
　12th Party Congress, 63, 75
　20th Party Congress, 250
　Politburo, 133, 233
　practices of, 11
　relations with the Communist Party
　　of Czechoslovakia, 6
　support of orthodox communists in
　　Czechoslovakia, 13
　tradition of relying on one person or
　　sphere, 16
Constantinescu, Miron, 240
Constantiniu, Florin, 253, note 35
Council for Mutual Economic Assistance
　(CMEA, COMECON), 20, 23, 44
Covasna, 253
Craiu, Ion, 240
Crimea, 9, 232
Croan, Melvin, 134, note 16
Cuban crisis, 16
Culcer, Rodica, 267, note 14
Cvik, Rudolf,

Cyrankiewicz, Józef, 121
Czech and Slovak Association of Canada, v
Czech
　communist elite, 89
　insincere, 108
　intellectuals, xxi, 33, 53
　interests, 88
　medal of Tomáš G. Masaryk, 122
　National Council, xix, 39
　scholars, xvi
　Jews, 109
　reformers, 33
　society, 31–32
　writers, 43
Czech Cycle, 189
Czech Republic
　Institute of Contemporary History,
　　194
　Masaryk Institute of the Academy of
　　Sciences, 273
　Minister of the Interior, Archival
　　Science Board, 274
Czech-Slovak
　assymetry, 53
　equal partners, 92
　federation, xx, 83
　relations, 62, 92
Czech Socialist Republic, 39, 84, 90
Czechoslovak (ia)
　Academy of Sciences, 56
　Act on National Committees, 64
　AGC (Archives of the ČSFR
　　Government Commission for the
　　Study of the 1967–70 Events), 1,
　　2, 12
　ambassador to the USA, 9
　army, 11, 28, 110
　borders of, 25
　Bulgarian Friendship, Cooperation
　　and Mutual Aid Treaty 176
　censorship (press), 7
　　abolished, 36, 56, 150
　　restored, 51, 75
　central communications, 48
　charge d'affaires in Hungary, 175

Index

Club of Non-Party Members, 40
Committee for the Preparation of the Act on Czechoslovak Federation, 83
Communist coup of 1948, 36, 57
Congress of the Union of Czechoslovak Writers, xxi, 54
consolidation of, xxx
Constitution of, 31
Constitution of May 9, 1948, 62
Constitution of the Czechoslovak Socialist Republic (ČSSR), July 11, 1960, 33, 63–4
Constitutional Act, No. 147, 1950, 62, adjustments in public administration, 63
Constitutional Act No. 125/1970, 84
Constitutional Committee for the preparation of the Act on Czechoslovak Federation, xii, 39
Constitutional Law No. 77/1968
Constitutional Law on the Federation of the Republic, No. 143, 1968, xix, xx, xxii, 39, 51, 84
creating a Czech National Council, 39
"Czechoslovakism," xxiii, 63, 93
delegation to Moscow, 50
democratization, xix, 33, 35–38, 41, 43, 46, 57, 58–9, 64, 72–4, 77, 83, 127, 144, 211, 262
dissolution of the federation, 39
economy, 32
embassy in Sofia, 190
Federal Assembly, 39
federation, 33
Five Year Plan (Third), 32
government, 61
flags, xv
freedom of expression (press), 32, 36, 43, 58–9, 92
hard-liners, 4
House of Nations, 39
ideological issues, 7
K-231 (Club of former Political Prisoners)

dissolved, 51
established, 56
KAN (Club of Active non-Party Members)
dissolved, 51
established, 56
Law on the National Front, 8, 21, 24
leaders, 3
military bases, 45
Ministry of Foreign Affairs, 1, 9, 177
legitimacy of the regime, 32
liberalization of, xxiii, 1, 58, 64, 71–3, 87, 89–92, 127, 142
multiparty democracy, 23
Ministry of the Interior, 22, 46, 51
military maneuvers (war games), 4–5, 13, 24, 45, 179, 212
Ministry of National Defense, 36
Ministry of State Security, 1
nation-state 88
National Assembly, xix, 32, 36–37, 49, 62
National Front, 37, 62, 177
national hockey team, 15
non-communist intellectuals, 33
"normalization," xvi, 1, 13–14, 16, 51, 74, 77, 83–5, 90–1, 97, 220, 224, 235
occupation of, 74, 76
option, 91
opposition political parties, 41
Organization of Former Political Prisoners, 40
Parliamentary elections (democracy), 62, 224, 235
party delegation, 41
Party of Freedom, 40
passive resistance, 12
Passport Act (1965), 32, note 2
People's Party, 40
pluralization of society, 57
political asylum, 37
political improvisation, 12
political inspectors, 38
political parties, 62

political pluralism, 22
political prisoners, 31
political purges, 31–32
political rehabilitation, 31, 53
"Popular Front" government, 61
press, 6–7
popular support
  for the intervention, 27
  for the reform movement, 58
public demonstrations, 51
public support, 57
puppet government, 12, 17, 49
pre-war capitalist system, 32
pre-war Czechoslovakia, 32
press and media war, xxvi
pro-Soviet Czechs and Slovaks, 26, 5
Press Agency (ČTK), 197
Prosecutor's Office, 1
reform movement in, 2, 6, 8, 74, 53
renewal of socialism, 8, 17, 24
restoration of capitalism, 22
revolutionary government of workers and peasants, xxx, 47
revisionism, xxvi
road to socialism, 47
"rovný s rovným," 88
social democracy, xxi, 6, 20
Socialist Party, 40
Socialist Republic (ČSSR), vii, 39, 71, 97, 172
Socialist Youth Movement, 70
Society for the Defense of Human Rights, 40
Soviet negotiations, 187
Soviet Treaty, 50
Stalin-Gottwald period, 31
State Security (StB) vii, viii, note 3; 48, 70
television, 2
trade unions, 7
Velvet Revolution, 267
Czecho-Slovakia, 87
  dissolved, 93
Częstochowa, 97, 122, 131

D
Dąbrowski, Witold, 114
Dacia (ii), 246, 252
Davis Center for Russian and Eurasian Studies, 271
Dawisha, Karen, xvi, note 23; xxix; 22, note 4; 23, note 9; 195, note 6; 205, note 3
Dean, Robert, xvi, note 23
Debré, Michel, 73
Děčín, 151, 156
de Gaulle, Charles, 242
Deletant, Dennis, 266, note 11
Demeter, Ion, 240
Democratic capitalism, 20
Democratic centralism, 40–41, 52
Der Spiegel, 154
Détante politics, 64, 150
Dautsche Welle, 190
Diamandescu, Tudor, 240
Dic-Dicescu, I., 240
Diedrich, Torsten, 139, note 6; 148, note 26
Dimitrov, Alexandar, 189
"divide et impera," 80
Dobre, Florica, 238, note 1; 242, note 8; 257, note 47
Dobrogeanu-Gherea, Alexandru, 240
Dobrynin, Anatoly, 9
Dolanský, Jaromír, 35
Doncea, Constantin, 241
Doskočil, Zdeněk, 51, note 72
Dragan, Oksana, xiv
Drăghici, Alexandru, 241, 257
Drejer, Michał, 120
Dresden, 160, 198
Dual Monarchy of Austria-Hungary, ix
Duda, Karel, 9
Dubček, Alexander
  admirers of, 65
  alleged naïveté, 65
  Brezhnev contacts, 5, 79
  clash with Novotný, xvii, 34–5
  career in Party, 65
  centrist, 226
  congratulatory telegram to, 197
  criticism of, 41–2, 77

defends reform, 74
disapproval of, 65, 72, 142
elder Dubček, 64
era, 171
First Secretary of the Communist
 Party of Czechoslovakia, xiv, note
 14, 64, 69, 89–90, 95, 196–7, 204,
 242
First Secretary of the Communist
 Party of Slovakia, xv, note 19, 63,
 69, 71, 89, 91
Hungarian support of, 203
increasing Slovak powers, 64, 70
internal and external enemies, 55–7, 71
leadership of, 13, 15, note 48
life in Soviet Union and in
 Czechoslovakia, 65
long-haired guys support, xviii, 8
meeting at Čierna nad Tisou, 80
meeting with Gomułka, 205
meeting with Soviet Politburo, 12, 206
memoirs of, 232, and note 21
moderate reform communist, 69, 77
Moscow's loss of faith in, 19–25, 27–8
negotiations with János Kádár, 204, 233
negotiations with Warsaw Pact,
 44–51, 208
personal archives of, 1
Polish questions about, 109
permanent apathy, 81
placard in support of, xiii
pluralist, 59
Presidium of the CC of the CPCs
radical reform of socialism, 65, 83,
 166, 241
replaced by Husak, xxx
resignation, 83
rise to power, 53
Soviet-trained, 91
Soviets lose faith in, xix, 3
student, 144
threatens to crack down, 8
trip to Moscow, 205
Dukla Hotel, viii
Dukla Pass, vii, note 2

Dygas, Maciej, 122
Dziady, xxiv, 96
Dzhurov, General Dobri, 184
Dzúr, General Martin, Czechoslovak
 Minister of National Defense
 prepared to use force, xviii, 8, 21
 tried to ascertain date of conclusion
  of war games, 5
 guaranteed no resistance to invasion,
  11
 threatened by Andrej Grechko, 12,
  16, 27
 signed Moscow Protocol, 50 note 67

E
East Berlin, 156, 159–60
East Central Europe, 274
Economic Committee, 39
Eisenfeld, Bernd, 160, note 57
Eisler, Jerzy, 100, note 8; 130
Elchovo, 183, 188
Ello, Paul, xvi
Embassy of the Czech Republic in Ottawa, v
Embassy of the ČSSR in Warsaw, 120
Embassy of the Slovak Republic in Ottawa, v
Epstein, Catherine, 166, note 6
Erdély, Károlyi, 206, 232
Erfurt, 160
Ermarth, Fritz, xxix; 195, note 6
Erz mountains, 157
Ernst, Hans, Lieutenant General, 155 and
 note 41
European Union, 267

F
Fabian Finkelstein, David, 240
Faculty of Arts, University of Ottawa, v
Falin, Valentin, 154
Federal Commission for the Stasi Files, 270
Federation & Federalization
 (Czechoslovak Republic)
 Action Program promises it, 3
 attitude of Communist Party of
  Slovakia towards, 91, 93
 asymmetrical, 64, 92

emasculated, 85
fictional, 52
victory for Slovak communists, xxiv; 77, 79, 93
Husák achieved federation, 78, 90
Husák amended Federation Act, xxiii
loose, 83, 85
realized, 51
Slovak demands for, xix, 35, 37–8, 62
taboo, 63
"Tatar figures," 38
tight, 84
Feher, Ferenc, 262, note 1
Fellow of the Royal Society of Canada, 271
Fejto, Francois, 134, note 16
Filipovici, Elena, 240
Fink, Carole, xvi, note 23
First Catholic Slovak Ladies Association, v
First Czechoslovak Army Corps, vii, note 2
Fischer, Mary Ellen, 263, note 3
Fock, Jenő, 215, 221, 223
Foitzik, Jan, 138, note 2
"For our and your slavery," 132
"For your and our freedom," 113, 121
Foriş, Ştefan, 240
Frank, Mario, 138, note 3; 165, note 1
French president, 242
Friszke, Andrzej, 125
Fulbright Fellow, 272
Fulbrook, Mary, 168, note 11

G
Galaţi Steel Combine, 244
Gassert, Philipp, xvi, note 23
Gazeta Robotnicza, 105
"Generals-diplomacy," 4
Gencheva, Colonel Alexander, 183
Genov, Eduard, 189
Geopolitical considerations, 7
George Washington University, 271
Geremek, Bronisław, 114
German Democratic Republic (GDR) (East Germany)
    accuses Czechoslovakia of counter-revolution, 57

"Aktion Sperrmauer" (Operation Dam Wall), 157
apologizes for invasion of Czechoslovakia, 202
Attorney General of, 161
Berlin Wall, 140–1
breach of international law, 154
calls for Soviet intervention; 134
closing of borders 140
combat readiness, 156
communists, 137
counter-weight to West Germany, 139
demonstrations against, 139
doubts about Dubček, 142, 166
established in, 139
expulsions from Party, 161
feared bourgeois liberals, xxvi
feared counter-revolution in Czechoslovakia, 143, 166
humiliated by Moscow, 167
jammed German-language broadcasts from Prague, 134
history of, 137
hoax, xxvii
invitation to Warsaw, 44
joined Warsaw Pact, 140
Lutheran Church disapproves of invasion, xxvii, 160
meeting in Dresdesn, 143
National Defense Council, 149
New Economic System of Planning and Leadership, 141
officers oppose invasion, 162, 168
opposition movement in, xxvii
President, 139
press war, 145
propaganda campaign against and restricts travel to Czechoslovakia, 134, 159
Protestant Church opposes invasion, 160
protests against the invasion, 159, 161
Pyrrhic victory, xxvii 169
radio broadcasts against Czechoslovakia, 146

Index

Reichsbahn (railroad), 157
reportedly invades Czechoslovakia, viii
secret police (Stasi), 169, 270
soldiers, 151, oppose the invasion, 160, 163
Socialist Unity Party of (SED), 137–40 and its Central Committee xxvi; 166
Soviet troops, 139–40
Soviets violated sovereignty of, 28
spying upon Czechoslovakia, 146
support for Dubček, 160
support of the USSR, 142
"tail" wagged the Soviet "dog," 167
the "68ers," 163
totalitarian, 168
victory parades, 157
German, (y) (s), vii, note 2; xxiii
Bundeswehr, 52
Communist Party of, 138, 165
diplomatic relations with, 206
Federal Republic of Germany (West Germany), xxix, 32, 103, 131, 142
influence of, 108
Military History Research Institute in Potsdam, xxvi, 275
Nazi Germany, xxiii, 28, 32, 61
Nazis, 165–6; revanchism, 44, 103
Soviet ambassador to, 154
Wehrmacht, 137, 151, 153, 160, 165
Weimar Republic, 165
Gheorghiu-Dej, Gheorghu
cult of personality, 263
ethnic understanding of the nation, 250
feared Soviet-backed Party coup, 250
flexibility of, 248
inner circle, 238
leadership style, 249
legitimacy problem, 251
liberalization, 237, 258, 262
misdeeds of, 240 249, 257
national communism, 238, 263
random terror, 250–1
regime, 240

Glassman, Ronald, 264, note 7
Glendon College of York University, 270
Global Uranium Corporation, v
Golan, Galia, xvi, note 23, 54, note 1; 89, note 4; 90, note 5
Goldstücker, Edvard, 116
Goma, Paul, Romanian dissident, 249 and note 24
Gomułka, Władysław (Wiesław)
anti-German phobia, 100, 134
at harvest festival in Warsaw, xxv, 121
concerned about counter-revolution, xxviii
co-author of 'Brezhnev Doctrine,' 99
convinced Brezhnev, 10
criticizes Czechoslovak party leadership, 41, 102
Cassandra-like speech, 95
fears Social Democratic Party, 52
feared liberal reforms, 100, 103
First Secretary of the United Polish Workers' Party, xxiv, 95, 99, 129
hard-line communist, 99
hostile towards 'Prague Spring,' 133, 194
incredible popularity, 100
ill-at-ease with Dubček, 95
KGB reports sent to, 8
limited responsibility, 125
met with Dubček in Ostrava, 95
meetings with Brezhnev, 100, 182
older generation, 135
out of his depth, 220
personal dislike of Dubček, 100
problems with students and writers, 96, 244
strengthens position in eyes of Kremlin, 100, 134
turned upon János Kádár, xxix
visits Moscow, 13
warns Dubcek, 95
Gorbachev, Mikhail
economic and political decentralization under, 266
failure of his *perestroika*, 52

Gorblicki, Julian, 123
Gordievsky, Oleg, 25, note 11
Gorzów, 123
Gosef, Isak, 187
Gosiorovský, Miloš, controversial *samizdat* publication of, 64
Gottwald, Klement, leader of the Czechoslovak Communist Party, 61
Gough, Roger, 229; 230, note 14; 231, note 17; 233–4
Goulash socialism, 83
Greek Catholic Church in Slovakia, xx
  Action Committee in Košice, xx, note 26
  Cathedral in Prešov, xx, note 26
Grant, Mr., ix
Great October Socialist Revolution, 34
Great War, ix
Grechko, Marshal Andrej A.
  Soviet defense minister, 12
    arrives unexpectedly in Czechoslovakia, 15–16
    debates gratitude with Dzúr, 27–28
    orders redeployment of East German troops, 157
    rumors of resignation, 110
Grieder, Peter, 165, note 2; 168, note 9
Grishin, V., 15, note 48
Grofu, Dumitru, 240
Gromyko, Andrei, 22–23
Guină, Nicolae, 240

H
Haas, John C., v
Hácha, Emil, 105
Hager, Kurt, 134
Hájek, Jiří, 177
Harghita, 253
Harrison, Hope, 167 and note 8
Havel, Václav, 41, 54–5, 59
Harvard Project on Cold War Studies, 271
Harvard's Kennedy School of Government, 271

Harvard University, xxix, 271
Hegedűs, András, 222
Heller, Ágnes, 222, 262, note 1
Hendrych, Jiří, 35
Herenčár, Robert, 70
Heydenmann, Günther, 140, note 9
Hermann, Konstantin, 43, note 15
Hertle, Hans-Hermann, 168, note 10
High Tatras, xiv
Hirka, Ján, xx, note 26
Hirszowicz-Bielińska, Maria, 98
Hitler, Adolf, 105, 107
Hochman, Jiří, xxi, note 27; 46, note 52; 47, note 56; 57, note 7; 58, note 8
Honecker, Erich, 166
Hoffmann, Army General, 148, 157
Hoffman, Karel, 48
Hradec Kralove, 118–20
Hric, Ján, xx, note 26
Hruškovič, Michal, 76
Hungarian (s), viii
Hungary, xxix, 31, 37, 41, 44, 203
  Academy of Sciences, 222, Research Groups for Sociology, 222
  ambassador to East Germany, 222
  apologizes for invasion of Czechoslovakia, 202
  army, 48, 82, 217, 219
  de-Stalinization, 203
  embassy in Prague, 231
  Institute for the History of the 1956 Hungarian Revolution, 269
  isolated negative reactions to the invasion, 222
  leaders welcome reforms in Prague, 203
  Minister of Defense, xviii, 5, 24
  minority in Slovakia, 227
  National Archives, 225
  New Economic Mechanism, 203, 225
  Polish solidarity with, 127

revolution of 1956, 220–21, 225, 253, 261
Soviet invasion of, xxix, 20–21, 27–28, 48, 228
Treaty of Friendship with Czechoslovakia, 207, 213
Warsaw Pact invasion, 225, 231
Hungarian Socialist Workers' Party, xxix
natural ally of CPCs, 203
Central Committee, 231
Politburo of, 206, 222–23, 225, 233
Husák, Gustáv
amended the Act on Czechoslovak Federation, xxiii, 84
bourgeois nationalist, 66
Chairman of the Board of Commissioners, 61
Chairman of the Committee for the Act on the Federation of the Republic, 83
condemned Warsaw Pact invasion, 12, 27
discussion with Brezhnev, 15, note 48
First Secretary of Communist Party of Czechoslovakia, xxx, 56, 83–4
First Secretary of Slovak Communist Party, 51, 90
flies to Moscow after the invasion, 49
"father of the federation," 84
liberal version of communist dictatorship, 224
memoirs of, 89, note 3
normalizer, 16
President of the republic, 52
purged in 1950's, 31, note 1
radical reform communist, 38, 77–8
rehabilitation of, 66, 71
secret meeting with Brezhnev, 50
Stalinist, 77
struggle with Vasil Biľak, xxii
vice-chairman of federal government in 1968, 39, 77
victory for, 79

Huszár, Tibor, 204, note 1; 215, note 33; 217, note 38; 220, note 44

I
Imperialism (western), 5–6
American, 44
Individual enterprises, 56
Indra, Alois
blocked formation of a Czech Communist Party, xx, 40
cooperated with invading forces, 49
"fifth column" for Moscow, 42
member of "healthy forces," 75
plots with conservatives to seize power, 47
signed letter of invitation for Warsaw Pact invasion, 11, 81
signed Moscow Protocol, 50, note 67
ultraconservative neo-Stalinist, 40
asked Moscow not to allow East Germans to invade, 155
Interhelpo, 64
International conference, v
International law, 110
Iron Curtain, xxii
Italy, 37
"Italian-type Marxists," 6

J
Jablonický, Jozef, 61, note 1; 89, note 3
Janáček, F., 78, note 28
Janák, Ignác, 77
Janík, Ján, 72, 75–6
Janus Pannonius University, 269
Jakeš, Miloš, 42; 50, note 67
Jakiel, Stanisław, 122
Jánošík, Juraj, xiv, vx, note 15
Jarausch, , Konrad H., 252, note 33
Jiu Valley, 245
John Jay College of Criminal Justice, 270
Johnson, Lyndon, 73
Josko, Anna, xxiii
Jowitt, Kenneth, 250 and note 29
Junker, Detlef, xvi, note 23

K

Kabul, 26
Kádár, János
  anti-Stalinist, 220
  Banquo's ghost, 228
  betrayed Dubček, 227
  biographer of, 229
  consumer socialism, 262
  conversations with Brezhnev, 2, 5, 177, 182, 207, 211, 227,232
  criticized "healthy forces" in Czechoslovakia, 221
  declared loyalty, 216
  denied counter-revolution in Czechoslovakia, 207
  diplomatic relations with West Germany, 227
  double-speak, 231
  "faux bonhomme," 230
  frightened Dubček and Černik, 217
  General Secretary of the Hungarian Socialist Workers' Party, 204, 225
  home consumption, 226
  insincerity of, 232
  meddling in Czechoslovakia's internal affairs, 227, 243
  mediator, xxix, 204, 213, 215, 217–8, 227, 229, 231, 233
  mentioned Slovak minority, 210
  messenger boy, xxx, 204, 227
  meeting in Yalta, 217–18, 232–3
  met with Dubček, 204–5, 215, 219, 233
  military solution a last resort, 215–16, 233
  myth propagated by, 228
  non-Leninist slogan, 225
  perpetuation of Party power, 235
  pragmatic politician, 226
  proposed compromise, 219–20, 235
  protest letters to Dubček, 229
  Quisling, 221
  reluctant ally, 230
  responsible for execution of Imre Nagy, 228
  restored order in Hungary, 220
  travelled to Moscow, 214, 223
  tried to steer Prague in the "right direction," 203
  two-faced, 226
  wanted political settlement, 217
  wanted to leave Bulgaria out of Dresden meeting, 199
Kalugin, Oleg, 25, note 12
Kamiński, Łukasz, xxiv–xxv; 95, 98, 129, 132–3, 270
Kafka, Franz, 134
Kapek, Antonín
  a leader of the CPCs, 8
  conservative communist, 47
  drafted a resolution on counter-revolution, 48–9
  "fifth column" for Moscow, 42
  signed letter of invitation for invasion, 11, 81
  supporter of Novotný, 35
Kaplan, Karel, 53; 54, note 4; 55 and note 4; 58 and note 9
Karl-Marx Stadt, 160
Karlovy Vary, 150–2, 156
Karner, Stefan, xvi, note 23; 147, note 24; 210, note 17; 316, note 35
Karta. 120
Katushev, K., 15, note 48
Katowice, 107, 122
Kenedi, János, 228, note 5; 231, note 18
Kersten, Krystyna, 114
Kessler, Heinz, Colonel General, 156
Kętrzyn, 120
Kirghiz Soviet Socialist Republic, 64
Kisielewski, Stefan, 114; 115, note 27; 116, note 29; 121, 131
Kiss, József, 228, note 3
Khrushchev, Nikita
  approves specific road for Yugoslavia, 47
  attempts moderate reforms, 72
  condemns crimes of Stalin, 250, 263
  General Secretary of the Communist Party of the Soviet Union, xvii

Kádár praised, 218
 liberalization under, 1
 ousted, 2, 32
 participated in 20th anniversary of SNP in Banská Bystrica, 89
 supported by Tito, 228
 visited Czechoslovakia, xvii
Khruschevite, 239–40, 250
King, Robert R., 263, note 5
Kirilenko, A.P., 9
Kirschbaum, Stanislav, xxiii; 87; 90, note 6; 93, note 10; 270
Kisielewski, Stefan, 131, note 5
Klokoč, Ondrej, 71
Klusák, Milan, 155
Kočtúch, Hvezdoň, 70
Kodaj, Samuel, 76
Kołakowski, Leszek, 98, 131
Kolder, Drahomír
 conservative communist, 40, 44
 member of the "healthy forces," 75, 177
 opposed Novotný 35
 refused to denounce the invasion, 48
 signed letter of invitation to invasion, 11, 47, 81
 signed Moscow Protocol, 50, note 67
 Soviet agent, 42, 50
Kolomyja airport, 183
Kornienko, G.M., 26, note 17
Komárno, 204, 206, 218
Komárom, 204, 215, 217
Kominek, Bolesław, 123, 131
Komócsin, Zoltán, 206
Konitz, Jacques, 240
Koblós, Elek, 240
Korcula, 222
Kořínek, O., 73–4; 82, note 34
Košice, self-immolation in, xxv
 Government Program, 61, note 2
 citizens protest invasion, xxviii, 184
Kosygin, Aleksei
 defends right to intervene in Czechoslovakia, 28
 equates Soviet with Czechoslovak borders, 7, 25
 met with Czechoslovak delegation at Čierna nad Tisou, 80
 Prime Minister of the Soviet Union, 6
 rumors about repenting for the invasion, 13
 supported by Soviet Ambassador S. Chervonenko, 8
 visited Czechoslovakia, 23
 met with Kádár at Yalta, 232
 met with Todor Zhivkov, 171
Koucký, Vladimír, 35; 50, note 67; 206
Kowalczuk, Ilko-Sascha, 163, note 71
Kozlowski, Krzysztof, 125
Krafcik, Patricia, xv, note 15
Krakow, 123
Kramer, Mark, vii, note 1; xvi, note 23; xviii, note 25; xxix; 133, notes 13 & 14; 142, note 12; 147, note 24; 172, note 3; 193, 271
Krasnay, Andrej, viii; xx note 26
Krasnaya Zvezda, 135
Kraus, Michael, xvi, note 23; xxi–xxii, 53, 271
Kremlin, the, 5, 8, 10, 14, 16, 22–26
Krenz, Egon, 168
Kretkowski, Sławomir, 127
Kriegel, František
 Chairman of the National Front, 46
 denounced the invasion, 48
 refused to sign the Moscow Protocol, 50, note 67
 tried to persuade Todor Zhivkov, 177–8
Kubadinski, Pencho, 181
Kučera, B., 50, note 67
Kultura, 132
Kultúrny život, 38, 90
Kun, Béla, ix
Kun, Miklós, 228 and notes 4 and 6; 230 note 13; 321, note 19
Kural, Václav, 42, note 32; 47, note 57; 48, note 48; 50, note 68; 66, note 10; 78, note 28; 99 note 7; 141, note 10; 142, note 12

Kusin, Vladimir, 54, note 1
Kuznetsov, M., 11, note 33

L

Labedz, Leopold, 135
Laluha, Ivan, 65
Larrabee, F. Stephen, 134, note 16
Last of the Mohicans, 71
Laštoviška, Bohumil, 35
Latin, ix
Latysh, Mikhail, xvii, xviii, xix, xx, xxi, 1, 19–25, 27, 272
Lederer, Jiří, 98
Legnica, 49, 148
Leipzig, 138, 160, 168
Leger, Peter, cartoon by, 144
Le Monde, 115
Lenárt, Jozef
    Chairman of the Slovak National Council, 63
    member of "healthy forces," 75
    neo-conservative, 77
    Prime Minister of the Czechoslovak Socialist Republic, 71
    signed Moscow Protocol, 50, note 67
    supported Novotný, 35
Leonin, Marcel, 240
Łepkowski, Tadeusz, 114
Letz, Róbert, viii, note 3
Leučík, Michal
    self-immolation, xxv, xxxiv
Levente, Mihai, 241
Liberal and conservative groups in Western Europe, 73
Lichtbalu, Leon, 240
Lindenberger, Thomas, 252, note 33
Linz, Juan J, 58
Lipták, Ľubomír, 91
Literární listy, xxx, 98, 213, 228
Literární noviny, 41, note 31; 43
Littell, Robert, xvi, note 20
Little Entente, 6
Litoměřice, 151
Londák, M., 64, 70
Longhi, Hugh, xvi

Lubianiec, Romuald, 127
Lukács, George, 222
Luža, Radomír, xxiii

M

Machcewicz, Pawel, 100, note 8; 133 and note 11
Magdeburg, 160
Magyar, ix
Mählert, Ulrich, 139, note 5
Majewski, Wacław, 123
Malenkov, Georgi, 228
Malycha, Andreas, 138, note 4
Mamatey, Victor S., xxiii
Mantsch, Lieutenant Colonel Werner, opposed invasion, 162
March 1969 ice hockey riots, 15, 27
Marin, Timotej, 240
Market economics, 92
Markiewicz, Tadeusz, 127
Marko, Miloš, 38
Markov, Georgi, xxviii, 189
Márkus, György, 222, 262, note 1
Márkus, Mária, 222
Marxism-Leninism, 28, 81, 239, 248
Masherov, P.M., 3
Martin, xiv, xv, 33
Matica slovenská, xv, 33
    Commemorative Medal, 271
Maťovce, 184
Maurer, Ion Gheorghe, 238, note 1
Maxim Gorky Institute of History, 263
May Day celebrations, 41
Mazowiecki, Tadeusz, 124–5
Mazurov, Kirill T. (alias General Trofimov), 12, 155
McGill University, 269
Mencl, Vojtěch, 51, note 71
Meetings of the 'five' 4, 211, 223–4
Micewski, , Andrzej, 124
Michálek, Slavomír, xiii, note 11; xxi, xxii, xxiii, 61; 73, note 18; 79, note 29; 87, 90–1, 93, 272
Michálkova, M., 99, note 7
Michigan State University, 275

Index

Mickiewicz, Adam, xxiv, 96
Miercurea Ciuc, 253–4
Middlebury College, xxi, 271
Mielke, Erich, 166
Migev, Vladimir, 194
Miklas, Dusan, v
Milovice, 15
Mimoň, 151
Mináč, Vladimír, 71
Minnesota caravan, xv
Mitrohkin, Vasili, 25, note 11
Mladenov, Petur, 172, 195–6
Mlynář, Zdeněk
    architect of the Action Program, 59
    autobiography of, 25, note 13
    Dubček's caution, 55
    interned in Moscow, 49
    revealed others' fear of openly
      defending invasion, 49, note 62
    radical reformer,14
    signed Moscow Protocol, 50, 67
    Soviet disdain for, 27; 71, note 17
Mycielski, Zygmunt, 115
"Modus vivendi," 24, 131
Moczar, Mieczysław, 135
Modoran, Vasile, 241
Modorcea, Grid, 252, note 33
Modzelewski, Jerzy, 122
Moldavia, 133, 252
Montclair State University, xxx, 273
Monteanu, Neculai Constantin, 257
Moravec, Jan, xxi, 34, note 9; 78, note 28; 83, note 38
Morawski, Stefan, 98
Móscicki, Aleksander, 122
Moscovici, Gelber, 240
Moscow, orders from, 137
    Protocol, xviii, xx, xxix, xxx, 12, 50–51, 220, 234
    State University, 272
Moskva, graffiti, xv
Mrożek, Sławomir, 115, 130
Mureş, 253,
Musiel, Franciszek, bishop, condemned the invasion, 123, 131

Musil, Jiři, 33
Munteanu, Neculai Constantin, 249 and note 26; 258, note 48

N

Naimark, Norman, 138, note 2
Nagórski, Wiktor, 127,
Nagy, Imre
    executed, xxx, 210, 221, 228
    fall of, 227
    Kádár protests article on, 229
    Prime Minister of Hungary, 213
Národnie noviny, xv
National Council for the Study of Securitate Archives (CNSAS), 273
National People's Army (NVA, "Red Prussians"), 139–40, 147–9
    7th Armored Division Dresden and 11th Motorized Rifle division Halle, 149
    did not invade Czechoslovakia, 151
    legend about participation in invasion, 153
    not deployed against its own people, 168
    "Prague Group," 151
NATO, 135, 145, 190, 267
Navrátil, Jaromír, viii, note 5; xxvii, note 32; 43, note 9; 54, note 2; 78, note 28; 80, note 32; 83, note 38; 99, note 7; 173, note 6; 175, note 12; 177, note 21; 178, note 25; 180, note 28; 181, note 31; 182, note 35; 187, note 50; 205, note 3; 216, notes 35 & 36; 220, note 44; 243, note 10
Navýchod, 274
Neagoe-Pleşa, Elis, 257, note 47
Nestorov, Christo, 189
Neubert, Ehrhart, 159, note 56
Neues Deutschland, 145, 150
New Jersey, xxx
New School for Social Research, 270
New York, 25
New York University, 273
Nichev, Bojan, 189
Nicolaescu, Sergiu, 252
Nicolau, Alexandru, 240
Nightfrost in Prague, 27

Nikolov, pettty officer Nikolai Cekov, 187
Nistor, Ioan Silviu, 253, note 36
Nomenklatura, 55, 238, 242, 249
Novaia I Noveishaia Istoria, 19
Nové slovo, 90
Novomeský, Ladislav, 71
Novotný, Antonín
    attack upon, 72
    chairs Presidium of CPCs, 63
    dictatorial powers, 34
    entourage of, 6
    expelled from CPCs, 42
    no support from Brezhnev, xvii, 2
    opponents of, 35, 70
    Party boss, 32
    personal problems of, 37
    President of Czechoslovakia, 31, 206
    rejects Soviet military bases, 45
    resignation (removal) of, 34, 36, 55, 64, 66, 71, 196–7, 205
    Slovak writers encounter wrath of, xxi
    Stalinist leader, 21
    supporters of, 35, 38, 71–2, 77
    very conservative, xix

O
Odessa, 187
Odorheiul Secuiesc, 253–4
Office of Public Education of the Polish Institute of National Remembrance (IPN), 270
Open Society Institute in Sofia, 193
Operation "Danube" (Dunaj), 49, 148
Orlík, 47
Orwellian absurdity, 263
Ostpolitik, 134, 144
Ottomans, 252
Ouimet, Matthew J., xviii, xix, 19, 272
Oxford University, 271

P
Paczkowski, Andrzej, 100, note 8; 132, note 10
Palach, Jan, self-immolation of, xxv, xxxiv, 122

Palárikovo, 205
Pangelov, Vasil, 175
Paris, 115, 132
Parrish, Michael, , xvi, note 23
Pashev, Apostol, 199
Paška, Juraj, 33
Pastor, Peter, xxx, 225, 273
Pastyřík, Miroslav, 35
Pataky, Iván, 217, note 39; 230, note 12
Patilineț, Vasile, 240
Pătrășcanu, Lucrețiu, 240
Pauker, Anna, 263
Pauker, Marcel, 240
Pauer, Jan, 56, note 6; 65, note 9; 82, notes 36–7; 99, note 7; 147, note 24; 154, note 40; 155, note 43
Pavel, Josef, 46
Pavlenda, Viktor, 72
Pavlík, Ondrej, 71
Pavlovsky, General Ivan., 11, 12, 182
Pawłowski, Antoni, bishop, supported the invasion, 123
Pécs, 269
Pelikán, Jiři, 2, 14
"Perestroika," 52, 59
personae non gratae, 46
Pešek, Jan, viii, note 3; 48, note 60; 70, note 15; 76
Petkov, Lieutenant Colonel, 185
Petržalka, xv
Petrescu, Cristina, 252, note 32
Petrescu, Dimitru, 241
Petrescu, Dragoș, xxx, 237; 252, note 33; 263, 265–6, 273
Pezlár, Ľudovít, 77
Philadelphia, 274
Philosophical Faculty of Pavol Jozef Šáfárik University, xiv
Pieck, Wilhelm, 139
Pikhoia, R.G., xviii, 1, 19, 20, note 1, 22, notes 4 and 5, 23, note 9, 26, note 15
Piller, Jan, 48–50
Piotrowski, Pawel, 205, note 5
Pitești Automobile Plant, 246
Płock, 123

Pluta, Wilhelm, 122–3
Plzeň, 151
Podgorny, Nikolaj V.
    East Germans did not invade Czechoslovakia, 155–6
    met with Kádár in Yalta, 232
    President of the Soviet Union, 6
Poland, Polish People's Republic
    accuse Czechoslovakia of counter-revolution, 57
    anonymous letters sent, 118
    apology for invasion of Czechoslovakia, 202
    anti-Czechoslovak propaganda, 103
    anti-Semitism in, xxvi
    Czechoslovaks invited to, 44
    de-Stalinization in, 31
    Dubček kidnapped to, xx
    hierarchy of, xxv
    March Events in, xxv, 97, 100, 117, 127, 130
    Marshal Yakubowsky in, xvii
    operation "Akcja", 126
    "Podhale" operation, 117, 125
    pro-Czechoslovak banners, 97
    Soviet Union did not invade, xviii
    student protests, 97
    threat to its borders, 100
    to invade Czechoslovakia, xxiv
    waiting for Dubček, 97
    war games in, 4
Poles (ish), viii
    abroad, xxvi
    Academy of Sciences (PAN), 114
    Association of Polish Writers, 115
    army, xxvi, 48, 102, 104–6, 135
    crisis of 1970
    Czechoslovak border agreement, 132
    Czechoslovak relations, 132
    Czechoslovakia did not suffer enough, 132
    disapproval of invasion, 105–6
    Dresden meeting, 3
    embassy in Prague, 98
    émigrés, 132

Institute of National Remembrance (IPN), 129
indifference to the invasion, 130
intellectuals protest the invasion, 113
invitations to Prague scientific institutions, 98
leadership, 52
leaflets protesting the invasion, 112–13
looked down upon Czechs ("Shveiks")
Martial Law, xxvi, 17, 26, 135
pacified, 127
press, 106
professors fired, 98
protests against Czechoslovak press, 100–01
reaction to the invasion, xxiv, xxvi
Roman Catholic Church, attitude towards invasion, 122–3, 131
Roman Catholic members (ZNAK) of the Polish Diet (Sejm), xxv; 124–5
Savings Bank (PKO), 111
scarecrow of West Germany, 134
Security Service (SB) of, xxiv; 98, 106–7, 111, 117, 120–24, 130
Stadium of the 10th Anniversary of the PPR, 121
solidarity with Czechs and Slovaks, 117
students expelled, 98
United Polish Workers' Party, xxiv, 15
    Politburo, xxiv
war with Soviets, 132
war with Ukraine, 132
Poleska, Sylwia, 127
Polish-Jewish Heritage Foundation of Canada, 275
Polityka, 131
Popescu, Dumitru, 242, and note 8
Poprad, xiv
Potsdam, 160
Povstalci, 92
Poznań, 97

Práce, 36
Prague
  Agreements, 62
  Brezhnev visited, xvii
  Bulgarian ambassador in, 189
  capital of Czechoslovakia, 90
  centralism, 53, 63, 72
  exchanged trade missions with Bonn occupied, 151, 156
  regional Party committees in, 44
  Regional State Archives in, xxviii, 274
  representative of Soviet Politburo in, 12
  Ruzyně airport, 48, 185–6
  Soviet assessments of what took place in, 7
  student demonstrations in, 15
Prague Spring
  an act against the revolution, 166
  and Poland, 129–30
  as seen from Prague, 31
  books written about, xvi
  Bulgaria's role in suppressing the, xxviii, 171
  clash between two groups, 54
  crisis triggered in the Eastern Bloc by, 164
  coined by western journalists, xv, note 19
  could have survived, 224
  deadly threat, 99
  demonstrated that reforming communism was impossible, xxiv, 17
  East Germans and, 137
  eight months of, 55
  enemies of, 134
  freedom of, xv
  heading towards western-style democracy, 25
  hopes and concerns of, 96
  Hungary welcomed the reforms of, xxix
  intriguing questions about, xvii
  ironies of, 20
  Kádár duplicitous during, 227
  Kremlin's response to, 24
  leaders of, 1, 6, 15
  liberalization of, 90
  meaning of, 91
  means counter-revolution, 21
  most Slovaks resent the term, xv, note 19
  nature of, xviii, 19
  Petro Shelest discussed impact of, 7
  Polish émigré press notices, 132
  "Prague heresy," 10
  reforms of, xxvi
  restoration of parliamentary democracy, 235
  role of the Czechs in, xix
  revisited, 53
  scholars have learned a great deal about, xxxi
  so-called, 64
  Soviet-East German relations during, 167
  suppressed, 154, 183, 255
  threat to political stability, 28
  well underway, 22
Prahova county, 256
Pravda, 71
Predvoj, 72
President's Office, University of Ottawa, v
Prešov
  anti-Russian posters, xiii
  Lutheran Lyceum in, ix
  martial law, xiv
  reaction of students and citizens to invasion, x
  roar of jackhammers in, vii
  resurrection of Greek Catholic Church, xx and note 26
Priess, Lutz, 141, note 10; 142, note 12; 147, note 24
Prozumenščikov, Michail, 147, note 25
Przemyśl, 121
Puzanov, Aleksandr, 199

Q
Quebec City, 271
Queen's University, 270
Quisling, 221

R
Radev, Valentin, 189
Radio Berlin International, 146
Radio Free Europe
  bellowing, 131
  broadcasts information on self-immolation of Siwiec, 122
  hostile towards Polish People's Republic, 100
  increase in interest in, 106
  Romanian desk, 249
"Radio Vltava" (Radio Moldau), 146
Raina, P., 122, note 37
Rainer, János M., 222, note 48; 226, 228, note 7
Rakowski, Mieczysław, 131, 135
Rau, Captain Joachim, opposed invasion, 162
Red Army
  auxiliary troops of, 151
  broke through the Dukla Pass, vii, note 2 and ix, note 7
  complete dependence upon, 147
  German communist support for, 138
  helped restore order in Hungary, 220
  Klement Gottwald returned in wake of, 61
  National People's Army modelled on, 140
"Rusi domov!" xv
Reșita, 254
Retegan, Mihai, 243
Rigby, T.H., 262, note 1
Rigo, Emil
  conservative communist, 42
  signed Moscow Protocol, 50, note 67
  Slovak Roma, 76
  voted against denunciation of invasion, 48
Rhodes Scholar, 271

Ripp. Zoltán, 228, note 3
Riveles, Stanley, xv, note 19
Rabotnichesko delo, 174
Rock, Claus-Dieter, 146, note 23
Roman, Laba, 262, note 1
Romania (n)
  ancient roots, 251–2
  apparatchiks, 266
  autarkic and unchallenged, 262
  bourgeois intellectuals, 263
  boycotts Sofia meeting, 41
  boycotts Warsaw meeting, xxix
  "brotherly help" extended to, 122
  closure, 237
  communes (*comune*), 253
  communists, 3, 6, 44, 99, 110, 237
  continuity, 251–2
  critical intellectuals, 249
  counties (*județe*), 235
  Declaration of April, 1964, 239
  de-Stalinization, 240, 249
  diplomatic relations with West Germany, 134
  districts (*raioane*), 235
  edge of Soviet intervention, 133
  embassy in Prague, 243
  ethnic Hungarians, 253
  films, 252
  four historical myths, 258
  Front of National Unity, 133
  Grand National Assembly, 252
  Gulag-style repression
  Hungarian Autonomous Region, 253
  historians, 251
  intelligentsia, 265
  liberalization, 266
  legitimacy, 237, 258
  mass rallies, 254
  member of Warsaw Pact, xxx
  Michael the Brave (*Mihai Viteazul*), 252, 254
  Military Academy, 245
  Mircea the Old (*Mircea cel Bătrîn*)
  nation-building, xxx 237, 258

national communism, 237, 251, 255, 258
national history, 251
nationalist-dynastic, 262
press, 243
Party of Greater Romania, 267, note 13
protochronism, 265
regions (*regiuni*), 253
Russians will possibly attack, 107
selective community-building, 237
socialist nation, 258
Stalinist state, xxx
Treaty of Friendship with Czechoslovakia, 246
Stephen the Great (*Ştefan cel Mare*), 254
three Principalities, 252, 255, 258
Union of Communist Youth, 256
Union of Fine Artists, 257
unity and independence, 251–2
unshakeable alliance with Czechoslovakia, 242
Romanian Communist Party (RCP), xxxi, 237
  activists, 240
  chief ideologue, 242
  Commission, 240
  collective leadership, 241
  delegation to Prague, 242, 246
  ethnic understanding of, 250
  First Secretary of, xxx
  "limited legitimation," 250
  nation-building process, 251
  Ninth Congress of, 255
  Plenum of the Central Committee, 239, 241–2
  propaganda machine, 258
  Stalinists, 250
Rožnava, xxviii, 184
Rozvan, Eugen, 240
Rudé právo
  reported Dubček replaced Novotný, 35
  published resolution condemning invasion, 49 and note 63
  Oldřich Švestka editor of, 231

Rusk, Dean, 73
Russia (n) (ns)
  AK-47 (Russian sub-machine gun), xv
  anti-Russian posters, xiii–xv
  generals, xvii, 3, 8, 21
  imperialism, 107
  Institute of Slavonic Studies, Russian Academy of Sciences, 272
  invade Czeshoclovakia, viii
  looting stores, x
  no Russian Communist Party xx, 15, 34, note 8
  people, 15
  tanks, ix–xii, xv
Russophilism, 49
Ruthenia, 49
Ružomberok, xiv
Rychlík, Jan, xiii, note 11; xix–xxii, 31; 32, note 2; 33 note 4; 53, 55–9; 84, note 39; 273
Rydz-Śmigły, Eduard, 107

S
Sabolčík, Michal, 71
Sádovský, Štefan, 35
Šalgovič, Colonel Viliam
  agent of the Soviet Security Service, 48
  appeared as a moderate reform communist 69
  Deputy Minister of the Interior and Chief of State Security, 48
  opposed reforms and supported invasion, 76
'samizdat,' 64
Savcenko, 81
Scînteia, 243
Schirdewan, Karl, 166 and note 3
Schröder, Wilhelm, 161, note 62
Schroeder, Klaus, 140, note 9
Schöpflin, George, 251 and note 31
Schwarz, Hans-Peter, 145, note 19
Schwarz, Wolfgang, 142, note 11
Scottish soldier, ix

Index

Securitate (Romanian Secret Service), 241, 256–7, 259, 265–6
Self-immolation, xxv
Selvage, Douglas, 207, note 12
Semerdzhiev, Atanas, 184
Šejna, General Jan, 36–37
Seyss-Inqart, Arthur, 105
Sfîntu Gheorghe, 253–4
Shafir, Michael, 265, note 9; 266 and note 12
Shawcross, William, 3, note 6; 59, note 14; 91, note 7;
Shelepin, N.A., 7
Shelest, Petro
 feared nationalist movement in Ukraine, 7
 First Secretary of the Ukrainian Communist Party, 26, 133
 generated tension, 13
 met with Todor Zhivkov, 200
 met with Vasil Biľak, 75, 81
 received letter of invitation for invasion, 47, 81
Sholtyseck, Joachim, 167, note 7
Šik, Ota, Chairman of Economic Committee, 39
 reforms of, 4
 right-wing "second center," 75
Sikorski, Marian, bishop approved of invasion of Czechoslovakia, 123
Sikora, Stanislav, xiii, note 11; xxi–xxiii; 61; 64, note 6; 77, note 24; 82, note 35; 87, 90–1, 93, 274
Simes, Dimitri, 7
Šimon, Bohumil, 50, note 67, 51
Šimůnek, Otakar, 35
Sindermann, Horst, 154
Široký, Viliam, 71
Siwiec, Ryszard, self-immolation of, xxv, xxxiii, 121
Skálová, Ivana, xxviii, xxix, 171, 193–4, 274
Skilling, H. Gordon, xvi, note 23; xvii, note 24; xxi, note 27; xxv, note 31; xxix; 59, note 12; 91, note 9; 133, note 14; 134, note 16; 135, note 17; 195; 205, note 3

Skwarnicki, Marek, 125
Slaba, Jaroslav, v
Slapka, Gejza, 76
Słonimski, Antoni, 96
Slovak
 Academy of Sciences, xxii, 272
 army, 48
 autonomy, 33, 36, 53
 bourgeois nationalism, xxiii, 33, 69, 71, 88
 citizens resisted invasion, 184
 Democratic Party, 62
 dissatisfaction with centralism, 33
 emigration from Hungary, ix
 ex-Ľudaks, 33
 Historical Institute, 272, 274
 independence, xxiii; 91–2
 institutions abroad, 33
 medal of the White Double Cross, 122
 Minister of the Interior, 69
 nation, 63, 88
 national emancipation (sovereignty), 25, 72
 nationalism, 34
 politics, 91
 question, xix, 33, 53
 resistance politicians, 62
 Roma, 76
Slovak-American International Cultural Foundation, Inc., v
Slovak Catholic Sokol, v
Slovak Community Circle of Oshawa, v
Slovak League of America Foundation, v
Slovak National Council (SNC)
 already existing, xx
 Board of Commissioners, 33, 61–2
 Chairman of, 38, 61, 63
 Czech equivalent, 39
 deprived of all its powers, 33
 full governmental and executive powers, 62
 negative attitude towards "Two Thousand Words," 44
 officially recognized by Edvard Beneš, 61

Presidium, 35–36
seeks codification of federation, 38
social organization, 63
useless organization, 63
Slovak National Uprising (SNP), 61
  Dubček participated in, 65
  20th anniversary celebrations, 89
Slovak Republic (1939–1945)
  semi-independent, xxiii–xxiv
  allied with Nazi Germany, 61
  communist uprising against, 89
Slovak Socialist Republic
  created, 39, 90
  loses powers, 84
  Party of Slovak Revival, 40
Slovakia
  ally of Germany, 132
  churches in, 41
  occupied small part of Poland, 132
  re-incorporated into Czechoslovakia, 87
Słowo, 114
Sme, 185
Smith, Timothy L., viii, ix, xiv
Smolar, Eugeniusz, 127
Smrkovský, Josef
  defended democratization, 42, 74
  denounced invasion, 48
  member of "second center," 75
  met with Brezhnev at Čierna nad Tisou, 80
  reform communist 12, 14
  reported on Moscow negotiations, 51
  revealed Party shakeup, 36
  signed Moscow Protocol, 50, note 67
Social Democratic Party (Czechoslovakia), 40
  Preparatory Committee, 41
  dissolved, 51, 52, 103
  movement, 274
Sofia, xxviii, xxix, 41, 175, 197–8, 204, 208
Solidarity labor movement, xviii, 168, 262
Sós, Vilmos, 222
Soviet, agents, 42, 50
  ambassador in Sofia, 199

ambassador to Washington, 9
anti-reform coalition, 145
anti-Semitism in, xxvi
army, 41, 48
archives, 198
bloc, 28, 47
commentators, 25
criticism, 74
delegation, demands, 55
diplomats, 197–8
East German relations, 167
embassy in Prague, 5–6, 9, 14, 27, 43, 77
embassy in Bulgaria, 175
general staff, 41, 45
government apologizes for invasion of Czechoslovakia, 202
intervention, 57
leadership, 41, 43, 45, 49, 57
led-invasion, 58
military administration in Germany (SMAD), 137–8
model, 139, 261
moral defeat, 135
occupation, zone (SBZ), 137–8
paratroopers, 48
prisoners 50
propaganda, 7
Politburo, xvii, xviii, xix, xxii, xxvii, 1, 2, 6–7, 10, 12, 19–20, 26–28, 46–48, 134, 177, 182
security forces, 228
soldiers, 82, 150, 157
Sovietized Europe, 255
sphere of influence, 28, 92
sponsors, 57
type organization, 253
Soviet Union
  army of, viii, note 5, 135
  captive Czechoslovak delegation, 219
  Ceaușescu broke with, xxxi
  Communist Party of, 44
  convergence of nations and nationalities, 63
  de-Stalinization, 89
  determined GDR policy, 139

Index

Dubček family moves to, 64
Dubček had lived in , 41
failure of "perestroika" in, 59
kidnapped Alexander Dubček, xx
KGB (Soviet Secret Police), 8, 20, 25
Klement Gottwald returned from, 61
network of agents in Czechoslovakia, xiv, 22, 48, 55, 70, 81
separatist tendencies of non-Russian nations, 63
stationing troops in Czechoslovakia, 83
working class of, 16, 28
writers protested the invasion, 130
Soviet-US relations, 9
Špaček, Josef, 13, 48, 50, note 67
Spanish Civil War, 222
Spilker, Dirk, 166, note 4
Stanová, Mária, vii, note 2
St. Kliment Ohridski University, 273
St. Nicholas Roman Catholic church, ix
Sts. Cyril and Methodius University, 273
Stalin, Josef
    cautious policy of, 135
    crimes perpetuated by, 250
    conservative process of, 73
Stalinist, Stalinism
    de-Stalinization, 31, 251
    era, 31
    denouncing, 95
    purges, 65
    rhetoric of, 47, 266
Stănescu, Ion, 257,
Stanley, John, 275
State University of New York at Plattsburgh, xxx
Status quo in Central Europe, 141
Steiner, Eugen, 22, note 3
Stepan, Alfred, 58
Stereotypes, 7
Štern, Jan, 36
Stodolniak, Teresa, 126
Stoica, Gheroghe, 240
Stolarik, Mark & Anne, v, vii, viii, ix, xiv, xxv, xxvii note 32; 274

Stomma, Stanisław, 125
Strausberg, 149
Strinka, Július, 38
Stulz-Herrnstadt, Nadja, 165, note 2
Strečno, viii, note 5
Štrougal, Ľubomír
    condemned invasion,12
    moderate normalizer, 16
    opponent of Novotný, 35
    pragmatic colleague,14
Šturák, Peter, xx, note 26
Sudetic, Chuck, 196
Suk, Jiří, 65
"Šumava" war games
    dress rehearsals for the occupation, xviii, 5, 24
    exercise in intimidation, xix, 23, 45
    GDR participated in, xxvi
    prelude to military intervention, 22, 45
    "sabre-rattling," viii, note 5
"Sum zero" logic of the Cold War, xix, 24
SUNY Plattsburgh, 270
Survey, 135
Suslov, Mikhail, 7, 80
Suspected criminal, 37
Švestka, Oldřich
    editor of *Rudé právo*, 231
    opposed resolution denouncing invasion, 48
    signed letter of invitation for invasion, 11, 47, 81
    signed Moscow Protocol, 50, note 67
Svitak, Ivan, xvi, note 23, 59
Svoboda, Ludvík
    appointed Gustav Husák vice-chairman of new government, 39
    Brigadier-General, vii, note 2
    disassociated himself from Dubček, 13
    fatal mistake, xx, 49
    guaranteed no resistance to invasion, 11
    hero of the Soviet Union, 37
    negotiated with Soviet leadership in Moscow, 155

President of Czechoslovakia, xv and
  note 17; 34, 37, 52
  signed Moscow Protocol, 50, note 67
  Soviets fail to win over, 12
  visited by Zdeněk Mlynář, 15
  wartime colleague, 4
Szeged University, 269
Szpakowski, Zdzisław, 124

T
Tanase, Stelian, 263, note 4
Tantzscher, Monika, 146, note 22; 159, note 54
Taylor, Philip, v
Tarkowski, Jacek, 118
Tarnów, 120
Ťažký, Anton, 70
Ťažký. Ladislav, 71
Tel Aviv, 264
Țepeneag, Dumitru, 249
The Trust for Civil Society in Central and Eastern Europe, 194
The Razum (Reason) Society, 194
Thirty Years' War, ix
Time-line, Czechoslovakia, 1968, xxxi
Timiș, 254
Timișoara, 254
Tismaneanu, Vladimir, 262, note 2
Tito, Iosip Broz, xxxi, 227–8, 242, 253, 264
Todorov, Stanko, 173, 181, 199
Tömpe, András, 222
Topoľčianky, 204–5
Tordai, Zádor, 222
Trans-Carpathian separatism, 7
Transregional Center for Democratic Studies, 270
Transylvania, 251–5
Trianon syndrome, 210
Trnava, xv, 271, 272–3
Trnavská univerzita, 271
Trybuna Robotnicza, 111
Tudor, Corneliu Vadim, 267, note 13
Tůma, Oldřich, 59
"Two Thousand Words" manifesto, 43–44, 54, 76, 179, 214, 228–9, 243

Tych, Feliks, 148, note 28
Tygodnik Powszechny, 125

U
Uher, Ján, 65, 69, 77
Uhl, Matthais, 140, note 8
Ukrainian
  partisans, 48
  party leader, 26, 47
Ukrainian Soviet Socialist Republic, 75
  Ivano-Frankov oblast, 183
  Mukachevski region, 183
Ulbricht, Walter, *alte Kämpfer*, 165
  "carrot and stick", 140
  "closet reformer," 141
  counter-revolution in Czechoslovakia, xxvii–xxviii
  criticized Czechoslovak Party leadership, 41
  elder statesman, 165
  enemy of Czechoslovak reforms, 4, 133, 137, 143, 147, 167, 194
  "faults and mistakes," 158, 230
  First Secretary of the Socialist Unity Party of Germany (SED), xxvi, 133–4, 139, 141, 166
  head of the "Berlin Group," 138
  "1938 Hitler–1968 Ulbricht," 153
  KGB reports to, 8, 10
  Marxist-Leninist, 141
  meeting with Brezhnev, 182
  meeting with Dubček, 150
  neo-Stalinist, 141
  older generation, 135
  proposed dictatorial solution, 220
  rule ended, 164, 169
  'schoolmaster," 144
  turned upon Kádár, xxix, 215
Uličný, Ferdinand, ix, note 6
Union of Slovak Writers, xxi
United Nations, 118
United States, 264
  Department of State, xviii, 9, 272
United States Steel Corporation, v
Université de Montréal, 270–71

Université Laval, 271
University of Bucharest, xxx, 273
University of California at Davis, 275
University of Leipzig, 275
University of Michigan, 275
University of Minnesota, vii, viii, 274
University of Nicolas Copernicus, 106
University of Ottawa, xvii, 270, 274
University of Paris, 270
University of Political Affairs of the CC of the CPSU in Moscow, 65
University of Sofia, 189–90
University of Toronto, xxvi, 270, 275
University of Warsaw, 275
University of Washington, 272
University of Waterloo, xxvii, 269
University of Wrocław, xxiv, 270
USA, xxxi, 9, 24, 26, 37, 107
    US-Soviet relations, 73
US, army, 52
    military hardware, 7
USSR, 11–13, 17, 25, 28, 41, 52, 142
Uzghorod, Užhorod, 46, 75
Uzunov, Konstantin, 192

V
Vaculík, Ludvík
    criticized communist regime, 54
    Czech writer, 43
    Warsaw Pact denounced his "Two Thousand Words" manifesto, 179
    "Two Thousand Words" manifesto, 43
Váh river, xiv
Valenta, Jiří, xxi, 23, note 9; 24, note 10; 182, note 34; 195, note 6
Vartanov, Valerij, 148, note 28
"Velvet Revolution," see Czechoslovakia
Verdery, Catherine, 265, note 9
Verner, Admiral Waldemar, 162
Vévoda, Rudolf, 131, note 7
Vida, István, 228, note 3
Vidich, Arthur, 264, note 7
Vietnam, 110
Viole, Aurel, 241

Vladislav, Jan, 54, note 3
Vltava river, 47
Volejník, O., 42
Volkszeitung, 134
Volker Neugebaure, Karl, 140, note 7
Vondrová, Jitka, 34, note 9; 65, note 9; 80, note 30; 83, note 38; 99, note 7; 173, note 6; 175, note 12; 177, note 21; 178, note 25; 180, note 38; 181, note 31; 182, note 35; 187, note 50
"Všetci ľudia na chodníku nemilujú republiku" (Communist slogan), x

W
Wagner, Armin, 140, note 8
Wallachia, 252
Warsaw
    capital city of, 126
    Club of Catholic Intelligentsia, 124
    Czechoslovak Cultural Center, 120
    Czechoslovak Party leadership invited to, 44
    Dubček meets with Brezhnev in, 15
    meeting of Warsaw Pact in, xxix
    Polish harvest festival in, 121
    Polish Institute of National Remembrance in, 270
    suffragen of, 123
    "Warsaw Five" meet in, 146, 215, approve the intervention, 234
    "Znak" club meets in, 125
Warsaw Pact
    bilateral consultations, 44–46
    collapse of, 22
    collision course with Czechoslovakia, xxii
    Communist Parties of, 44
    departure from, xxi, 20, 52
    Dresden Meeting ("Tribunal"), xvii, xxiv, xxvi, xxviii, 3, 21–22, 41, 44, 46–7, 57, 73–4, 98–9, 133, 198, 204, 207, 227, 244
    diktat of February 1967, 207
    five "fraternal" parties, 10, 42, 211, 219

gap in, 44
GDR joins, 140
generation gap in, xxvi, 134
intervention (invasion, occupation)
   of Czechoslovakia, xx, xxiii, xxxi,
   27, 58–9, 77, 82, 87, 91–2, 151, 234,
   247, 252, 261
July summit, 1968, 179, 230
Kádár mediates with, xxix
meeting in Sofia, 98
military maneuvers (war games), viii,
   xvii, xix, 4–5, 13, 24, 45, 179, 212
occupation ineffective, 19
Politburos of, xxvi, 134
Political Advisory Committee, 41,
   171, 198
remains within, 23, 45
Romania did not invade, xxx
Statutes of, 110
the "Five," 44, 48, 217
the "Six," 73, 98, 217, 220
Unified Armed Forces of, 140
USSR engages in conflict with, 16
Wasilewski, Marek A., 96
Weber, Max, 250; 264, note 6
   concept, 248, 265
   theory of legitimacy, 263–4
Weit, Irwin, 195, 200
Wenzke, Rüdiger, xxvi, xxvii, 137; 140,
   note 7; 147, note 24; 148, note 26 & 28;
   151, note 35; 155, note 42; 156, notes
   46 and 48; 157, note 52; 163, note 68;
   165–6, 169, 275
West European Left, the "Third Way," 73
Western scholars, publications of, xvi, 7,
   13
Western-style democracy, 25
White House official, 9
Wieczorek, Wojciech, 124
Wilke, Jürgen, 161, note 64
Wilke, Manfred, 141, note 10; 147, note
   24; 205 note 5
Williams, Kieran, 58, note 10; 205, note 3;
Włocławek, 123
Woodrow Wilson Fellow, 272

Wolle, Stefan, 150, note 32; 154 and note
   38, 160, note 58
World communist movement, 13
World War II
   biggest military action since, 82, 129
   celebrating end of, xvii
   defeat of Nazis in, 28
   Czechoslovak government-in-exile
      during,132
   desertions during, 48
   making a film about, 7
   Slovak resistance politicians during, 62
   unconditional surrender of German
      Wehrmacht in, 137
Woroszylski, Wiktor, 114
Wróbel, Piotr, xxvi, 129, 275
Wrocław, 123, 131
Wysínszki, Stefan Cardinal
   advised bishops and Catholic "Znak"
      club not to protest against the
      invasion, 125, 131
   Primate of Poland, 122
   remained silent about invasion, xxv

Y

Yakubovsky, Marshal Ivan I.
   commander-in-chief of Warsaw Pact
      forces, xvii
   explained the non-participation
      of East German troops in the
      invasion, 155–6
   prematurely ordered the invasion of
      Czechoslovakia, 4, 22–3
   prepared East Germans for the
      invasion, 148–9
Yale University, 271
Yashkin, General G., 4, 22
Yershov, I., 11
York University, xxiii
Young intellectuals, 32
Yugoslavia
   Belgrade Declaration, 47
   break with the Soviet bloc, 47
   Ceauşescu visited, 253, and compared
      to Tito in, 264

dissident from the Soviet bloc, 107
Dubček proposed consultations with, 44
General Šejna fled via, 37
Hungarian philosophers and sociologists attended conference in, 222
member of "Little Entente," 6
Stalin did not invade, 135
stance of, 110
violated Moscow Orthodox rules, 99

Z

Zablocki, Janusz, 125
Zabrze, 124
Zaolzie, 106–7, 110, 115
Zalic, Alter, 240
Zatlin, Jonathan, 166, note 5
Zero-sum logic, 26, 28–29
Zhivkov, Todor
  anti-Semitic, 200
  attacked Kádár's position, 216, 230
  "belated antagonism," 195
  denied urging military force, 191, 196
  Dresden meeting, 173
  faith in Dubček's leadership, 176, loss of such faith, 177–8
  feared change, 197
  First Secretary of the Bulgarian Communist Party, 171
  KGB sent special reports to, 8
  met with Leonid Brezhnev, 171, 182, 198
  met with Alexei Kosygin, 171
  opposed Dubček's leadership, 196
  proclaimed situation in Czechoslovakia "counter-revolutionary," xxviii–xxix, 171–4, 177–8, 190, 195
  proposed dictatorial solution, xxx, 220
  recommended military dictatorship in Czechoslovakia, 201
  recommended use of armies, 10, 172, 178, 180–1, 196, 198, 200–1
  satrap of the Kremlin, 192
  supported "healthy forces," 178, 180
  supported Gomułka and Ulbricht, rejected Kádár, 179
  unfulfilled ambition, 192
  "wait-and-see attitude," 195
  visited Czechoslovakia, 177
Zhivkov, Zhivko, 199
Zhnatino, 183
Zissu, Petre, 240
Žilina, viii, note 5
Zionism (ists)
  anti-Polish propaganda by, 100
  Prague reformers accused of, xxvii, 6, 124
  scarecrow of, 135
  will lead the world to war, 109
Znak Club, 124
Zündorf, Irmgard, 140, note 7
Zupka, František, 70, 76
Zvolen, "Tri Duby" airport, 185
Zrak, Jozef, 70

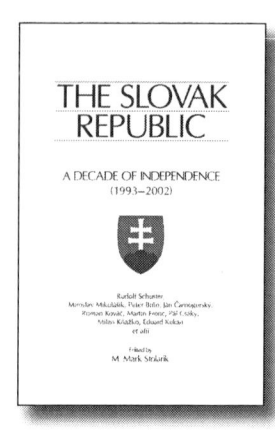

The Slovak Republic
A Decade of Independence

xiv + 168 pp. (2003) 6" x 9" Paperback, ISBN 978-0-86516-568-7

Rudolf Schuster, Miroslav Mikolášik, Peter Brňo, Ján Čarnogurský, Roman Kováč, Martin Fronc, Pál Csáky, Milan Kňažko, Eduard Kukan
and
Paul Dubois, Anton Jura, Thea Herman, George Fodor, Piotr Dutkiewicz, Paul R. Magocsi, Martin Votruba, Ron Halpin

Edited by M. Mark Stolarik

The Slovak Republic: A Decade of Independence is Slovakia's first "white paper," a statement of position and its first "progress report." It outlines Slovakia's remarkable progress and promising trends of the past ten years:

- its fertile ground for foreign investments
- its strategic value to the West as the geographic heart of Europe
- actions taken towards growth and development in the wake of Nazi and Communist occupation
- its support of the goals of the U.S., UN, and NATO

The book is a collaborative document: nine papers written by Slovakia's president and eight of his high level government officials, with commentaries by eight North American scholars.

This document will serve well as a basic introduction to Slovakia's primary institutions, its "prime movers," and its potential in work force and resources.

Slovakia is a new political entity that evolved in the twentieth century. Its people, however, document their ethnic existence for over a millennium. In the past six centuries they produced a unique syncretism in culture and Weltanschauung. Their oral traditions have been written down and translated into multiple languages; their social and political philosophy is available in many volumes in Latin. Their past century under the yoke of several "isms" has given their writers a fertile field for growing modern literature that deserves to be translated into other languages. Now, after Nazism and Communism, Slovakia looks to the world for partnership.

Slovakia's entry as an equal partner into the rest of the Western world will prove mutually beneficial, as is maintained by Steve Forbes in a recent *Forbes Magazine* article on Slovakia, "Investors' Paradise" (August 11, 2003).

These nine essays represent a commitment to a Slovak political, social, and economic platform written by President Schuster and eight of his high level government officials. The eight commentaries by North American scholars give this "white paper" a reality check. Steve Forbes' independent article corroborates the claims of great progress, and recommends Slovakia as an "Investors' Paradise."

WWW.BOLCHAZY.COM

Illustrated Slovak History
A Struggle for Sovereignty in Central Europe

xii + 420 pp., 321 Color Images (2006)
Paperback, ISBN 978-0-86516-426-0 • Hardbound, ISBN 978-0-86516-500-7

Enhanced English version of *Dejiny Slovenska: na ceste k sebauvedomeniu* (1992, 1999) by Anton Spiesz, Ph.D.
Afterword by Dusan Caplovic, Ph.D.
Edited by Ladislaus J. Bolchazy, Ph.D.
in collaboration with Translators Joseph J. Palus, Jr., M.A.; Albert Devine, Ph.D, J.D.; David Daniel, Ph.D.; Michael Kopanic, Ph.D., and Ivan Reguli, Ing.

Notes: Michael Kopanic, Ph.D., et alii

Academic Consultants: Martin Votruba, Ph.D.; Albert Devine, Ph.D., J.D.; Milan S. Durica, Ph.D.; Frantisek Vnuk, Ph.D.; Ivan Reguli, Ing.; Charles Sabatos, M.A.; Patrick Romane, M.A.; John Karch, Ph.D.; Zdenko G. Alexy, Ph.D.; et alii

Associate Editors: Albert Devine, Ph.D., J.D.; Patrick Romane, M.A.; and Richard Wood, B.A.

The latest scholarship in the context of an on-going historical debate on the Slovak *ethnie* in Central Europe

Features • Collaborative English translation of two historical works: one by Anton Spiesz, the other by Dusan Caplovic • Annotated with new additions: • Copious Notes on controversial issues • Extensive Bibliography • Index with various spellings of names • 7 color maps • Foreword by President Ivan Gasparovic • Survey of the historiography of Slovak historians • Updates to 2005 • Original 321 Color Images

Who are the Slovaks? What is their contribution to the history and culture of Central Europe? Situated at the geographic and cultural crossroads of Europe, the Slovak Republic has emerged as an independent nation with membership in the EU and NATO and has been hailed as an "investors' paradise." This book explores the origins and the development of the Slovak *ethnie* within the context of Central Europe and provides copious notes and bibliography on controversial issues—Beginnings to 2005.

"... merits are threefold: first is the translation of the history of Slovakia by the late Anton Spiesz, a respected Slovak economic historian who passed away just before the creation of the Slovak Republic in 1993; secondly, there is the wealth of magnificent illustrations that cover the entirety of Slovak history since ancient times; and thirdly there are additional materials like an afterword by Dusan Caplovic, notes by Michael J. Kopanic, a chronology of major events since the creation of the second Slovak Republic (to 2004), and a selective bibliography...."
– Stanislav J. Kirschbaum, *Jednota*

WWW.BOLCHAZY.COM

Night of the Barbarians
Memoirs of Communist Persecution of the Slovak Cardinal

492 pp., 10 color photographs (2002) Hardbound, ISBN 978-0-86516-537-3

Editors: Richard Gaughran, Emil Vontorcik, and Ivan Reguli; **Translators:** Peter-Paul Siska with Richard Gaughran and Jeff Schmitz; **Contributors:** Preface: Peter-Paul Siska; **Forewords:** Vaclav Havel, John Paul II, and Theodore Cardinal McCarrick; **Introduction:** Viliam Judak; **Epilogue:** Peter Liba; **Footnotes:** Emil Vontorcik and Peter-Paul Siska

First book in English featuring the values of a top Jesuit, top churchman, and a prominent Slovak.

First exposé of Communist persecution of religion and failure of Communist principles in Slovakia.

Another totalitarian system began vigorously marching across the borders of Central Europe. Violence, collectivization, mandatory atheist education, crude interrogations, and imprisonment were just a few of the many experiences that profoundly affected the life of Slovak people. Cardinal Jan Chryzostom Korec, S.J.'s book leads us vividly into the middle of this reality. The *Night of the Barbarians* is an honest and sincere account of events as they began to unfold in front of the author's eyes beginning the night of April 13, 1950, and ending December 8, 1968. This English translation includes a new foreword, introduction, notes, and epilogue.

Jan Chryzostom Cardinal Korec, S.J. (1924–), the Slovak cardinal, was secretly ordained a priest in 1950, consecrated a bishop in 1951 at the age of 27, and named a cardinal in 1991. In 1960 he was sentenced to twelve years in prison. He has authored over 100 publications on theology, philosophy, and social policy.

> "Thank you very much, Lord Cardinal, that you eternalized your memories of your eight year imprisonment under the Communist oppression in this book. This testimony is extremely needed."
> – John Paul II

> "Cardinal Korec guided his severely tested Church... Today we are thankful to him for his example and the stand he took, even here in the Czech Republic, where he survived the most crucial moments of his life in Valdice prison."
> – Vaclav Havel

> "Cardinal Korec is one of my heroes....He writes of events in history—moments that changed the world, like the Communist takeover of Eastern Europe, or the Second Vatican Council....I am truly honored at being invited to write this brief Foreword to Cardinal Korec's book. It is a way of saying 'Thank You' for his inspiration and his life."
> – Theodore E. Cardinal McCarrick

WWW.BOLCHAZY.COM

Slovak History
Chronology and Lexicon

380 pp (2002)
Hardbound English, ISBN 978-0-86516-444-4
Hardbound Slovak, ISBN 978-0-86516-445-1

By Dusan Skvarna, Julius Bartl, Viliam Cicaj, Maria Kohutova, Robert Letz, Vladimir Seges

The history of Slovakia is part of the rich tapestry of the course of human events at the geographical and strategic crossroads of Europe. Yet, very little contemporary scholarship on Slovak history exists in English or is readily accessible to North American and Western European readers. This title thus fills an important gap in historiography and knowledge of events and developments throughout Central Europe over the last fourteen centuries.

"**A collaborative work** of Dusan Skvarna, Julius Bartl, Viliam Cicaj, Maria Kohutova, Robert Letz, and Vladimir Seges, *Slovak History: Chronology & Lexicon** is a highly methodical presentation of Slovak history, ranging from primeval times to 2000 A.D., while highlighting and summarizing key historical events throughout the descending centuries.

Also included is a concisely written and plainly presented **lexicon of historical figures and terms** key to Slovakia.

Enhanced with **appendices** providing genealogies and leadership lists for ruling royal dynasties and republican regimes, *Slovak History* is a masterpiece of scholarship.

Deftly **translated into English** by David Daniel and prepared for an American readership by English Language Editor Albert Devine, Slovak History is a tautly written reference excellent for basic research and quick lookup of facts."
— *Midwest Book Review*, May 2003

*Original Edition: *Lexikón Slovenských Dejín* (Slovenské Pedagogické Nakladateľstvo, 1997 & 1999)

WWW.BOLCHAZY.COM

Slavic Myths

168 pp. (Forthcoming) 97 B&W Illustrations, Paperback, ISBN 0-86516-503-3

Ivan Hudec & Dusan Caplovic
Illustrator: Karol Ondreicka
General Editor: Ladislaus J. Bolchazy
Translators: Emma Nezinska & Jeff Schmitz with Albert Devine & Patrick Romane

Slavic Myths* is a revised and enhanced version of *Tales from Slavic Myths*.

It presents careful re-tellings of essential Slavic mythology, and is the first collaborative work in English. This new edition also includes a pantheon of Slavic gods and deities, bibliography, index, six maps of prehistoric Slavic cult sites, captions, and comprehensive introduction.

The world of Slavic myths is now accessible to English-language readers.

These myths, now supplanted by Christian belief, are important to understanding the development of Slavic civilization and character. This book is an incomparable general introduction to the topic. Additionally, this book features Professor Ondreicka's outstanding artwork which showcases the high artistic culture of the Slovak Republic.

"Ivan Hudec's *Tales From Slavic Myths* is an impressive, informative, and highly entertaining compendium of Slavic folktales and legends and ably translated for English readers by the collaborative efforts of Emma Nezinska, Jeff Schmitz, and Albert Devine. Beautifully illustrated in color by Karol Ondreicka and with an informative afterword by Dusan Caplovic, *Tales From Slavic Myths* is an impressive addition to any personal, school, or community library mythology collection."
– *The Midwest Book Review*

"This is an eminently readable book and fills a lacuna in the literature of world mythology. No other comparable work on Slavic mythology exists in the English language. In addition to filling an existing need for any library's holdings on mythology, it can mark an important starting point for those interested in pursuing further research on the topic."
– Michael Kopanic, *Jednota*

"*Tales from Slavic Myths* will also well serve readers and admirers of other Slavic literary and cultural works, such as Russian and South Slavic heroic eposes, operas, and paintings, for the comprehension and appreciation of such works demands knowledge of the Slavic myths.
– Mila Saskova-Pierce, *Kosmas: Czechoslovak and Central European Review*

*Original title: *Báje a Mýty Starých Slovanov* (Martin, Sk, 1994)

WWW.BOLCHAZY.COM